I0884871

The Holy Spirit before Christianity

The Holy Spirit before Christianity

John R. Levison

BAYLOR UNIVERSITY PRESS

© 2019 by Baylor University Press
Waco, Texas 76798

All Rights Reserved. No part of this publication may be reproduced, stored in a retrieval system, or transmitted, in any form or by any means, electronic, mechanical, photocopying, recording, or otherwise, without the prior permission in writing of Baylor University Press.

Unless otherwise stated, Scripture quotations are from the New Revised Standard Version Bible, copyright 1989, Division of Christian Education of the National Council of the Churches of Christ in the United States of America. Used by permission. All rights reserved.

Cover design by Savanah N. Landerholm
Cover image: Exodus, 1999 (oil on canvas), Mcbee, Richard (b. 1947) (Contemporary Artist) / Private Collection / Bridgeman Images
Book design by Scribe Inc.

The Library of Congress has cataloged this book under ISBN 978-1-4813-1003-1.

Printed in the United States of America on acid-free paper with a minimum of thirty percent recycled content.

To Priscilla

So fair art thou, my bonnie lass,
So deep in luve am I;
And I will luve thee still, my dear,
Till a' the seas gang dry.

CONTENTS

LIST OF EXCURSES

ACKNOWLEDGMENTS

After yet another gratifying Tuesday evening Hebrew class, instead of tucking my laptop away and heading home, I decided to check e-mail. The date, I remember, was October 25, 2016. Radu Bordeianu had written to invite me to deliver Duquesne University's Annual Holy Spirit Lecture. I would lecture in the evening and spend the following day behind closed doors amid the critical gaze of rabbis, Orthodox theologians, a Roman Catholic Dead Sea Scrolls expert, and a Pentecostal scholar.

I was all in, and I knew immediately what the topic would be. Twenty-one years earlier, in a Society of Biblical Literature seminar paper titled "The Angelic Spirit in Early Judaism," I had proposed that something dramatic took place in Israel's understanding of the spirit in the literary corpora of two prophets, Haggai and Isaiah 56–66. Between then and now, I would touch on the theme once or twice more, but I had never worked the idea out fully. Now was the time. This was the occasion.

A year later, I left Pittsburgh, the home of Duquesne University, with a headful of fresh ideas for this book—and a few essential words of caution—thanks to the able participants of the colloquium: Rachel Sabath Beit-Halachmi, Radu Bordeianu, Bogdan G. Bucur, Silviu Bunta, James A. Gibson, Angela Kim Harkins, Wilfred Hildebrandt, and Paul Tuchman.

The experience of writing that lecture and this book has allowed me to play the student in an environment that is ardent about education. That environment includes the Bridwell Library of Southern Methodist University, which sits a pleasant stone's throw from my office. I have spent not hours but days in the Bridwell, scouring and scanning, finding and fetching articles and entries and books. It is a magical place, the Bridwell, at least for someone who no longer crams for exams or scurries to write papers. The staff, too, are magnificent. I leaned heavily on David Schmersal, a friend and colleague; we often searched together the physical and virtual worlds afforded by the Bridwell. Jane Elder, Sally Hoover, and Roberta Schaafsma, too, were forbearing companions in what proved to be occasional, arcane forays into esoterica. The staff of the Bridwell never wavered; in fact, they love the challenge of learning and, for that reason, are themselves a stellar group of colleagues.

I have also engaged with several Perkins School of Theology colleagues on this project. I think here in particular of Billy Abraham, a quick-witted, brilliant philosophical theologian. Billy and I taught simultaneous classes in Houston, so we often hopped on the same Southwest Airlines flight and debated along the way. Billy never held back an opinion, and I never wanted him to. I owe him much more than a few feeble notes on divine agency. Other Perkins faculty and administrators have lent their expertise to this volume, as well: Roy Heller; Jim Lee; Bruce Marshall; academic dean Evelyn Parker; and Dean Craig Hill, who authorized a yearlong research leave, one of those rare indulgences of the academic life.

Not to be missed in any accounting of this book is Andrew Klumpp, who is far more than a graduate assistant. Reliable, intelligent, and efficient, Andrew does indispensable research, often of the most tedious sort, and he does it capably and affably. In concrete terms, he is responsible for the lion's share of the bibliography and the indexes, but to limit his work to these, appreciable though they be, is to underestimate the scope of his influence on this research.

I found new colleagues at SMU but not at the expense of old ones. When it came time to ask someone to read a few sections of my conclusion, I turned to Daniel Castelo, professor of theology at Seattle Pacific University. I also consulted Martin Abegg, a leading Dead Sea Scrolls scholar and professor at Trinity Western University; Marty patiently worked out lacunae and possible reconstructions of the most essential texts for this study; his expertise is pivotal to this analysis. My friend from graduate school days and now a trustworthy colleague from afar, Amy-Jill Levine, pushed me, as she should have, on what nomenclature to adopt, especially about the relationship between Israel and early Judaism.

Others I did not yet know also lent their expertise to this project. I wrote to scholars of Antiquity, out of the blue, to ask about possible Persian influence on Israelite conceptions of the spirit—and received enlightening responses. Both Bruce Lincoln, Caroline E. Haskell Distinguished Service Professor Emeritus of the History of Religions in the Divinity School of the University of Chicago, and Jason Sion Mokhtarian, associate professor in the Department of Religious Studies and Borns Jewish Studies Program at Indiana University, replied carefully. They deserve my thanks, though we have never met face to face.

When it came time to consider a publisher, I turned to Carey Newman at Baylor University Press. I did not know he would put me through my paces. Carey gave me writing exercises to sharpen my focus, each of which I found more fascinating than the prior one. He also told me to write *abductively*, which I did—once I understood what the word meant. I followed Carey's advice assiduously; this is a better book for it. I am indebted to Carey and his terrific team at Baylor University Press, which includes Cade Jarrell, Savanah Landerholm, Jenny Hunt, Steffi Hoffman, and Kingsley East. I visited this remarkable coterie of colleagues more than once en route from Dallas to Georgetown, Texas; they are an impressive, energetic, and collaborative lot, and I am grateful for what they have accomplished, from soup to nuts, as Carey says. I should also add my thanks to Carrie Watterson for her meticulous copy editing.

Then, of course, there is the amiable orbit of my family. Both of my adult children, Chloe and Jeremy, moved to Dallas shortly after Priscilla and I did. Their conviviality rims my vocation, giving me so much to enjoy when I am not at my desk—and revitalizing me to return to it.

And now, even as I strain in what can only be a futile effort to compose these final words about her, my wife Priscilla's bare feet are tucked up along my ribs, as we stretch together along the couch this rainy autumn afternoon. She is writing her own book; I am finishing mine. Three years ago, Priscilla uprooted her life and moved from Seattle to Dallas to be by my side in prayer and in service, as we had vowed at our wedding more than thirty-six years ago. Now our offices are barely more than thirty-six feet apart, along the third floor of Selecman Hall. I take exquisite delight in the company of this woman, whose gait and golden hair I first noticed decades ago, whose intellect I tap on a daily basis, whose wisdom I cherish perennially, and whose gaze I crave, still.

Chapter 1

THE EMERGENCE OF THE SPIRIT
Recasting Exodus: The Font of Pneumatology

The son of a rural pastor wrote a prize-winning manuscript on the holy spirit at the University of Straßburg,[1] left it in Darmstadt with a publisher in 1916, and headed to war, first as a machine gunner on the western front, then as a lieutenant in charge of a regiment in the east, in Galicia, and ultimately as a company commander. Back on the western front, he engaged in a brutal tank battle in Cambrai and was awarded the Iron Cross.

Hans Leisegang corrected his manuscript while fighting in the First World War—eventually with an injured right hand. "It was not easy to make the corrections outdoors," he mused, "in rain and sunshine, in quarters loud with the noise of comrades, and finally to write with my left hand in a military hospital."[2] The hardships of war and wounds notwithstanding, Leisegang managed to complete his prodigious *Der heilige Geist: Das Wesen und Werden der mystisch-intuitiven Erkenntnis in der Philosophie und Religion der Griechen*. The book saw the light of day a year after the war ended, exactly a century ago, in 1919.[3]

As I contemplate my own study of the holy spirit, it is inevitable that I cast a protracted glance backward a full century, to a time drenched with war but flush, too, with intellectual promise. I see there in rat-infested trenches and hospitals lined with the beds of the wounded sheer tenacity. To many of their readers, books are static storehouses of knowledge tidied up for posterity, electronic or paper records of disembodied thought. A good book is something altogether different. It is the expression of intellectual passion. It is the culmination of a single idea, hatched at some now-forgotten moment, that at the time raised a distant possibility. This possibility emerged frame by frame, step by tentative step, only as far as the headlights shone[4]—and always in the to and fro of real life.

The Holy Spirit before Christianity

Hans Leisegang posed a deceptively simple but significant question in this book: "Is the teaching of the Holy Spirit of Greek or oriental origin?" By this he meant to pinpoint whether the origin of pneumatology lay in the ancient Greek or Jewish worlds.[5] More to the point, with this question, he wrested pneumatology from the grasp of Christianity and set it instead in the context of other, earlier religious traditions. His was a classic study along the vein of the *Religionsgeschichtliche Schule*, which set *theological* topics in their *historical* contexts.

The century that separates the publication of this book from Leisegang's can do little to tamp down the resonance between them. Both are earnest efforts to trace the origin of pneumatology on a historical plane. Both agree that the origin of pneumatology is found in cultures that preexisted Christianity. And both challenge a proprietary form of pneumatology that privileges Christian concerns to the neglect of its historical antecedents.

Leisegang must be credited with asking an essential question, even if the answer he gave was ill-advised. A philosopher with a keen interest in Neoplatonism, he argued in no uncertain terms that the origin of pneumatology lay in *Greek* culture. Even the Greek Old Testament, the Septuagint, was a vehicle of Greek, rather than Hebrew, conceptions of the spirit—or so he thought. "Perhaps even the theologians and learned of the hellenistic era approached the Old Testament with a concept of the Holy Spirit already fully worked out in Hellenism, and they believed to have found it afresh in the πνεῦμα ἅγιον of the Septuagint."[6] The origin of pneumatology, in short, lay neither in Christianity nor in Judaism but in "the essence and being of mystical-intuitive knowledge in the philosophy and religion of the Greeks."[7]

Leisegang believed he could peel off the veneer of Judaism from the Greco-Roman conceptual world that lay beneath it, the way one might peel an orange or a banana. This is not true, if the findings of this study, one hundred years later, are themselves true. The origin of pneumatology belongs to a world that existed before hellenistic culture flourished, before Jews populated swaths of the Greco-Roman world, and long before Christians emerged as a licit religion of the Roman Empire. Unprecedented conceptions of the spirit, of *rûaḥ*, emerged earlier within a world embattled by the dual, and equally challenging, crises of exile and restoration.

There, in trauma borne of the caprice of the Babylonian and Persian Empires, Israelite voices recalled a dark, destitute, and despairing landscape. They remembered how they had eked out an existence at the whim of another ancient empire—only, one day, to escape. Their escape was wonderful, miraculous even, but it led them to a terrifying wilderness, where they nearly starved and where they wandered for years on end. Yet, as they remembered the story, they did not wander alone. God was inevitably, incontrovertibly present in a menagerie of mysterious entities that led them along the way. There were pillars of cloud by day and fire by night, clouds that lifted and descended on them, a terrifying angel to lead the way. Even a strange face, like the *pānîm* of a god, led them—until the ragtag band reached a land flowing with milk and honey, where they lived, if not happily, at least with intermittent solace, for many years.

Even as they remembered these early traumatic days of peril and provision, Israel nursed a tandem belief that God was present with them as *rûaḥ*. For more than half a millennium, from eighth-century prophets Hosea, Micah, and Isaiah, to the book of Daniel, written in response to the horrors of Antiochus IV Epiphanes—six full, rich centuries—Israelite and Jewish authors embraced the presence, power, and promise of *rûaḥ*. With the composition of Haggai 2:4-5 and Isaiah 63:7-14, however, something shifted. The author of an otherwise typical communal lament in Isaiah 63, at some point after 586 BCE, and the prophet Haggai, at some point after 539, accomplished something unique.[8]

Prophecy and Innovation

Drawing on the exodus tradition, in which a pillar and angel had stood in Israel's midst, Haggai encouraged his compatriots with the claim that now, centuries after the exodus, *the spirit stood in their midst*. Until this point in time, Israelites believed that the spirit had undertaken many activities—resting upon, rushing upon, being upon, falling upon, hovering over, filling—but never had the spirit *stood*.

The developments in the lament of Isaiah 63 are even more daring—and certainly more intricate. Drawing as well on the exodus tradition, this prophet fused two figures that stood in tension with one another: the angel and the presence or face or *pānîm* of God. God and Moses had tussled fiercely over who would lead Israel, the angel or the *pānîm*, and, by the end of their intense negotiation, were no nearer to a resolution. The prophet of the lament resolves the tension by fusing angel and *pānîm*: the angel of God's presence saved them. Then, with barely a pause, the prophet identifies this angel with the holy spirit, whom God had put into Israel's midst. Drawing yet one more time on the exodus tradition, in which God's presence or *pānîm* would give Israel rest, the prophet of Isaiah 63 claims that the *rûaḥ* of the Lord had given Israel rest.

This fusion was unprecedented. In one fell swoop, a pair of Israelite prophets realized that something no less magnificent than the great angel, no less magical than the pillars of cloud and fire, no less mysterious than the *pānîm*, had been there all along. They had called this presence *rûaḥ—spirit*—and now they realized, for the first time, that this spirit was what had rescued—they would say *redeemed*—them and led them through the wilderness. This spirit was stronger than any unholy force that infested the wilderness, physical or figurative, through which they now trekked.

Once they realized this, that the pillar and angel and *pānîm* were actually this spirit, they did not, as one might expect, rejoice. The prophet of lament—the poet of Isaiah 63:7-14—grieved the spirit's absence. *Where?* asked the prophet of lament. Where is the one who had, in ages past, put the holy spirit within them?[9]

That aching sense of absence was not the only response they had to this discovery. Through the auspices of a more benevolent ruler, they returned home, or at least to their ancestral home, where they became mired in the muck of drought and discouragement. But despair would not, this time, be the last word. *The word I cut with you when you came out of Egypt. My spirit stands among you. Do not fear!*[10] Not pleas or prayers or laments but a promise, this time, would be the final word. A promise that took this small group of Jews back to the dark days, maybe even the darkest day of all, when Israel stopped, crumpled between an Egyptian shore and an enemy camp. There, during the darkest night of all, the pillar and angel moved from the front to the rear, from fore to aft, to shield the slaves for one last night. Now, the prophet knows, the spirit stands as the pillar and angel once did. There is no need to fear. There is only the need, as in the days of old, to forge ahead.

The Future of Pneumatology

These innovations took place sometime between 587 and 445 B.C.E.—long before the heyday of Greco-Roman mysticism and longer still before the emergence of Christianity.[11] This chronology is significant. These prophets spoke of the spirit as standing, as giving rest, even as becoming the target of Israel's rebellion, more than five centuries before Jesus walked the earth or the apostle Paul sailed the Mediterranean, more than eight hundred years before the Christian Council of Nicea in 325, more than nine centuries—nearly a millennium—before the Council of Chalcedon in 451, no less than twenty centuries before the filioque issue came to a head, and two and a half millennia before the rumblings at Azusa Street, which catalyzed the wildfire expansion of global Pentecostalism.

The priority of Israelite tradition at the headwaters of pneumatology calls into question the proprietary nature of Christian pneumatology, to which some Christians have clung stubbornly with errant distinctions that bolster Christian identity at the expense of their Israelite and Jewish ancestral literature. For example, the convenient possibility of viewing the spirit in the Old Testament[12] as an *intermittent* presence and the spirit in the New Testament as a *permanent* one becomes a nonsensical distinction in light of Haggai's clear conviction that the spirit stands in Israel's midst[13] or the prophet's lament for a spirit that had been, at one time, an enduring and reliable guide to the promised land.[14] The equally convenient but misleading distinction between the spirit as a *power* in the first testament and a *person* in the second evaporates in the face of the prophet's lament and Haggai's promise, whose evocative plea and promise belie this bland distinction.

More trenchant and subtle critiques of pneumatology will emerge in the course of our study; to survey them now would be premature. Yet it is not premature to suggest, at the outset, that the enterprise of pneumatology may need to change in one key respect, which it would be disingenuous to ignore at the start. If ancient Israelites on the cusp of Judaism were responsible for humankind's first glimpse of the spirit as an agent of the exodus acting in concert with God, then it may not be too much to suggest that Christians begin to regard pneumatology as a collaborative enterprise, whose richness should be explored in the company of Jews and their reserve of ancient texts.[15]

This straightforward goal may be difficult to achieve. From interpretations of the biblical book of Acts to the letters of Paul, from Roman Catholic bishops to Pentecostal storefront preachers, from the *veni sancte spiritus* to speaking in tongues, the holy spirit is typically the sine qua non of Christian spirituality. To expect Christians to share that identity, this experience, with Jews may be too much to ask—except that at the headwaters of pneumatology lies Israelite insight into the holy spirit. Perhaps Christians should begin to ponder what other insight along the way they may have forfeited along their solitary path—and what insights they stand to gain along a shared path.[16]

Woven into this study is the fierce—others might call it naïve—conviction that a single observation can shift an entire paradigm, especially if that observation plunges one into the headwaters of a tradition. Of course, change rarely takes place in this way, with the advent of a simple observation, as a colleague, Bob Fine, whose expertise lies in palliative medicine, cautioned me. As we sat on his front porch and I told him about this book, Bob told me the story of Barry Marshall, the hardscrabble Australian doctor who bucked the medical consensus with his certainty that ulcers were the result not of acid but of bacteria. Marshall and his colleague Robin Warren repeatedly presented their findings to gastroenterologists, who just as repeatedly ignored and rejected them. With letters to the *Lancet*, presentations to gastroenterologists in Perth and microbiologists in Brussels, and a paper soundly rejected by the Gastroenterological Society of Australia, Marshall and Warren made no headway. Finally, in desperation, Marshall drank a broth with the bacteria called *Helicobacter pylori* and, not long afterward, came down with a peptic ulcer. He and Warren published a full report in the *Medical Journal of Australia* in 1985, yet the hypothesis hung limply for several more years—entropy fueled by the entire discipline of gastroenterology and a $3 billion pharmaceutical industry dependent upon the notion that acid causes ulcers.[17] There simply was too much vested interest in the older perspective. Still, in 2005, Marshall and Warren received the Nobel Prize in Physiology or Medicine for their hard-earned discovery.[18]

This is a cautionary—and now infamous—tale. I cannot (nor would I want to) muster the evidence of my own peptic ulcer to satisfy every stripe of theologian and scholar or to move entire communities toward fresh experiments in pneumatology. Still, it is not outlandish to suggest that there may be ample observations in this book to prompt even modest consideration of the possibility that Jews preceded Christians by centuries in their reflection upon pneumatology. Resistance to this thesis will be inevitable, skepticism requisite, and correction necessary, yet I hope these values will not shrink into recalcitrance, suspicion, and cynicism. That response would blunt and block the very horizon along which prophets millennia ago ably peered when, setting the spirit at the epicenter of divine deliverance, they explored—and discovered—God's elusive presence.[19]

Chapter 2

THE ESSENCE OF THE SPIRIT
Retelling Exodus: The Precursors of Pneumatology

With almost indiscriminate devotion, Israel hung its fate, like harps on exilic willows, on the conviction that God was present and active from the beginning, when a rabble of slaves ascended out of Egypt. From stories in the crevices of Exodus to the Persian-era prayers of Nehemiah, from the dogma of Deuteronomy to the poetry of Psalms, from the pedestrian prose of Numbers to the elevated verse of exilic Isaiah—Israel saw God, obliquely but unmistakably, at the cusp of liberation from Egypt. There was no memory that did not include the mien of God's presence.

But how? How was God present at the Egyptian seashore? If the answer were too confident, we could mock the gullibility of ancient faith. Too crisp, and it might sound contrived. Too confused, and we could dismiss these stories as by-products, pollutants of the vagaries of Antiquity.

Israel found an answer that was neither too confident nor too confused—and certainly not too contrived—to be taken seriously. Through the mists of communal reminiscence, Israel clung doggedly to the conviction that God had acted—walked and looked and defended and shied away—along the shores of the Sea, in the desert, at the mountain, and on the eastern banks of the Jordan River. The conviction that God was present then, if not in their own latter-day turmoil, circulated in Israel's bloodstream.

While it may seem peculiar to begin a study of the spirit *not* with the spirit but with a discussion of divine presence, this is exactly where a study of the spirit should begin. The prophet whose lament frames the next chapter is apoplectic at the prospect—actually, the actuality—of divine absence. *Where?* the prophet asks. Three times, in fact, the prophet asks, *Where?*

Where is the one who brought them up out of the sea with the shepherds of his flock?

Where is the one who put within them his holy spirit,
who caused his glorious arm to march at the right hand of Moses,
who divided the waters before them to make for himself an everlasting name . . .
who led them through the depths?

Where are your zeal and your might?[1]

A tradition in which God is so palpably present, the exodus tradition, raises for later generations, those who traipse bereft to Babylon or return to a temple in shambles, the question of God's absence. It is here, in this question, where pneumatology begins—not in affirmation or confidence or creed but in a question, panicked perhaps and plaintive, certainly. *Where is the one who put within them his*[2] *holy spirit?*

To probe the matter of God's presence, it is elemental to acknowledge that this conviction did not emerge as a perfect whole, faultlessly contoured, tidy and neat. Instead, Israel saw in this conviction a collection of divine agents through which God acted, in which God was present, on which God rode. Traditions of these agents invariably clash with one another in the texts as they now stand, which is how it should be if we regard Israelite literature "not simply as a succession of texts but a competition of voices."[3] Competition or concurrence, choir or cacophony—the sweep of Israel's composers affirmed the presence of God through different divine agents: pillars of cloud and fire, an extraordinary angel, God's own presence—literally, face—and a dense cloud.

This company of complementary agents of divine presence populates Israel's traditions within the sacred confines of the Torah, clashing among various literary strands of modern scholarship: the Yahwist, Elohist, Deuteronomist, and Priestly authors. These agents appear, too, well beyond the books of Moses. After a long hiatus, the angel of Sinai materializes unexpectedly in the book of Judges, of all places.[4] The cloud and fire, in various guises and to differing ends, appear as well in Israel's hymnody, both in the psalter and an extended public prayer in the book of Nehemiah.[5]

The memory of God's presence was persistent—but never static. Sometimes God is present in pillars of cloud and fire. Sometimes just in fire or a cloud. Sometimes God is present in an angel. Sometimes as the weight of God's glory. Sometimes God is present in God's presence, God's face. And sometimes these agents are combined, like a James Bond martini—shaken, not stirred—such as when Moses, in a panicked effort to rescue Israel from a murderously angry God, throws the whole gamut in God's face. If God kills Israel, Moses remonstrates, then the nations will hold God in contempt, "for you, O Lord, are seen face to face, and your cloud stands over them and you go in front of them, in a pillar of cloud by day and in a pillar of fire by night."[6] Moses offers a menagerie of divine agents to forestall annihilation and ensure survival.

Is Moses' last-ditch appeal contrived? Confused? Confident? Hardly. It is, however, enough, this time at least, to stave off the divine rampage.

All of this is confusing—and enlivening. No one sat down during the void of Babylonian exile and ironed out the creases. No one returned to Palestine in 538 B.C.E. and excised alternative traditions. No one censored allegedly obsolete ones. And certainly no one developed a doctrine of divine presence, a creed, an orthodoxy for a cataphatic or apophatic God. For all the vying and jockeying of the Persian era, with its opposing visions that simultaneously championed the outcasts or eschewed them, for all of this, rival conceptions of God's presence thrive not just on the surface but in the marrow of Israel's memory.

Put in a scholarly way, one documentary source has not erased another. If the Priestly authors were the last to put their stamp on the story, they did not squash or silence prior perceptions of God's presence. Cloud and fire, pillars of fire and cloud, a guiding angel, even God's face itself—all of these vie for attention. None of them dissipates. The putative traditions of the Yahwist, the Elohist, the Deuteronomist, and the Priestly authors each have a stake in God's presence, as do poets and prophets. An enduring conviction about God's presence, in other words, comprised the bedrock of Israel's corporate memory of its birth and early years.[7]

That bedrock, this sense of divine presence, lies at the foundation of pneumatology. But no single, seamless conviction lies there, an extraction of the faultless and coherent nature of divine perfection. A consciousness of the holy spirit—what the spirit did and who the spirit was—grew genetically from the variegated traditions of the exodus. Presence is no abstraction in Israel's traditions, nor is the spirit an abstraction, floating independently of a world populated by pillars and angels and God's face.

It is not possible to divvy up divine presence. Divine agents in the book of Exodus—not to mention Numbers, Deuteronomy, Nehemiah, Judges, Psalms, and Isaiah—are, to put the matter generously, *untidy*. In Exodus, for example, the pillar of cloud and angel seem simultaneously to offer protection from Egypt, with an odd redundancy; *both* move from the front of the camp to the rear to stand between escaping Israel and the Egyptian army.[8] This oddity raises the question of whether the angel and pillar are one and the same or separate expressions of divine presence. In a slightly later example, the pillars of cloud and fire seem to merge—this time *without* the angel—allowing God to look through one pillar and to send the Egyptian army into a panic.[9] Finally, this angel disappears, integral though it be to Israel's liberation. It reappears at Sinai, carrying divine authority[10] but, then, later still, becomes just a shadow presence of God.[11] Perhaps that does not matter because, by the end of the story, pillars and angel alike are set aside for the cloud—*just* the cloud—which covers the tabernacle.

These twists and turns in the traditions about God's presence emerge from centuries-long groping over the very question of how God is present in the push and shove, the tug and pull of human history. For all the talk of revelation in the Jewish Scriptures, for all the affirmation of God's love, mercy, and anger, for all of the centrality of Mt. Sinai in the Torah, the question still lingers, and it lingers especially in times of crisis. *How* is God present among us? In crisis, especially then, Israel asks this question. The psalmists ask this best, or at least most. But a close reading of Israel's stories, its poems, its prophecies, can be summed up in the simple question of how God accompanies God's people. Period.[12]

This memory—these memories—of divine presence, disordered though it may have been, is the ancestral home of pneumatology. Israel would change over the centuries, through wrenching experiences, but carry with it the aboriginal conviction that God was present in an array of agents—even if that memory, over the years, changed, too. An unprecedented change, in particular, would occur no more dramatically than in two prophetic writings—Haggai 2:5 and Isaiah 63:7-14—to which it is possible to trace the birth of the holy spirit or, expressed in more acceptable theological terms, the origin of pneumatology.[13] The authors of these texts introduced the spirit into the traditions of the exodus, in which God had rescued Israel from Egypt through a cadre of divine agents—pillars, an angel, and God's own face. Now, claimed these prophets, the spirit took on the role of those agents by standing in Israel's midst and guiding them to the promised land.

In a real sense, that unprecedented change was also a homecoming, leading Israel to where they began or, better yet, to the slightly muddled but unerring conviction of divine presence, which they carried with them over the centuries. The sense that God had led—*could* lead—Israel through pillars, an angel, and God's own presence, lingered, matured, even mutated, as Israel confronted ever more crises. To grasp the force of this conviction—to drill to the bedrock of pneumatology—it is not essential to analyze every agent or element that accompanied divine presence in the Hebrew Bible. Only those that funded the origin of pneumatology, particularly in Isaiah 63:7-14 and Haggai 2:4-5—the pillars, the angel, the presence-face of God, and, only by association, the cloud—appear in this study. There were other agents and elements, but the pillars, angel, and presence-face provide both ample focus and parameters. It is necessary to divvy up these agents, though always with the acknowledgment of their porous borders.[14]

The Pillars

In the itinerary of liberation, Egypt's slaves "set out from Succoth, and camped at Etham, on the edge of the wilderness," at which point God told them "to turn back and camp in front of Pi-Hahiroth . . . by the sea"[15] Simple enough directions, but *how* did God communicate them? The answer is given parenthetically, dropped somewhere between Exodus 13:20 and 14:1, between Etham and Pi-Hahiroth, in a narrative aside with explosive significance for understanding divine presence and, eventually, pneumatology.

> The LORD was traveling in front of them in a pillar of cloud by day, to lead them along the way, and in a pillar of fire by night, to give them light, so that they might travel by day and by night. Neither the pillar of cloud by day nor the pillar of fire by night left its place in front of the people.[16]

These pillars are the baseline of God's presence.[17] The rest of Jewish Scripture offers variations on this theme, but, at this point at least, the nature of God's presence is straightforward and solid.

One aspect of this scenario is unavoidable: God travels. In this initial version of the story, God travels in or with or simply by means of the pillars. No appreciable distinction separates God from the pillars, though no great effort is made to pinpoint that relationship either, if that were even possible. The ambiguous Hebrew inseparable preposition makes sure of that.

Ambiguity heightens overnight. By the morning after liberation, the two pillars have merged into one pillar of fire and cloud and stopped by the shores of the Sea: "At the morning watch the LORD in the pillar of fire and cloud looked down upon the Egyptian army, and threw the Egyptian army into panic." Gone are the simple days when God traveled in front of itinerant Israel in a pillar of cloud and a pillar of fire. The pillars are now one, and that pillar has now stopped.

Despite these changes, the place of the presence of God may be clearer still. Whether God is atop the pillar, in it, or behind it may not be possible to say.[18] Yet God looks *through* it. This pillar is the window through which God looks in order to send Egypt into panic.[19] Again, then, God's presence is attached to the pillars—this time, *one* pillar—so intimately that God is able to watch Egypt through it, as through a window.

Once God has driven the Egyptian army into chaos, God goes on the move again. God is itinerant in later traditions, as well. The book of Deuteronomy recollects a God "who goes before you on the way to seek out a place for you to camp, in fire by night, to show you the route you should take, and in the cloud by day."[20] This recollection, though offering no more precision than its forebear, continues to affirm God's itinerancy.[21]

In Israel's poetry, in contrast, God may *not* be on the move. One psalmist recalls how God "in the daytime led them with a cloud, and all night long with a fiery light."[22] The pillars travel, but God may not. God's presence could be near or far; God could lead by acting as a distant director or a fellow traveler. There is ambiguity here, unknowing. Not uncertainty—God *is* there—but the details of

God's presence are, as perhaps they should be, ultimately unknowable. Conviction, in Israel's poetry, is harnessed to inscrutability.

For another of Israel's poets, itinerancy dissolves in a litany of liberation, in which God directs Israel while standing apart. God "stretched a cloud for a partition, and fire to give light by night."[23] The image of God as Israel's intimately present and itinerant pillar-God has vanished, supplanted by a more palatable image: God stretches a cloud and fire for Israel. God does not travel *in* pillars of fire and cloud.

The latest and last portrait of the pillars in the Jewish Scriptures leads back to the earliest. The pillars of cloud and fire resurface in a prayer in the Persian-era book of Nehemiah, in which Ezra says to God, "You led them by day with a pillar of cloud, and by night with a pillar of fire."[24] The resemblance between Ezra's prayer and the primary appearance of the pillars in the Torah is striking. There are, in both texts, two pillars. The pillar of cloud leads by day, and the pillar of fire illuminates by night. Even the verbs that describe leading by the pillar of cloud during the day and lighting by the pillar of fire at night are identical in both texts. This iteration of the exodus story is, then, less innovation than preservation—with one possible exception. Ezra's prayer lacks the potentially awkward image of God's traveling before Israel in the pillar of cloud and the pillar of fire. "*You* have led them with . . ." prays Ezra, not "You traveled in front of them," as Exodus suggests. Apart from the omission of this anthropomorphic inelegance, which may be inadvertent, Ezra's prayer provides a version of the pillars that lacks any clear signs of innovation. Ezra's prayer offers clear evidence of the long shelf life—until well into the fifth century B.C.E.—of the belief that God led the Israelites with, perhaps even *in*, two pillars.

This realization—that God is intimately connected to the pillars—raises the question of what God *does* in or through the pillar(s).[25] The purpose of the pillars at first is unambiguous: with God, who travels in them, they *lead* the people day and night.[26] The pillar of cloud would "lead them on the way." The pillar of fire would illumine them by night.[27] In this way, the Israelites could outpace the Egyptian army.[28] If Israel is to escape, they need guides both day and night.[29]

This was not an evanescent presence, a glimpse of God on Sinai,[30] a glimmer of glory in passing,[31] an ephemeral episode of prophesying by a band of inspired elders.[32] The unusual verbs in this description of God and the pillars say otherwise. The LORD *was traveling* in front of the people.[33] Yet that is not all. There is a surfeit of repetition in this first telling of the story. The story is told, succinctly but fully, in Exodus 13:21. Exodus 13:22, otherwise redundant, functions as an exclamation point to underscore the persistence of the pillars. Neither pillar *would leave its place* at the front of the people.[34] In Israel's memory of their flight from

Egypt, God *was journeying* in front of them, and the pillars *would not leave* their place in front of them. There is an enduring quality to these verbs, their moods and tenses, that suggests durability, solidity, unshakable presence.[35]

This permanence may seem pedestrian. *Of course* God was present with the Israelites in those early days. Not so. This sense of stability fractures soon after the slaves arrive at Sinai. After a phase of unusual patience on God's part while Israel journeyed in the wilderness,[36] now, during the golden calf fiasco, God is quick to say, "I will not go up among you, or I would consume you on the way."[37] Later, while the Israelites travel from Sinai to the promised land, God's anger ignites a fire on the outskirts of the camp,[38] causes a plague,[39] rises against Aaron and Miriam so that Miriam contracts a skin disease, and flares again when Israel, intimidated by the report of the spies who return from Canaan, refuses to enter the land. "I will strike them with pestilence and disinherit them,"[40] threatens God. Against the background of these threats to God's presence, the emphasis upon reliability—God *was journeying* and the pillars *would not leave*—is poignant. At the base of their experience, according to Israel's collective memory, lay the belief that God led Israel constantly, dependably, and *improbably*, in a pillar of cloud by day and a pillar of fire by night.[41]

All this talk of the pillar(s) may appear to have little to do with the origin of pneumatology, but it is, in reality, an essential task of drilling to its bedrock. A detailed discussion will clarify that point later in this study, with a full-scale analysis of the prophetic claim, "My spirit abides among you; do not fear."[42] At this point, it is important simply to point out that the exodus tradition, in which the pillar(s) travel(s) in front of and shield(s) Israel, is the peculiar soil in which the rare, even exotic, seed of Israel's belief in the spirit as a deliverer would take root.

This lucid tradition, simple in its lines, is soon churned up, like the waters of the Red Sea. Even before the Israelites pass through the Sea, the tradition tilts:

> The angel of God who was going before the Israelite army moved and went behind them; and the pillar of cloud moved from in front of them and took its place behind them. It came between the army of Egypt and the army of Israel. And so the cloud was there with the darkness, and it lit up the night; one did not come near the other all night. . . . At the morning watch the Lord in the pillar of fire and cloud looked down upon the Egyptian army, and threw the Egyptian army into panic.[43]

Several actors crowd this scene: the angel, the pillar of cloud, the cloud, the Lord, the (single) pillar of fire and cloud.

The angel, who is new to the story, and the pillar, which is not, stop leading. They are not automatons, like a mechanical rabbit at dog races, but autonomous agents. They *pull out*.[44] Now, with Egypt breathing down the slaves' necks, the angel and pillar pull up stakes, moving from front to behind, from fore to aft, to occupy a defensive post, wedging themselves between the slaves and their pursuers. This defense takes another form: the cloud illuminates the night, so that neither camp approaches the other.[45] Then, at morning light, God looks in or through—as through a window—the pillar and throws Egypt into panic.

According to Israel's complicated memory, various agents led and defended the refugee slaves even prior to Israel's liberation from Egypt. The memory that Israel carried with it—perhaps cherished the most over the centuries—was the simple one of leading. Even long after the return from Babylonian exile in 538 B.C.E., in what may be the latest reference to the pillars in the Jewish Scriptures, Ezra's prayer preserves not so much an iteration as a reiteration of the baseline version: "You in your great mercies did not forsake them in the wilderness; the pillar of cloud that led them in the way did not leave them by day, nor the pillar of fire by night that gave them light on the way by which they should go."[46]

Still, Israel's memories were malleable, so that subsequent iterations varied ever so slightly. Moses' frenzied plea en route to the promised land reproduces the tradition in prayer form: "In a pillar of cloud you *are traveling in front of them* by day, and in a pillar of fire by night."[47] Yet the pillars are not the star of the show here; Moses appeals first to the cloud that overshadows Israel and the divine presence or *pānîm*, which allows God to be seen face to face. God, argues Moses, continues to travel in Israel's midst, continues to protect and stand over Israel through a cloud, continues to communicate eye-to-eye, and continues to go in front of the people in dual pillars of cloud and fire. Moses takes a desperate, determined plunge into the tradition and, in one fell and final swoop, concocts a recipe intended to reverse God's course and preserve, yet again, the people he has led from slavery to a long-promised homeland. The pillars are but two ingredients of this hastily but artfully crafted recipe.

According to still another iteration, God did more than identify the route; God also found places to encamp. The first version may have given the impression that Israel traveled day and night—an unsustainable practice. In this one, God also discovered places for Israel to rest.[48]

The psalms could be simultaneously slavish and innovative in their recitation of the story. "In the daytime he led them with a cloud, and all night long with a fiery light."[49] The psalmist, in a subtle development, emphasizes that the fire gave light *all night long* by combining, perhaps, the fiery pillar's ability to lead with the pillar of cloud's ability to function as a searchlight to prevent attack.[50]

Other poets proved more inventive. According to a litany reprising liberation from Egypt, God "stretched a cloud as a partition, and fire to give light by night."[51] The word *partition*, typically translated in this psalm as "covering"—God spread a covering[52]—is principally a reference to various partitioning *screens* in the tabernacle complex: the screen at the court gate,[53] the screen at the entrance to the tent, and the screen stretched over the ark of the covenant. In this respect, it is rich with reminiscence of Exodus 14:19-20, when "the pillar of cloud moved from in front of them and took its place behind them. It came between the army of Egypt and the army of Israel."[54] Against this fertile background, the simple statement that God "stretched a cloud as a partition" creatively recollects that moment when the cloud moved to Israel's rear flank and protected the camp from the Egyptian army.[55] Protection in this poem supplants itinerant presence.[56]

Both psalms, then, refract the memory of leading (Exodus 13:21-22) through the curtain of protection (Exodus 14:19-20). One poet may do so subtly by underscoring that light lasted throughout the night; the other does so overtly by depicting the cloud as a screen, a partition.

The vitality of Israel's traditions pulses in these recollections of Israel's agents of liberation. The figures themselves merge and diverge in the course of retelling, as do their activities. Yet the conviction they relay, that God was unusually present in or through or with these agents, pervades them all. No less significant, this conviction of divine presence through an assortment of agents—the pillar(s), in particular—would, during periods of colossal crisis, define Israel's understanding of the spirit.

The Angel

The pillar(s), so palpable and present during Israel's escape from Egypt, are not the sole agents of deliverance. On the night before liberation, with Israel perched between the Sea and the Egyptian army, an angel appears out of the blue to play a critical but cameo role.

Perhaps, on second thought, it is not such a critical role. The angel mirrors the action of the pillar of cloud, and so is, in a sense, superfluous. The angel moves from the front to the rear of the Israelite camp.[57] This seems momentous but for the detail that the "pillar of cloud moved from in front of them and took its place behind them." The rest of the story has to do with the cloud—and the pillar of fire and cloud. The angel is a footnote, a detail dropped into the story, then dropped altogether.[58]

The angel may be a redundancy—but not an incidental one. The angel does what God does. God is traveling in front of the camp; the angel, too, is traveling in front of the camp. Both *were traveling* in front of Israel. The angel may appear and just as quickly disappear. The angel may be a blip, perhaps the residue of a different version of the same story.[59] Yet something significant is to be garnered from its brief moment on the stage: God and the angel took exactly the same action in Israel's liberation. Any effort to grasp the relationship between God and this angel must take seriously this auspicious if fleeting first appearance.

Ephemeral though its appearance may be, this angel is not just "a poor player that struts and frets his hour upon the stage and then is heard no more."[60] The angel will indeed be heard of again, in further iterations that accentuate its eminence. It will appear as well in a lament, in which its prerogatives and accomplishments will pass to the holy spirit—or, as the prophet says as well, the spirit of the Lord.[61] It will materialize, in short, at the fountainhead of pneumatology. A reader's deceptively brief first encounter with this angel is but an adumbration of seismic shifts that lie ahead, in which the tectonic plates of angel and spirit will collide in the context of severe, if not final, crisis.[62]

Long before that moment, this angel resurfaces in a divine promise issued at Mt. Sinai. Toward the end of Israel's oldest law code,[63] God promises that an angel will lead the people. This is not just promise; it is warning, as well:

> I am going to send an angel in front of you, to guard you on the way and to bring you to the place that I have prepared. Be attentive to him and listen to his voice; do not rebel against him, for he will not pardon your transgression; for my name is in him. But if you listen attentively to his voice and do all that I say, then I will be an enemy to your enemies and a foe to your foes. When my angel goes in front of you, and brings you to the Amorites, the Hittites, the Perizzites, the Canaanites, the Hivites, and the Jebusites, and I blot them out, you shall not bow down to their gods, or worship them, or follow their practices, but you shall utterly demolish them and break their pillars in pieces.[64]

These words, tucked awkwardly into the Book of the Covenant, provide a lesson in call and response, divine initiative and human accountability.[65] The angel performs four verbs. The Israelites, too, must perform four verbs

The actions of the angel are pure, inescapable—and of enormous benefit to Israel. The angel will *protect* Israel on the journey; what it offered on that first propitious night along the shores of the Sea, it now provides perpetually.[66] The angel will *bring* them to the place God has prepared; the angel, in short, will finish the job begun in Egypt;[67] as if this note of assurance might be lost, this verb occurs not once but twice.[68] The angel will *speak* to the Israelites; God commands them to "listen attentively to his voice." The angel *travels in front of* the Israelites; the prerogatives of God and the pillars, here at least, belong equally to the angel.[69]

If there is a call, there is also a response. What response should Israel have to this angelic agent of God? Sheer and utter obedience, for starters. They must *pay careful attention* to this angel; in an arresting turn of phrase, the Israelites are to *watch out* for the angel who *watches out* for them.[70] They must *listen* to the angel's voice. They must *not rebel* against the angel.[71] Again, they must *listen* to—obey—the angel's voice; it is not possible to overemphasize the need for attentiveness to the angel.[72] Listening, *right* listening, shades into sheer obedience, submission even, in the Jewish Scriptures.[73] That is why this concatenation occurs: "*Listen* attentively to his voice and *do* all that I say."

Why is inattention so pernicious, distraction so dangerous? Because the angel's words are God's: "If you absolutely listen attentively to *his* voice and do all that *I* will say." To pay careful attention to the angel's words is to put God's into practice.

In this call and response, the consequences of rebellion are unavoidable: "For he will not pardon your transgression; for my name is in him." The presence of God's name in the angel evinces a remarkable level of intimacy, perhaps even identity, between God and the angel.[74] Medieval Jewish commentator Ibn Ezra adopted the analogy of the reflection of the sun in the moon to interpret the relationship of God with the angel.[75] Later in the story, though still at Sinai, the footing for this relationship will begin to slip under the pressure of Israel's distant will, but for now it is sure. Israel must not rebel against this angel because he will not forgive their sins—and he has that prerogative because God's name is in him.[76]

The angel has become much more than the figure who moved from Israel's front to its rear on the eve of the exodus, even though the angel's intervention, at that point, brought enormous dividends by providing a protective shield for the vulnerable band of refugee slaves. Israel's deference toward the angel now determines God's stance toward Israel. To disobey the angel is to displease God. There will come a time in Israel's experience when this prerogative will be the holy spirit's, when the prophet claims, "But they rebelled and grieved his holy spirit; therefore he became their enemy; he himself fought against them."[77] This will not occur because the angel forfeits its prerogatives to the spirit but because the prophet will see them as one and the same. For now, however, in the story of the exodus, the holy spirit is not yet in view; those prerogatives belong exclusively to an angel, whom God promises as a guide that will lead Israel to possess the promised land.

Vaunted and commanding now, the angel slips from eminence in short measure. After God has given the Israelites the ten words, followed by a full-fledged theophany, the Book of the Covenant, and initial instructions on the tabernacle, Israel responds by manufacturing a golden calf, which they create because they doubt that Moses will ever descend from the mountain. God is furious; Moses talks God from the ledge so that the people will not be destroyed.[78] Yet Moses, now furious himself, descends and throws the tablets down,[79] commands the Levites to slaughter the people, of whom three thousand die,[80] then heads back up the mountain to see if he can cover for their sin.[81]

With Israel in the throes of rebellion and punishment, God repeats the promise of an angel: "Whoever has sinned against me I will blot out of my book. But now travel, lead the people to the place about which I have spoken to you; see, my angel shall go in front of you. Nevertheless, when the day comes for punishment, I will punish them for their sin."[82] Following this old promise, this new *warning*, God sends a plague on the people.[83] The repetition of the promise of the angel, then, is cradled in conflict.

Despite the disaster of sin, killing, and plague, the promise remains—though with a vicious twist. God commands Moses, "Travel, lead."[84] Both verbs are pungent with reminiscence, providing a direct link to the tradition. God had originally led Israel in the pillars: "the LORD *was traveling*[85] in front of them in a pillar of cloud by day, to *lead* them[86] along the way."[87] Now, however, God relinquishes the responsibility of leading and places the task squarely upon Moses' shoulders—though not before recalling the promise made earlier. The promise is not new, though in a new context of utter rebellion, death, and plagues, with both God and Moses furious, it is perhaps surprising that God holds true to the original promise of an angel at all.

Along with the renewed promise comes warning: when the day comes, God will account for Israel's sin. (This day comes, at least in part, immediately, in the form of a plague.)[88] This warning, though framed in different words, recalls the gist of the angelic promise: the angel, if rebelled against, will not lift Israel's transgression. Both promise and warning, then, reemerge in what will become a memorable tussle between God and Moses: the angel will travel in front of Israel but with the threat of punishment hanging over Israel's head.

God shoos Moses away from Sinai, and everything looks to be in good order. In a single statement, God condenses the broad sweep of history: the promise to the ancestors, the promise of the angel, and the promise to drive out the inhabitants of Canaan. "Travel, go up from this place, you and the people whom you have brought up out of the land of Egypt, and go to the land of which I swore to Abraham, Isaac, and Jacob, saying, 'To your descendants I will give it.' I will send an angel before you, and I will drive out the Canaanites, the Amorites, the Hittites, the Perizzites, the Hivites, and the Jebusites."[89] This is a more sweeping version than the original command and promise—but for two disturbing details. First, God, in a strange twist, attributes the exodus to Moses: "The people whom you have brought up out of the land of Egypt." It looks as if God may be subtly relinquishing responsibility. Second, God does not call the angel *my* angel. The pronoun may subtly suggest a growing rift between God and Israel.[90]

At first blush, God's unwillingness to go up among them—in their midst—looks like God is pulling the pillars out from under them, for it was in the pillars that God traveled in front of Israel[91] and through the pillar of fire and cloud that God looked down and threw Egypt into a panic.[92] But that cannot be the case because the pillars appear subsequently, as the story unfolds. What God's recalcitrance does suggest is that the angel, which once shared responsibilities and prerogatives with God, is reduced to acting "as a surrogate for an absent, infuriated Yahweh."[93] "The people sought a substitute for Yahweh, and now he gives them one."[94]

Earlier on, the story had accorded a much higher status to the angel. The angel's word was God's word. Obedience to the angel was obedience to God. Rebellion against the angel brought punishment from God. The affiliation between God and the angel, once intimate and integral, now cleaves in two, like the Sea through which Israel once walked unhindered and unharmed. The liaison between God and Israel cleaves in two as well, despite Israel's harrowing, and apparently sincere, penitence in the following scene.[95]

Israel does travel. Moses does lead them. When, finally, a generation later, Israel reaches Kadesh and needs to travel through Edom to cross the Jordan and arrive in the promised land, the angel becomes the only agent of divine deliverance Moses chooses to include in an extremely brief review of Israel's experience. In a message to the king of Edom, Moses says: "Thus says your brother Israel: You know all the adversity that has befallen us: how our ancestors went down to Egypt, and we lived in Egypt a long time; and the Egyptians oppressed us and our ancestors; and when we cried to the LORD, he heard our voice, and sent an angel and brought us out of Egypt; and here we are in Kadesh, a town on the edge of your territory."[96] Moses' review is clipped, with large swaths of Israel's experience reduced to a few catchwords.[97]

The inclusion of this angel reveals just how deeply embedded an angelic guide must have been in Israel's corporate memory. The book of Numbers exhibits no interest in such a guide, given its focus on the tabernacle, on which a cloud descended. Even when his back is to the wall in a desperate effort to save his people, Moses does not make the slightest mention of the angel. Then, at a point in the story when there is no need to mention the angel—the pillars or presence-face or cloud would do nicely—it materializes as the agent by which God liberated Israel.

Moses chooses only the angel in this laconic recitation of Israel's past. Perhaps this is because the angel is the only agent, among all the agents of divine presence, associated with the destruction of enemies in the new land.[98] Or perhaps because stories of Israel's rebellion—a pivotal theme in the various promises of the guiding angel—frame this message.[99] Perhaps even simply because of the compelling persona of this angel. The angel—forceful and not at all forgiving—in the traditions of exodus, wilderness wandering, and land taking may have been so deeply embedded in Israel's traditions that it rose occasionally but not randomly in stories that filled Israel's collective memory. Whatever the reason for its stubborn persistence in the tradition, this angel surfaced, too, in prophetic writings—Isaiah 63, in particular—where it became the basis for the emergence of the spirit as an agent of the exodus.

After an appreciable hiatus, the angel of the exodus reenters the scene, as something of a surprise, particularly as he[100] arrives via a strange itinerary: "Now the angel of the Lord went up from Gilgal to Bochim."[101] In principle, this could be any angel, any messenger, but this angel is not just any angel.[102] This is the angel of the exodus, who claims, "I brought you up from Egypt, and brought you into the land that I had promised to your ancestors. I said, 'I will never break my covenant with you. For your part, do not make a covenant with the inhabitants of this land; tear down their altars.' But you have not obeyed my command. See what you have done! So now I say, I will not drive them out before you; but they shall become adversaries to you, and their gods shall be a snare to you."[103] This must be the angel of the exodus.[104] Now, however, this angel is not merely a protector,[105] an emissary charged with leading the people from Sinai to the promised land,[106] or perhaps even a poor substitute for God.[107] This angel claims the whole sweep of liberation, from Egypt to Canaan, for himself.

The transformation in this denouement is stunning.[108] The angelic prerogatives are sweeping. This angel is the deliverer and the covenant-maker himself. Further, the angel does not give the slightest hint that he is speaking on God's behalf; the angel speaks on his own behalf. In Exodus, there is identity—and ambiguity—between the voices of God and the angel: "If you listen attentively to *his* voice and do all that *I* say, then I will be an enemy to your enemies and a foe to your foes."[109] There is no ambiguity here: the angel who delivers Israel and has the power to continue delivering Israel speaks with complete and utter authority.

At this later point in the tradition, the significance of the angel has grown. The angel lays claim to what God, elsewhere in the tradition, has done: brought Israel from Egypt and into the promised land, kept covenant, watched Israel fail to obey, and drove out the inhabitants of the land. Throughout Exodus, Numbers, and Deuteronomy, these are divine prerogatives. In Judges, however, these are the angel's claims. The claims of Exodus 23:20-23 appear full-blown in Judges 2:1-5, as if the step back in Exodus 33:2 were a negligible whisper, barely a stumble, in the tradition. Now across the Jordan and in the land, the angel takes full credit for liberation, for covenant, and for what would have been but for Israel's unwillingness to drive out the nations of the promised land in a complete and quick conquest. The angel has come of age, and it is to Israel's detriment that they have kept covenant not with the angel but with the inhabitants of the land.

The Presence-Face

The emergence of the spirit as an agent of the exodus owed its existence to the pillar(s) and angel of the exodus—and also to the mysterious *pānîm* or presence-face of God.[110] This agent competes with the pillar and angel. On the one hand, it occupies a key place in the tradition, perhaps even the paramount place among God's agents in the story of the exodus. In a prophetic lament that lies at the base of pneumatology, on the other hand, God's presence-face shares this elevated position with the angel—and *both* fuse to create an equally imposing figure known, perhaps for the first time in Israel's history, as the holy spirit.[111] To engender an appreciation for the significance of that prophetic fusion, it is essential to trace the emergence of this figure in the context of a spellbinding negotiation between Moses and God.

The scenario could not become more complicated, the conversation more turgid, a sense of divine presence more convoluted, than it does in Moses' exchange with God at Sinai.[112] This level of complication reflects what is at stake in this conversation. With the debacle of the golden calf fresh in their minds, Moses and God have a serious tête-à-tête. A dialogue in which the stakes are so high, the investment of resources so extraordinary, the relationship so close is bound to progress by fits and starts. In fact, what transpires is less of a dialogue than a protracted negotiation. Too much is at stake. Too much binds the partners together. To part now is not simply to leave but to tear the fabric of covenant, care, and compassion. Naturally, then, the dialogue is heated, manipulative, and, to those who listen in, both dazzling and bewildering. And, naturally, the role of the agents of divine presence becomes confused in the process.

God begins the negotiation by twice repeating the promise of the angel, even if the second entails God's refusal to travel with Israel.[113] Rooted as this promise is in the baseline vocabulary of accompaniment, the premise of the negotiation is indisputable. The angel will lead Israel along the way, all the way to Canaan. God is not about to renege on that promise.

Then follow two extraordinary scenes, which stall the negotiation. In the first, the Israelites wholeheartedly repent; they proceed, whatever it may mean, without ornaments.[114] The second scene narrates a typical, companionable occurrence—how Moses regularly would meet God outside the camp at the tent of meeting, where the pillar of God would descend, and speak to God as a friend.[115] This is a misleading calm at the eye of the hurricane, a respite unworthy of trust.

No sooner does this serene scene of ordered homage and conviviality between Moses and God end than Moses and God square off again. In a tangled and tortuous conversation, Moses, who knows he has found favor with God, begs for someone to accompany them and for God to "consider too that this nation is your people."[116] Divine acquiescence is immediate: "My presence-face will go with you, and I will give you rest."[117]

Immediate—but inadequate. God's response refers again only to Moses with the second-person-singular rather than to Israel with the second-person-plural suffix.[118] Again, direct divine guidance for Israel is off the table in this negotiation, though Moses himself apparently continues in God's good graces. Unsatisfied by this state of affairs, Moses takes his turn by minimizing "the partial concession in order to press for the full request."[119] He demands that the compass of God's care encompass the people: "If your presence will not go, do not carry *us* up from here. For how shall it be known that I have found favor in your sight, *I and your people*, unless you go with *us*? In this way, *we* shall be distinct, *I and your people*, from every people on the face of the earth."[120] Moses' point is clear, emphatic, unambiguous, so God relents yet again: "I will do the very thing that you have asked."[121] This concession "is a brilliantly arresting conclusion to a magnificent narrative sequence, dazzlingly effective in its brevity, masterfully bold in its presentation of a Yahweh who is so secure that he does not mind being upstaged by his own servant Moses."[122]

Brilliantly arresting, yes. Masterfully bold, certainly. But lucid? Not exactly—at least not concerning divine agents. While it is clear that God's angel and presence-face are not the same, their relationship is not equally apparent. It is easy enough to infer that the presence-face is superior to the angel. The impression of superiority rises from Moses' demand to see God's presence-face despite the sure promise of angelic accompaniment.[123] To Moses, at least, the presence-face is preferable to the angel, notwithstanding the angelic prerogatives that God had delineated earlier on Mt. Sinai.[124] Since the angel leads Israel but God will not, Moses demands something else, probably something *more* of God—God's presence-face.[125]

Divine concession is not the end of the story. (It is not yet time for the reader to let out his or her breath.) Moses presses his advantage and asks God, "Cause me to see your glory, please."[126] This is mostly command; Moses might have used the polite and pleading Hebrew jussive form but instead adopts the imperative.[127] He is not entirely successful. With a rhetorical folding of the arms, God retreats into the aloofness of formulaic language—the intimacy of intense argument slips away for a moment—and responds, "I will make all my goodness pass before you, and will proclaim before you the name, 'The LORD'; and I will be gracious to whom I will be gracious, and will show mercy on whom I will show mercy."[128] This is a return to normalcy, divine reclusion, where God began in the burning bush. It looks as if Moses pushed too far. Too hard. Too relentlessly. God will now reveal God's goodness, but not apparently God's glory; the name of God Moses already knows, so this is hardly a bequest.

The negotiation has stalled. God withdraws to the familiar but aloof realm of divine decree, in which God selects objects of grace and covenant faithfulness. God ends the drama, full stop, with refusal: "you cannot see my presence-face;[129] for no one shall see me and live."[130] What seems like the end of the story, however, is not. God cradles Moses while the glory Moses requested passes by. Once God takes God's hand away, Moses does see—not God's presence-face but what lies behind God. Moses sees God from behind.[131]

The narrative does not clarify the relationship between God's presence-face and God's angel. Presumably, in Exodus, presence-face is something more than the angel, though how much more is simply not clear.[132] God has, in a remarkable concession, had a change of mind, thanks to Moses' intercession, and offered unmediated access.

Like so much of this negotiation, the answer to this question is shrouded in ambiguity.[133] When Moses demands, "Show me your glory," God's response is absolutely negative.[134] Yet, in the blink of an eye, God, apparently fickle, relents: "See, there is a place by me where you shall stand on the rock; and while my glory passes by I will put you in a cleft of the rock, and I will cover you with my hand until I have passed by; then I will take away my hand, and you shall see my back."[135] Moses will, then, experience God's glory, if fleetingly, obtusely, and not with his own eyes. Finally, notwithstanding this concession, and others God has made, God terminates the discussion in no uncertain terms: "My presence-face shall not be seen."[136]

There is an exacting realism in this negotiation. Neither stands upon terra firma. Both jockey for position. God issues threats and promises, reneges on both, and concedes parts of both. Moses makes demands of his own, pressing for every advantage, without winning ground. In the end, it is not clear what is left. Has Moses seen God's glory? God's presence-face? Or neither? And how can God's presence-face accompany the people without being seen?[137]

This conversation is tortured, manipulative, a series of strategic ploys by which Moses tries to wrest from God the settled presence that gives him authority among the uncooperative people he now must lead through the wilderness. It is also inconclusive. God relents to an extent, and Moses has gained ground, though it looks as if he has lost territory, too.

And yet, despite this ambiguity, the final stages of the negotiation suggest that Moses, with Israel's immense infidelity still fresh on his mind, has gained something. Not an unbridled theophany. Not grander promises to Israel. Not even ground gained—but territory *not lost*. In short measure, Moses climbs the mountain, where he is permitted, a second time, to cut two tablets of stone like the first.[138] God promises no guides better than the angel and the pillar(s). Israel becomes no more obedient, as the book of Numbers will detail. Moses is no more patient. But God is, or promises to be. God descends in a cloud—perhaps the pillar of cloud—and *stands*, as the pillar of cloud *stood* to protect Israel on the eve of liberation from Egypt,[139] then reveals God's name again, and, finally—in a magnificent word play evocative of Egypt—*passes*[140] before Moses and says: "The Lord, the Lord, a God merciful and gracious, slow to anger, and abounding in steadfast love and faithfulness, keeping steadfast love for the thousandth generation, forgiving iniquity and transgression and sin, yet by no means clearing the guilty, but visiting the iniquity of the parents upon the children and the children's children, to the third and the fourth generation."[141]

Perhaps this negotiation led nowhere. Or perhaps maintaining one's place can be counted as success in the midst of a nation on the verge of sedition.

This was not a failed negotiation in the sense that it lay fallow and forgotten. It was not an embarrassment to Israel, with God reneging and Moses begging. Before its late eighth-century demise at the hands of Assyria, the northern kingdom would join the southern kingdom in preserving it, though with a simplicity that belies its density: "And because he loved your ancestors, he chose their descendants after them. He brought you out of Egypt with his own presence-face[142] by his great power."[143]

This iteration gives no indication of how tangled and tortuous the negotiation between Moses and God was. There is not a hint of the tension between God's promise, "My presence-face will go with you, and I will give you rest,"[144] and God's subsequent refusal, "I will make all my goodness pass before you. . . . But . . . you cannot see my presence-face; for no one shall see me and live."[145] The agony, the manipulation, the negotiation become, in Deuteronomy, a simple statement that God's presence-face was a powerful agent of liberation during the exodus.

This version also traces the activity of God's presence-face to the exodus itself. In the original story, Moses and God tangled later, during the sojourn at Mt. Sinai, about whether God's presence-face would accompany Israel—or perhaps just Moses—from that point on. The ability to trace the activity of God's presence-face all the way back to the exodus is a departure from the tradition—still another sign of its expansiveness and elasticity.

In this way, a fragile sliver of promise in the tradition, that God's presence will accompany Moses—a promise that, in short measure, is withdrawn, when Moses is told he cannot see God's presence-face and live—expands. God's presence-face comes to be associated not with guidance on the journey and the validation of Moses but with the sheer power that rescued Israel from Egypt. Yet something too is lost in this retrojection of the presence-face: the tenor and tension of argument and debate, which made the presence-face of God, in its earliest iteration, a latecomer—an auspicious and inaccessible latecomer, to be sure—among the cadre of divine agents that led Israel from Egypt to Canaan.

An even more irenic appropriation of the exodus tradition is discernible in a prophetic lament, in which the angel and the presence-face of God fuse amiably, as if there had been no debate at all, into a single figure, the angel of God's presence.[146] The tense dispute about the angel and the presence-face dissolves in this lament, where no evidence remains of God and Moses' heated exchange at Sinai. Something even more dramatic is apparent in this lament: the angel and presence-face of God fuse not only with one another but with the holy spirit. That unprecedented development will soon be the subject of further discussion.

The Cloud

It is difficult to leave this passionate negotiation without a sideways glance and upturned brows—perhaps, too, a sigh of relief. How this heated exchange is like speaking to a friend is hard to imagine. This negotiation, rather, marks the height of tension that permeates the tradition of God's accompaniment during Israel's early years. Did God journey with them (Exodus 13:21-22; 33:2-3)? Were there two pillars (13:21-22) or one (14:19-20, 33:9-10) or one made up of both cloud and fire (14:24), or was there a cloud that would luminesce at times—or luminesce constantly but be visible only in the darkness (14:19-20)? What was the primary purpose of the pillar(s)? To guide and guard Israel (13:21-22; 14:19-20; 14:24), or to descend on the tent outside the camp (33:9-10)? And what of the angel, the severity of whose initial gravitas diminishes as Moses' penchant for the presence-face of God increases (14:19; 23:20-23; 32:34; 33:2-3; 33:14-15)?

The picture is, if not confused, at least confusing, full of overlap and ambiguity. Add to that the intermittent presence of a cloud that exhibits some of the characteristics of the pillars. Unlike the pillars or angel or presence-face, the cloud is more locale than agent. Nor does it reappear in Isaiah 63:7-14 and Haggai 2:4-5. Yet the cloud appears often enough and with enough association with these agents to demand attention.[147]

In its first appearance, God is said to appear in *the* cloud, as if a reader would be familiar with this cloud, though no cloud had previously appeared on the horizon of Israel's story: "And as Aaron spoke to the whole congregation of the Israelites, they looked toward the wilderness, and the glory of the LORD appeared in the cloud."[148] A second oddity in this snippet is the location—or lack of location—of the cloud. The Israelites "looked toward the wilderness." They are *already* in a wilderness, though perhaps this phrase "at least implies the wilderness of Sinai, the place of the greatest theophany."[149]

Whatever can be made of this unusual appearance of God in this cloud, it is clear that the cloud has no agency. It does not lead. It does not travel. It does not protect. It is simply the locale of God's glory. The same can be said of the cloud in which God appears at Sinai in Exodus,[150] as well as the cloud in which God descends to stand with Moses.[151] These clouds provide a place for God's descent and appearance, yet they perform no actions of their own. Not a single verb describes their activity apart from *covering* the mountain;[152] this is a verb that can describe any cloud, theophanic or otherwise.[153]

The appearance of the same cloud above the tabernacle closes the book of Exodus:

> Then the cloud covered the tent of meeting, and the glory of the LORD filled the tabernacle. Moses was not able to enter the tent of meeting because the cloud settled upon it, and the glory of the LORD filled the tabernacle. Whenever the cloud was taken up from the tabernacle, the Israelites would set out on each stage of their journey; but if the cloud was not taken up, then they did not set out until the day that it was taken up. For the cloud of the LORD was on the tabernacle by day, and fire was in the cloud by night, before the eyes of all the house of Israel at each stage of their journey.[154]

This cloud bears a striking resemblance to the pillars—though with significant differences. The cloud eclipses the itinerant pillars that traveled before Israel, though the cloud does not signal *where* to go; it indicates only *when* they should set off on their journey. Its presence by day and fire *in* the cloud by night also recalls the eve of deliverance, throughout which a pillar of cloud protected Israel by illuminating the night. The cloud also functions as a barrier—Moses cannot enter the tabernacle—like the angel and pillar on the eve of deliverance[155] or the partition the pillar is said to provide in the psalms.[156] And though the images are not quite the same, the descent of the cloud over the tabernacle mirrors the descent of the pillar of cloud over the tent of meeting, though, again, with an appreciable difference: the pillar signaled to those in the camp that Moses had entered the tent of meeting, while the cloud and glory mean he *cannot* enter.[157]

These similarities are an indication of how effectively the final paragraph of Exodus gathers elements from elsewhere in the book. Yet not all of those elements appear, and those elements that do appear, given the sweep of Exodus, are awkward—signaling when to leave but not where to go and keeping Moses from entering the tent. This awkwardness in the epilogue to Exodus is no doubt due to the need to preserve the journey—this is a tabernacle, after all, not a temple—but in a context whose focus lies elsewhere, in a mirror image of the Sinai experience. After all, "the function of the Tabernacle was to create a portable Sinai."[158] While the final paragraph of Exodus, then, preserves key elements of guidance and protection, ultimately it hamstrings the vision originally associated with the itinerant pillars of cloud and fire, as well as the angel and God's presence-face.[159]

Traditions in Motion

In the uneven furrows of Israel's collective memory of deliverance from Egypt, a protracted sojourn at Sinai, an interminable journey through the wilderness, and a contested settlement in Canaan, divine agents play a vital role in answering the question, *How is God present with us?* A dense cloud, pillars of fire and cloud, an angel, and God's presence-face appear and reappear, like a boat thrashing on a stormy horizon, in the prose and poetry that Israel would eventually collect, edit, and cherish.

The spirit is none of these agents. There is not even a hint of the spirit's presence as an agent in the spate of stories that focused upon the exodus, the wilderness wanderings, and settlement of the promised land. Yet these stories ignited prophetic imaginations in crisis to embrace the traditions of the exodus and to modify them, not least by introducing into them the figure of a spirit standing in Israel's midst, becoming the object of Israel's recalcitrance, and giving Israel rest. These stories, in short, provided the raw material for the emergence of the spirit as an agent of God's deliverance.

The character of the exodus tradition made this unprecedented transformation possible. The exodus tradition was never static; it was *elastic*, prone simultaneously to preservation and modification. This is precisely what occurred in the lament in Isaiah 63:7-14 and the promise of Haggai 2:5. Nor were the agents of the exodus—the pillar(s), angel, and presence-face—so inflexible and autonomous as to prevent intersection. This proclivity for *interaction* between them made it not only possible but likely that further metamorphoses, such as the fusion of angel and spirit, would take place. Finally, the exodus tradition was nothing if not *persistent*; that it would intersect with belief in the spirit, and change both in the process, is credible and probable. Before turning to the intriguing innovations of Isaiah 63:7-14 and the promise of Haggai 2:5, it may prove beneficial to look, one last time, at the qualities of the exodus tradition that made it the supple source of an unprecedented metamorphosis of both the exodus tradition itself and belief in the spirit of God.

Elasticity

The elasticity of the role played by divine agents in the exodus tradition begins nearly at the start. The tradition of two pillars, one of cloud by day, the other of fire by night,[160] quickly metamorphoses into one pillar consisting, in some mysterious way, of both cloud and fire.[161] Not much later—merely the time it takes to travel from Egypt to Sinai—the metamorphosis continues, as the pillar of cloud descends at the entrance of the tent of meeting so that God and Moses can talk face to face.[162] The horizontal movement of leading from the front has changed to vertical movement, to ascent and descent on the outskirts of the camp. Only a sliver of the earlier tradition remains in Exodus 33:7-11: the realization that the pillar of cloud could create a partition. Yet even this bit of continuity is scarcely enough to obfuscate the element of discontinuity; there is no apparent danger outside the camp,[163] certainly no threat akin to the relentless Egyptians, who had cornered Israel between their chariots and the Sea.[164] The threat of the exodus proved ephemeral; the greatest threat now to Israel is God and their own disobedience.

By the end of Exodus, the vertical dimension has eclipsed the horizontal; divine presence from above has supplanted divine presence in front of Israel en route to the promised land (Exodus 40:34-38). The cloud descends upon the tabernacle. If there is a hint of the journey ahead, it lodges awkwardly in the detail that the descent of the cloud signaled encampment and its ascent, the journey. But to where? That issue is not resolved until the book of Numbers, where God's command supplies the *where* of the journey, while the cloud's ascent signals the *when*. There is a clash in the tradition between the dynamic pillars and the static—and the many permutations that characterize them along the way.

No matter how strong the impulse was to attach the cloud and fire to the tabernacle, no matter how keen the effort to localize God's agents, the dynamic quality never dissipated. The centuries that may have separated the original narratives from their northern versions, for example, could not eviscerate the initial dynamic impulse. Alongside something new—God went before the Israelites in a fire by night to find a place for them to camp—occurs something old—God traveled in a cloud by day to show them the route.[165] The psalms, too, would reshape these traditions, adding touches such as the presence of a fiery light "all night long."[166] In Psalm 105:39, the cloud protects Israel, while the fire illumines their way.

The tradition of the angel, too, proved elastic. Introduced as a guardian, alongside the pillar of cloud, who moved fore to aft to protect Israel from the Egyptians,[167] the angel would be introduced again as Israel's guard, the bearer of God's name, and a figure not to be trifled with or rebelled against.[168] Yet just chapters later, and with no geographical movement—they are still at Sinai—the angel looks less like the bearer of God's name and more like a surrogate supplanted by God's presence-face.[169]

That is where the situation is left at the end of Exodus, where the cloud over the tabernacle and the glory within draw all of the attention—and the angel, none. Even in Numbers, Moses, with his back to the wall yet again, collects traditions intended to recollect the intimacy between God and Israel, but the angel is not there. The cloud is. The pillar of cloud by day and the pillar of fire by night are there, too. But not the angel, though the angel reappears, of all places, in a missive to the king of Edom, in which Moses pleads for passage.[170] Finally, the angel appears in full force in Judges 2:1-5, where he claims to have effected liberation and safe passage by himself, as if the full orb of God's power were entirely and exclusively his. The tradition, in an unexpected way, is resurrected on the outer lip of the promised land.

Intersection

Within any of these traditions, there is development and divergence, so that it is not possible to speak of any given tradition as a static whole. These traditions reflect the ebb and flow of Israelite memory.

Traditions about divine agents are difficult to corral for another reason: their borders are porous. What separates them from one another is like a membrane, which absorbs dimensions of the various agents. The pillars of cloud and fire that lead Israel in Exodus 13:21-22 show up, for instance, simply as cloud and a fiery light in Psalm 78:14 or as a protective partition-cloud and fire by night in Psalm 105:39. These pillars (or just one pillar of cloud), which are linked to movement and guidance in their first iterations,[171] become static in later appearances on Sinai.[172] Sometimes the pillars are reduced to one, a pillar of cloud, through which God speaks,[173] or simply a cloud over the tabernacle.[174]

These iterations are elusive. The cloud that descends over the tabernacle, for instance, is fiery by night, like the pillars of cloud and fire that led the way[175] or the protective pillar in Egypt.[176] Is the cloud by night that covers the tabernacle a remnant of the two pillars or simply a reflection of an altar fire? The author of Numbers seems aware of this tension in the tradition, for he writes, in his summary of what typically took place, that the cloud had the *appearance* of fire.[177] The fiery *manifestation*, in other words, was different from the *actual* pillar of cloud and pillar of fire that went before Israel at the start.[178]

There may be a better word than *intersection* to describe these traditions. *Overlap*, perhaps. *Porosity*, even. *Membraneity*—were that a word. Whatever the phenomenon is called, the tendency of traditions to diverge and merge throughout the centuries evinces both a complexity and a vitality that ought not to be missed in any study of the exodus tradition. These agents are not the same, yet they cannot be separated from one another without causing a tear, or at least a slit, in Israel's memory. This state of affairs makes it impossible to detect clear strands, detached traditions in Israel's understanding of divine presence. The pillars, the angel, the cloud, God's presence itself—these are neither altogether discrete nor necessarily identical dimensions of Israel's memory.

Persistence

Alongside the qualities of elasticity and porosity, the divine agents of the exodus tradition evince a stubborn persistence. The tradition of an angel, for example, nearly disappears but rises from the ashes of oblivion—and with a vengeance—in Judges 2:1-5. This should not be surprising, as the stubbornness of the angel tradition is evident already in Numbers 20:16, where, for reasons that are difficult to fathom, Moses mentions this angel in his letter to the king of Edom, though the angel plays no other role in the book of Numbers.

The northern kingdom, centuries after the initial narratives came into being, simultaneously preserved and adapted a variety of traditions. God's traveling—even the participial form remains—in the dynamic pillar of fire by night and cloud by day[179] reappears in pillars that direct Israel's itinerary, though now with the element of finding rest by night.[180] The presence-face plays a role, too, among northern traditions—perhaps even a more formidable role, since northern traditions trace its agency, contrary to Exodus 33:14-15, all the way back to the exodus.[181] The pillar of cloud, understood along the lines of Exodus 33:7-11, descends and stands at the entrance to the tent.[182] Even syntax proves significant; ancient trajectories, from Exodus 13:21-22 to Deuteronomy 1:33 and Numbers 11:14-15, discernible across centuries, hold a participle in common: these agents *were traveling* in front of Israel.

The pillars of cloud and fire, the pillar of cloud, the cloud, the cloud and the fiery light, the angel, the presence-face of God—these appear and reappear, from Torah to Psalms. The permutations of the exodus tradition provide an essential datum: while numerous agents played key roles in the exodus tradition, the spirit did not. Pillars of various sorts, different types of clouds, the presence-face of God, an angel, even God, play assorted roles in leading Israel from Egypt to the promised land. Not, however, the spirit. Not, that is, until someone sang or spoke or composed Isaiah 63:7-14 and Haggai 2:5. In these prophetic texts, the spirit does not just take its place *alongside* these agents; the spirit takes their place altogether.

Chapter 3

THE ABSENCE OF THE SPIRIT
Recalling Exodus: The Dawn of Pneumatology

Demetrius of Phalerum—so the story is told—was the royal librarian in Alexandria.[1] Charged with bartering and buying all the books in the world, he amassed a library of more than two hundred thousand volumes and, bolder still, promised King Ptolemy he would reach half a million in short order. Among those, Demetrius had heard, ought to be the Jews' writings. Translation would be tricky, he admitted, because the Jews had their own language, like Syriac, but not quite. So the king, enthused by the prospect, wrote to the high priest and invited seventy-two Jewish elders—six from each tribe—to Alexandria.[2] Feted for seven days while the king posed impromptu philosophical questions, to which they responded with aplomb and perspicacity, the elders then headed to a Mediterranean island to translate the Torah from Hebrew into Greek.

The story grew, as stories did, in the annals of Jewish Antiquity. For starters, the element of inspiration ousted the congenial labor of translation. Originally, the sages came up with a common text by comparing their translations with one another.[3] In another version, the elders did not compare translations at all; they went instead into separate rooms and, voilà, came up with the same translation, word for word.[4] In still another, the seventy-two elders became seventy, like the seventy elders who accompanied Moses on Mt. Sinai and prophesied in the desert, when a dollop of the spirit that rested upon Moses came to each of them.[5]

Accretions and aggrandizements aside, the story of the translation of the Hebrew Torah into the Greek Pentateuch at some point during the second century B.C.E. stands. Eventually—though little is known of specifics—other Hebrew books, along with those of the Apocrypha, would find their way into Greek, too.

Another aspect of the original story stands as well: the Greek translation was the product of consultation and comparison. The translators, whoever they were, proved to be intelligent interpreters adept at resolving conundrums in the original Hebrew texts. In Joshua 22:19, for instance, Phinehas warns some Israelites against building an altar other than the LORD's altar. The Hebrew has the same word for *altar* in both instances, but the translators distinguished between an Israelite altar and a non-Israelite one by adopting different words. The Greek translation engenders, in a way the Hebrew does not, the sanctity of Israel's altar; it preserves, unlike its Hebrew forebear, a sense of the sacred.[6]

Translators resolved a more pressing issue in Genesis 2:3, which, in Hebrew, implies that God worked on the Sabbath when it says that God *completed* God's work on the seventh day (like finishing homework in class). The translators dispensed with this issue swiftly and succinctly by saying instead that God completed God's work on the *sixth* day. Problem solved.

The Source of Salvation

No less thorny a conundrum materializes, though less conspicuously than Genesis 2:3, at the tail end of the book of Isaiah, in a moving lament.[7] This Hebrew lament, both rich with praise and plaintive in tone, pivots nearly midway, where the word, *Where?* twice reveals deep grappling not just with divine apophasis but with divine absence:

> I will recount the gracious deeds of the LORD,
> the praiseworthy acts of the LORD,
> because of all that the LORD has done for us,
> and the great favor to the house of Israel that he has shown them
> according to his mercy,
> according to the abundance of his steadfast love.
> For he said, "Surely they are my people, children who will not deal falsely";
> and he became their savior in all their distress.
> *The angel of God's presence saved them;*
> in his love and in his pity he redeemed them;
> he lifted them up and carried them all the days of old.
> *But they rebelled and grieved his holy spirit;*
> therefore he became their enemy; he himself fought against them.
> Then they remembered the days of old,[8] of Moses his servant.
> Where is the one who brought them up out of the sea with the shepherds of his flock?
> *Where is the one who put within them his holy spirit,*
> who caused his glorious arm to march at the right hand of Moses,
> who divided the waters before them to make for himself an everlasting name,
> who led them through the depths?
> Like a horse in the desert, they did not stumble.

> Like cattle that go down into the valley, *the spirit of the* L*ORD* *gave them rest.*
> Thus you led your people, to make for yourself a glorious name.[9]

This lament is critical to a proper perspective on pneumatology. Its deceptively simple poetry may, in fact, lead back, through centuries of doctrinal and theological brush, to the headwaters of pneumatology, where the spirit is, for the first time in Israel's history, an active agent. With one reference to an angel and three to the spirit, including two to God's *holy* spirit, this lament holds promise for the origin of pneumatology.

One line in particular, couched in a context of tribute, marks a decisive point in the emergence of pneumatology, though it is shrouded by uncertainty because of the difference that separates the Hebrew and Greek versions. The Hebrew reads:

> became their savior
> in all their distress.[10]
> *And the angel of his presence saved them;*
> in his love and in his pity he redeemed them;
> he lifted them up and carried them all the days of old.

This is an English translation of the *Hebrew* version. The *Greek* translation, in contrast, affirms that God

> became to them salvation
> out of all affliction.
> *It was no ambassador*[11] *or angel but the Lord himself that saved them,*
> because he loved them and spared them; he himself ransomed them
> and took them up and lifted them up all the days of old.

What emerges from the difference between these versions is disquieting. In the Hebrew version, the source of Israel's liberation is unequivocal: *the angel of God's presence saved Israel.* In the Greek, the source of Israel's liberation shifts from the angel to the Lord: *only the Lord saved Israel.* In essence, the Greek negates precisely what the Hebrew asserts: the angel of God's presence saved Israel.

The notion of an angel, like the angel promised in Exodus,[12] leading Israel to safety is gone from the Greek version. Equally filleted is the notion that God's presence—the presence-face once promised to Moses on Mt. Sinai—accompanied Israel in safety.[13] This translational move is less communication than assault. It is not merely translation from one culture to another; it is transposition, in which God alone supplants the actors of the exodus. The translators accomplished this not by ignoring the angel or presence and simply omitting the difficult line, *"and the angel of his presence saved them,"* but by importing a polemical contrast: *"it was no ambassador or angel but the Lord himself that saved them."*

The sharpness of that contrast reveals how explosive the affirmation that "the angel of God's presence saved them" might have been to a Jewish translator during the Greco-Roman era. The attribution of salvation to an ambassador or angel rather than to God was anathema, a conviction not just to be avoided but to be resisted, to be unmasked even at the cost of the Hebrew text.

No less consequential, the Hebrew version demands that the spirit in subsequent lines be understood as an angelic presence; the Greek does not. In the Hebrew, the three references to the spirit that follow in quick succession must be understood in terms of "the angel of God's presence," which "saved them." The Greek, in contrast, distinguishes God, who saves, from the holy spirit. The shift in the Greek version from angel-as-savior to God-as-savior, troubling enough on its own, proves elemental to an understanding of the origin of pneumatology.

The three references to the spirit, it should be said, can be understood on their own to portray an agent of God, robust as they are with reminiscence of the exodus, but a measure of their meaning is lost with the Greek translation. "God alone became their savior," tempers the edge of the angelic presence in Israel's remembered history. Perhaps to say this is to say too little; it may be more accurate to say that the Greek translation, "God alone became their savior," effaces the presence of the angel and, with that, erases the clear association of angel and spirit in the subsequent lines of the Hebrew version.

To make this point more bluntly: this poem *in Hebrew* fuses two agents of the tradition, the angel and God's presence, and identifies this figure, produced by that fusion, with the holy spirit. This swift sequence, this easy transition from angel to spirit, does not occur in Greek, where the angel is absent, the presence-face gone missing, and God, God alone, liberates Israel, loves Israel, pities Israel. The choice of the Greek over against the Hebrew, then, has significant implications for comprehending the spirit.[14]

A daunting array of interpreters gives priority to the Greek against the Hebrew although, oddly enough, few of those interpreters substantiate their claim. The reasons they proffer, it would seem, can be boiled down to three. To begin with, the Greek is more felicitous, with three clear pairings:

> He became to them a savior / in all their affliction
> Not a messenger or an angel / his presence saved them
> In his love and in his compassion / he himself redeemed them.[15]

Additionally, the expression *the angel of his presence*, is unique—too distinctive, in fact, to be original. Finally, the theology of the Greek, in which the accent lies upon the work of God alone, without the aid of messengers and angels, fits Isaiah 63:7–64:14—the passage that cradles this lament—better than does the Hebrew. There is simply no room for a mediator in this passage; God alone redeems, lifts, and carries Israel. The Greek, therefore, preserves the original text.

The question of whether the Greek preserves the more original text is pivotal for grasping the origin of pneumatology. If the Greek is original, then the spirit may, *but need not*, be seen to take on the role of the angel of God's presence. If the Hebrew is original, then the spirit *should* be seen to take on the role of the angel of God's presence.[16]

The Case for a Hebrew Lament

As a preamble to this essential lament, a brief but technical discussion is inevitable—perhaps even profitable—because Hebrew Isaiah 63:9, followed, as it is, by three references to spirit (*rûaḥ*), lies at the base of pneumatology. Several bits and pieces cohere to form a compelling case for the originality of the Hebrew rather than the Greek.

The first bit of evidence comes from the shores of the Dead Sea. The Qumran text of Isaiah, the earliest extant version of Isaiah 63:9, preserves the expression *the angel of his presence saved them*.[17] Even the Targumic tradition reads, *an angel sent from before him [God] saved them*.[18] Given the strength of this textual evidence, substantial countervailing evidence is required to opt for the Greek version. That evidence does not exist.

Another consideration has to do with the Greek version of Isaiah 63:8-9, which shows signs of being more than just a bit of translational tinkering.[19] It looks rather like a deliberate effort to interpret a difficult Hebrew text. The shift from "distress" (צָר) to "ambassador" (πρέσβυς, צִיר in Hebrew) is due to difficult Hebrew in this context. This is not a natural step, as "ambassador" (צִיר) is not written defectively (צָר) elsewhere, except in Isaiah 57:9.[20] Another sign of tinkering is apparent in the addition of "but" (ἀλλά); there is no corresponding conjunction in the Hebrew text, so this looks like a deliberate attempt to make an unmistakable point about the unmediated relationship between God and Israel: "not an ambassador or angel *but* the Lord himself saved them."[21] Finally, the climax of this deliberate effort to preserve the relationship between God and Israel is the metamorphosis of the Hebrew, "his presence saved them" (פָּנָיו הוֹשִׁיעָם), into "the Lord himself saved them" (αὐτὸς κύριος ἔσωσεν αὐτούς). This is hardly a literal rendering. Nor is the transformation subtle, a quiet instance of translational prose intended delicately to undermine the presence of mediator figures. Something bolder and more polemical is going on in the Greek when "his presence" is rendered, with the addition of the emphatic demonstrative pronoun, by "the Lord *himself*."[22] This translation slams the door in the face of the angel and preserves an unmediated relationship between God and Israel.

There is also a case to be made against regarding the phrase *angel of his presence* as too unique within the Hebrew Bible—it is unattested elsewhere—to be original.[23] If all of the original expressions in Isaiah 63:7-14 were deleted, the poem would disintegrate, since other of its phrases are equally inventive: *rebelled against his holy spirit, shepherds of his flock, established them in his presence, his holy spirit, YHWH's spirit gave them rest,* and *to make for yourself a glorious name.*[24] Since Isaiah 63:7-14 is rife with originality, riddled with novelty, the phrase *angel of his presence* should not be rejected by dint of its originality. Its uniqueness hardly provides a reliable reason to opt for the Greek, "it was no ambassador or angel but the Lord himself that saved them," rather than the Hebrew, "the angel of his presence saved them."

In light of how patently the Greek translators reshaped Isaiah 63:8-9 into a pristine statement of unmediated divine presence, through the repointing of a word (πρέσβυς: צִיר for צָר), the insertion of an adversative particle "but" (ἀλλά) in a Hebrew clause that lacks one, and a robust statement of how God alone saves (αὐτὸς κύριος ἔσωσεν αὐτούς), it is understandable why interpreters prefer it to the Qumran text, the Targums, and the Masoretic text. Yet this emphasis upon the exclusive agency of God is due to a good deal of tidying up in the Greek translation of this lament. Elsewhere, ancient Jewish translators made it clear that God could not be worshiped on a pagan altar and that God had *not* worked on the Sabbath; here certain translators made it clear that God, and God alone, rescued Israel from Egypt. The shift from Hebrew to Greek nipped in the bud the possibility of multiple saviors and manifold gods.

This reluctance to associate angels too closely with God and God's work, in fact, is not unique among Greek translations of the Hebrew text. In the keynote promise of the angel,[25] the Greek translators temper the threat that the angel "will not pardon your transgression." In the Greek, the angel will, in a more benign warning, not *draw back.*[26] Pardoning is not, in the Greek, one of the angel's rights, as it is in the Hebrew. On a subtler note, the Greek eliminates the vacillation of pronouns that serves to link divine and angelic authority. The Hebrew reads: "If you listen attentively to his voice and do all that I say." In the Greek, God alone—not the angel—has authority: "If by paying attention you listen to my voice and do all that I tell you . . ." In this key promise, the authority of the angel in the Greek is attenuated. In essence, the Greek translators do not allow for the blurring of lines between divine and angelic prerogatives that is palpable in the Hebrew text. Analogously, in the Greek of Isaiah 63:9, the line between divine and angelic authority is rigid; salvation is *not* one of the angel's prerogatives, as it is in the Hebrew text.

A similar reluctance rears its head in the Greek versions of Judges 2. In the Hebrew, the angel claims to have delivered Israel from Egypt. The translator of Greek version A modifies the first-person pronoun, by which the angel claims to have led the people from Egypt, to "the Lord, the Lord brought you up from Egypt and brought you into the land that he had sworn to your fathers to give to you." God, not the angel, effected exodus. Greek version B, by prefacing the quotation with the words, "this is what the Lord says," clarifies that God, not the angel, speaks, in the first place, of deliverance and guidance. The angel, in effect, simply quotes God. In Judges 2, then, the Greek translators of both versions transfer responsibility for the exodus from the angel—as in the Hebrew—to God. In precisely the same way, the Greek translators of Isaiah 63:9 strip from the angel of God's presence responsibility for the exodus. The similarity in translational strategy is uncanny. In the Greek translations of both Judges 2 and Isaiah 63, only God—not the angel—delivers Israel.[27]

The conclusion to be drawn from this brief discussion is that *the Hebrew of Isaiah 63:8-9 is a better representative of the original text than the Greek.* The Greek may ring truer in theological terms to contemporary interpreters and translators, as it apparently did to some ancient ones, because it eschews divine agents and adopts a pristine theology, in which God alone rescues Israel. But the Greek text contains evidence that its translators grappled with several elements of a difficult text and ultimately rejected one of its fundamental tenets: salvation through the angel of God's presence. While translators of the Greek may have excised this angel, it remains stubbornly in Qumran Isaiah, the Targums, the Vulgate,[28] and the Masoretic Text.

Here, then, in a Hebrew lament easily overlooked in a corpus that sports elevated poetry, grand global visions of salvation, and a servant figure that fired the imagination of Jesus, lies the seedbed of pneumatology. Yet that pneumatological impulse did not emerge without preparation. As so often happens, the time was ripe, the scenario suited to something trailblazing.

The Jolt of Crisis

One protracted series of events catalyzed this climax in creativity, with its unique amalgamation of otherwise competing elements of the exodus tradition—the angel and the presence-face. One series of unfortunate events precipitated this burst of originality: *the Babylonian onslaught in the early 500s B.C.E.* The inevitability of Babylonian hegemony cast a spell over Israel's southern kingdom and overshadowed Israel's communal psyche for more than a century and a half—long after Persia overpowered Babylon and authorized a band of exiles to return to their homeland. Even then, the footprint of Babylon on Israel's neck would be noticeable, the scars of distant tragedy unmistakable.

Adumbrations of that crisis can be traced to the Battle of Carchemish, in 605 B.C.E., when Nebuchadnezzar of Babylon soundly defeated Egypt. Babylon was on the rise. More abstrusely but just as ominously, the seeds of crisis can be found even earlier, in the soil of another battle, at Megiddo in 609 B.C.E., when a stalwart King Josiah intruded between Assyria and Egypt. Pharaoh Neco II killed Josiah and unleashed a string of more fickle and less fearless kings.

Josiah's successor, Jehoahaz, lasted three months before being trundled off to Egypt.[29] Pharaoh Neco replaced Jehoahaz with Jehoiakim, who bet on Babylon and rebelled.[30] His short-lived successor, Jehoiachin, lasted a mere three months before Nebuchadnezzar, in a campaign to subdue Syro-Palestine, took him into exile and set up Zedekiah as king.[31] Though he reigned for more than ten years, sources are sparse, except that "Zedekiah rebelled against the king of Babylon."[32] That rebellion launched a crisis of great moment.

For two years, Babylon besieged Jerusalem, precipitating a dire famine. As the Babylonians breached the city walls, Zedekiah and his military fled. Caught near Jericho and abandoned by his army, Zedekiah watched his sons murdered before being blinded and bound for Babylon.[33] Shortly afterward, Nebuzaradan, captain of Babylon's bodyguard, wreaked havoc on Jerusalem.[34] The catalog of devastation is breathtaking, ending simply, "so Judah went into exile out of its land."[35]

From this point on, events are a blur.[36] Threnodies embedded in Lamentations and the prophecies of Ezekiel—"Our bones are dried up, and our hope is lost; we are cut off completely"—point to the wrenching experience of forced deportation.[37] Some Judeans voluntarily exiled themselves to Egypt rather than endure involuntary exile in Babylon.[38] Others, once settled in Babylon, could buy and sell, plant and harvest, though they never rose to the upper echelons of society.[39]

The experience of those fortunate enough not to be deported is accessible through pottery shards and scattered glimpses in a few biblical books. Worship continued, modestly but uninterrupted, at a shrine in Mizpah, less than ten miles north of Jerusalem. Life for many, especially those in remote settings, went on, unbroken. Finances, in fact, may have improved for the rural poor, since the deportation of the wealthy merchant class brought with it the dissolution of debt. Ironically, Babylon brought about what Israel never could: a year of Jubilee.[40]

Life in Babylon and Palestine alike was more fluid and robust than a binary scenario of near-total exile and an empty land would suggest.[41] This was an era of economic opportunity in Palestine and the start of scratching out an existence in Babylon, which many of the exiles appear to have done, if texts from a century later are any indication. It was an era when Babylonian exiles gathered and edited texts, composed psalms, and produced some of Israel's most compelling prophetic images—though composition may have taken place in Judea, as well, among the literate who remained behind, working and worshipping in small urban centers such as Mizpah. In short, the Babylonian era, both in Babylon and Palestine, was rife with a combination of crisis and displacement that proved fertile ground for a creative reimagining of Israel's cherished traditions.[42] One of those creative imaginings, tempered by grief, like so many exilic and postexilic imaginings, is the lament in Isaiah 63:7-14, with its strange appeal to the angel of God's presence, followed by three references to *rûaḥ*, the spirit of God.

Exodus on the Edge of Exile

The disruption prompted by Babylonian subjugation dislocated Israel's traditions, the exodus chief among them. Centuries earlier, eighth-century prophets in both the northern and southern kingdoms had looked back amiably, even nostalgically, to the exodus experience. In the north, Amos could pit Israel's greed and oppression against Israel's unique relationship with God: "Hear this word that the LORD has spoken against you, O people of Israel, against the whole family that I brought up out of the land of Egypt: You only have I known of all the families of the earth; therefore I will punish you for all your iniquities."[43] Hosea, through the lens of dysfunction, admittedly, planned to allure his estranged wife—Israel—"and bring her into the wilderness, and speak tenderly to her." This time, he knew, she would "respond as in the days of her youth, as at the time when she came out of the land of Egypt."[44] He could recall bittersweetly, "When Israel was a child, I loved him, and out of Egypt I called my son."[45] These were, in Hosea's troubled memory, tender days. These positive prophetic recollections mirror the quintessential characteristic of the northern tradition expressed in the book of Deuteronomy: "It was not because you were more numerous than any other people that the LORD set his heart on you and chose you—for you were the fewest of all peoples. It was because the LORD loved you and kept the oath that he swore to your ancestors, that the LORD has brought you out with a mighty hand, and redeemed you from the house of slavery, from the hand of Pharaoh king of Egypt."[46]

Prophets of the southern kingdom affirmed with no less appreciation the divine rescue from Egypt. Like Amos' God in the north, Micah's in the rural south is apoplectic: "O my people, what have I done to you?" asks God. "In what have I wearied you? Answer me! For I brought you up from the land of Egypt, and redeemed you from the house of slavery; and I sent before you Moses, Aaron, and Miriam."[47] Isaiah parallels the imminent destruction of Assyria with the fall of Egypt: "The LORD of hosts will wield a whip against them, as when he struck Midian at the rock of Oreb; his staff will be over the sea, and he will lift it as he did in Egypt. On that day his burden will be removed from your shoulder, and his yoke will be destroyed from your neck."[48]

Benign reminiscence disintegrated in the years encircling the first deportation of 597. In his famed temple sermon, Jeremiah reframed the exodus tradition dramatically, in light of Judah's abuse of the temple. "For in the day that I brought your ancestors out of the land of Egypt," claims God, "I did not speak to them or command them concerning burnt offerings and sacrifices." God demanded only obedience—mere obedience—but they "did not obey or incline their ear." In one fell swoop, gone is the entire sacrificial system that had been established, in the scope of the Torah, at Mt. Sinai. In fact, the history of the exodus, from where Jeremiah stood, was one of protracted recalcitrance: "From the day that your ancestors came out of the land of Egypt until this day, I have persistently sent all my servants the prophets to them, day after day; yet they did not listen to me, or pay attention, but they stiffened their necks. They did worse than their ancestors did."[49] Vanished is any pretense to prophetic reminiscence of a tender time in Israel's past. The drama at the beginning of the sixth century demanded more, even if that *more* radically altered the exodus tradition itself.

This recalibration of the tradition is no more evident than in Ezekiel's gruesome and sexually explicit surveys of Israel's past, in which there was *never* a moment of obedience, *never* a hiatus in defiance, where election and redemption evaporate in the heat of God's disgust.[50] Ezekiel dares even to transplant Israel's origins from Egypt to "the land of the Canaanites," where their Amorite father and Hittite mother threw Israel away: "On the day you were born your navel cord was not cut, nor were you washed with water to cleanse you, nor rubbed with salt, nor wrapped in cloths. No eye pitied you, to do any of these things for you out of compassion for you; but you were thrown out in the open field, for you were abhorred on the day you were born."[51] Like Jeremiah, Ezekiel, panicked by the menace of Babylon, alters the tradition of sacrifices, though with a vicious twist. Jeremiah traded sacrifices and offerings for none—God had given no such commandments—but Ezekiel presents God, in an act of desperation fueled by Israel's defiance, challenging Israel at its own evil game. "I gave them statutes that were not good and ordinances by which they could not live," blusters God. "I defiled them through their very gifts, in their offering up all their firstborn, in order that I might horrify them, so that they might know that I am the Lord."[52] In the metaphor of the two sisters—the northern and southern kingdoms—Oholah was unfaithful from the start. "She did not give up her whorings that she had practiced since Egypt; for in her youth men had lain with her and fondled her virgin bosom and poured out their lust upon her";[53] her sister Oholibah proved to be no better. In Ezekiel's hands, then, the exodus tradition undergoes a gruesome metamorphosis, fueled by Ezekiel's feverish effort to turn Israel from its practice and, in this way, to avoid the final swipe of Babylon's sword.

The sacred tradition is itself defiled, mocked, altered—perhaps distorted—by the desperation of Jeremiah and Ezekiel's God. Tortured by the perfect storm of Babylonian menace, divine disgust, and human insubordination, prophets could not simply preserve the tradition or tinker with it. They *changed* it because Judah paid attention to nothing less. The imminence of full-blown exile, especially during the years after Ezekiel's own exile alongside the River Chebar, detonated an era of explosive creativity, which left its mark inevitably on Israel's most cherished tradition.

Spirit on the Edge of Exile

The crisis of exile, impending and actual, brooded darkly over conceptions of the spirit as well. Ezekiel's prophetic corpus contains a flurry of images related to *rûaḥ*: *rûaḥ* in whirling wheels that moved in every direction at once,[54] *rûaḥ* that lifted him in visionary transport,[55] the falling of *rûaḥ* upon Ezekiel,[56] *rûaḥ* sprinkled like water,[57] the promise of a new *rûaḥ* and heart,[58] the infilling of bleached bones through the *rûaḥ*-breath and the rush of the four *rûaḥ*-winds,[59] and the outpouring of *rûaḥ* on the reconstituted people in the land.[60] The miseries of exile did not dampen Ezekiel's conviction that the spirit was—and would be—present among the exiles.

Ezekiel's corpus is a kaleidoscope of references to *rûaḥ*, in which a metamorphosis unfolds, step by disheartening step, before a reader's eyes. In particular, as Babylon breathed down Israel's neck, some Israelites naturally, perhaps justifiably, raised the question of responsibility in the form of a proverb: "The parents have eaten sour grapes, and the children's teeth are set on edge."[61] Ezekiel responds by demonstrating at length that each individual's sin or obedience determines his or her destiny. This lengthy response to the maxim concludes with a candid challenge: "Cast away from you all the transgressions that you have committed against me, and make yourselves a new heart and a new spirit![62] Why will you die, O house of Israel? For I have no pleasure in the death of anyone, says the Lord GOD. Turn, then, and live."[63] Ezekiel commands the people to *make for themselves* a new heart and spirit. These are realities that the Israelites can bring about themselves, a condition they can ensure. Individuals have it under their own control not only to repent but even to develop in themselves a new heart and a new spirit.

Ezekiel returns to this theme in a series of visions, by which point the sins of the temple have become progressively more grotesque.[64] In this context, he promises a fresh gathering of Israelite exiles with one heart and a new spirit within:

> Thus says the Lord GOD: I will gather you from the peoples, and assemble you out of the countries where you have been scattered, and I will give you the land of Israel. When they come there, they will remove from it all its detestable things and all its abominations. I will give them one heart, and put a new spirit[65] within them; I will remove the heart of stone from their flesh and give them a heart of flesh, so that they may follow my statutes and keep my ordinances and obey them. Then they shall be my people, and I will be their God.[66]

Despite temple abominations, Ezekiel is still hopeful. Once they remove the causes of sin, God will give to the restored exiles a single heart and a new spirit to enable them to be fully God's people.

Command (Ezekiel 18:30-32) and promise (Ezekiel 11:17-20) share a conviction: the Israelites are capable of putting away their sins and setting aside their idols. In the third iteration, following a jarring and decade-long submission to Babylonian power, which ended for many in exile, the dark side of Israel's character rules out human initiative:

> I will take you from the nations, and gather you from all the countries, and bring you into your own land. I will sprinkle clean water upon you, and you shall be clean from all your uncleannesses, and from all your idols I will cleanse you. A new heart I will give you, and a new spirit I will put within you;[67] and I will remove from your body the heart of stone and give you a heart of flesh. I will put my spirit within you,[68] and make you follow my statutes and be careful to observe my ordinances. Then you shall live in the land that I gave to your ancestors; and you shall be my people, and I will be your God.[69]

In the aftermath of 586 B.C.E., God could not simply promise that Israel would be restored to the land, for that community would be a collection of Israelites whose earlier actions had led to the fall of Jerusalem. Exiled Israel could no longer be asked to repent[70] or to make for themselves a new heart and a new spirit.[71] They had their chance and showed themselves incapable of penitence.

The canonical book of Ezekiel offers a glimmer of the creativity that rose with the rise of Babylon, that emerged with the inevitable emergence of foreign hegemony. No less than three perspectives on the promise of a new heart and spirit within, all of them conditioned by the imminence and actuality of exile, materialize in the book of Ezekiel. In response to the proverb about sour grapes (Ezekiel 18:30-32), Ezekiel lays responsibility for recreation at his hearers' feet; hope lies with human beings. Elsewhere, in a protracted vision of the tainted temple (Ezekiel 11:24-31), Ezekiel links divine initiative to human. God *will* give a new heart and a new spirit within when the nation puts pollutants aside; hope lies in collaboration between God and humans. Then, in the wake of 586 B.C.E., with any hope of human tractability gone, Ezekiel lays hope for a new heart and a new spirit wholly at the feet of God.[72] Hammered on the anvil of Israel's recalcitrance,[73] this final version yields a promise[74] that is also, implicitly at least, a lament for the absence of the spirit in the here and now. With the privation of human fidelity, the hope of a new heart and spirit is thrust into the future.

These two streams—exodus and spirit—would merge in a poem that mourned the absence of God, the absence of the angel of God's presence, the absence of the holy spirit, the absence of the spirit of the Lord, each of which played a pivotal role, in the purview of this lament, in the exodus. This amalgamation of exodus and spirit would prove to be unprecedented. Yet the elements of this alchemy already percolated during the Babylonian era, certainly among the exiles and possibly among those who remained in the land. With exile impending or descending upon Judah, traditions changed. The exodus, once the hallmark of tenderness, election, and covenant, became one long, gruesome history of divine grace and human disgrace. The spirit became a thing of the past—or the future. Crisis, in short, stimulated a surfeit of creativity; loss was the catalyst of this astonishingly inventive lament.

Lament and Divine Absence in Isaiah 63:7-14

In the harshness of the crises posed by geopolitical shifts, not least Babylon's mercurial rise and precipitous fall to Persia, Israel had the option of jettisoning their traditions, dismissing them as unrealistic, unattainable, entirely forgettable. They took another tack by evaluating their own failure in light of those traditions[75] and, in a move that would prove indispensable for their understanding of the spirit, reinventing those traditions in the teeth of disappointment, even despair. Creativity rather than capitulation, vitality rather than evisceration, ruled the day, at least in the writings that survive the tumultuous sixth and fifth centuries.

Angel of God's Presence

One of those creative appropriations occurs in an unobtrusive lament tucked into a passage of uncertain date—Isaiah 63:7–64:11—in the tail end of a corpus that could easily have ended earlier, and arguably more climactically, with chapter 55. The reinvention of Israel's tradition in Isaiah 63:7-14 erupts first in the simple and unique phrase *the angel of his presence*. Better yet, the creative *amalgamation* of two figures from Israel's traditions—plural—in Isaiah 63:7-14 erupts in the simple and unique phrase *the angel of his presence*.

The angel held a robust place in the story of the exodus, wilderness wanderings, and settlement in the promised land. Nearly from the start,[76] God and the angel traveled similarly at Israel's crest; there is continuity, if not identity, here. Then, on the cusp of liberation, the angel moved, alongside the pillar, to Israel's rear, wedging itself between the oncoming Egyptian marauders and the refugees in flight.[77] Later in the story, with Israel safely entrenched at Mt. Sinai, divine sanction, so far implicit in the story, sealed the angel's status:

> I am going to send an angel in front of you, to guard you on the way and to bring you to the place that I have prepared. Be attentive to him and

> listen to his voice; do not rebel against him, for he will not pardon your transgression; for my name is in him. But if you listen attentively to his voice and do all that I say, then I will be an enemy to your enemies and a foe to your foes. When my angel goes in front of you, and brings you to the Amorites, the Hittites . . .[78]

Twice more in close succession, God iterated this vaunted promise. "My angel shall go in front of you," pledged God.[79] Then, in the wake of a short-lived but devastating plague, God promised again, "I will send an angel before you, and I will drive out the Canaanites, the Amorites, the Hittites, the Perizzites, the Hivites, and the Jebusites."[80] No measure of recalcitrance, apparently, could prompt God to withdraw this promise.

Later still, on the cusp of entry into the land sworn to Israel's ancestors, in a letter Moses wrote to pass through Edom, the angel became not a companion to the pillars but the sole agent of liberation in the sweep of Israel's tragic history: "You know all the adversity that has befallen us: how our ancestors went down to Egypt, and we lived in Egypt a long time; and the Egyptians oppressed us and our ancestors; and when we cried to the Lord, he heard our voice, and sent an angel and brought us out of Egypt."[81] The crescendo continued when the angel spoke in the first person in words that, if delivered freestanding, without any indication of the speaker, would be attributed readily to God: "I brought you up from Egypt, and brought you into the land that I had promised to your ancestors. I said, 'I will never break my covenant with you.'"[82] The angel, in this powerful précis, is deliverer, guide, and covenant-maker. In short, the angel takes on the role of God.

This is not the whole of the story. The angel is robust but not unambiguously so. Already at the start, the angel accompanied the pillars, which played a more prominent and enduring role in Israel's liberation from Egypt. When the angel became Israel's rearguard, it was *alongside* the pillar of cloud, which offered protection by illuminating the night. What the angel accomplished is less apparent.

The pillars eclipse the angel elsewhere in the Torah. Moses, his back against the wall, appealed to a jumble of reasons why God should not destroy Israel: "You, O Lord, are seen face to face, and your cloud stands over them and you go in front of them, in a pillar of cloud by day and in a pillar of fire by night."[83] God may be overtly present in the pillars in Moses' desperate plea, but the angel is not. The psalmists, too, would remember liberation, but by pillars and clouds—never at the hand of an angel.[84]

Neglect may be a fate preferable to the inference to be drawn from Moses' intense negotiation with God at Mt. Sinai, where Moses disregards God's promise altogether and orders, "See, you have said to me, 'Bring up this people'; but you have not let me know whom you will send with me."[85] Whatever God thought of the angel—and this is clear in each of the three promises—Moses is unimpressed. So God offers something better, or so it seems. "My presence-face will go with you . . ." to which Moses retorts, "If your presence-face will not go, do not carry us up from here."[86]

The rift is clear, the distinction evident. To Moses' mind, at least, the angel was inferior, the presence-face a preferable guide and companion in the trek to the promised land.

Yet the scenario unraveled further when Moses pressed to see God's glory. Apparently, this was beyond the pale. "You cannot see my presence-face; for no one shall see me and live."[87]

This negotiation, for all of its intensity, resolves little and, arguably, raises more questions than it resolves. From the start, the relationship between the angel and the presence-face is vague. The angel was inferior, at least to Moses' mind, but how inferior is simply not clear. To God's mind, the angel may have been equal to the presence-face, but God's willingness not to press Moses on this point but instead to relent—whether in agreement with Moses is not apparent—obscures God's own point of view. Accompanying this question is another: whether the angel or the presence-face of God would accompany Israel as a whole or just Moses is also left unresolved, no matter how hard Moses pressed God. Moses never received a satisfactory resolution to his demand that the angel or presence-face accompany *all* Israel. Finally, the question of how God would accompany Moses or Israel remained unanswered, even as Moses stepped into the cleft of the rock and glimpsed God's glory from behind. It is not at all clear whether the angel or the presence-face of God were palpable modes of God's presence, even if it is clear that Moses—every other human with him, too—could not see God's presence-face and live to tell the story.

Three questions, then, go unanswered in Moses' dialogue *coram deo*: *which* will accompany, the angel or presence-face; *whom* that angel or presence-face will accompany, Moses or Israel; and *how* the angel or presence-face will accompany. These questions are left to languish—or linger in Israel's memory of the sojourn at Sinai. None comes to a tolerably clear conclusion. It is as if the negotiation has fallen apart and, as we determined earlier, left Moses no further ahead—and no further behind, either. In the next scene, he was allowed to cut two tablets of stone but only to replace the ones he shattered in a fit of pique.

Answers to all three questions rise in lament in Isaiah 63:7-14 in the figure of *the angel of God's presence*. This is a unique expression in the Hebrew Bible, but its coinage is understandable as a creative resolution to the tortured figures of the angel and the presence-face of God, which feature in Moses' confrontation with God at Sinai. Their uneasy relationship is resolved amicably in this simple sobriquet. The angel and the presence-face are not competing realities, as they were in Moses' negotiation, with its unsatisfying outcome.

The angel and the presence, in this lament, are one and the same: the angel *of* God's presence. The presumed pecking order vanishes; aspersions of inferiority disappear. This is not altogether implausible, since God and the angel traveled in the same way,[88] God's voice was the voice of this angel,[89] and the angel later spoke without rancor, as Israel's liberator, guide, and covenant cutter.[90] That in Isaiah 63:9, this angel, now identified with God's presence, delivers Israel should come less as surprise than satisfaction at the way in which the tradition of the angel should come to fruition.[91] In light of the tradition of exodus, the angel of God's presence acts—*saves* Israel—as if that angel of God's presence were God.[92] The uncertain conclusion to which Moses' standoff with God ultimately led, with its unresolved concoction of presence-face, goodness, and glory, comes to rest in this lament, where the presence-face of God is the divinely authorized angel, whom God promised to lead Israel.[93]

This lament also answers the question of *whom* the angel of God's presence will lead: the "angel of his presence saved *them*; in his love and in his pity he [God] redeemed *them*; he [God] lifted *them* up and carried *them* all the days of old."[94] The point of negotiation that drove Moses to distraction, whether God would accompany all of God's people, is neatly expressed in this lament. The tension, the ambiguity, the posturing, the posing, the redirecting—these evaporate in the harsh sun of reality: there was a time when the presence of God in the angel of God's presence led Israel. That time is no longer. The vagaries of the tradition, the debate, the inconclusiveness are no longer relevant in light of this profound realization—the angel of God's presence saved them.

The lament answers another question—*how* the angel of God's presence saved Israel—dimly. The angel, which had protected Israel on the shores of the Sea by becoming a barrier between them and the Egyptian army, accomplished something else.[95] The angel of God's presence *saved* Israel. This root, יָשַׁע, though hardly unusual in the Hebrew Bible, occurs only twice in the book of Exodus and only once in the story of the exodus.[96] It occurs precisely where a reader of this lament might expect: on the shores of the Sea. As the story is told, "Moses stretched out his hand over the sea, and at dawn the sea returned to its normal depth. As the Egyptians fled before it, the Lord tossed the Egyptians into the sea. The waters returned and covered the chariots and the chariot drivers, the entire army of Pharaoh that had followed them into the sea; not one of them remained. But the Israelites walked on dry ground through the sea, the waters forming a wall for them on their right and on their left."[97]

Then comes the codicil, which clinches the deal: "Thus the Lord saved [וַיּוֹשַׁע יְהוָה] Israel that day from the Egyptians; and Israel saw the Egyptians dead on the seashore. Israel saw the great work that the LORD did against the Egyptians. So the people feared the LORD and believed in the LORD and in his servant Moses."[98] God, and God alone, saved Israel—a reality to which the Egyptians' corpses bore testimony. What *God* had accomplished, according to the narrative of the exodus, *the angel of God's presence* had accomplished, according to the lament. Not only did the angel and the presence-face fuse, but the prophet attributed to this angel of God's presence the very salvation that, according to the narrative of the exodus, God alone had accomplished.[99]

Still, notwithstanding the magnitude of this shift, this is only the beginning of the metamorphosis in this lament. More emerges in what ensues—more that is essential for the origin of pneumatology. The remarkable role of the angel of God's presence in Israel's liberation—and Israel's tortured relationship to this angel—surfaces in the following lines, in words spoken not of an angel but of God's *spirit*. The alchemy that blended the angel and presence-face now emerges in a peculiar fusion of that angel with the holy spirit.

Rebellion against the Holy Spirit

The lament's first indictment of Israel comes out of the blue, or so it would seem, when the prophet recollects how Israel

> rebelled and grieved his holy spirit;
> therefore he became their enemy;
> he himself fought against them.[100]

Without apparently laying any groundwork, the prophet introduces God's holy spirit. This may be the earliest reference to God's *holy spirit* in Israelite literature. If not, it is still only one of three:

> But they rebelled against and grieved his holy spirit.[101]
>
> Where is the one who put with them his holy spirit . . . ?[102]
>
> Do not cast me away from your presence, and do not take your holy spirit
> from me.[103]

The first two, from the lament in Isaiah 63, and the third, from Psalm 51, comprise the totality of references to *holy spirit* in the Hebrew Bible. All are found in poetry. Each is found in lament.

The sequence of this lament suggests that the holy spirit is none other than the angel of God's presence.

> In all their distress, there was to him (no) distress.[104]
> The angel of his presence saved them;

in his love and in his pity he redeemed them;
he lifted them up and carried them all the days of old.
But they rebelled against
and grieved his holy spirit;
therefore he became their enemy;
he himself fought against them.[105]

There is a clear sequence in this portion of the lament—from angel to spirit.[106] There is not, however, a spirit, and certainly not a *holy* spirit, to be found among the agents of the exodus. Perhaps an ancient prophet or poet added this spirit de novo to the coterie of agents that were active during the exodus. This is not impossible, given the creativity that emerged in the wake of Babylonian conquest.

Not impossible, no, but unlikely. More likely is another scenario, in which the prerogatives and accomplishments attributed to the angel of the exodus transferred to the spirit.

This is apparent in the initial verb associated with this holy spirit—Israel *rebelled against* God's holy spirit, which has its roots in the first promise of the *angel* delivered at Mt. Sinai. What is said of God's *holy spirit* in the lament was said earlier of God's *angel* in the divine promise, in which God warned Israel not to rebel against the promised angel.[107]

Yet the lament offers an unexpected twist, catalyzed perhaps by the Babylonian crisis. God's reaction to Israel's rebellion—God becomes Israel's *enemy*—provides another rationale for an interpretation of the lament in which the prerogatives of the angel promised on Mt. Sinai are transferred to God's holy spirit. Since Israel rebelled against and grieved God's holy spirit, God "became their enemy; he himself fought against them."[108] The drama in this reversal of the divine posture toward Israel surfaces principally against the backdrop of the promise of the angel: "But if you listen attentively to his [the angel's] voice and do all that I say, then I will be an enemy to your enemies and a foe to your foes."[109] In the lament, God takes a posture originally intended against Israel's foes—enmity—and turns it toward Israel. If Israel had listened attentively to the angel, God would have become an enemy to Israel's enemies. Instead, Israel rebelled against the angel—the holy spirit in the lament—so God became *Israel's* enemy.

The shift is precise, the inversion of the promise terrifying—now with the spirit in place of the angel. Israel rebelled against God's *holy spirit,* although they had been warned not to rebel against the *angel.* Angel and spirit are one and the same; neither is to be trifled with.

The straightforward line, "they rebelled against and grieved his holy spirit," has further implications because it draws an intense association not only between the angel and the spirit but, even more dramatically, between God and the holy spirit. This association was implicit, of course, from the start in stories of the angel.[110] According to the earliest iteration of the exodus tradition, the angel and God traveled in the same way, and the angel's voice was God's voice.[111] God and the angel, in short, were intimately, if not precisely, related to one another.

To the strength of this association can be added the realization that, throughout Israelite literature, God is typically the object of opprobrium.[112] In fact, the two verbs, *rebel* and *grieve*, which feature in this lament, in another song of exile or restoration, describe Israel's misguided response to God: "How often they rebelled against him in the wilderness and grieved him in the desert!"[113] According to the psalm, Israel rebelled against and grieved God; according to the lament, Israel rebelled against and grieved God's holy spirit. The holy spirit has taken over not only the role of the angel of God's presence to save Israel but the role of God as the object of Israel's contempt. The overlap between rebellion against the angel and rebellion against God is substantial, if ultimately abstruse.

With this explosive line, we arrive at the headwaters of pneumatology. In this single line, the prophet introduces the phrase *holy spirit* into literature perhaps for the first time in Israel's history—perhaps in *human* history. The prophet also identifies this holy spirit with the angel of the exodus, whom the prophet has just as innovatively identified with God's presence-face in the expression *the angel of his presence*. Yet this is not the totality of innovation in this lament. The prophet inverts the ancient promise that God would become the enemy of Israel's enemies by saying that God became *Israel's* enemies—not now, however, by their reaction to the *angel* but by their reaction to the *holy spirit*. Finally, the prophet draws an unbreakable association between God and the holy spirit, since both liberate Israel and both are the object of Israel's contempt. If the spirit takes on the role of the *angel* of God's presence, this spirit also takes on the role of *God*.

The Holy Spirit in Israel's Midst

Israel's past is testimony to "the praiseworthy acts of the Lord," to "great favor to the house of Israel," to God's "mercy," to "the abundance of his steadfast love."[114] The opening of the lament makes this much clear. But the paean to God as loving redeemer ends, and praise for the angel of God's presence, which saved them, evaporates, eclipsed by the trenchant awareness that, the opening volley of praise notwithstanding, these are a thing of the past. Israel has dealt falsely with God; even in days gone by, they rebelled against and grieved God's holy spirit. More punishing, now, in the prophet's age of anguish, there is nothing to grieve more than God's absence.

> Where is the one who brought them up out of the sea with the shepherds of his flock?
> Where is the one who put within them his holy spirit,
> who caused his glorious arm to march at the right hand of Moses,

> who divided the waters before them to make for himself an everlasting name,
> who led them through the depths?[115]

This is no elusive presence—nearby but evasive. This lament crescendos in questions. Where? Where is the one who, once upon a time, led them through troubled waters?[116]

From the wrack and ruin of Israel's present, the past is still visible. And prominent among those memories is God's holy spirit. Yet this is a strange memory. Unforeseen, even. Unexpected. The exodus tradition itself is nearly bereft of that spirit, which the prophet unblinkingly locates within Israel.

It is possible that the question, "Where is the one who put his holy spirit within them?" in the latter-day lament was prompted by the memory of Moses, who must have, it can be assumed, possessed the spirit, since he laid his hands upon his protégé, who was full of a spirit of wisdom.[117] This narrative detail is slender, however, just a splinter of a reference, a slim implication, too oblique to offer a plausible foreground to the lament. It is unlikely that the ancestry of this conviction—God put within them God's holy spirit—lies with Joshua's inspiration at the hands of Moses.

It is also possible that the question, "Where is the one who put within them his holy spirit?" was prompted by the magnificent skills of Bezalel and Oholiab, architects of the tabernacle, whom God filled "with divine spirit, with ability, intelligence, and knowledge in every kind of craft?"[118] But these inspired artisans were a select few. It is unlikely their story would have prompted a question so generally framed, without parameters, of *all* Israel.

It is possible, too, that the sense of loss in this lament was prompted by the prophet's memory of the seventy-two elders, who prophesied in the wilderness. Yet that story depicts the distribution of the spirit *upon* elders rather than the setting of the spirit *within* Israel. This is not an insuperable difference, but it is a difference nonetheless. Also, God parceled out the spirit that was upon Moses to a highly select group of elders.[119] As with the story of the artisans, it is unlikely that this story prompted a question about the spirit within Israel *as a whole.*

The most compelling argument against accepting any of these stories as the source of the question, "Where is the one who put within them his holy spirit?" comes from another quarter. The reason why none of these stories from the exodus tradition rises to the surface is simple: the lament, at this point, has nothing to do with Moses' protégé, Joshua, or the architects of the tabernacle or the inspired elders in the wilderness. These figures, important though they were, lie outside the purview of this portion of the lament, the sole focus of which is one event, and one event alone: *deliverance through the Sea.* The prophet grieves the absence of "the one who brought them up out of the sea," "who divided the waters before them," "who led them through the depths." Three phrases and one event—rescue through the sea—lie at the heart of the lament.[120]

Wedged into this context, and its preoccupation with deliverance through the Sea, is the plea, "Where is the one who put within them his holy spirit?"[121] The difficulty with this question, at first blush, is simply that God did *not* put the holy spirit within Israel during deliverance through the Sea. The agents of deliverance were the pillars and the angel. The angel "moved and went behind them" to shelter them from the advancing Egyptian army.[122] On the eve of liberation, the angel moved from helm to hind, setting itself in Israel's midst as a rearguard. The angel and the pillar protected Israel and made possible, the following day, rescue through the Sea.

The transposition of the angel of God into the holy spirit is hardly sudden. Already the prophet had, in quick succession, identified the angel of God's presence with God's holy spirit. Now the prophet asks where that holy spirit is: "Where is the one who put within them his holy spirit," while Israel prepared to plow through the depths of the Sea? Where is that angel now? Where is that holy spirit now? Where is that God now?

Salvation through the Sea, which the prophet expresses so many times in the short compass of this poem—bringing up Moses and the shepherds, dividing the waters, leading Israel through the depths—is no longer a cause célèbre. It is the source of lament, the stuff of lamentation. The salvation, the angel of God's presence, the love, the pity, the redemption, the holy spirit, the glorious arm, the divided waters, the march through the depths—now sting. Memories once cherished now serve to amplify divine absence. Yet these testify, too, to the vitality of the traditions, as recollections rise now in unanswered prayers.

The Spirit Giving Rest

The bitterest pill to swallow comes last: the people rested. Energy expended in taciturn prayers, like the prophet's, did not deplete the vigor of that first generation, whom God redeemed in love and pity. Though they had rebelled against God's holy spirit, still, despite that lapse in devotion, "the spirit of the LORD[123] gave them rest."[124] That rest, the grace of human repose, has metamorphosed in this lament into angst over divine absence. The spirit of the LORD, present then, is now elusive.

There is no place in the exodus tradition, however, for a spirit that led Israel or caused Israel to rest. Yet the turgid negotiation between Moses and God, which is stubbornly and unforgettably wedged between two sets of stone tablets, provides a point of origin for the prophet's belief that "the spirit of the LORD gave them rest."

That negotiation begins straightforwardly, as God iterated the promise of the angel—not once but twice. Then the process starts to unravel. To the second promise, God appends, without apparent warning, the threat that God will not go with Moses. Moses will have to go it alone—or, at least, with the angel alone to guide him.[125] After a brief hiatus, the conversation heats up, and the negotiation takes place in earnest.[126]

Moses begins with two volleys over the bow. He does not know whom God will send with him, and he does not know whether God will accompany the people as a whole. In tense jockeying for position, God tells Moses, "My presence-face will go with you, and I will give you rest." Moses reacts, "If your presence-face will not go, do not make us travel up from here."[127] Only if God goes will the uniqueness of Moses and the people be apparent to everyone on the face—the pun may be intentional—of the earth.

This posing and parrying is difficult to track, but God's two promises are not. The angel will accompany Moses, if not Israel. This does not satisfy Moses, so God promises that God's presence-face will go with Moses (perhaps also Israel) and that God will give Moses (Israel too perhaps) rest. The second promise supersedes the first. At the center of divine accompaniment, then, is the presence-face, and the impact for Moses (Israel perhaps as well) will be rest.

Patent in all of this to and fro is the intimate association between the presence-face of God and rest. "My presence-face will go with you, and I will give you rest." This salient promise is the sole plausible precursor to the recollection in the lament, "the spirit of the Lord gave him [them] rest."[128] The spirit of the Lord is said, in the later lament, to have accomplished what the presence-face of God would, according to the promise in the exodus tradition.[129]

More than once in the short compass of this otherwise inconspicuous lament, the spirit has taken on the role of an agent of the exodus. Rebellion against the angel, in this lament, becomes rebellion against God's holy spirit.[130] The protecting angel along the shores of the Sea the night before liberation becomes God's holy spirit in Israel's midst.[131] Now the spirit of the Lord takes on the role of the presence-face of God, as Israel—Israel in the poet's past, not the anxious present—rests.[132]

Yet there is a twist in the lament, and not an altogether subtle one. In the negotiation between God and Moses, the promised presence-face does not give rest. *God* does. "My presence-face will go with you, and I will give you rest." Within the compass of the lament, the spirit of the Lord gave Israel rest. Though the logic should not be pressed too hard—this identification may be more inadvertent than intentional—the obvious conclusion to be drawn is that, yet again, the *spirit* fulfilled the promise of what *God* would do when the presence-face accompanied Israel. This is not the first time in the lament when an agent takes on the role of God. The angel of God's presence saved Israel. Now, in the lament's closing lines, the spirit of the Lord gave Israel rest.

Divine Absence Made Present

The trenchant awareness of divine absence might have led to a rejection of tradition. God *never* redeemed Israel. An angel of God's presence *never* saved Israel. Israel *never* paced unharmed and unhindered through the Sea. But this was not the tack Israel took despite the havoc Babylon wreaked. Instead, they trusted the tradition more than their own contemporaneity. The tradition hung around their necks, like slaughtered infants would in the days of Antiochus IV Epiphanes,[133] not as an albatross but as an anchor, not as a vestige of faith but as a vigorous reminder of God's stubborn presence. If the spoken pleas in this lament are any indication, these questions also express what Israel hoped to discover again. "Where is the one who brought them up out of the Sea with the shepherds of his flock? Where is the one who put within them his holy spirit, who caused his glorious arm to march at the right hand of Moses, who divided the waters before them to make for himself an everlasting name, who led them through the depths?" Though veiled, muted, and muffled by grief, these questions—interrogations perhaps, even protests—are signs of a pulse, indicators of a tradition alive and well, even if Israel was not.

Not just alive and well but malleable, too, capable of durability and transformation at the same time. This otherwise ordinary communal lament, tucked discreetly into the final chapters of Isaiah, contains just such a remarkable and unprecedented combination of preservation and innovation.

The full scope of praise and anguish in this lament is drenched in the exodus tradition. Yet not the exodus tradition in a pristine form, brittle and intractable. In this lament, the exodus tradition, while preserved for posterity in the guise of grief, undergoes sweeping metamorphoses, which prove essential to the origin of pneumatology—to an understanding of the spirit as an active agent. These metamorphoses are so ample that they cascade, like wadis flush with spring rains, down the strophes of this poem. Each transformation feeds and fuses with the next.

The first dramatic transformation of the exodus tradition involves the amalgamation of the angel and the presence-face of God. In earlier tradition, the angel and presence-face vied with one another, or, more to the point, God and Moses vied with one another in a negotiation over which one would guide God's people. God promises the angel—though without God's going along—while Moses demands God's presence-face. In the lament, angel and presence-face merge into the unique figure of *the angel of God's presence*.

The next transformation is no less dramatic: the author shifts almost imperceptibly from this angel to the holy spirit: "The angel of his presence saved them . . . but they rebelled against and grieved his holy spirit." That the angel and the spirit—God's holy spirit—are now one is apparent, not only in this quick shift from angel to spirit but also in how Israel responded to God's holy spirit. They rebelled against God's holy *spirit*; rebellion against the *angel* in the divine promise becomes, in this lament, rebellion against the holy *spirit*. Yet that is not all. God's reaction to Israel's response also underscores the identity of angel and spirit. In the original promise of the angel, God had promised to become the enemy of Israel's enemies if they did not rebel against the *angel*. In the lament, God becomes Israel's enemy because of their rebellion against the *spirit*. While this metamorphosis is complex and subtle, the point is straightforward: *the holy spirit takes on the role—even as the object of rebellion—that belongs to the angel in the exodus tradition.*

This fusing of the holy spirit with the angel of God's presence paves the way for the prophet to ask, "Where is the one who put within them his holy spirit?" There is no *spirit* of this sort in the exodus tradition, but the *angel* stood with Israel as its guide and, on the cusp of liberation, rearguard. With a sea before and an army behind, the angel shielded Israel the night before they traipsed through the Sea to safety. Where is that spirit—once so present, so protective, so propitious—now?

With the lament nearly complete, another metamorphosis propels the poetry forward. The spirit of the Lord takes on the role of the *pānîm* or presence-face of God: the rest God promised at the behest of the presence-face, during an episode of intense diplomacy, becomes in this lament the rest the spirit of the Lord gave. The wrestling in this ultimately unsettling negotiation fades away in the memory of rest—rest that eludes the prophet and the Israelites who lament, asking, *Where? Where?*

It may seem reasonable, as studies of the spirit tend to do, to slice and dice *rûaḥ*, to categorize its meaning as wind or breath or spirit or Spirit—or some combination of these. Yet the word cannot be categorized so easily in this lament, where the exodus tradition takes on new life. The agents that once played pivotal roles in the tradition are fungible. Their prerogatives become the prerogatives of the spirit, God's *holy* spirit. Their actions become the actions of the spirit. Where the angel—now the angel of God's presence—once met with their opprobrium, now the holy spirit is the object of rebellion. Where God had once set the angel in Israel's midst, now the holy spirit is within Israel. Where the *pānîm* had once been promised to give rest, now the spirit of the Lord gives Israel rest. The spirit is wind, yes, and breath and spirit and Spirit, too, but none of these words captures the agency of the spirit, which emerged with salience, even exuberance, despite the tenor of lament, when Israel remembered the salvation wrought by the angel of God's presence and recalled how that salvation—and the human rebellion that inevitably attended it—lay within the province of God's spirit.[134]

Chapter 4

THE ASSURANCE OF THE SPIRIT
Rekindling Exodus: The Force of Pneumatology

"Since the Most High God has appointed me king of the habitable world," decreed Cyrus, first in a series of formidable Achaemenid rulers, "I am persuaded that He is the god whom the Israelite nation worships, for He foretold my name through the prophets and that I should build His temple in Jerusalem in the land of Judaea."[1] This is what Cyrus said, though *not exactly*. Cyrus actually wrote, "I resettled upon the command of Marduk, the great lord, all the gods of Sumer and Akkad whom Nabonidus has brought into Babylon to the anger of the lord of the gods, unharmed, in their (former) chapels, the places which make them happy."[2]

Flavius Josephus can be forgiven perhaps for baptizing Cyrus in the waters of Jewish politics and piety. Josephus had, after all, weathered the storm of the Jewish Revolt and lived to tell the story, fancifully and egocentrically, admittedly, but tell the story nonetheless. In *his* version, if not Cyrus', the Persian ruler knew what he had to do because he had read "the book of prophecy which Isaiah had left behind two hundred and ten years earlier." When Cyrus read the prophecies about himself, "he wondered at the divine power and was seized by a strong desire and ambition to do what had been written."[3]

The rest, as they say, is history. With a nod to Marduk, rather than Israel's god, Cyrus sent some of the Jews home with his backing. Though we have no record to say so, Cyrus' support must have resonated with Josephus, who now wrote a version of Jewish history under the powerful patronage of the Flavian dynasty. Josephus knew firsthand what it was like to live in two worlds. He understood divided loyalties.

That effort simultaneously to occupy two realms defined the world in which the prophet Haggai cajoled and criticized, advised and assured the people of

Yehud, a small Persian province, in an all-out effort to rebuild the temple. This was Cyrus' mandate; Haggai, a devoted Jew and loyal Persian, was bound and determined to make sure it happened.

This was no simple matter, given the unsettling atmosphere in which Haggai articulated the deceptively simple claim, *my spirit stands among you.* Judah's situation was more than a matter of drama conjured from the spell of an uncertain future. Judah's condition was the product of ethnic crises, religious skirmishes, and events of historic proportion. It is all too easy to talk glibly of exile and restoration, as if these were two distinct eras, the former anguished and the latter optimistic. The complexion of Palestine, in the wake of Cyrus' decree, was knottier and more gnarled than that. The situation that spawned this unique promise was itself unique—and complex, protracted, disquieting to the generations charged with the task of restoration.

Dawn of a New Epoch

Still decades ahead of a return from exile, a prophet subject to the tyranny of Babylon discerned in the rise of the Achaemenid ruler Cyrus a messiah, God's anointed one,[4] but expectations were not universally high among Israel's exilic population. Whether rooted in a desire to remain in Babylon, as the prophet Jeremiah had advised,[5] or in a latent hostility toward foreign overlords, the prophet's contemporaries offered stiff resistance to his largesse.

On balance, the prophet, Isaiah of the exile, was right in his claim that God had selected Cyrus to be "my shepherd," who would "carry out all my purpose." He saw what others did not, that Jerusalem would "be rebuilt," and was prescient in his belief that the temple had a bright future: "Your foundation shall be laid," he knew, against all odds.[6]

Cyrus' policies bear out these prognostications. Even taking into account the propagandistic purpose of his cylinder—Esarhaddon and Nabonidus, too, had claimed to gather the scattered and to restore ancient shrines—it is beyond doubt that Cyrus did return willing Judean exiles to their homeland, with the mandate to rebuild the temple in Jerusalem.[7] Persia's positive posture toward Israel was, at least in part, the product of political expediency. Egypt remained troublesome, even for an empire as vast as Persia.[8] It would have been beneficial to return loyal exiles to Yehud in order to provide a buffer against Egypt.[9] So return the Judean exiles Cyrus did.

Meanwhile, Persia continued to extend its vast borders. Though a foreign empire, Persia provided relative security and stability; its enemies were too far flung to pose a credible threat. Under Darius I, Persia attained a surprising unity, with Aramaic as the lingua franca, a standing army, a courier service, royal coins, and extensive trade.

Yet in a small province, Yehud—little more than a pinprick, albeit a strategic one, on the body politic of Persia—strident *disunity* prevailed.[10] The period after the exiles' return from Babylon after 539 B.C.E. proved tense, and the people—both the descendants of those who had remained in the land and the descendants of those who had been banished to Babylon—were fractured.[11] For good reason. These groups inherited divergent histories. The returnees' exiled grandparents had experienced intense trauma, while those who had remained in the land may have benefitted from the expulsion of affluent landowners.

Small wonder, then, that the offer of help from the people of the land—those who had not been exiled—was soundly rebuffed by the returning exiles.[12] According to the book of Ezra, a product of Persian loyalists, the people who had remained in the land raised constant opposition to the temple project throughout the reigns of Cyrus, Darius, Ahasuerus (Xerxes I, perhaps), and Artaxerxes.[13]

This tension was also rooted in the Torah. Those in exile presumably cultivated a deep commitment to the Torah, while those who remained in Palestine intermarried and, at least in the eyes of the returnees, assimilated Canaanite culture at the expense of Israelite faith. While in exile, those who now returned seem to have rediscovered the stringent perspective of Deuteronomy, with its harsh attitudes toward assimilation with the Canaanites. Participation in celebration of the Passover, for instance, was limited to those "who had returned from exile, and also . . . all who had joined them and separated themselves from the pollutions of the nations of the land to worship the LORD, the God of Israel."[14] Even at the tail end of rebuilding, Nehemiah vigorously purged Yehud of perceived sins, including intermarriage: "And I contended with them and cursed them and beat some of them and pulled out their hair; and I made them take an oath in the name of God, saying, 'You shall not give your daughters to their sons, or take their daughters for your sons or for yourselves.'"[15]

At the heart of this tension, though probably more symptomatic than causal, lay the project of rebuilding the temple. The texts, biased and scant as they are, point to a jagged and protracted process, despite an early initial dedication. Apparently, Sheshbazzar, governor of the Persian province, began restoration under Cyrus; Zerubbabel completed the initial restoration under Cambyses and Darius I.[16]

The protracted nature of restoration suggests how competing visions arose in decades of starting and stopping.[17] Haggai and Isaiah 56–66 are two of the voices, perhaps contemporaneous but possibly not, that sought to determine what shape a restored people of God would take. Both championed the restoration of the temple but disagreed about who would lead worship—or what worship should look like.

The people to whom Haggai appealed, on the one hand, included the returnees, who held to a strict form of worship, led by authorized priests and enacted in ways that would promote ethnic purity. The authors of Isaiah 56–66, on the other hand, championed the poor and outcasts, foreigners and eunuchs, who, they hoped, would play a more conspicuous role in the future of worship in Jerusalem. There is no place in the imagination of the prophets responsible for Isaiah 56–66 for such exclusion—rejection, actually. On the contrary, eunuchs and foreigners will keep Sabbath, minister in the temple, offer burnt offerings and sacrifices, and pray in the temple, because, God promises, or warns, "my house shall be called a house of prayer for all peoples."[18]

Both prophets concur on one matter: the need for healthy worship in a restored temple. Haggai's first words following a list of recipients are these: "Thus says the LORD of hosts: These people say the time has not yet come to rebuild the LORD's house."[19] What plagues them—their excuses for why they cannot yet rebuild—is in fact the result of their not building, claims Haggai. Famine is no excuse for delay; famine is caused by delay! "Is it a time for you yourselves to live in your paneled houses, while this house lies in ruins? Now therefore, thus says the LORD of hosts: Consider how you have fared. You have sown much, and harvested little; you eat, but you never have enough; you drink, but you never have your fill; you clothe yourselves, but no one is warm; and you that earn wages earn wages to put them into a bag with holes."[20]

Why is there famine and drought, according to Haggai? "Why? says the LORD of hosts. Because my house lies in ruins, while all of you hurry off to your own houses. Therefore the heavens above you have withheld the dew, and the earth has withheld its produce. And I have called for a drought on the land and the hills, on the grain, the new wine, the oil, on what the soil produces, on human beings and animals, and on all their labors."[21] Portions of Isaiah 56–66 also show an urgency about the temple. Abundant grain and wine are to be celebrated, God claims, "in my holy courts."[22] Sword and slaughter will be the fate of "you who forsake the LORD, who forget my holy mountain."[23]

Yehud suffers, according to Isaiah 56–66, not, as from Haggai's perspective, because of a delay in rebuilding the temple. For this prophet, a debilitating partnership between greed and injustice—fasts without integrity and Sabbath keeping without mercy—is the cause for delay in the advent of God's salvation. In typical prophetic fashion, the prophet charges the people with false fast days, on which they continue to oppress workers.[24] He then inquires:

Is not this the fast that I choose:
    to loose the bonds of injustice,
    to undo the thongs of the yoke,
to let the oppressed go free,
    and to break every yoke?

> Is it not to share your bread with the hungry,
> and bring the homeless poor into your house;
> when you see the naked, to cover them,
> and not to hide yourself from your own kin?[25]

Only then, when yokes are broken and the oppressed let free, will salvation visit Yehud:

> Then your light shall break forth like the dawn,
> and your healing shall spring up quickly;
> your vindicator shall go before you,
> the glory of the LORD shall be your rearguard.
> Then you shall call, and the LORD will answer;
> you shall cry for help, and he will say, Here I am.[26]

Still, in a future that is similar to Haggai's, parched places will become gardens, bones strong, and "your ancient ruins shall be rebuilt; you shall raise up the foundations of many generations; you shall be called the repairer of the breach, the restorer of streets to live in."[27] This will occur because

> the LORD will guide you continually,
> and satisfy your needs in parched places,
> and make your bones strong;
> and you shall be like a watered garden,
> like a spring of water,
> whose waters never fail.[28]

This is not a simplistic vision. It combines images of the pillar and angel as vanguards and rearguards, evoking the exodus tradition, and the rebuilding of ruins, which is precisely the goal to which Haggai moves his people.[29]

Haggai and the prophet of Isaiah 56–66, possibly two Persian-era prophets, share a vision that the temple will be restored and the city rebuilt, but they offer, if not competing, at least complementary ways to achieve this goal.[30] Haggai put the people to work on the temple; to a limited extent, they achieved their goal when the temple was dedicated between 520 and 515 B.C.E.[31] Isaiah 56–66 evinces far less preoccupation with the physical temple and far more interest in who can participate in worship: foreigners, eunuchs, and outcasts.[32]

Something significant for the origin of pneumatology, it may be important to note in passing, emerges in this simple observation about Haggai and Isaiah 56–66. Despite their diverging visions for the restored temple, both prophets understand the spirit in a fresh way that unites them. For both prophets, the spirit is a divine agent that was active in guiding Israel during the exodus from

Egypt. In two different prophets, possibly representing disparate sets of national experiences, remaining in the land or being exiled, and embracing disparate visions of temple worship, a singular perspective on the spirit as a divine agent surfaces—giving testimony to the enduring power of belief in the spirit and a lasting esteem for the relevance of the exodus traditions.

Though often dismissed as an era that brought about the end of prophecy and the emergence of priestly legalism, in fact the Persian era after 539 B.C.E. was a period of creativity. For centuries, the people of Israel had lived in the shadow of threatening empires, and for decades with Judah's leading citizens in enforced exile. Now Persia permitted them to exist, neither in the shadow of a hostile empire nor in exile, but as a politically legitimate province of an acceptable empire, whose leaders had not only let them return voluntarily to their homelands but authorized them to rebuild their cities and their house of worship.

Exceptional during this era were the constraints under which Israel would now be forced, for the first time in its history, to live. Though with a measure of political independence and imperial support, they blazed new trails with no hope for a restoration of the monarchy. The temple and its worship? Yes. The city? Yes, again. But the monarchy? No. Yehud was to be ruled only by authorized governors, so hopes for a Davidic king that might have arisen with return from exile simply could not be met.[33]

Unmet expectations demanded *fresh* expectations. This is precisely what Judah discovered in the disorientation demanded by living under altogether new circumstances that were jarring especially for those who returned from exile. Compounding this disorientation were inner tensions, too, about the shape that the restored community, the restored temple, and restored worship would take. This effort, contested by disparate factions, contributed as well to a creative impulse that carved out of crisis an enduring future.

That creative impulse yielded something extraordinary: a people whose existence outlasted Babylon and Persia alike. The onslaught of Babylon in 586 B.C.E. had unleashed "a uniquely creative epoch in Judean history," as "the survivors of the Babylonian conquest sought to examine the causes of the calamity that had destroyed their holy city and the Jerusalem temple and had made so many homeless and impoverished."[34] Now, half a century later, other prophets would rise up, prophets of a different stripe, prophets like Haggai and the authors of Zechariah 1–8 and Isaiah 56–66. These prophets labored in "the unique circumstances of the restoration period and Persian governance," which demanded what might be called restrained creativity, in which they reconciled their new situation with their enduring sacred traditions. "If they seem to point in a new direction, it is because there was no turning back. If they seem too committed to supporting the powers that be, it is because the alternative was to oppose the mightiest power of the day, which probably would have led to the destruction of much that was valuable in their national heritage."[35]

To put this another way—and it is not possible to put too fine a point on this—the era following return from exile, though often characterized as spiritually arid and legalistic, in fact proved combustive. Memory of exile remained fresh and raw for many. "Like a drumbeat, the biblical text reminds us of their exilic past. They are the 'exiles,' 'the captive exiles,' 'sons of the exile,' and 'the assembly of exiles.'"[36] Notwithstanding the agony of exile, those who returned shaped a vision of a new people. They were not alone. Apparently, so did others, some of them perhaps those who had remained in the land. These visions variously bounced off of one another and fused. These visions were pragmatic but never static, careful but always kinetic.

These visions, most important of all, birthed Judaism—a religion shaped without a visible and viable theocracy but with a cherished collection of texts. The northern kingdom had fallen to Assyria, the south to Neo-Babylonia. Sometime during exile, the last king died. So those in Judah, but particularly those in exile from Judah, forged a future built ultimately on their Torah. Haggai was part of this transformation of the past into a fresh future, not only because he urged and insisted and cajoled and pressed his people to restore the temple, but also because he brought the old wine of Israel's traditions into new wineskins: "Work, for I am with you, says the LORD of hosts—the word I cut with you when you came out of Egypt: my spirit stands among you; do not fear" (Haggai 2:4-5).

Traditions in Transition

Haggai did not frame these words unprompted. Though extraordinary in significance, what Haggai said was not entirely without precedent. Before Cyrus' decree and after, authors and prophets energetically transposed their traditions: revitalizing the exodus tradition; reshaping belief in the spirit; and combining exodus and spirit. Seen from this standpoint, Haggai's prophetic promise, *My spirit stands among you,* is significant but not surprising, unprecedented but not unexpected.

A New Exodus

Even as the freshness of exile dawned upon the Judeans in Babylon, Ezekiel, according to the book that bears his name, could not relinquish hope that God would, as God had at the beginning, lead Israel from slavery to the wilderness. "As I live, says the Lord GOD, surely with a mighty hand and an outstretched arm, and with wrath poured out," Ezekiel tells his exiled compatriots what God has to say, "I will be king over you. I will bring you out from the peoples and gather you out of the countries where you are scattered, with a mighty hand

and an outstretched arm, and with wrath poured out and I will bring you into the wilderness of the peoples, and there I will enter into judgment with you face to face."[37] The promise is terrifying. Ezekiel has just demonstrated in a revision of Israel's early history how God repeatedly stayed a hand, despite Israel's recalcitrance in the wilderness. Now freedom from slavery will bring—this is hard to miss—wrath and judgment. "As I entered into judgment with your ancestors in the wilderness of the land of Egypt, so I will enter into judgment with you, says the Lord GOD."[38]

There will, it is clear, be a second exodus. But Ezekiel refuses to sanitize the first, and he will not disinfect the second. Still, though the cloud of judgment turns the scene gray, one thing is sure: there will be release from exile in the form of a second exodus.

The book of Ezekiel ends, in fact, with a magisterial vision of a temple restored. Wall by wall, corner by cornerstone, Ezekiel rebuilt the temple and its liturgy in the imaginations of those in exile.[39] Permeating this vision is the unshakable sense that this new temple is built upon a new Eden,[40] a new Zion, too,[41] but also a new Sinai—with Ezekiel a prophet like Moses.[42]

The parallels between Moses and Ezekiel are arresting. Ezekiel and Moses are the only figures in the entire Hebrew Bible to deliver priestly instruction.[43] Ezekiel and Moses alike receive revelation on a mountain.[44] Ezekiel delivers a detailed plan for the temple, just as Moses delivered a blueprint for the tabernacle.[45] No other building, not even Solomon's temple, is described in such detail. And, like Moses, who was permitted to see the promised land from a mountain but not enter, Ezekiel was permitted to see the restored temple from a mountain but not worship in it.[46]

To these observations may be added a variety of others.[47] The *dating* of Ezekiel's vision on the tenth day of the first month[48] marks the day on which God told "Moses and Aaron in the land of Egypt" to command Israel to prepare lambs for the Passover. Ezekiel's vision of the purified temple mirrors Israel's escape from Egypt.

The *content* of Ezekiel's Torah has much in common with Mosaic Torah, particularly those regulations that were given to Moses between his command to ascend the mountain on the border of the promised land and his death.[49] These include the liturgical calendar and rules of sacrifice,[50] the allocation of land,[51] Levitic land and cities,[52] and rights of inheritance.[53] The legal elements of Ezekiel's vision, then, mirror many of the same issues in Numbers 27–36.[54]

Ezekiel's vivid imagination was unbounded, but it was also seriously tethered to Israel's traditions. The impression given in the book that bears his name is that Ezekiel is a prophet like Moses, even a *new* Moses, whose blueprint for a renewed temple, which he received on a high mountain, contains the provisions for God's glory in the context of liberation from Babylon, even as Moses' blueprint for the original tabernacle, which he received on Mt. Sinai, contains the provisions for God's glory in the context of liberation from Egypt. Ezekiel's blueprint does not match that of the Torah exactly, given Ezekiel's idiosyncrasies and imagination, plus the new and imposing challenges of exile, but the figure who promulgates it does match the original prophet, lawgiver, and visionary—Moses.

Ezekiel's temple vision is, then, at least in part, an appropriation of the exodus tradition, inspired by disaster and dislocation, and directed toward a new future. It functions as a baseline, of sorts, for the Persian-era authors of the books of Ezra and Nehemiah, as well as later prophets, such as so-called Second Isaiah and Haggai. Haggai's assurance that a spirit stands in Israel's midst—the word God had cut with them when they ascended from Egypt—is a descendant, not an altogether distant one, of Ezekiel's vision of the new temple as a new Sinai.

Less flamboyantly, Jeremiah touched upon the possibility of a new exodus. After predicting that God would hurl the people of Judah "out of this land into a land that neither you nor your ancestors have known," Jeremiah predicts the certainty of restoration: "Therefore, the days are surely coming, says the Lord, when it shall no longer be said, 'As the Lord lives who brought the people of Israel up out of the land of Egypt,' but 'As the Lord lives who brought the people of Israel up out of the land of the north and out of all the lands where he had driven them.' For I will bring them back to their own land that I gave to their ancestors."[55] Here there are no visions of a new temple, no contrived linguistic echoes of the language of exodus, no typologies. There is just a promise, simply stated, but a promise nonetheless.

Implicit in Jeremiah's famed expectation of a new covenant, written on hearts rather than stone, is the prospect of a new exodus. "It will not be like the covenant that I made with their ancestors when I took them by the hand to bring them out of the land of Egypt—a covenant that they broke, though I was their husband, says the Lord."[56]

Expectations of a new exodus hardly abound in the book of Jeremiah, and what little is there may be the product of later Deuteronomic editing. Yet these promises are there, unexpected perhaps, forthright certainly. Taken with the book of Ezekiel, they provide a possible baseline for the flourishing of new exodus hopes in the decades to follow.

Flourish is what this expectation did, as liberation drew near, with the Persian defeat of Neo-Babylonia and the rise of Cyrus. Toward the end of exile, a prophet emerged with extraordinary vision and a pro-Persian stance that offered a way forward. Emblematic of this creative burst is the resurgence of exodus language in Isaiah 40–55, where liberation from Babylon—or Egypt or elsewhere in the diaspora—mirrors liberation from Egypt, wilderness wanderings, and entry into Palestine.[57]

In an intrepid condemnation of Babylon—Babylon was still the regnant empire even if Persia soon would be—the prophet's God promises to break Babylon and transform their shouting into a dirge. This God, "the LORD, your holy one, the Creator of Israel, your King," is the one:

> who makes a way in the sea,
>   a path in the mighty waters,
> who brings out chariot and horse, army and warrior;
> they lie down, they cannot rise, they are extinguished, quenched like a wick.[58]

Allusions to the exodus are unmistakable; to read this is to remember the triumphant trail of escapees in the Sea and the Egyptian chariot-riders, with their horses lying dead along the same path. Allusions to the desert sojourn are only slightly more muted.[59] God promises to "make a way in the wilderness and rivers in the desert." God promises, too, to "give water in the wilderness, rivers in the desert."[60] The parallel between Egypt and Babylon is striking; hope is rooted in past protection. In fact, the prophet uses participles, rather than the past tense, to describe God's actions, giving them a timelessness that allows past and future to fuse in the crucible of hope. God *did* not make a way. God *will* not make a way. God *makes* a way.[61]

The prophet returns to this theme with a sense of urgency when he commands the exiles:

> Go out from Babylon, flee from Chaldea,
> declare this with a shout of joy, proclaim it,
> send it forth to the end of the earth;
> say, "The LORD has redeemed his servant Jacob!"
> They did not thirst when he led them through the deserts;
>   he made water flow for them from the rock;
>   he split open the rock and the water gushed out.[62]

Typically command and promise are joined at the hip, as in Haggai 2:4-5, where a promise that the spirit stands in Israel's midst supports the command to work. In Isaiah 48:20-21, command is followed not so much by promise as recollection. Remembering what God did, recalling the water that God provided, is the ballast the exiles need to pull up stakes, leave their houses, and flee Babylon in an unsettling swirl of geopolitical events.[63] The prophet does not reveal an awareness that Cyrus will send the exiles home, that the results will be peaceful if arduous. The prophet does know, from the reservoir of tradition, that God will make provision along the prolonged and onerous journey home.[64] To put it more colloquially: the politics of Isaiah 40–55 are vague, the theology unambiguous.

The exodus tradition, which funds the prophet's confidence, fuses with the mythology of creation when the prophet rouses the arm of God to unusual alertness and action *as in the days of old*:

> Awake, awake, put on strength,
> O arm of the LORD!
> Awake, as in days of old,
> the generations of long ago!
> Was it not you who cut Rahab in pieces,
> who pierced the dragon?
> Was it not you who dried up the sea,
> the waters of the great deep;
> who made the depths of the sea a way
> for the redeemed to cross over?
> So the ransomed of the LORD shall return,
> and come to Zion with singing;
> everlasting joy shall be upon their heads;
> they shall obtain joy and gladness,
> and sorrow and sighing shall flee away.[65]

In this beautiful poetry,[66] the mythology of creation—Rahab and drying up the waters of the sea, the great deep—becomes the reality of exodus: the redeemed cross the depths of the sea. "It is hard to imagine a more poignant reminder to a wavering people that neither the cause of world justice nor their own safety rested upon human self-help projects but solely upon the power that created the universe by repelling the forces of chaos, called Israel forth from bondage to peoplehood, and even now was preparing to return the exiled community to Zion" with joy and gladness.[67]

Of decisive significance for any analysis of the exodus tradition in Haggai 2:5 and Isaiah 63:7-14 is a recapitulation of the exodus tradition:

> Depart, depart, go out from there!
> Touch no unclean thing;
> go out from the midst of it, purify yourselves, you who carry the vessels of the LORD.
> For you shall not go out in haste, and you shall not go in flight;
> for the LORD will go before you, and the God of Israel will be your rear guard.[68]

Resonances of the exodus permeate this petition.[69] The carrying of vessels—temple vessels moved to Babylon earlier in the sixth century B.C.E.—is reminiscent of the Israelites' flight from Egypt, laden with silver and gold.[70] The promise not to leave in a hurry offers a direct contrast to the exodus and the need to leave in haste.[71] The promise that God will go before them as they leave Babylon evokes the complex memory that the LORD traveled before the Israelites in the pillars of cloud and fire[72] and that an angel, too, led Israel.[73] Isaiah's statement is simpler but not, for that reason, less significant: the LORD will travel before the exiles.

It is difficult to know whether to interpret this promise as an effort to supplant the agents who went before Israel at the exodus or to recapture the grandeur of what had happened when God traveled before the Israelites in pillars of cloud and fire—or both. The tradition is, we have seen, fluid. The prophet of the exile may be promising that only God will lead the exiles, absent other agents, or simply reminding them that God will travel before the exiles, as God had done at the exodus through a variety of agents. In either case, this promise confirms that the exodus tradition, according to which God traveled before the Israelites, was alive just decades before Cyrus released the exiles to return to Judah and Haggai pressed the inhabitants of Yehud to rebuild the temple in earnest.

More stirring even than the promise of God's traveling *before* the exiles is the resuscitation of the concept of the *rearguard*.[74] This is a claim to divine protection, though not for the first time. In Exodus 14:19-24, the angel and pillar of cloud moved from the front of the Israelite camp to its rear in order to protect them from the Egyptians. This tradition was alive, as well, in the Psalms, where the cloud becomes a protective screen and fire illumines the night.[75]

Like the angel in front and the angel behind, like the pillar(s) in front and the pillar behind, the LORD travels in front of the exiles, the God of Israel is their rearguard. They have no need to fear, no reason to hesitate, no rationale for remaining in Babylon. God will lead them home and follow behind to ensure that no one, not even the Babylonians, will launch an attack from the rear to keep them from leaving. The exiles have no need to fret their security; their sole preoccupation should be their purity. Most of the imperatives in Isaiah 52:11 have to do with purity of faith and worship; none has to do with military strategy or travel plans.

With this creativity toward the end of Babylonian captivity, the exiles were well prepared for a return to Jerusalem. If they were prone to remain in Babylon, amid the gardens they had planted, the children they had birthed, and the houses they had built, this plea comes as a challenge to move ahead, to move out—to depart tremulously. For those prone to leave, fueled by the traditions that were gathered and edited in exile, ablaze with distant memories of a distant homeland, this plea comes as a promise to move ahead, to move out—to depart audaciously.

Depart they did, if not audaciously, at least obedient to the dictates of Persia. Yet little happened by way of restoration, even in the days of Haggai, who would cajole the inhabitants of Yehud to rebuild, with the promise that God's spirit stood among them. Decades later—how many it may not be possible to know—Ezra returned and led the people in the reading and interpretation of the Torah. The hues of this return, though less vibrant than the oracles of exilic prophets, are those of the exodus. The accomplishments of Ezra, in other words, correspond to early acts of liberation and the occupation of Canaan. The character of restoration as a new exodus is apparent in the understated ways in which the exodus story is woven into the tapestry of Ezra's story. This is no denouement. It is a subtle surfacing of the exodus tradition.

Already the opening scene portrays the return from exile as a new exodus. The description of the exiles as people who "were *brought up* from Babylonia to Jerusalem" adopts a key verb that described the slaves, whom God brought up from Egypt.[76] The detail that "their neighbors aided them with silver vessels, with gold, with goods, with animals, and with valuable gifts, besides all that was freely offered," suggests a parallel scenario to the days when the Egyptians voluntarily gave the fleeing slaves their possessions.[77] Even the return of vessels to the temple, clearly not an element of the exodus narrative, became part of the hope in the new exodus during exile;[78] in Ezra that hope would come to pass.[79] Right away, then, the author of the book of Ezra "presents the return from Babylon as a 'second exodus,' an act of God's grace comparable with the very birth of the nation itself. From an historical point of view it is likely that the return was a long drawn out and rather unspectacular affair. The use of typology, however, opens the eye of faith to the hand of God behind the historical process. To those who may have been tempted to play down the significance of what had happened, our author invites the thought that it may be described as no less than a rebirth of the nation."[80]

Later in the story, further reminiscences of the exodus surface. Again, they *ascended* from Babylon. This they did on the first day of the new year—a date reminiscent of the exodus.[81] The attribution of this particular date to Ezra's study—the return began then "*because* Ezra had set his heart to study the law of the LORD, and to do it, and to teach the statutes and ordinances in Israel"—suggests that the choice of this date may have been intentional.[82] Ezra chose it, on the basis of his study of the Torah, so that the exit from Babylon would mirror the date of the exodus from Egypt.[83]

Taken together with the oracles of Ezekiel and Jeremiah, at the start of exile, and the poetry of Isaiah 40–55, toward the end of exile, the book of Ezra gives testimony to the depth of conviction that the God of the exodus was now the God of restoration. The events would not be exactly the same. The personnel would differ, as would the topography of return. But the fundamental core of belief in God's deep desire—and ability—to liberate Israel endured for more than a century of sustained crisis. In that context, Haggai would resurrect belief in the exodus, though with a twist that positioned the spirit at the center of that tradition.

Spirit in Transition

The appearance of the spirit in Haggai's promise is abrupt, but it rises nonetheless like the crest of an ocean swell. Israel had long since busied itself with the spirit. While no transformation quite like the one in the lament of Isaiah or the promise of Haggai occurs elsewhere in the vast and varied tracts of Israelite literature, this realization should not obscure the reality that *rûaḥ*, in its various semantic domains, played a pivotal role in how Israel perceived itself and its leaders. Particularly salient is the resurgence of interest in the spirit in the Persian or postexilic era. Typically characterized, by ancient and modern thinkers alike, as the era that brought the last of the prophets, the withdrawal of the spirit from Israel, and the rise of priestly legalism, in reality attention to *rûaḥ* did not diminish or disappear in the Persian era. The book of Zechariah, 1–2 Chronicles, the book of Joel, and the later chapters of Isaiah contain significant references to the spirit as the source of justice, reconciliation, inspired speech, and the reordering of all flesh.[84] If a keen interest in *rûaḥ* spanned more than half a millennium, it is crucial to acknowledge as well that this interest remained vibrant and vital after return from exile, when Haggai extended the promise: *My spirit stands among you.*

It would be cumbersome to trace all of these developments in detail. Three will suffice to illuminate the kinetic energy that provided the crucible in which Haggai framed his unique promise of the spirit: the rushing of the spirit, the resting of the spirit, and the outpouring of the spirit.

Among the most ancient stories of the spirit in the Jewish Bible are those of the judges, upon whom the spirit came to liberate Israel. The baseline is straightforward: the spirit came or rushed upon or clothed the judges—Othniel, Gideon, Jephthah, and Samson[85]—who led oppressed Israel to freedom.[86] When the spirit pressed upon its leaders, the troops were mustered and oppressors thwarted. This pattern holds even for Israel's first king. "The spirit of God came upon Saul[87] when he heard" about a plot to gouge out Israel's eyes, so he cut a yoke of oxen and sent it as a battle cry to the tribes of Israel. A total of 370,000 troops responded to his ultimatum by gathering for battle.[88]

This sort of inspiration lay dormant for centuries, according to what appears in Israel's literary heritage,[89] only to resurface in 1–2 Chronicles, where the language of inspiration associated with the judges and Saul rises to the surface without any apparent prompt in 1–2 Samuel and 1–2 Kings, of which it is a revision.[90] When it resurfaces no less than four times, it does so considerably changed.

The spirit clothed[91] "Amasai, chief of the Thirty," a group of legendary warriors, as it had Gideon.[92] Unlike Gideon, Amasai did not prepare for battle but waxed poetic in support of David—enough to mollify his potential adversary.[93] In a second instance, "the spirit was upon Azariah son of Oded," as it had been upon Othniel and Jephthah.[94] Like Amasai, but unlike judges Othniel and Jephthah, Azariah delivered a prophetic speech[95] rife with allusions to Israel's traditions and support for the king. In the third instance in 1–2 Chronicles, "the spirit of the LORD was upon Jahaziel,"[96] whose directives exhibit an astute combination of precise military strategy and the sort of encouragement a priest would deliver to the troops before battle.[97] While the verb is the same, the impact of the spirit once again is unlike its impact upon Othniel and Jephthah. Finally, "the spirit of God clothed Zechariah son of the priest Jehoiada," as it had Gideon.[98] In contrast to Gideon, Zechariah indicted the people. Rather than face the reality of Zechariah's charge, they stoned him, tragically, *ironically*, in the temple court.[99]

This creative resurfacing of the language of the spirit in relation to the judges and Saul gives testimony to an avid interest in the spirit during the Persian era, when Haggai too would offer his word of promise to the disheartened people of Yehud.[100] Notwithstanding the verbal clues that tie these stories in Chronicles to the stories of Israel's early judges, they reappear modified. In the book of Judges, the spirit inspired astonishing acts of liberation; in 1–2 Chronicles, the spirit inspires speeches, including one urging the people of Judah *not* to fight. In the book of Judges, the spirit appeared in arenas that were free from the corridors of official power; in 1–2 Chronicles, the spirit speaks only in the arena of public politics. Finally, the spirit in Judges came upon or clothed a ragtag coterie of judges—the feeble Gideon, the bastard Jephthah, the fickle Samson; now, those who receive the spirit are people of pedigree—Amasai, chief of the Thirty warriors; Azariah, who delivers a prophecy directly to the king; Jahaziel, a trained musician and a descendant of Asaph; and Zechariah, a courageous priest.[101]

This shift from the judges, among the first of Israel's leaders, to the prophet-priests of the Persian era underscores again the symbiosis that existed, when it came to the spirit, between tradition and creativity. Old formulae reemerge in fresh ways, in the midst of new communities, in relation to new speakers, and at the base of practical and prophetic messages. Precisely this combination of old and new, tradition and innovation, lies at the base of Haggai 2:4-5—Isaiah 63:7-14, too—to which the origin of pneumatology can be traced.

Israel's tendency to preserve and adapt its conception of the spirit, even during the Persian era, can be illustrated by a conception of the spirit outpoured. Whether in times of political uncertainty or decades of sheer anguish, Israel's prophets believed that the spirit outpoured would refresh nature,[102] turn God's people into a green tree in a vast desert,[103] bring Israel home,[104] transform slave-girls into prophets,[105] and evoke unprecedented remorse in the wake of political violence.[106] A glance at these texts, which span as many as four centuries, will serve nicely to uncover how ably prophets adopted and adapted the traditions they received.

Sometime during the late eighth century B.C.E., Isaiah accused women, in particular, of complacency during a failed harvest. These women, Isaiah urged, should beat their breasts in funerary mourning for the death of their fields and vines. Palace, city, fields, and vines would lie desolate

> until a spirit from on high is poured out on us,[107] and the wilderness becomes a fruitful field, and the fruitful field is deemed a forest. Then good judgment will dwell in the wilderness, and justice abide in the fruitful field. The effect of righteousness will be peace, and the result of righteousness, quietness, and trust forever. My people will abide in a peaceful habitation, in secure dwellings, and in quiet resting places.[108]

Two centuries later, in the harsh light of Babylonian supremacy, another prophet issued a promise that the spirit would be poured out.

> For I will pour water on the thirsty land, and streams on the dry ground; I will pour my spirit upon your descendants,[109] and my blessing on your offspring. They shall spring up like a green tamarisk, like willows by flowing streams. This one will say, "I am the LORD's," another will be called by the name of Jacob, yet another will write on the hand, "The LORD's," and adopt the name of Israel.[110]

This promise to descendants and offspring recalls the promise of blessing to Abraham and Sarah. From smallness comes national prominence; from insignificance arises a great people. Like the prophet responsible for the word of assurance in Haggai 2:4-5, this prophet, too, lunges forward by reaching back, offering promise for the future by grasping the roots of tradition. This is not an entirely new promise; it is a *renewed* promise.[111]

These are not the sole promises anchored by hope for the spirit outpoured. As exile strangled Judah, Ezekiel promised an outpouring by which God would gather exiles into their own land.[112] Joel, possibly during the neo-Babylonian or Persian eras, imagined a staggering obliteration of the status quo for all flesh, with a privileging of slaves, women, and the elderly, which hardly funds the exacting hierarchy so often associated with Judean life during the Persian era.[113] The Persian-era author of Zechariah 9–14 promised the outpouring of a spirit of compassion and forgiveness that would bring deep grief—but also reconciliation in the wake of a brutal stabbing.[114]

> And I will pour out a spirit of compassion and supplication on the house of David and the inhabitants of Jerusalem, so that, when they look on the one whom they have stabbed, they shall mourn for him, as one mourns for an only child, and weep bitterly over him, as one weeps over a firstborn.[115]

This is a powerful prediction, rooted in a violent act of stabbing and rife with the language of grief. At the opposite end of the spectrum from Joel, the recipients of this outpouring are limited to the house of David and inhabitants of Persian-era Jerusalem.[116] Therefore, this is not a sweeping outpouring. It is unlike the outpouring that will cause justice to dwell in the wilderness,[117] the outpouring that will come in torrents and initiate an influx of citizens,[118] the outpouring upon all flesh that will reach from the elders to female slaves.[119] This is a constricted outpouring of a spirit of compassion and supplication upon a particular group of people who are responsible for a violent act of stabbing.

The impact upon the Persian province of Yehud will be striking. The spirit will instigate compassion or favor; the houses of David, Nathan, and Levi, in other words, will replace violence with favor. As a result, the houses of David, Nathan, and Levi will seek forgiveness from the one whom they stabbed. This spirit effects a two-way street of favor and forgiveness between former opponents. The perpetrators of evil, further, will be utterly overcome by grief; the Hebrew root itself, *mourn* or *grieve*,[120] occurs no less than three times in this brief set of sayings, while the power of grief is expressed twice by the objects of grief: an only child, a firstborn. Utter desolation. Utter grief.

The timing of this prediction, "on that day," is vague. Nonetheless, what gives this text a force that may extend beyond other visions of outpouring is its specificity. Other earlier promises are magnificent, but this prediction is rooted in an actual political event, a violent, vile act. This is no ethereal vision of lions and lambs lying at peace together; this is a vision in which violent politicians, priests, and court prophets of the Persian era are moved to embrace a former opponent, against whom they have acted with unspeakable violence. Precisely because this vision is about actual politics and politicians, its vision of the force of God's spirit, a spirit outpoured, a spirit that effects a complete turnaround, that encloses whole families in utter grief, is unforgettable, as memorable as the grieving of the Egyptians for their only children, their lost firstborn.

The ability to imagine God's spirit outpoured extended through at least four centuries—from the eighth to the fourth, from an era of Assyrian domination to the apex of Persian power. Though persistent, this theme was never static. The emptying of the spirit upon Israel[121] became, in later centuries and situations, the occasion to gather foreigners,[122] to restore Israel to its land,[123] to inspire all flesh, bottom to top, to prophesy,[124] and to prompt remorse among political rivals during the Persian era.[125] The promise of the spirit outpoured, then, offers an apt illustration of how deftly prophets conserved earlier traditions, though with fresh modifications that addressed new challenges. Haggai's situation, as we have seen, was utterly disorienting, pungent with hope but not for a monarch, full of potential but only within the confines of the Persian province known as Yehud. It was an era ripe with the possibility of a fresh vision anchored in ancient traditions duly modified. Haggai would provide just that sort of vision for his beleaguered tribe of Yehudites.

A third conception portrayed the spirit of God not as rushing upon or pouring over but resting upon individuals. From the 700s to the 400s B.C.E., the fate of Judah prompted serious metamorphoses in this conception of the spirit, which took root in the late eighth century B.C.E., during an era of political vacillation, when Isaiah imagined an inspired ruler:

> The spirit of the Lord shall rest on him,
> the spirit of wisdom and understanding,
> the spirit of counsel and might,
> the spirit of knowledge and the fear of the Lord.[126]

Clothed with justice as his belt and faithfulness as his undergarment, this ruler would bring about justice not with violence but with the rod of his mouth; his inspired words alone would destroy the wicked.[127]

Nearly two centuries passed before a prophet picked up the themes of Isaiah's vision. With the monarchy eviscerated, it was not now a ruler but a servant upon whom the spirit rests: "Here is my servant, whom I uphold, my chosen, in whom my soul delights; I have put my spirit upon him."[128] The servant's message is characterized as *torah*, "teaching" that will reach the coastlands;[129] he will be "a light to the nations, to open the eyes that are blind, to bring out the prisoners from the dungeon, from the prison those who sit in darkness."[130]

This expansive view of inspired leadership narrows in the final chapters of the book of Isaiah, though not with rigid nationalism: "And as for me, this is my covenant with them, says the Lord: my spirit that is upon you, and my words that I have put in your mouth,[131] shall not depart out of your mouth, or out of the mouths of your children, or out of the mouths of your children's children, says the Lord, from now on and forever."[132] This Neo-Babylonian or Persian-era promise, written in prose, looks at first blush prosaic and predictable. It is not. It differs dramatically from earlier covenants made with Israel, such as those in the books of Ezekiel and Jeremiah, which are directed to the nation as a whole, or at least the segment in exile.[133] This promise is made to an individual, not now a Davidic king,[134] as in Isaiah's initial vision,[135] but a prophet, in whose mouth are God's words.[136]

Not many lines later, the prophet claims: "The spirit of the Lord GOD is upon me, because the Lord has anointed me; he has sent me to bring good news to the oppressed, to bind up the brokenhearted, to proclaim liberty to the captives, and release to the prisoners; to proclaim the year of the Lord's favor, and the day of vengeance of our God; to comfort all who mourn; to provide for those who mourn in Zion."[137] This mission is rooted in the understanding and wisdom of the inspired ruler[138] and the justice that lies at the core of the exilic servant's teaching.[139] Now, however, it is not the nation itself or other nations that are preeminent but the poor *within* Israel: the prophet preaches good news to the oppressed, release to prisoners, comfort for those who weep in Jerusalem, the frayed and fragmented center of Yehud.

This series of texts evinces a blend of preservation and modification that is similar to other strands of belief in the spirit. A single figure lies at the base of this conception, but this figure changed over the centuries, moving from an anointed ruler[140] to a beloved servant[141] to a prophetic recipient of the covenant[142] to a champion of the oppressed.[143] As political anxiety[144] turned to exile[145] and the challenge of rebuilding during the Persian era,[146] the universal tendency hinted at in Isaiah 11 swelled to encompass proselytes from distant coastlands[147] and then narrowed, though not in a parochial way, to an intense preoccupation with the debt-poor in Israel.[148]

A span of half a millennium or more led, through the vicissitudes of Israel's politics, to profound creativity in matters related to the spirit.[149] This tendency toward innovation characterized the Persian era as well, when the resting of the spirit upon key figures led to covenant renewal and the proclamation of good news to the poor.[150] The book of Zechariah as a whole contains three innovative messages: not by might but by God's *rûaḥ* would the nation be built;[151] a retrospective view, in which it was claimed that the spirit had spoken to a rebellious nation through a succession of prophets;[152] and the outpouring of a spirit of compassion and pleading in the wake of a vicious stabbing.[153] Even 1–2 Chronicles evinces rich innovation, when its author applies a traditional formula associated with ancient judges to four men of impeccable pedigree, who deliver inspired speeches that at once contain allusions to Israel's traditions and perspicacious political and military counsel.

Attention to *rûaḥ* did not evaporate during the Persian era in the face of priestly stratification, a penchant for purity of heritage, and Persian pressure. Even traditions that lay dormant, such as the rushing of the spirit upon the judges, reemerged freshly reconfigured. It would be a grave mistake to accept a view of the Persian era as sterile and legalistic. Haggai's promise alone is enough to dispel that caricature. Yet, as we have seen, Haggai was *not* alone.

Spirit and Exodus in the Service of the Future

This thumbnail sketch, highly selective and altogether too brief, may be enough to demonstrate that creativity came to a head after the cataclysm of 586 B.C.E. In the wake of this catastrophe and the formidable challenge of rebuilding, Israelites returned to familiar traditions—creation, exodus, deliverance through judges, temple, spirit—and framed a viable if unlikely future. The era after 586 B.C.E., punctuated by the return of a smattering of exiles after 539 B.C.E., proved to be a heady time, swirling with traditions that, when put to new uses, provided both the ballast and winds that were necessary to sail into an uncertain future. The spirit, *rûaḥ*, with its amorphous temperament and malleability, would play perfectly into this complex need for stability and temerity.

This realization strengthens the likelihood that Haggai was in a position not only to retrieve but also to extend the exodus and *rûaḥ* trajectories by combining them in creative ways. The *exodus tradition* became not only hope for but also, in the book of Ezra, the actualization of a *new* exodus, while *conceptions of rûaḥ* framed a future marked by resilience, refreshment, and restitution for Israel's oppressed. Israel's preoccupation with a future forged on the anvil of a new exodus and the reality of God's spirit was not desultory. It was, on the whole, assiduous, dynamic, and widespread.

The Promise of the Spirit in Haggai

"Work, for I am with you, says the LORD of hosts, according to the word that I cut with you when you came out of Egypt," urges Haggai. He then adds promise to command, "My spirit stands among you; do not fear." Though perhaps not at first blush, certainly at a second glance, this word of assurance is baffling. God had spoken many words with Israel when they came out of Egypt: the Ten Words; the designation of Israel as a kingdom of priests, holy, set apart;[154] commands to follow; sacrifices to make; offerings to give; tents to build.

Word after word after word. Promise following command. Command following promise. Words for the whole community. Words whispered in secret just to Moses—some in the conviviality of companionship, others through gritted teeth. So many words spoken when they came out of Egypt.

Just not this one: *my spirit stands among you*. That one God did *not* say. That word God did *not* cut. That pledge God did *not* make. Yet that is the word of assurance, which lies, alongside Isaiah 63:7-14, at the base of pneumatology. Lament—Isaiah 63:7-14—and promise—Haggai 2:4-5—frame the door to unprecedented oracles that engendered a conception of the spirit as a unique agent, which embedded God's invisible and inescapable presence in the drama of human history.

This promise, however, is plagued by a serious issue: the preceding words, *the word that I cut with you when you came out of Egypt*, occur in the Masoretic text but not in several ancient versions, including the Old Greek, Vetus Latina, and the Syriac Peshitta. In the Masoretic Text, exodus is the primary point of reference, in the other versions, not necessarily.

HEBREW	OLD GREEK
Yet now take courage,	And now, be strong,
O Zerubbabel, says the LORD;	O Zorobabel, says the Lord,
take courage, O Joshua, son of Jehozadak, the high priest;	and be strong, O Iesous the son of Iosedek, the great priest,
take courage, all you people of the land, says the LORD;	and let all the people of the land be strong, says the Lord,
work, for I am with you,	and act, for I am with you,
says the LORD of hosts—	says the Lord Almighty,
—the word that I cut with you when you came out of Egypt.	
My spirit abides among you; do not fear.	**and my spirit is present among you; have courage.**

In light of this textual conundrum, a preliminary brief discussion is in order, especially since a salient argument of this study is that exodus and spirit fuse in the promise of Haggai 2:4-5.[155] Two alternatives present themselves. Either the earliest Hebrew tradition, represented by the Masoretic Text, included the line, *the word that I cut with you when you came out of Egypt*, and translators omitted it, or, alternatively, the line was never there in the earliest Hebrew, and scribes responsible for the Masoretic tradition added it. It was either added, in which case the shorter Old Greek, Vetus Latina, and Syriac Peshitta represent the earlier form, or it was omitted, in which case the longer Masoretic version represents the earlier form.

The argument that the line, "the word that I cut with you when you came out of Egypt," was added in the Masoretic tradition—and is consequently not original—has three alleged pillars of support. It is, first of all, syntactically awkward. It begins abruptly in Hebrew with a particle that indicates a direct object, אֵת. The opening phrase, אֶת־הַדָּבָר, poses a problem because there is no verb in the preceding context in need of a direct object.[156] This line, then, is a later, awkward insertion, according to this line of argument. Another oddity is the phrase, "the word [matter] that I cut" (אֶת־הַדָּבָר אֲשֶׁר־כָּרַתִּי). Typically, God cuts not a *word* but a *covenant* with Israel.[157] The third awkward element is thought to be how it disrupts the flow of thought in Haggai 2:4-5, in which God twice, in close succession, promises sustained presence: "I am with you . . . my spirit stands among you." The reference to Egypt, so the argument goes, is intrusive. For reasons such as these, the line, "the word which I cut with you when you came out of Egypt," is considered a later insertion. If this is so, then the indisputable allusion to the exodus, which would bolster the argument that exodus traditions and spirit language merge in Haggai 2:5, did not exist in the earliest Hebrew version.

This is, however, a questionable line of argument, which violates a common-sense rule of thumb, that "although there are thousands of differences between

[MT] and the translations, only a fraction of them were created by a divergence between [MT] and the *Vorlage* of the translation. Most of the differences were created by other factors that are not related to the Hebrew *Vorlage*. These are inner-translational factors, especially in the area of exegesis."[158] In short, "one should probably not look to a different parent text as the cause for most differences."[159]

The absence of this line, if possible, should be attributed not to a different parent text but to the need to dispense with a troublesome text.[160] It is more feasible to suggest that this collection of oddities in the Hebrew—especially the introductory sign of the direct object (אֶת) and the occurrence of *word* rather than *covenant* with the verb *to cut*—prompted translators, who were keen to excise difficulties, to omit this Hebrew phrase altogether. The difficulties of the Hebrew text, in short, led to its omission.

As to the matter of disruption—a subjective criterion at best—this line is disruptive only if the integrity of tandem promises rests upon their immediate succession without anything significant intervening. In this instance, however, the putative intrusion serves to underscore the gravity of the promise of God's presence with a clear allusion to the exodus. The line in Hebrew cements the promises rather than interrupting them.[161]

To these commonsense arguments may be added text-critical ones. Mur88, the sole text from the Judean Desert containing the book of Haggai, is "one of the most conservative of all the biblical scrolls orthographically and morphologically and is virtually identical to the MT textually."[162] The text is extremely fragmentary, but the spacing of Haggai 2:5 in Mur88, lines 25-26, looks solidly like a reading resembling the Masoretic Text. "The MT rather nicely fills out the lines (ll. 25-26), leaving Mur88 22:27 blank." This first-century C.E. manuscript represents the Masoretic tradition rather than the Old Greek; were it not fragmentary, spacing tells us, it would contain this line.

The Aramaic Targums corroborate the originality of the Hebrew, too, with the paraphrase: "The word I cut with you when you came out of Egypt, and my prophets (are) teaching among you. Do not fear."[163] The whole of the Masoretic Text, including what is absent from the Old Greek, is represented by this paraphrase. The words "my prophets" are an obvious paraphrase of "my spirit;" "teaching" substitutes for "stand."

The allusion to the exodus in Haggai 2:5 features, then, in both Mur88, of the Dead Sea Scrolls, and the Aramaic Targums. Arguments for the priority of the Greek, therefore, must be grounded in more credible evidence than allegedly awkward syntax and putative interruptions, both of which are preserved even in the Targums,[164] despite their authors' inclination to interpret the original text with a rich measure of freedom. In light of the questionable criteria espoused to argue against the Masoretic Text, it is more judicious to accept the Hebrew as the original text and to assume that the awkward line, *the word that I cut with you when you came out of Egypt*, was omitted because of the challenges it posed to translators.[165]

The bewildering aspect of the exodus reminiscence in Haggai 2:5 is that, among the 377 other references to *rûaḥ* in the Hebrew Bible, plus an additional eleven in Aramaic, there is not a single one to *rûaḥ* standing. The spirit rushes upon, is upon, pours out, empties upon, blows, clothes, rests upon, guides—along with a host of other actions. But the spirit does not *stand*.

This association of *rûaḥ* with standing is unique in the Hebrew Bible. Like the phrase *angel of his presence*, it belongs to those innovations that emerged at some point following the destruction of Jerusalem, perhaps even after the return to Jerusalem. Many interpreters, we noted, considered the phrase *angel of his presence* too unique to be original, too innovative to be authentic, so they opted for the Old Greek, which shifted the emphasis away from the angel with the translation "not an angel but he himself saved them." Haggai's promise is equally formidable in its originality, but, absent a textual issue, there is no reason to jettison it. It must be dealt with straightforwardly.

Like the phrase *angel of his presence*, rebellion against the spirit, and the spirit's giving Israel rest—all elements of the lament in Isaiah 63 that blend exodus and spirit—Haggai's promise, *my spirit stands among you*, is the product of the fusion of exodus and spirit. In Haggai's promise, the intonation is slightly different from the lament. The lament fused exodus and spirit in a wistful look to the past, while Haggai's promise fuses the parallel convictions, which we briefly reviewed, that God is at work in a new exodus, and the spirit shapes Israel's future.

To compose a promise that would simultaneously assure and motivate, Haggai, like prophets before him, remembers the exodus, with its coterie of divine agents. One of them emerges, like a butterfly from a chrysalis, with singular clarity in Haggai 2:5, in the choice of the verb עמד, "to stand," to evoke the spirit's presence at a particularly threatening moment in Israel's distant past—the exodus from Egypt. Pinned between the Egyptian army and the Sea, Israel faced annihilation. Yet pillars of cloud and fire accompanied them. All of a sudden, as evening set and peril reared its head:

> The angel of God who was going before the Israelite army moved and went behind them; and the pillar of cloud moved from in front of them and *stood* behind them. It came between the army of Egypt and the army of Israel.[166]

The pillar of cloud *stood* between Israel and the Egyptian army, hot in pursuit, and protected them, on the cusp of escape, for one more necessary night.[167] The pillar's standing as safeguard was the sine qua non of Israel's existence. Without this movement from fore to aft, without the pillar's shift from guide to rearguard, Israel would never have crossed the Sea, traversed the wilderness, and settled the land. This was a singular moment of salvation.

The pillars were the baseline of God's presence, the vehicle of God's transport: "The LORD *was traveling* in front of them in a pillar of cloud by day, to lead them along the way, and in a pillar of fire by night, to give them light, so that they might travel by day and by night. Neither the pillar of cloud by day nor the pillar of fire by night left its place in front of the people."[168] Neither the pillar nor cloud would leave its place.[169] Until, of course, the pillar of cloud pulled out and moved from the front, where it led Israel, to the rear, where it stood guard.

Not just storytellers but Israel's poets, too, remembered this moment of supreme protection. One reprised the memory of how God "in the daytime led them with a cloud, and all night long with a fiery light."[170] All night long—like that first long night along the Sea. For another poet, the cloud was a partition and the fire a night light.[171] This adjustment, through which the cloud becomes a partition, akin to the screens in the tabernacle, allows the protective stance of the pillar on the eve of the exodus to surface in poetic praise of God's powerful acts in history.

Prophets—*this* prophet at least—understood the potential in this portrait of the pillar, so pried out of it a promise.

> Yet now take courage, O Zerubbabel, says the LORD; take courage, O Joshua, son of Jehozadak, the high priest; take courage, all you people of the land, says the LORD; work, for I am with you, says the LORD of hosts—the word I cut with you when you came out of Egypt: my spirit stands in your midst; do not fear.

The inhabitants of Yehud had not gotten the job done. Paralyzed by drought, preoccupied by reasonable self-interest—homes needed to be built more than a temple—confronted with a strange new land they had never before seen and a precarious political Persian landscape they had never before known, they hesitated. It is difficult not to empathize with their hesitation, given needs that may have seemed to them, at least, more pressing than a shrine or sanctuary.

In short, they had fear. Fear of scarcity. Fear of the threat posed by others in the land. Fear of Persia, with a new policy of allowing exiles to return home but without a restoration of the monarchy. If Ezekiel had seen the temple as the epitome of a new exodus, if the prophet of Isaiah 40–55 had seen redemption as a new exodus, if Ezra, later still, would see return as a new exodus—then the underside of exodus, of new exodus, confronted the first to return from Babylon. The promise was fulfilled, but the challenge remained.

So Haggai transforms the first exodus into *their* exodus. There is no visible pillar, no illumination throughout the night, no intimidating angel to oust enemies. They carry with them, nonetheless, a longstanding belief in the spirit as the shaper of the future. They embrace an enduring memory of the exodus. Haggai urges them to recognize, too, that this moment is a new exodus, in which the spirit stands where the pillar once did. There is no need to fear.

How this realization relates to the word God cut with them when they came out of Egypt is not immediately apparent, since God made no promise about the spirit when they came out of Egypt. Yet precisely here is where the complicated memory of the divine agents comes to a head. No, God spoke no word of a spirit standing when the slaves emerged unscathed from Egypt. Yet Haggai's promise may be tethered, tenuously perhaps, but tethered nonetheless, to some of the words God spoke when the slaves emerged unscathed from Egypt.

At Sinai, toward the tail end of the Book of the Covenant, God had promised to send an angel "to guard you on the way and to bring you to the place that I have prepared." It is possible that this is the word to which Haggai refers: a word of assurance that the angel, understood now, in tandem with the pillar, to be the spirit, is present through guarding and leading the people to the place God had established. That angel had once led Israel, had wedged itself, along with the pillar, between Israel and the onslaught of the Egyptians. That angel, ineluctably related to the pillar as partition and protection in Israel's traditions, is now present as God's spirit among them. There is no need to fear.

This association is feasible because Haggai's promise of the spirit's standing in relation to the exodus is tied principally to one text: Exodus 14:19, where the pillar and the angel moved from front to rear, and the pillar stood. By implication, the angel stood, too, though the text does not say so explicitly. Yet we have seen, time and again, how the activities of the divine agents of the exodus fused with one another, how their personae intersected, how memories of them overlapped. The close association of pillar and angel at the exodus is a prima facie example of this sort of fusion, which may have led a later interpreter, such as Haggai, to connect the pillar and angel who stood at the exodus with the angel God promised at Sinai—and to identify this coalescence with the spirit.

This metamorphosis, or series of metamorphoses, lies near at hand to Isaiah 63:7-14. The author of that lament combined the angel of the exodus with God's presence-face to create the angel of God's presence, who saved Israel. The author then went on to identify this angel with the spirit. Something similar may occur in Haggai, if Haggai associates the pillar of cloud with the promised angel—and both with the spirit. Whether this in fact occurred is not possible to say. It is possible to say with rather more certainty that Haggai identified the pillar of the exodus tradition with the spirit, who now stands in the pillar's stead.

These elements emerge from the exodus story: the pillar moved and stood to protect the escaping Israelites; the angel moved and, by implication, stood alongside the pillar; God promised the angel as guard and guide. From these elements, it is a short step to Haggai's words: *work, for I am with you, says the* Lord *of hosts—the word I cut with you when you came out of Egypt: my spirit stands in your midst; do not fear.* The dots are there. Haggai connects them.

That Haggai should connect them in this way is to be expected. Past and present fold together in Haggai's promise. The word God cut—in true Deuteronomic fashion[172]—is for Haggai's people and not just those whom God rescued from Egypt: this is the word I cut with *you* when *you* came out of Egypt. The people of the restoration are the people of the exodus. Haggai's people, not a generation long past, are the recipients of God's word, the object of God's protection.

The conviction that return from Babylon was a new exodus, that return to Yehud was a new taking of the land, that *this* is the generation of the exodus, whom God addresses directly, is not limited to this promise. The prophecy concludes with a word that the governor will be God's signet ring, because, promises God, "I am about to shake the heavens and the earth, and to overthrow the throne of kingdoms; I am about to destroy the strength of the kingdoms of the nations, and overthrow the chariots and their riders; and the horses and their riders shall fall, every one by the sword of a comrade."[173] Hope takes on the guise of exodus. Destruction of the nations will mirror the annihilation of Egypt, when God overthrew chariots and riders.[174] At the end of the book, as in the promise of the spirit, future salvation is portrayed with language redolent of the exodus.

The pillar that protected the escaped slaves from the marauding Egyptian army reappeared at other moments of particular presence and providence during Israel's early days. In one of those episodes—the tortured conversation between God and Moses—the pillar of cloud stands again. This is a protracted and fierce negotiation over who—the angel or God's presence-face—will accompany Israel. As we saw, the conclusion is unsatisfying, an instance of maintaining rather than gaining ground. The debate is also puzzling, interrupted as it is by a quaint scene, in which God talked with Moses face to face, presence to presence, the way a person talks to a friend. On those occasions, "when Moses entered the tent, the pillar of cloud would descend and stand at the entrance of the tent, and the Lord would speak with Moses. When all the people saw the pillar of cloud standing at the entrance of the tent, all the people would rise and bow down, all of them, at the entrance of their tent."[175] Twice the pillar is said to stand at the tent's entrance. When the people saw the pillar of cloud standing there, they bowed down at their own tents. The pillar, in short, signaled the presence of God in Israel's midst, while Moses and God talked face to face. Like the earlier scene, in which the angel and pillar moved to become a partition between Israel and its pursuers, in this scene, too, the pillar of cloud functions as a partition, this time to shield God and Moses from the Israelites.[176]

For Haggai, there is no palpable pillar to which he can point during the early years of rebuilding after Cyrus' mandate to return and rebuild, no corporeal cloud that exists to signal God's presence. But there is something else that can stand in Israel's midst and signal God's presence. There is spirit, *rûaḥ*. It is possible that the standing of the spirit points to this bucolic and peaceful scene outside the camp, but the precarious situation in which the Yehudites found themselves suggests that the standing of the spirit reverberates more effectively, resonates more richly, against the wall of Egyptians that had surged toward their ancestors along the shore on that final, fateful, fearful night.

Do not fear are common enough words in the Hebrew Bible, occurring nearly eighty times. Yet one foothold in the tradition may anchor Haggai's promise. Returning his hearers perhaps to the cusp of the Sea, he uses exactly the same words as Moses: "*Do not fear*, stand firm, and see the deliverance that the LORD will accomplish for you today; for the Egyptians whom you see today you shall never see again. The LORD will fight for you, and you have only to keep still."[177] This word would prove true. God commands Moses to lift up his staff, stretch out his hand, so that the Israelites might pass. Before they do, they have one more harrowing night—made less harrowing by the initiative of the pillar and angel. It is not possible to know, given how recurrent and global the command not to fear is, but it should be pointed out that, no sooner does Moses tell the people on the verge of liberation not to fear than the angel and pillar pull up stakes and—the pillar, at least—stand as Israel's rearguard: "The angel of God who was going before the Israelite army moved and went behind them; and the pillar of cloud moved from in front of them and *stood* behind them. It came between the army of Egypt and the army of Israel. And so the cloud was there with the darkness, and it lit up the night; one did not come near the other all night" (Exodus 14:19-20). There are indeed memorable nights. This may have been one of them. Memorable enough perhaps to infuse, centuries later, courage into a hesitant and fainthearted people.

Fissures and Fusion

Cyrus, administratively able, perhaps even benevolent, but not theologically progressive, probably could not have imagined the creativity, innovation, and resourcefulness of the people he commissioned to return home and to rebuild the temple. Cyrus' god Marduk was keeper of the status quo. It was Marduk, after all, who authorized Cyrus "to march against his city Babylon" and who traveled "at his side like a real friend." When it came time to fight, Marduk "delivered into his (i.e., Cyrus') hands Nabonidus, the king who did not worship" Marduk.[178]

While Cyrus busied himself with the industry of an empire, the exiles returned to Jerusalem, where one of them, at least, continued along a vein of ingenuity that his predecessors in exile, perhaps in Palestine as well, had explored. Like the prophet of lament (Isaiah 63:7-14), Haggai tested the mettle of his tradition by fusing its cornerstone, the exodus, with belief in the inevitable if invisible presence of the spirit of God. Both prophets poured old wine into new wineskins, which burst to create an unprecedented conception of the spirit as an independent agent capable of saving and giving rest and standing—and, in darker times, becoming the object of opprobrium.

Haggai faced a timorous people, whose foundation had slipped again, even if in a good way. The gardens they had planted, the homes they had built, the modest niche in the imperial economy they had occupied, perhaps even the children they had raised, this doughty band of believers left behind. Indomitable they would seem until confronted with drought, with people who had settled in their ancestral plots and worshiped in what had once been their parents' shrines, with the challenge of a whole new political order, led by governors rather than kings, organized in provinces rather than tribal lands.

The ability to discover ancestral traditions that would meet the challenges that lay ahead must have been daunting. Perhaps the paucity of prophetic texts from this era is an indication of how few were capable of meeting that challenge. Haggai may not have been alone, but he was nearly so. Once more unto the breach he charged, taking his place between the vicissitudes of empires and belief in Israel's God. Confronted by entropy, provoked by inertia, Haggai insisted it was time to rebuild the temple. Cyrus or Cambyses or Darius would expect it. The God of Israel would demand it. No trepidation or cowardice, and certainly no selfishness, insisted Haggai, should be allowed to stand in the way.

To move them to action, Haggai makes grand promises from a God who will shake the heavens, so that riches will flow to the new temple, then shake the heavens to throw chariots and riders into the sea and install Yehud's governor, Zerubbabel, as a signet ring—though not as a king.[179] This is a grand promise but one that appeased the Persians, too. "We dream on a budget," playwright J.M. Barrie quips in *Finding Neverland*, when young Peter sees actors rehearsing with wooden swords. Haggai dreams on a budget, too, generating hope within strict Persian parameters, captured in the simple line, "From this day on I will bless you."[180] Blessing must not entail aspirations to monarchy.

Twice in the brief compass of this prophetic exhortation, Haggai offers simple words of assurance. "I am with you," the Lord utters without fanfare.[181] Then again, "I am with you,"[182] though this time followed by a rare, and ultimately strange, appeal to Israel's history: *the word I cut with you when you came out of Egypt. My spirit stands in your midst.* A bolt out of the blue, syntactically speaking, the line bursts onto the scene. This is no wisp of memory, a glimpse of bygone days, a hint of the past. It is one of those memories that jumps out, wrenched into existence by a scent or a scene or a sensation. It is déjà vu. Not first exodus. Not second exodus, either. But *our* exodus. God cut a word with *us* when *we* came out of Egypt. God's spirit stands in *our* midst.

The book of Haggai reveals the eye of a pragmatist, content to rebuild in the shadow of Persia, consigned to collaborate with leaders hamstrung by anxiety. Haggai meets them with simple language, straightforward questions, and conventional promises. Except for this one, in which the tradition speaks to a timid folk face to face, like Moses and God wrestling over the fate of Israel in that desert tent. *The word I cut with you when you came out of Egypt: my spirit stands in your midst.*

In this anamnesis, the diaphanous border between past, present, and future disintegrates. There is only the presence of God, who cut a word with *us,* the trickle of exiles who dared return to Yehud. There is only the presence of God in the solidity of the spirit's standing—not rushing or pouring or clothing or breathing or blowing but *standing,* a spirit-pillar wedged between our camp and theirs, between annihilation and escape.

Chapter 5

THE SIGNIFICANCE OF THE SPIRIT
Rediscovering Exodus: The Future of Pneumatology

It might be possible to dismiss these observations as relics of a bygone era or isolated exegetical notations that change nothing, leaving the discipline of Christian pneumatology intact. To disparage its significance in this way would be an egregious error because this was an historic phenomenon rooted in historical crises that led to a fresh understanding of both the exodus tradition and the spirit. It is not so much biblical, in the sense of canonical, as *historical*—an actual innovation that emerged from the compression of historical events that were inevitably tied to subsequent historical events. The remainder of the history of pneumatology is dependent upon it, like a door on a hinge. To appeal to tradition to maintain the status quo is neither possible nor optimal because the shape of that tradition is dependent upon understandings and misunderstandings at its source. If the attribution of the spirit's agency first to Christianity is a misjudgment—a misapprehension of history—it is incumbent upon bearers of the tradition to analyze the impact of that misunderstanding and to offer course correctives that better reflect the impulse that lay at the origin of that tradition.

Think of Amos' plumb line, the third of five visions that led a prophet from the bucolic south to the relatively urban north in order to prosecute the people of Israel—king, priest, and people—for their failure to live as God's chosen people.[1] The plumb line is the central vision, at which point Amos shifts from being the people's advocate to being their prosecutor. Amos could remonstrate about the first two visions of locusts and fire, but the plumb line spoke for itself. Amos could not protest the clear message of a crooked people set against the plumb line of the tradition, rightly understood. In a similar way, the ability to hold up a plumb line consisting of the prior Israelite understanding of the spirit as an agent has the potential to reveal where Christian tradition is crooked, off kilter, in need of correction.

A fitting analogy may be drawn from the English word *helpmeet,* which translates a single pair of Hebrew words in such a way as to offer both a text and pretext for a particular understanding of gender. As a *helper,* the woman was man's aide. When, however, Phyllis Trible demonstrated that the word *help* refers almost exclusively in the Hebrew Bible to God, she inscribed at the headwaters of tradition an impulse that undercut the view of woman as subordinate rather than savior, as complement rather than cocreator.[2] In this instance, a fresh exegetical perspective functioned as a plumb line alongside which the limits, possibly even the misdirections, of the tradition could be measured. When traditions do not change—and many traditions have not changed based upon exegetical advances—their exegetical source stands nonetheless as an indictment against that element of the tradition. Once the exegetical observation is out in the open, always the question remains of what tradition and practice would look like if their source had been understood or interpreted correctly from the start. Even more pressing is the question of what tradition and practice would look like if they were brought *now* into closer conformity to that source.

While the essence of this study is exegetical, it impinges—infringes, too—upon theology. Three dimensions of Christian pneumatology, in particular, can benefit from a fresh appraisal in light of what we have disclosed in this book. These reappraisals are complex and significant, but it is possible briefly to pinpoint their points of departure.

Christians have tended to describe the spirit as a hypostasis, which suggests the progressive rendering of an internal attribute as an external entity. Over the course of time, by way of analogy, God's quality of wisdom, it is said, became a hypostasis, an independent reality known as Wisdom. This may be an appropriate way to understand the emergence of Wisdom—Christ as the wisdom of God, as well—but it is an inadequate way to understand the origin of pneumatology, which occurred when two prophets encountered and countered crisis by fusing a robust belief in the presence of *rûaḥ* with the rich tradition of the exodus. It is now time to unmask the inadequacy of the concept of hypostasis in light of the actual historical origin of pneumatology.

No less essential to the future of pneumatology is the realization that it is not an exclusively Christian enterprise. At its point of origin, in fact, pneumatology was an Israelite enterprise. It is time to rediscover that dimension of pneumatology and, with it, to rekindle an appreciation for the Israelite world—its Jewish legacy, too—that gave birth to the understanding of the spirit as an agent.

Pneumatology grew first in the soil of history, of crisis, of community. Pneumatology may for Christians eventually be about the divine economy in the trinity, the inner logic of father, son, and holy spirit, but it cannot begin there because it *did not* begin there. If contemporary pneumatology is to be faithful to its point of origin, then it ought to explore as one of its central loci—this is the third mandate—the relationship of the spirit to historical crisis, to catastrophe, the birthplace of the holy spirit.

These desiderata will occupy us for most of the remainder of this book. Yet the question may still remain of whether an analysis of *Israelite* texts should have any impact upon *Christian* pneumatology. The interpretations of the spirit championed in Haggai 2 and Isaiah 63, we shall see, did not even hold the day in postbiblical Jewish writings. How much less should these texts be considered influential in the shaping of *Christian* pneumatology? Not *less* at all, as it turns out. A burgeoning segment of Antiquity did in fact adopt this innovative view of the spirit as the preeminent agent of the exodus. Their embrace of the view of the spirit espoused especially in Isaiah 63 became a subterranean force in their elucidation of the life of Jesus and the life of faith. Rather than languish, the connection between the spirit and the exodus exploited in Haggai 2 and Isaiah 63 came to fruition subtly but unmistakably in the gospels and letters of the New Testament. What cataclysm had birthed during the century after the fall of Jerusalem to Babylon—the spirit understood as an agent of the exodus—reignited during the century when Jerusalem would fall again, this time to Rome.

Hypostasis and the Future of Pneumatology

Exactly one hundred years ago, scholarship thrummed with interest in the spirit. Hermann Gunkel's *Die Wirkungen des heiligen Geistes nach der populären Anschauung der apostolischen Zeit und nach der Lehre des Apostels Paulus*[3] had opened the floodgates, bursting the dam of German Idealism, which had for decades tamed the spirit, constricting it to the principle of human consciousness.[4] Not the human—or natural—spirit, contested Gunkel, but the *supernatural* spirit, which eclipses human potential, lay at the heart of early Christian pneumatology. Though Gunkel himself was a child of his age,[5] he refused to hold early Christianity captive to late nineteenth-century Idealism, so he discerned the most palpable presence of the spirit not in the cultivation of an intellectual or ethically conscious life but in the phenomenon of glossolalia.[6]

With the dam now breached, other voices chimed in with related studies of the spirit. Heinrich Weinel brilliantly assayed Gunkel's emphasis upon the effects of the spirit through the late second century in *Die Wirkungen des Geistes und die Geister im nachapostolischen Zeitalter bis auf Irenäus*.[7] Oscar Holtzmann asked, *War Jesus Ekstatiker?*[8] A year later, W. R. Shoemaker's copious article, "The Use of Ruach in the Old Testament, and of Pneuma in the New Testament: A Lexicographical Study," appeared in the *Journal of Biblical Literature*.[9]

Then, within three years of one another, a spate of significant studies from three distinct quarters shone light on the spirit. Regius Professor of Divinity at the University of Cambridge H. B. Swete penned *The Holy Spirit in the New Testament*[10] and, just three years later, *The Holy Spirit in the Ancient Church: A Study of Christian Teaching in the Age of the Fathers.*[11] Paul Volz, professor of theology in Tübingen, in *Der Geist Gottes und die verwandten Erscheinungen im Alten Testament und im anschliessenden Judentum,* looked uniquely at the spirit in the Hebrew Bible and early Judaism.[12] A Welsh-born rabbi in England, Joshua Abelson, created a compendium on the topic of *The Immanence of God in Rabbinical Literature,* in which he explored the *shekinah,* though not without devoting more than one hundred pages to the holy spirit, with such questions as "In what respects is the rabbinic treatment of Holy Spirit an advance upon the Old Testament treatment?"[13]

In the decades to follow, some of Germany's finest minds turned to the spirit. Hans Leisegang's *Der heilige Geist: Das Wesen und Werden der mystisch-intuitiven Erkenntnis in der Philosophie und Religion der Griechen,* which I noted in passing at the start of this study, saw the light of day in 1919;[14] on its heels, Leisegang published *Pneuma Hagion: Der Ursprung des Geistbegriffs der synoptischen Evangelien aus der griechischen Mystik.*[15] In the first of these volumes, as we saw, Leisegang posed the question of whether the teaching on the holy spirit is Greek or Oriental (as he put it) in origin. To answer this question, he looked principally to Alexandrian philosopher Philo Judaeus as the nexus of Greek and Jewish conceptions of the spirit—though Leisegang was not satisfied to identify this nexus; he was determined rather to peel off the Jewish veneer in Philo's writings to discover the Greek ideas that lay underneath in order to settle Jesus into the world of Greek ecstasy.[16]

Furious opposition to Leisegang arose from several corners; two studies appeared, in fact, in 1926. Friedrich Büchsel framed an immense retort, in which the whole of Jesus' life—his prophetic authority, ascetic bent, and visionary experiences—flowed from his consciousness of being a Jewish *Pneumatiker.*[17] Heinrich von Baer set the spirit into a three-part scheme of salvation history, grounded in the history of Israel rather than a sphere of Greco-Roman ideas.[18]

The flames of the spirit burned brightly—then burned out, due perhaps to the simultaneous rise of National Socialism, with its devaluation of all things Jewish, alongside the theological thrust of Karl Barth and company, which drew attention away from the History of Religions approach to the spirit, with its keen eye toward cultures of origin. Still, a crevice had opened, and the question of origins had already yielded rich dividends. Leisegang, by banking on the Greco-Roman origin of Christianity, launched a serious effort among his detractors to situate the inspiration of Jesus in its Jewish context. More broadly, and even more significant from our standpoint, Paul Volz drew a direct line from the Hebrew

Bible through early Judaism to the New Testament; early Christianity, contended Volz, rose from continuity with Judaism rather than a rejection of Judaism.[19] This perspective would prove revolutionary, too radical perhaps for an era soon to spawn National Socialism, with its concerted and largely effective effort to uproot Christianity from its fertile Jewish soil.[20]

Following the lead of his predecessors, Hermann Gunkel and Heinrich Weinel, Volz devoted a substantial portion of his study to the effects (*Wirkungen*) of the spirit, such as inspired speech, inspired poetry, inspired translation (e.g., the Septuagint), and inspired wisdom. He looked, too, at "pneumatische Personen," from Moses, in the distant past, to relative contemporaries of Christianity—Ben Sira, Philo Judaeus, apocalypticists, and rabbis—and further to those figures reserved for the eschatological future, including the messiah and the people of salvation. The whole pneumatological sweep of history, and beyond, fell under Volz's thoughtful gaze.

Volz accomplished something else of equal significance. He explored not only the *effects* but also the *nature* of the spirit. A sizeable portion of his book, therefore, beginning with analyses of Isaiah 63:7-14 and Haggai 2:5, is devoted to "Die Geisthypostase," the Spirit-hypostasis.[21] It is here, with the notion of a Geisthypostase, that we begin to explore in earnest the implications of our own study, now more than a full century since Gunkel, Weinel, Swete, Volz, and Abelson studied the spirit with a keen eye and attentive gaze—and exactly one hundred years, somewhat propitiously, since Leisegang attempted to peel the Jewish veneer off of authors whose spirituality rose, or so Leisegang thought, from the spring of Greco-Roman mysticism.

Nineteenth-century commentators had already identified the spirit in Isaiah 63:7-14 as a hypostasis.[22] Influential British interpreter T. K Cheyne discerned in Second Isaiah a "tendency in this book to hypostatize the Divine Spirit (which it mentions no less than seven times) with special distinctness."[23] In their commentaries on Isaiah, Bernard Duhm and D. Karl Marti—the scholars responsible for the hypothesis of a Third Isaiah—discerned in the spirit of Isaiah 63:7-14 "an independent being similar to the hypostasis of prophecy and administration."[24] Duhm found support for this interpretation in the provoking of the spirit in Isaiah 63:10. One can only grieve or afflict the spirit when it is understood to be a hypostasis.[25]

The ability to be grieved or rebelled against does not, notwithstanding Duhm, a hypostasis make. In Psalms, the people of Israel exasperated Moses, either by making his spirit bitter or rebelling against his spirit;[26] either way, the impact was clear: Moses "spoke words that were rash."[27] In this psalm, this grieving or rebelling does not require that Moses' spirit be a hypostasis. On the contrary,

Moses' spirit is his self, his whole person. When they rebelled against *him*—his spirit—he responded by speaking rashly.

Within a decade of the publication of Marti's commentary, and within two of Duhm's and Cheyne's, Paul Volz explored this vein more attentively. He admitted from the start the difficulty in identifying a hypostasis. Is the spirit an organ moving *within* God, he wondered, or something that is projected *outside* of God?[28] Jews doubtless believed that the spirit was this sort of hypostasis, but when, he speculated, did this belief take root? The answer he gives is clear: during the postexilic era in a cluster of texts, including Isaiah 63:7-14 and Haggai 2:5. The close monotheistic connection between the spirit and God catalyzed the hypostatization of the spirit during the postexilic era.[29]

The exploration of such a remarkable development demands definition—something commentators Cheyne, Duhm, and Marti had not proffered. Volz delivers on this when he defines the Spirit-hypostasis as "the outward projected abstraction of the inner being of God, a power separated from God. . . . It is not a person but a personified abstraction, indeed it is thought of as an independent, existing-in-itself power next to Yahweh and apart from people."[30] This definition is essential, even if, as we will soon see, errant. With it, Volz identifies the spirit as a hypostasis resulting from the projected abstraction of the inner essence of God.[31] That abstraction is *not* a person but is *personal* (*personhafte*) and an abstraction *personified* (*personifizierte*).[32]

The lament in Isaiah 63:7-14 is the linchpin of this interpretation.[33] In this lament, notes Volz, the spirit is a massive presence in the community of Israel, which works powerfully in Moses and his successors—but is never bound to Israel and its leaders. Despite its presence in the community, the spirit remains an independent presence from a higher world.[34]

The lament in Isaiah 63 is just the beginning of a long process, cautions Volz.[35] The reticence of the language in Isaiah 63 adopted to express the hypostatic character of the spirit demonstrates that Israel was just on the threshold of the process of hypostatization that would, in time, produce a full-orbed understanding of the spirit as a hypostasis.[36]

The spirit, notes Volz, is a powerful communal presence as well in the prophecy of Haggai, where the spirit protects and guides Israel as a whole, giving Israel its peculiar place in the world.[37] This power does not rise from the heart of Israel; it is rather an independent power that *stands* in Israel's midst. The spirit's posture of standing is precisely what gives the spirit a personal quality. So too, for Volz, does the relationship between the promise, "I am with you," in Haggai 2:4, and the spirit: "the spirit appears through this word, which proceeds without mediation, as something independent next to Yahweh."[38]

Isaiah 63:7-14 and Haggai 2:4-5 are of a piece. In both, suggests Volz, the spirit is an independent presence, a personification of God, which influences the entire community of Israel. The only difference between the lament and promise is that Haggai accepts as a matter of faith that the spirit is present, while the lament rues the absence of the spirit that once was present.[39] The spirit in both lament and promise, Volz is certain, is a hypostasis, even if the nature of that hypostasis is still expressed hesitantly.

Volz adds to this cluster Zechariah 7:4-6, in which the spirit utilizes the organs of the prophets. This is enough, he surmises, to suggest that the spirit is independent of God. So too is the use of the word *good* in the prayer of Ezra in Nehemiah 9:20: God gave the *good* spirit to instruct Israel during their wilderness sojourn. This same spirit, later in Ezra's prayer, is said to have been in Israel's midst, though Israel would not listen.[40] The epithet *good*, alongside the spirit's presence in Israel, smacks, for Volz, of "the hypostatic character of the spirit."[41]

Together, concludes Volz, this cluster of Hebrew texts offers "a unified portrait of this spirit-hypostasis, which stands and works in Israel."[42] This portrait exhibits salient features, like a museum room full of similar paintings—French impressionists or cubists, for example:

- The spirit is a *hypostasis*, understood as the personification of the divine essence; this hypostasis, however, is not a person but a personification.[43]
- The spirit has a special relationship with prophets, though its impact is not limited to the use of their mouths as organs of divine speech.[44]
- The spirit influences the people as a whole; the spirit functions principally within the community rather than individuals.[45]
- The notion of a hypostasis is not so developed that the spirit is active alongside or in place of God; God works through the spirit, convincing and instructing the people in order to ensure their success.[46]
- The primary sphere of the spirit is the religious-ethical life, understood particularly in the life of Israel as a whole.[47] The spirit is more *passive* than God, who is more active in the national life of Israel.[48] In this respect, the spirit is not identical to the angel of God's presence of Isaiah 63:9; the angel is more active in the sphere of national help and leading than the spirit.[49]
- The spirit rises to fill the gap between the sense of an unmediated era long ago, when people knew their limits and had unlimited access to God, and the present; now the spirit mediates God to Israel, especially through prophets.[50]

A similar sort of language materialized in subsequent commentaries on the lament in Isaiah 63:7-14, though rarely in commentaries on Haggai 2:5, whose contribution to ancient conceptions of the spirit tends to be overlooked. Before returning to engage Volz's rich discussion of the spirit as a hypostasis in Isaiah 63:7-14 and Haggai 2:5, it will be informative to touch upon a few twentieth-century commentators in order to grasp, by way of illustration, just how persistent—and imprecise—this characterization of the spirit continues to be.

Walther Eichrodt characterized the Persian era as a period when "everything which earlier generations had learned and enunciated about the working of the spirit of God came alive more than ever before, and exerted a direct influence on the conduct of daily life." This is an impeccable description of that era. Eichrodt continues: "This may be seen first of all in the development by which the spirit of God is made markedly independent, so that it can now be portrayed as a so-called hypostasis, that is, to say, a separate entity which acts of its own motion, and is of itself concerned with human affairs."[51] This, too, is an exceptionally perceptive portrayal, except for his inexact reference to a *so-called hypostasis*.

Pierre Bonnard determined that this spirit "is certainly not a divine person that would approximate trinitarian dogma but the personification of a divine attribute: the Power of God."[52] Like Volz, Bonnard did not discern in the Isaianic lament a person, certainly not a person akin to the trinitarian spirit, but he did detect a personification, a power, and a principle. Bonnard's language is fluid, suggesting how difficult it is to pinpoint precisely how the poet who penned this lament conceived of the spirit.

R. N. Whybray described the spirit with similar imprecision: "God's Holy Spirit, dwelling within his people (verse 11), leading them through the desert to their destined home in Canaan (verse 14), but then grieved by their rebellion, is here personified more clearly than anywhere else in the OT, and is on its way to its later full development as a distinct hypostasis in late Jewish and in Christian thought."[53] The spirit is here *personified, on its way* to a *distinct hypostasis*. The impression Whybray gives, without explanation or evidence, is of a monolithic trajectory from personification to hypostasis.

Joseph Blenkinsopp discerned a similar trajectory in this lament. "The association of the Spirit with the Presence or the Face of God (also in Ps 139:7)," noted Blenkinsopp, "indicates that the Spirit (*rûaḥ*) has now become the object of theological reflection, a kind of hypostasis similar in that respect to the Face (*pānîm*), the Angel (*mal'āk*) and, later in the Targum, the Word (*memra'*). We are at the beginning of a development that will eventuate, on the one hand, in the Christian doctrine of the Holy Spirit and, on the other, the rabbinic concept of the *rûaḥ* haqqodeš as the spirit of prophecy (*rûaḥ hannĕbû'â*)."[54] This description, though perceptive on the whole, drips with imprecision—an indication of how thorny it is to put language to reality. *Theological reflection* conjures myriad images, many of them Christian. With the words, *a kind of hypostasis*, imprecision again rears its ugly head; the spirit is presumably a hypostasis known principally by similarities it shares with the presence-face and angel of God—though how these clarify what sort of hypostasis the spirit is, is simply not clear. The genetic trajectory from this sort of relatively undefined—*a kind of*—hypostasis to the Christian doctrine of the holy spirit and the rabbinic spirit of prophecy, though plausible, begs for qualification and substantiation.

Brevard Childs cautiously noted that "the spirit here is the holy presence of Yahweh, which is a form of his outward manifestation to Israel theologically retrojected to the period of the nation's inception. Although the holy spirit is here still far removed from its later New Testament understanding, there is nevertheless an adumbration in the Old Testament of the identity of the God of Israel both as the transcendent and immanent presence in creation and redemption."[55] This description, like the others, is rife with ill-defined jargon, such as *outward manifestation, theologically retrojected,* and, in particular, *adumbration.* What precisely is an adumbration?

Whatever Childs meant by adumbration, it raised the hackles of John Goldingay, spurring him to pen a passionate comment in response:

> Christian interpretation is inclined to see an "adumbration" of Christian thinking in this line, but this understanding obscures the significance of the line more than it clarifies it. To say that the Israelites hurt Yhwh's spirit no more implies that Yhwh's spirit is a hypostasis than would be implied if someone spoke of hurting a human being's spirit.[56] Speaking of Yhwh's holy spirit does not imply any personification of the spirit as if it were a hypostasis in some way separate from Yhwh. "Basically it is an emphatic expression for 'him,' as if to draw attention to God's presence and activity."[57] While the phrase helped early Christians nuance their understanding of God, this does not imply that the expression itself "foreshadowed" the Holy Spirit as understood in Christian faith. The development of that understanding issued essentially from reflection on events that took place in the life of Jesus and subsequent decades, whose nature Old Testament expressions such as this one helped the early Christians to articulate. This does not mean that the connotations that come to attach to the phrase are somehow contained or implicit within the expression, and Christian interpretation consistently shows how this framework of thinking obscures understanding of the Old Testament by conforming to the New.[58]

Interpreters from Volz to Childs discern in Isaiah 63:7-14 the embryonic stage of the spirit as a hypostasis. Goldingay demurs. For him, the term *hypostasis* strikes a raw nerve, so that the term *holy spirit* is nothing more than an expression for God, "as if to draw attention to God's presence and activity." The phrase, apparently, *helped* Christians to nuance their understanding of God and to *articulate* that understanding, though how, Goldingay does not say. Instead, he draws a line in the sand: Christian understanding of the holy spirit developed essentially not from texts such as Isaiah 63:7-14 but from the life of Jesus and events from subsequent decades. There is no sense, no sense at all, in which a Christian understanding of the holy spirit was *contained* or *implicit* in this Hebrew lament. Goldingay's keen resistance to distorting the first testament by conforming it to the second prompts him, when it comes to the holy spirit, to throw the baby out with the bath. No personification in Isaiah 63. Certainly no hypostasis. No direct influence from Old to New Testament. Not even adumbration. Help, yes. Aid in articulation, to be sure. But how, Goldingay does not—no doubt *will* not—say because Christian thinking of this sort *obscures*—he adopts this verb twice—the interpretation of this Hebrew line in the service of Christian theology.

A great deal is at stake in the interpretation of the holy spirit in this ancient lament. That much is indisputable. The holy spirit in this lament is deemed to be either the embryo of a hypostasis, a personification destined to develop into the holy spirit of Christian theology, or a distant foreground that helped Christians to articulate but not to generate their conception of the holy spirit. This is a substantial impasse.[59]

To grasp the nature of this impasse, and to remedy it, we return with a critical eye to Paul Volz's formidable study. Volz was not the first to formulate the notion that the spirit in Isaiah 63:7-14 is a hypostasis, but he has been, through more than a century of scholarship, a lasting proponent of this point of view. His is the work to be reckoned with, the book to be taken into account. To revisit Volz critically is not to denigrate him. Volz's view of Judaism proved prescient in an era riddled by insidious anti-Semitism. Rather than taking the path of least resistance by portraying Judaism as a negative foil for the rise of Christianity, as had such a luminary as Hermann Gunkel, Volz contended that the tendency to compare a deteriorating form of Judaism with a vigorous form of Christianity always leaves Judaism wanting. This, he protested, is historically misleading. It is far more likely that the new religion arose out of a period of religious stirring rather than out of a torpid and dying one.[60]

Volz's identification of the holy spirit in Isaiah 63:7-14 and Haggai 2:5 as a hypostasis is the best of exegesis and the worst of exegesis. With unusual perspicuity, he situated the holy spirit in the world of nascent Judaism, where it belongs. By adopting the language of Geisthypostase in his thoughtful exegetical analysis, however, Volz supplied the ballast that enabled subsequent commentators and interpreters to promulgate similar language—and with it unnecessary imprecision. Given the durability of Volz's study, a return to it will reap rich dividends.

The conception of a hypostasis suggests, as Volz phrased it, an outward projection of an inward essence. By way of illustration, the hypostatization of wisdom can be understood in this way. God was believed to be wise; in the course of centuries, God's wisdom took on an independent aura and became, as in Proverbs 8, God's aide-de-camp. Along the same vein, the belief that God possesses both holiness and breath or *rûaḥ*, led, over the course of centuries, to belief in an independent being that, like wisdom, expressed God's presence within the community.

For interpreters like Duhm, Volz, Marti, Eichrodt, Bonnard, Whybray, Childs, and Blenkinsopp, a convenient view of hypostatization or hypostasis has generated a misguided conception of the holy spirit in Hebrew texts. The conceptual framework they embrace makes sense as a metanarrative of sorts, but it lacks an exegetical toehold in either Isaiah 63:7-14 or Haggai 2:5, the contexts of which suggest an altogether different provenance. A more trustworthy conception lies along a different trajectory.

That trajectory encompasses the prophets—certainly Ezekiel, Jeremiah, Second Isaiah, and Haggai—who explored and exploited their traditions. Time and again, we saw, they took those traditions, occasionally distorted them, but consistently utilized them to generate messages intended to break through Israel's numbness.[61] Chief among those traditions was the exodus, which we have explored in some depth. Here, in the appropriation and reappropriation of the exodus, lies the key to understanding the spirit, which came to be understood as a presence independent of but related to, perhaps even identified with, God, not through a process of hypostatization— projecting an internal dimension of God into the world of Israel—but through a process of what might loosely be called *prophetic exegesis*.

In the guise of both lament and promise, exodus becomes the defining moment of divine presence. Exodus is the magnet to which the filings in Israel's memory are drawn, the pivot around which Israel's recollections spin. There may be occasional hope for a Davidic restoration or anticipation of a renewed covenant with Abraham and Sarah, but no conviction permeates and persists, twists and turns through the literary heritage of Babylonian and Persian-era prophets, more readily and robustly than the exodus.

When the prophet, therefore, expresses a biting sense of divine absence, the disparity he articulates is between the intense presence of God at the exodus and the crushing absence of his own era. "Where is the one who brought them up out of the sea with the shepherds of his flock?" he pleads. "Where is the one who put within them his holy spirit, who caused his glorious arm to march at the right hand of Moses, who divided the waters before them to make for himself an everlasting name, who led them through the depths?" he presses. The question is not, "Where is the one who made a covenant with Abraham?" Or "Where now is David, dancing with the ark?" Or "Where is the one whose glory once filled our temple?"

Grief transposes, but does not efface, the exodus tradition. In the form of lament, presence is a bitter pill, exodus an agonizing therapy. Yet in the throes of throbbing and aching, exodus comes to new life and, with it, the angel, the presence, and the spirit. This is not merely rote memorization, a litany of loss, but the emergence—resurrection may be a better term—of saviors. This is the revival of a once-loved Broadway play brought to new life even in the midst of old tears, of memories that still sting.

The re-formation begins with the fusion of two figures over whom initially God and Moses nearly came to blows. In this latter-day revival of exodus, the angel, whom God promised but Moses rejected, merges with the presence-face of God into the unique figure of *the angel of God's presence*. This simple phrase recaptures and rekindles the memory of guidance, protection, and intense presence. Moments later, the prophet recalls the angel again—and Israel's tortured relationship with it: "The angel of his presence saved them . . . but they rebelled against his holy spirit." The transformation is almost, like the spirit, ineffable. Where Israel once rebelled against the angel—*that* angel—now the prophet recalls that it was the spirit, the *holy* spirit, against whom they had rebelled.

There you have it: arguably the first time in history the spirit comes to be understood as an angelic presence occurs during a wrenching reemergence of the exodus tradition. In the alchemy of this transformation of the exodus, the holy spirit is not just any angel; the holy spirit is the formidable angel of the exodus: who led Israel alongside the pillars; who wedged itself between Israel and the marauding Egyptians; whom God authorized to lead them to the promised land and vanquish their enemies; who, God threatened, should not be rebelled against; and who, an exasperated God warned, would lead them without the company of an irate God.

Yet even this is not enough, the prophet knows, to calculate what has been lost. The holy spirit takes the place of not just any angel, nor exclusively the angel of the exodus, but also of God's presence. God's presence, once pitted against the angel, for which Moses had bargained and bartered—and lost. This presence, denied once to Moses, is now known as the holy spirit. The angel of God's presence saved them.

This, the prophet remembers, is the holy spirit whom God put within Israel. This, the prophet recalls, is the spirit of the Lord, who led Israel to rest. In one final strophe, the fusion is complete, the synthesis absolute. The spirit of the Lord takes on the role of the *pānîm* or presence-face of God: the respite God once promised through the presence-face, the lament now ascribes to the spirit of the Lord. Long gone is the question of whom the *pānîm* would lead, Moses alone or the people, too; now, in the lament, the spirit of the Lord led all of them to rest.

The fierce negotiation is bygone, the golden calf fiasco forgotten, the tension between angel and presence-face lifted. This prophet remembers only the surge of presence that occurred when the three—the angel of the exodus, the presence-face of God, and the holy spirit—were one. This is not hypostatization, the outward projection of God's inner essence. It is a simple but bold fusion of the spirit with the agents who led Israel during the exodus. It marks an effort to recall, in even brighter hues than other stories and psalms of exodus, a time in Israel's life when angel and presence-face and spirit—a spirit absent from the narratives and poems of exodus but present in so many other life-giving ways throughout Israel's literature—came together in a single, seamless memory of divine presence. This conception of the holy spirit is, at its core, exodus-generated. It is, simply put, *exegetical.*

This transformation also marks an effort to express despair—but not only despair. In the transposition of exodus in this lament, with the spirit active yet invisible, present if unseen, there is still hope. Hope of salvation. Hope of divine presence in the community. Hope of leading and rest. Hope, in short, in the presence of the holy spirit, promised so often in the prophets and now, in this lament, inserted easily into the story of the exodus. This is not the product principally of abstraction or theological invention or projection; this is the product of prophetic exegesis, of old traditions made new.

Haggai confronted a different reality. Once emboldened, now vanquished not by Persian overlords but by drought and discouragement, the people left the temple to languish. Time's up, Haggai challenges them. If they can remember the former glory of the temple, then they should recognize, too, that God has ever more glory in store. They must reckon with the reality that God is with them *now.* They know this not because of the temple's splendor or the monarchy's return or the governor's courage or even Persia's benefaction. They know this because of the word God cut with them when they came out of Egypt. They know this, in short, because of the exodus tradition. When Haggai grapples, when he looks for an anvil on which to forge a people of courage and initiative, he turns, as prophets so often did, to the exodus tradition.

There may not have been a more malleable tradition than the exodus. The exodus: a cipher for redemption. The exodus: a symbol of Israel's sustained disobedience. The new exodus: an icon of hope.

Like a lightning bolt, therefore, Haggai urges his people to work because, somehow, *the word I cut with you when you came out of Egypt. My spirit stands among you. Do not fear!* Whatever may be the relationship between command and promise, between words past and present—the syntax is strained—Haggai has hit bedrock: God cut a word not just with refugees in ages past but with them—the Yehudites on the precipice of restoration. The word I cut with *you* when *you* came out of Egypt.

Then the denouement: my spirit stands among you. *Stands.* Any number of verbs would have sufficed: comes upon, rushes upon, is outpoured over, rests on, fills. But *stands* is novel in a repertoire of verbs that Israel adopted to describe the spirit's presence. Novel, yes, but surprising, no. On the eve of exodus, the angel and pillar led the people to the Sea. With the Egyptian army on the prowl, the pillar and angel moved to the rear and *stood* there. It was an act of exquisite protection. Without it, Israel could never have crossed the Sea.

The effort to rebuild, Haggai knows, is intimidating. Overwhelming, even. So he plumbs the depths of his tradition and culls the one unshakable moment, the single saving night along the shores of the Sea, and says simply, *My spirit stands among you. Do not fear.*[62]

The choice of this verb does not arise from the prophet's ability to imagine the spirit as an outward projection of the inner being of God. This spirit is not a hypostasis in the sense of a theological abstraction. It is not the personification of a divine attribute. This spirit represents Haggai's creative and sustained effort to steel nerves and stall inertia by absorbing his dispirited people in the story of the exodus. If the spirit is independent or hypostatic or personified, it is because the spirit now does what the pillar and angel once did: stands as safeguard between threat and safety, slavery and liberation, exile and restoration.

Hypostasis, therefore, is a flawed category. It is riddled by imprecision. It suggests, inaccurately, that impersonal qualities—presumably divine breath and holiness in this instance—attained an independent character when they were personified as the spirit. It represents a tendency to minimize the exegetical strategies in the texts themselves, whose transformation of the exodus tradition allowed the spirit to do what pillar or angel or presence-face once did.

Hypostasis is a flawed category for another reason. It is principally a Christian concept when interpreted in relation to the Holy Spirit. It conceals the Israelite roots of Christian pneumatology and, consequently, usurps from its parent religion an essential mode of expressing the presence of God. To the troubled relationship between Judaism and Christianity, therefore, it is now necessary to turn.

Judaism and the Future of Pneumatology

Prophets in Israel, whether during the Neo-Babylonian or Persian eras, first understood the spirit, even the *holy* spirit, as an agent that saved, stood, and led Israel to rest. Yet this realization, rather than tidying the matter up, raises new questions because, tangled up in theology in general and pneumatology in particular, is the perennial challenge of vocabulary.

Unfortunately, interpreters have often adopted the word *hypostasis* to describe this spirit, not least with respect to Isaiah 63:7-14. By doing so, they have bypassed the exegetical underpinnings of this momentous development en route to a convenient but imprecise mode of expression. It is not even clear—nor is it ever made clear—what element or essence of God is personified to create the spirit. Is it breath? Wind? Vitality? Soul? Yet the liability of imprecision pales in relation to the reality that *hypostasis*, when used in relation to the holy spirit, has *Christian* overtones.

The precise meaning of hypostasis was never entirely clear—hence, it occasioned protracted discussion. The word, hypostasis, itself was used frequently in arenas as diverse as construction, where it was a foundation, and philosophy, where it might mean a separate individual existence.[63]

Origen may have been the first Christian theologian to develop the meaning of hypostasis in relation to the trinity—and thus the spirit.[64] Against the backdrop of Valentinian Gnosticism, Origen seems to have expressed his belief that every human being has its own hypostasis while sharing with all human beings a nature or essence.[65] He also criticized certain *haeretici*, who denied that the father and son have the same essence or nature (οὐσία, φύσις), and proposed his own view that each person of the trinity had its own individual substance or hypostasis, while they shared a common essence or nature.[66]

The conception of hypostasis, worked out in relation to the spirit, came into particular focus among the fourth-century Cappadocians—Basil the Great, Gregory of Nyssa, and Gregory of Nazianzus. The translation of *hypostasis* into Latin by its literal equivalent, *substantia*, had aroused in the West the suspicion that those in the East were Arians, while the translation of the Latin, *persona*, into the Greek, πρόσωπον, had the effect of making the West sound Sabellian to those in the East. The Cappadocians were instrumental in resolving the impasse by espousing the trinitarian formula, "three hypostaseis in one ousia," that is, three entities in one essence.[67] Each person of the trinity, which shares a common ousia with the others, is a hypostasis by virtue of what differentiates that person from the other two. For instance, the son shares ousia with the father but is a separate hypostasis because he was begotten, while the father is unique in being the one who begets. Gregory of Nyssa, in discussing the nature of living bodies, "remarks that their hypostasis is derived from a fusion of physical elements, but that, in respect of their ousia, their physical grossness enjoys an association with the simple incorporeality of the soul."[68] In this way, the groundwork was laid for a distinction between one ousia, shared by the trinity, and three hypostaseis.

This solution would not be met with universal acceptance, due in some measure to the distinction between Latin and Greek. Like some of his predecessors, Jerome was suspicious of this Greek distinction because it sounded so similar to Arian teaching.[69] Augustine exhibited a similar resistance to this Greek distinction, in part because of how ambiguously it could be translated into Latin; the same word, *substantia*, could be translated both as "hypostasis" and "ousia."[70]

A lengthier rehearsal of Christian theology is hardly necessary to demonstrate that the word *hypostasis*, when used in relation to the spirit, is embedded in centuries of Christian trinitarian discussion. This sort of Christian theology is a far cry from Haggai 2 and Isaiah 63. Separated from Origen and the Cappadocians by dint of language (Hebrew versus Greek), chronology (seven centuries or more), empires (Persia versus Rome), and theological commitments (monotheism versus trinitarianism), a great deal distinguishes the Cappadocians from Neo-Babylonian and Persian era prophets. There is little to commend introducing a term brought to currency by Origen, refined by the Cappadocians, and debated by Jerome and Augustine, into a discussion of Israel's prophets. To do so is to connect distant dots. Discovering a hypostasis in the literary legacy of Hebrew prophets, absent clear evidence that it is the earliest development on the threshold of a path that led eventually to a full-blown hypostasis, is anachronistic.

More urgently, the use of the word *hypostasis* to describe the spirit in the Jewish Scriptures has the unwanted effect of subsuming Israelite innovations under the umbrella of Christian theology. This was undoubtedly not the intent of a scholar such as Volz, who attempted to study Judaism for its own sake. But the language he adopted was largely Christian, particularly when at stake was the character of the holy spirit, which, in Christian theology, is believed to be one of the three hypostaseis of the trinity.

This tendency to assimilate Judaism to Christianity, to see the former as an adumbration of the latter, riled Goldingay. Yet, as we saw, his reaction was no more precise than Childs or Eichrodt or Volz. In fact, Goldingay overreacted to Christian overreach by reducing the holy spirit in Isaiah 63:7-14 to "an emphatic expression for 'him,' as if to draw attention to God's presence and activity." By doing so, he, no less than those he criticized, overlooked the exegetical impulse of the lament and the way in which the holy spirit took on the activities and characteristics of the agents of the exodus.

If these alternatives—identifying the spirit as a hypostasis or reducing the spirit to an emphatic expression for God—do not adequately describe the spirit in these early iterations, the resolution lies elsewhere, in the exegetical activity underlying the lament in Isaiah 63:7-14 and the promise in Haggai 2:5. The deep rootedness of these texts in the exodus tradition provides a significant clue about what to call, and how to conceive of, the spirit.

In the quest for vocabulary, an apt category is *divine agency*.[71] In the lament of Isaiah 63:7-14 and the promise of Haggai 2:5, the spirit takes on the role of divine agents in the story of Israel's exodus from Egypt. In essence, the spirit becomes an agent of the exodus—not any one of those agents but something more intense, more present, especially in the lament, where the spirit takes on the roles once attributed to the angel of the exodus (they rebelled against it), the presence-face of God (which gave them rest), and the angel of God's presence (which saved Israel). Since the birth of pneumatology took place in this context, with the amalgamation of these specific biblical traditions—the exodus and the spirit—it is essential to adopt or, if need be, *create* an adequate vocabulary to express the quality of the ancient exegetical effort that led to this innovative understanding of the spirit. For Christian theologians, the term must no longer be *hypostasis*, which imports, inadvertently or purposefully, into Israelite literature nuances of Christian trinitarian debate. A more adequate vocabulary must reflect the earliest impulses that first led to the discernment of the spirit as an agent, a *hyperagent* of sorts, of the exodus.

Another consequence of this study has to do with modern assessments of early Judaism. Paul Volz discerned rich vitality in Judaism, from the prophecy of Haggai to the rabbis, and contended that Christianity was not the upstart opponent of Judaism but its heir, the beneficiary of its vitality. Eichrodt, too, discerned a generative impulse in the Persian era. Yet, time and again, scholars took a tack different from Volz by referring to a belief, which they would attribute to ancient Jews, that prophecy had ceased and the holy spirit withdrawn. They constructed this belief from an assemblage of disparate texts.[72]

In Kittel's *Theological Dictionary of the New Testament*, for example, Erik Sjöberg referred to "a widespread theological conviction" that the holy spirit had withdrawn.[73] Geoffrey Lampe's entry in the *New Interpreter's Dictionary of the Bible*, the resource for a generation of interpreters, read, "In the main, the Spirit continues to be thought of as being, pre-eminently, the Spirit of prophecy, manifested in the distant past in such great figures as Elijah (Ecclus. 48.12) or Isaiah (vs. 24), but which was now no longer present in Israel."[74] In his massive and immensely influential study of the spirit in the writings of Paul, which shaped an emerging cadre of Pentecostal scholars, Gordon Fee asserted, "Noticeably missing in the intertestamental literature . . . is the sense that the Spirit speaks through any contemporary 'prophet.' This is almost certainly the result of the growth of a tradition called 'the quenched Spirit,' which begins in the later books of the Old Testament and is found variously during the Second Temple period."[75]

Several scholars have challenged this view of prophecy and the spirit in late Israel and early Judaism.[76] Consequently, it is no longer de rigueur to skirt Philo Judaeus' ample and unabashed claims to prophetic inspiration or to assemble the usual ancient texts in order to characterize the Persian, Hellenistic, and Roman eras as ones during which Jews widely affirmed that the spirit had withdrawn and prophecy ceased. This perspective has not, however, disappeared entirely. N. T. Wright has recently championed it. Like Volz, Wright has a deep appreciation for the contributions of Second Temple Judaism. Consequently, a claim against a portion of Wright's impressive, imposing, and extensive oeuvre is by no means a critique of the whole. Yet at this point, in the arena of pneumatology, Wright may have exchanged the vitality of Judaism for the originality of the apostle Paul.[77] His interpretation, so cogently argued, deserves to be challenged, since so much is at stake.

Wright sets out from Paul's experience. He supposes that

> when Paul, like the other early Christians, experienced that renewal [of the heart], and saw others experiencing it, they must have realized how badly it had been needed. Here, too, Paul found the clues in scripture, where Israel had been warned about its own hard-heartedness. But he went looking for those clues, we may surmise, because of the revised monotheism in which the spirit of the one God, the spirit of Jesus, had produced previously unimagined effects on hearts and minds, not only his own but those of converts from every kind of background.[78]

These believers, Paul says in no uncertain terms, are a temple of the holy spirit. From this image of the church, Wright infers that, "when Paul speaks of the individual Christian, or the whole church, as the 'temple' in which the spirit 'dwells,' such language from a second-Temple Jew can only mean (a) that YHWH has returned to his Temple as he had promised and (b) that the mode of this long-awaited, glorious, tabernacling presence is the spirit."[79] "No ex-Pharisee could write this without intending to say that the founding and building up of the church through the gospel constituted the long-awaited rebuilding of the Temple, and that *the indwelling of the spirit constituted the long-awaited return of YHWH to Zion*."[80]

The indwelling of the spirit in the church is rooted, suggests Wright, in the long-held Jewish belief that the shekinah had indwelt the tabernacle and temple. The indwelling of the spirit in the church "can only mean—must only mean—some kind of identification of the divine spirit with the long-awaited returning Shekinah. For the divine spirit to take up residence in the church is for Exodus 40 and Ezekiel 43 to find a radical, unexpected and even shocking new fulfilment. But there can be no doubt that this is what Paul meant to say."[81] Wright claims that "the church, as it stands, is thus already the new Temple, and the spirit that dwells within is the new Shekinah. It is hard to see how a second-Temple Jew could give the spirit a higher value than this."[82]

In a comment on Paul's letter to the Ephesians, according to which the holy temple is built together in the spirit, Wright's observations come to a crescendo: "In context, both of Ephesians and of second-Temple expectations, this too can only mean one thing. The hope that one day YHWH would return to Zion, to dwell in the renewed Temple for ever, has now been fulfilled—but in a radical, shocking and unexpected fashion. The role of God's living presence, the glorious Shekinah, is taken by the spirit. Once again, in second-Temple Jewish terms there cannot be a higher pneumatology than this. The spirit is incorporated within the divine identity, the identity which is shaped particularly by the eschatology of YHWH's return."[83]

Wright discovers something "radical, shocking and unexpected" in Paul's revision of monotheism at the expense of Second Temple Judaism, in which he situates the apostle Paul.[84] Jews awaited but presumably did not experience the spirit, which God had meant to constitute "the further, and ongoing, manifestation of the personal presence of the one God."[85] The principal flaw in Wright's project is that earlier Israelite prophets—half a millennium earlier—had already connected the spirit with the agents of the exodus and, in what might be considered a "radical, shocking and unexpected" way, had accorded the spirit a status and agency it had never before possessed.[86]

Haggai's simple promise, *my spirit stands among you,* is no less a "radical, shocking and unexpected" portrayal of the spirit than the apostle Paul's. To motivate a beleaguered band of citizens in the province of Yehud to reconstruct their temple, during years of wrenching transition, Haggai holds out this simple promise: the spirit stands among you—as you build the temple. Haggai glances back at the exodus with a keen awareness of the spirit's *presence,* standing and guarding, as it did on that auspicious night along the Sea, even as the lament in Isaiah 63 looks back to the intense presence of the holy spirit during the exodus with a trenchant awareness of its *absence.*

These prophetic texts demand a recalibration of Wright's portrayal of Paul—and of any portrayals of Christian pneumatology that fail to reckon with the radical, shocking, and unexpected portrayals that emerged in the crises of exile and restoration. At that time, amid severely perplexing challenges, prophets understood the spirit afresh as an agent of the exodus—saving, giving rest, standing, even becoming the object of rebellion. Wright's verdict, that a spirit-filled temple "can only mean" the return of the long-awaited shekinah as spirit, is only partly true. Paul's understanding of the church as a spirit-filled temple does not require the belief that the entire Jewish world was empty, awaiting the shekinah's denouement, anticipating the spirit's return. This was certainly not Haggai's view. Against all hope, against the evidence of a disheartened community, from governor to priest to people of the land, against the near impossibility of rebuilding in a time of drought and despair, Haggai lays audacious claim to the presence of the spirit. He does not claim that the spirit once present can be present again. He does not claim that the spirit will be present only in the eschatological future. He claims that the spirit is active *now,* as he removes the veil dividing past and present and makes the simple, unassailable claim and command: *the word I cut with you when you came out of Egypt: my spirit stands among you. Do not fear!*

In two unfortunate ways, Christianity has encroached upon the world of Judaism. These are critical, in particular, because they are *not* the product of blatant anti-Semitism or shoddy scholarship. Yet somehow, they have seeped into the vocabulary of Christianity and, all too often, Christian scholarship.

On the one hand, the vocabulary adopted to describe the spirit in its emergence as an independent agent—hypostasis—is drenched in Christian concern for the place of the holy spirit in the trinity. Christianity has encroached upon the world of Judaism at the base level of language; whether someone adopts this language or, like John Goldingay, rejects it, the use of Christian language sets the stage of debate and the direction of discourse. It is time, in light of Isaiah 63:7-14 and Haggai 2:5, to jettison such vocabulary.

On the other hand, the ability to characterize early Judaism as a religion that looked for the restoration of the spirit but did not engage that spirit in its quotidian experience provides a convenient but errant foil for emergent Christianity. The prophetic lament and promise that have preoccupied us put the lie to this characterization of Judaism. At the fountainhead of Judaism, beliefs in exodus and spirit fused, forming an agent that took over the prerogatives of the pillar, the angel of the exodus, the presence-face of God, and a new figure, the angel of God's presence. This was a remarkable transformation, and there is no evidence that, in the years to follow, Jews rejected the spirit and projected it exclusively onto a distant future. It is time, therefore, to jettison errant characterizations of ancient Judaism.

It may be appropriate to suggest, in light of these realizations, that the search for vocabulary, the recovery of history, the quest for *understanding*, ought to take place in a sustained collaboration between Judaism and Christianity. Perhaps it is time for Christians, who have too easily encroached on Judaism and misrepresented Jewish Antiquity, to study pneumatology in earnest as if the Hebrew Bible, and Judaism as a whole, made indispensable contributions to a far-reaching understanding of the spirit. Perhaps it is time to embrace Jewish Scripture, too, as more than foreground or prolegomenon to the study of Christian pneumatology.

This is not a request for a spate of studies that parse the Hebrew word *rûaḥ* to arrive at an analysis of Pauline theology or the book of Acts. It is rather a mandate that Christians delve into pneumatology per se—the spirit as an agent that saves, gives rest, and stands—in consort with Jews. By the same token, it may be time, in light of this study, for Jews to reclaim—perhaps *salvage* is a better word—the heritage of the spirit, and to do so in the company of Christians who are open to explore the character of the spirit with them. After two thousand years of discussing in separate corners, those who partner in this venture may discover together a mutual world of glory, an intensity of divine presence.[87]

Crisis and the Future of Pneumatology

Jews and Christians share a common history refracted through a mutual recollection of election and exile, redemption and restoration. We have seen, too, that they share a common pneumatology wrought by the exigencies of historical events. An authentic pneumatology, which takes historical points of origin seriously, reflects the reality that pneumatology sprouted shoots first in the soil of crisis. Even the agents of liberation—precursors to pneumatology proper—materialized first in flight, with the Egyptians hot in pursuit. It is never quite clear whether Israelites believed that a pillar or two or an angel or God's presence-face or all of them or none of them—just God alone—led Israel to the Sea and wedged themselves between the slaves and their former overlords. How God was present, Israel did not clarify. *That* God was present, Israel did. Crisis engendered a sense of God's inexorable presence—a confused, cacophonous, mildly implausible sense of God's presence in itinerant pillars and a somewhat superfluous angel. Israel never managed to simplify this memory; the initial chaos remained, the opening crisis endured in their prose, in their hymnody, in their prophecies.

Nor could Israel leave well enough alone. Their collective memory compounded the confusion and raised the cacophony to a deafening roar when, they remembered, after the crisis of the golden calf and consequent death of thousands, Moses and God went at it tête-à-tête. This memory is muddled, a bit confused—or confusing, at least. It is never clear who would lead Israel—angel or *pānîm*—or whether one would lead Israel at all. Moses, perhaps alone, would be the beneficiary of God's guidance. This heated negotiation muddies the matter of divine accompaniment. Once again, crisis—this one determined by the impatience of Israel's mistrust that Moses would return—yields confusion, at least as Israel remembered the experience.

Yet crisis can also breed unusual clarity. Whether in the throes of exile or the tangle of restoration, one prophet brought atypical lucidity to the matter of divine presence—or, better yet, divine absence. In praise turned into plaintive pleas, the prophet formed from two former rivals, the angel and *pānîm*, a solitary angel of God's presence. Then, in quick succession, this angel became the holy spirit, against whom the people rebelled, the holy spirit in Israel's midst, and the spirit of the LORD, who gave Israel rest. The qualities of the angel, the abilities of the *pānîm*, converge with singular clarity and extraordinary inventiveness in the unsettling alchemy of crisis and despair.

Haggai, too, in the erratic rhythm of restoration, brought singular clarity to God's presence in crisis. Haggai promised: *My spirit stands among you.* No drought, no rivals, no empires, not even the entropy borne of communal self-preservation, could forestall the return of God's glory to the temple. The algebra is simple: as the pillar—perhaps the angel, too—moved, stood, and guarded Israel from the onslaught of the Egyptian army on that night of nights, now the spirit stands in Israel's midst. There is no room for fear.

This is history experienced, confessed, and adapted—history as a concoction of politics, tradition, and reflection. With their backs against the wall, in the throes of crisis, one prophet found in an earlier crisis experiences worthy of lament, while another found words worthy of promise. In crisis, they recalled crisis. In history, they recalled their history. During their excruciating saga, they recalled their saga of liberation. From that recollection emerged a conception of the spirit that changed everything—or should have. In crisis, while remembering crisis, these prophets conveyed afresh belief in the spirit, not the spirit outpoured like water or rushing like wind or inspiring like breath or resting like oil. They discovered the spirit standing, like the ancient pillar, and the spirit giving rest, like the ancient *pānîm*.

The most important moments for the origin of pneumatology were rife with historical uncertainty and historic insecurity. For prophets confronted by a painful present and an indeterminate future, crisis remembered became the pathway to crisis confronted. In the memory of what happened once upon a time inhered, for the prophet of lament, the hope of what might be. In the memory of emancipation inhered, for Haggai at least, the hope of restoration. Crisis, in short, generated innovation.

If we take our cue from Haggai and Isaiah 63, then we are compelled to acknowledge, too, that this was crisis experienced by a *community*. When the prophet of lament recalls the exodus, he or she remembers the work of the spirit principally in the community.[88] Israel, not Moses, is the object of salvation. Israel, not Moses, rebels against the holy spirit.[89] Even more telling, despite the inherent ambiguity of the conversation between God and Moses on Mt. Sinai, the spirit gives Israel rest. Haggai's promise is clear about this, too: my spirit stands among you—*plural*. This Persian-era generation, the whole of it, is the one of whom it can be said, "The word I cut with you—*plural*—when you—*plural*—came out of Egypt." Haggai does not say that the spirit fills the governor or rests upon the high priest but that the spirit stands in *Israel's* midst. In brief, the origin of pneumatology took place in a context preoccupied, as Volz noted, with community.[90]

The acknowledgment that the birth of pneumatology came with the pangs of communal crisis provides a corrective to overly individualized conceptions of the spirit's impact. The effectiveness of the spirit as an agent, active and influential, was evident, according to the earliest voices that expressed the agency of the spirit, in *communities* in desperate need of help. It would have been easy to couch pneumatology in individualistic terms—artisans and architects and prophets and poets filled with the spirit, anointed rulers upon whom the spirit rests, liberators upon whom the spirit rushes—but at the headwaters of pneumatology, when the spirit is first seen as an agent, the spirit is active on behalf of *communities*.

This realization, that pneumatology emerged in communities in crisis, provides a corrective to Volz's insistence that the spirit's influence, according to the lament in Isaiah 63, is limited principally to the religious-ethical sphere.[91] Both lament and promise see the spirit actively engaged in liberation. The angel of God's presence, identified in the lament with the holy spirit, saved—liberated—Israel from Egypt. The spirit was among them as well during their trek through the Sea. And the spirit gave them rest. This is not primarily a religious or ethical series of actions, and it certainly is not limited to the prophetic word; these actions bring freedom from slavery and possession of the land. Whether this lament was composed during exile or restoration, under the heavy hand of Babylon or the lighter touch of Persia, its political thrust cannot be muted. The prophet looks to a time when the angel of God's presence, God's holy spirit, saved, when God stretched out a mighty hand, when Israel walked through the depths of water, and the spirit of the Lord gave them rest in the land.

Nor does Haggai, whose attentive gaze rests on rebuilding the temple, sequester the spirit in the religious or ethical sphere. The spirit protects the fragile community in Yehud so that they can roll up their sleeves, gird their loins, and build. The spirit stands as the pillar once did, a rearguard, a beacon in the night. The stature of the spirit soars not because it influences the religious and ethical spheres but because it stands as an implacable partition between destruction and salvation.

The origin of pneumatology is embedded in *history*—the fragile and fungible nature of Israel's status amid the overpowering geopolitical shifts of the Neo-Babylonian and Persian eras. These situations catalyzed a lament that contains an unprecedented portrayal of the spirit, as well as an unparalleled promise of the spirit's protection and power in a politically unstable era. They accomplished this, during epochs of historic crisis, by looking back to their own histories, to the crisis they believed brought them into existence. Historic crises, perhaps not long after the fall of Jerusalem to Babylon, and certainly after the return to the Persian province of Yehud, led Israel back to the celebrated crisis of the exodus.

For theologians who situate the locus of pneumatology in the trinity, history may be irrelevant. The goal of pneumatology is principally to understand the relationship of the holy spirit to father and son. Pneumatology, in essence, is an intra-trinitarian affair. This study mandates a recalibration of that approach—not a dismissal of trinitarian discussion among Christians, but an assessment of origins and the implication of origins for the development of pneumatology. Since pneumatology took shape in *history*, in *crisis*, in *community*, the starting point of contemporary pneumatology ought equally to lie in history, crisis, and community.

This suggestion is hardly unique. Theologian Jürgen Moltmann explicitly roots pneumatology precisely in history, crisis, and community. To appreciate Moltmann's approach to pneumatology-as-history, and also to identify its limitations, it is essential to pause over his instrumental work, *Der Geist des Lebens: Eine ganzheitliche Pneumatologie*—a holistic pneumatology. Moltmann resists any truncation of the scope of pneumatology, chief among them what he considers to be a false alternative between divine revelation and human experience in the dialectical theologies of Karl Barth, Emil Brummer, Rudolf Bultmann, and Friedrich Gogarten. "The Holy Spirit," contends Moltmann, "is not simply the subjective side of God's revelation of himself, and faith is not merely the echo of the Word of God in the human heart. The Holy Spirit is much more than that. It is the power that raises the dead, the power of the new creation of all things; and faith is the beginning of the rebirth of human beings to new life."[92] The spirit is, in short, the power of God *in history*.

Nor can the spirit be truncated as *Spiritus sanctificans*, to the exclusion of *spiritus vivificans*. "In both Protestant and Catholic theology and devotion," notes Moltmann, "there is a tendency to view the Holy Spirit solely as *the Spirit of Redemption*. Its place is in the church, and it gives men and women the assurance of the eternal blessedness of their souls. This redemptive Spirit is cut off both from bodily life and from the life of nature. It makes people turn away from 'this world' and hope for a better world beyond. They then seek and experience in the Spirit of Christ a power that is different from the divine energy of life, which according to the Old Testament ideas interpenetrates all the living."[93]

The Old Testament[94] puts the lie to such a malformed pneumatology. "The experience of the eschatological reality of the Spirit," writes Moltmann, "leads to the conclusion that this is the same Spirit in whose power the Father, through the Son, has created the world, and preserves it against annihilating Nothingness: 'When thou takest away their breath, they die and return to their dust. When thou sendest forth thy breath, they are created; and thou renewest the face of the ground' (Ps. 104:29-30). This means that the Spirit is the efficacious power of the Creator and the power that quickens created beings."[95] Redemption is joined at the hip to creation, eschatology to protology, avoidance of annihilation to inspiration.

This Old Testament affirmation is only the starting point for a holistic understanding of pneumatology. If the breath of life is also the spirit of salvation, then history—beginning with *Israel's* history—is the sphere of the spirit. Moltmann titles his analysis of the spirit in the Old Testament "Historical Experience of the Spirit." "By a historical experience of God," he explains, "we mean an experience of God which happens to people in the medium of history through historical events, and which is perceived in terms of time."[96]

At the heart of Israel's history lay three principal experiences: exodus, covenant, and entry into the promised land. "Through historical remembrance, the God of the Exodus, the covenant and the promised land becomes present to such a degree that as the Creator of the world and the Lord of human liberty he determines the present. The historical experience of God is always tensed between the remembrance and the expectation which frame that experience. Remembrances of God and expectations of God make the experienced presence of God a historical present."[97] The study we have undertaken confirms how accurate

Moltmann's affirmation is. While a prophet of lament looked from an experience of absence to God's presence in the experiences of exodus, Sinai, and land taking, a prophet of promise addressed his people as if they had come out of Egypt, as if the spirit were standing not along the distant shores of the Sea but in the ruins yet to be rebuilt by an apparently inconsequential group of Yehudites. We have seen, too, that claims to both absence and presence did not float freely; these were not efforts to circumscribe an apophatic God. Lament and promise grew from the soil of history; both are alert to the intensity of God's presence in those early days, even if one laments the absence of divine presence in his own day and the other champions the inescapability of divine presence in his.

There is a limitation, nonetheless, to Moltmann's robust pneumatology, because he unnecessarily delays agency until the postbiblical era. Pivotal to the triune experience of exodus, covenant, and promised land, suggests Moltmann, is the power of the spirit. Power, indeed. A force to be reckoned with. The "divine energy of life."[98] The "*creative power* of God."[99] Even "the space of freedom in which the living being can unfold."[100] The Jewish Scriptures describe the spirit as a power but not a person; they ascribe to the spirit activity but not agency.

Only later, in postbiblical Judaism, does the spirit attain "an 'immanent transcendence'" through its association with wisdom. "In the form of Wisdom," explains Moltmann, "the Spirit is a kind of counterpart in God himself, and is at the same time the divine presence in creation and history."[101]

The activity of the spirit in the realm of Israelite history is as a power, a creative force, a divine energy of life—but *not* an agent. The spirit is breath, tempest, impulse, but only later "a kind of counterpart in God" through its association with wisdom. Yet divine presence does exist as a counterpart to God in the Jewish Scriptures, though not as the holy spirit. God's counterpart is not the spirit, argues Moltmann, but the shekinah. Especially following the onslaught of the Babylonians, when the shekinah could no longer inhabit the temple in Jerusalem, did the shekinah rise to prominence.

The vocabulary most Christian theologians adopt to depict the Holy Spirit, Moltmann believes, "is actually much more closely related to the idea of the Shekinah, the descent and indwelling of God in space and time, at a particular place and a particular era of earthly beings and in their history."[102] The shekinah represents God's peculiar presence in Israel's history, God's suffering presence in Israel's history, God's abiding presence in Israel's history. The spirit reflects, represents, and reveals God's presence by dint of association with that shekinah. Moltmann is quick to append "and the spirit" to statements about the shekinah, but he does not do the reverse.[103]

The shekinah, not the spirit, lies at the heart of Israel's perception of divine presence in history.[104] The relationship between shekinah and spirit cannot even be called symbiotic. Parasitic perhaps, or derivative: the spirit draws its empathy, its sensibility, its kenotic capacity from the shekinah.[105] Even in the Gospels, when the spirit rests upon Jesus at his baptism, "the phraseology about the 'descent' of the Spirit on Jesus, and its 'resting' on him, suggests that the Spirit should be interpreted as *God's Shekinah*."[106]

It was in historical crisis, contends Moltmann, especially the protracted crisis of exile and restoration, that "the efficacies of all God's works came to be ascribed to the Spirit, so that the historical bond linking these works and God's acts was seen in the uninterrupted operation of God's Spirit." At this point in Israel's history,

> Yahweh's *ruach* no longer dwells and rests merely in the temple. His dwelling place is the people and its history. In this way Yahweh's *ruach* became the expression for Yahweh's presence and Shekinah, outside the cult on Zion too. And this meant that after the fall of the temple, Israel was able to console herself with the accompanying presence in her history of her God. That is the reason why God's historical activity in and for Israel was then ascribed to Yahweh's *ruach*. Yahweh's *ruach* accompanied Moses—it divided the waters of the Reed Sea—it led the people through the wilderness: 'Like cattle that go down into the valley, the Spirit of the Lord gave them rest. So thou didst lead thy people, to make for thyself a glorious name' (Isa. 63.14; see the whole context, Isa. 63.7-19).[107]

Moltmann's hypothesis is uncannily close to what occurred in Israel sometime after 586 B.C.E. History did generate a burst of creativity. Crisis did catalyze a torrent of reflection on Israel's devastation, though not exactly in the way Moltmann imagines when he inserts the shekinah into this flurry of reflection on the exodus. To grasp what has gone wrong, we must take a few steps back to the beginning.

The spirit in the Jewish Scriptures, claims Moltmann, is a creative and vital power that gives life. This force is not a person or agent—or any other, to use Moltmann's language, "counterpart in God." Moltmann is forced by this perceived state of affairs to introduce the shekinah, which has agency, into his discussion of the spirit, which lacks agency.[108] The shekinah is personal, sensible, even kenotic. By association with this shekinah, the spirit becomes personal, sensible, and kenotic. During the throes of exile, the spirit, Moltmann seems to claim, took on the characteristics of the shekinah. "That is the reason why God's historical activity in and for Israel was then ascribed to Yahweh's *ruach*."[109] Later still, the spirit became God's counterpart by its association with wisdom personified.

As perceptive as Moltmann may be, he is not quite correct. The authors of the lament in Isaiah 63 and the promise in Haggai 2 portrayed the spirit as an agent active in history, present in crisis. The angel of God's presence had saved the slaves from Egypt, yet Israel had rebelled against that holy spirit, which God had set in them, and which, rebellion notwithstanding, would, like the promised *pānîm*, lead them to rest in the promised land. The prophet of lament grieves the absence of this spirit, whom God had authorized to save and lead Israel.

Haggai reaches, too, into the exodus tradition, not to grieve the spirit's absence, but to champion the spirit's presence. The spirit stands among you, he claims, like the pillar, that protective partition on the eve of exodus. Whatever word, whatever thing, God had cut with Israel when they came out of Egypt, God now cuts with the inhabitants of Yehud, declares Haggai, who understands the spirit not primarily as a reality of the past, as it is in the lament, but as the quintessence of divine presence. My spirit stands among *you*, promises God through Haggai. Yes, God was present in the very real rescue of Israel from slavery in Egypt, but God, believes Haggai, is present, too, in the very real, if less dramatic, challenge of rebuilding the temple, stone by shattered stone.

The origin of pneumatology—the understanding of the spirit as an agent—is not dependent upon an association with shekinah or, later still, wisdom. It is due rather to the impress of crisis upon the traditions of Israel, by which pillars and angels and *pānîm* yielded to the spirit, which already had its own massive and malleable history of interpretation even before the onset of exile. The emergence of the spirit as an agent, which took place with the metamorphosis of Israel's traditions, occurred under the intense heat and pressure of historic crises, when prophets fused two grand convictions—the presence and promise of *rûaḥ* and the unassailable datum of liberation from Egypt through the accompaniment of a coterie of divine agents.

With this correction in mind, we can embrace Moltmann's keen effort to ground pneumatology not first in the hypostatization of a divine attribute but in the pressures of the exilic and postexilic eras. The origin of pneumatology lies in innovation borne of crisis, metamorphosis in the clutch of historic failure, the merging of past, present, and future in anamnesis. The spirit that emerges, when the dust of crisis settles, as if it ever does, is liberator, protector, presence, and guide. The spirit who emerges from massive failures of political will, from futile monarchical strategies, from imperial decrees beyond Israel's control, was present once in divided seas and unforgiving deserts, according to the prophet of lament, and is present again in the rubble awaiting restoration, according to another prophet, who deftly negotiated the tension between constraint and promise inherent in Persian rule. The spirit who emerges, both in lament and promise, from all of this upheaval and angst, demands a new relative pronoun altogether: not which but *who*.

Exodus and the Future of Pneumatology

During periods of exile or rebuilding, the prodigious traditions of exodus and *rûaḥ* fused. While this exegetical innovation may have been significant in its own day—Haggai was apparently successful in prompting his comrades to rebuild the temple—it is entirely possible that its ongoing significance was trivial. After all, swaths of Second Temple Judaism tapped into the exodus tradition without offering the slightest nod to this innovation; the spirit, in these texts, is nowhere to be seen. Perhaps, then, we have studied texts—Isaiah 63:7-14 and Haggai 2:4-5—that had no afterlife and therefore only negligible significance. Perhaps this is an exegetical tempest in a teapot. This might be the case were it not for the impact of this innovation on a corner of first-century Judaism that adopted this construal of the exodus tradition. Precisely this take on the exodus tradition provided the footing for a new understanding of history, rooted now in a conviction that God had again acted, this time to raise Jesus of Nazareth from the dead and to translate his followers from slavery to freedom.

The New Testament is not the apex of interpretation. It is not the ultimate goal of these ancient Hebrew texts. It is not the sole telos of the Jewish Scriptures. Yet it does form a collection of texts for which the spirit would be understood as an agent of the exodus. The New Testament does, in other words, demonstrate that this understanding of the spirit extended into the Roman era in a community whose legacy gave rise, eventually, to the Christian church. The realization that the innovations in Isaiah 63 and Haggai 2 combusted in this community offers Christian pneumatology another rationale for seeing the spirit, first of all, as an agent of the exodus. To gain proper perspective on the impact of this innovation and, equally important, its lack of impact, we will touch upon a few Jewish texts through the first century, in which key details of the exodus story that proved so essential to Haggai and the author of the lament in Isaiah emerged in various guises.

Closest in time lay the composition of a Persian-era prayer embedded in the book of Nehemiah. In this prayer, Ezra narrates Israel's history in two matching parts. Ezra recalls how "you led them by day with a pillar of cloud, and by night with a pillar of fire, to give them light on the way in which they should go";[110] he then repeats how "you in your great mercies did not forsake them in the wilderness; the pillar of cloud that led them in the way did not leave them by day, nor the pillar of fire by night that gave them light on the way by which they should go."[111] Twice Ezra refers to the pillars of cloud and fire. While there is nothing particularly innovative in this recollection, Ezra refers as well to the spirit, how "you gave your good spirit to instruct them, and did not withhold your manna from their mouths, and gave them water for their thirst."[112]

The point of reference to the spirit in the exodus story is not entirely clear. Perhaps the inspiration for this addition is the story of the architects of the tabernacle, whom God filled with a spirit of wisdom,[113] or their leaders, Bezalel and Oholiab, gifted architects of the tabernacle, whom God filled with knowledge, skill in every craft, and the spirit of the Lord, to accomplish an extraordinary task under unprecedented duress.[114] Or perhaps this is a reference to inspiration at Mt. Sinai, since, in this prayer, the gift of Torah and the gift of the spirit occur in parallel: the pillars to guide, Torah or the spirit to instruct, the gifts of manna and water to sustain. If this is so, if Torah and spirit correspond to one another, then the nature of their relationship is apparent in the infinitive *to instruct*,[115] the root of which had already occurred just a chapter earlier, when, on the first day of the seventh month, "they read from the book, from the law of God, with interpretation. They gave the sense,[116] so that the people understood the reading."[117] The next day, "the heads of the ancestral houses of all the people, with the priests and the Levites, came together to the scribe Ezra in order to *interpret* the words of the Law."[118] The correspondence in Ezra's prayer between the gift of Torah and the gift of the good spirit suggests that the spirit was active in the process of interpretation, of instruction, of teaching the people torah. God gave the words *and* the means to understand them.[119]

As intriguing as this recapitulation of the exodus story is, the spirit is not, in Ezra's prayer, a surrogate for the pillars—or the cloud, angel, or *pānîm*—as in the promise of Haggai and the lament of Isaiah. The pillars lead along the wilderness way; the good spirit instructs. While the pillars and spirit occur in close association, the spirit does not take over their prerogatives and responsibilities. The spirit, in short, does not stand in the pillars' place.

About three centuries later, the exodus story reemerged in the book of Jubilees, where the story is told, surprisingly perhaps, through the mouth of the angel of the presence. That same angel, which the translators of the Old Greek had studiously effaced—*not an angel but God's presence saved them*—appears in Jubilees as *angelus interpres*, the very angel who mediates world history, from creation to Sinai.[120] God tells the angel of the presence to dictate the story in Jubilees.[121] This is the angel who led Israel; there is not the merest mention of the pillars, the cloud, the *pānîm* as guides—or the spirit, for that matter. Just the angel.

Toward the end of the story, the angel of the presence tells how Prince Mastema inspired the Egyptians—chariots, horses, and a huge multitude—to pursue the escaped slaves, at which point, "I stood between the Egyptians and Israel, and we delivered Israel from his hand and from the hand of his people. And the Lord brought them out through the midst of the sea as through dry land."[122] Gone is the pillar that moved from front to rear and stood between the

Egyptians and Israelites; now it is only the angel of the presence who stood there and, with the other angels, delivered Israel.[123] Protection by the angel, implicit in the story of exodus in the standing of the pillar, is now transferred from the pillar to the angel—exclusively.

Jubilees offers prima facie evidence for the persistence of the fusion of angel and presence in Second Temple Judaism. Those who opt for the originality of the Greek reading of Isaiah 63:9, which lacks a reference to the angel of God's presence, must reckon with Jubilees, in which the fusion of angel and presence is not only adopted but elevated. In Jubilees, the angel of the exodus *alone* survives—going before Israel and standing between them and the Egyptians.[124] This is not just any angel; this is the angel of the presence, whose preeminence Isaiah 63:9 seems to have generated.[125]

The ins and outs of historical detail in the exodus story held little appeal for leading first-century Alexandrian citizen, philosopher, and Torah interpreter Philo Judaeus. Still, his interpretation of Exodus 13:21-22, in which he summarizes the story in this way, reveals a rich level of coherent thought: "A cloud shaped like a tall pillar, the light of which in the daytime was as the sun and in night as flame, went before the host, so that they should not stray in their journey, but follow in the steps of a guide who could never err."[126] Philo tidies the uneven furrows of the biblical texts:[127] there is one cloud shaped like a tall pillar, with bright light in the day and flame at night. Yet this is not all. He wonders further whether "perhaps indeed there was enclosed within the cloud one of the lieutenants[128] of the great King, an unseen angel, a forerunner on whom the eyes of the body were not permitted to look."[129] Philo offers serious reflection here, though it is not easy to parse. It may be that he interprets God's riding in the pillars in Exodus 13:21-22 as an invisible angel. Or it may be a combination of the pillars of Exodus 13:21-22 with the angel of Exodus 14:19. Or it may be that he has merged Exodus 13:21-22, Exodus 14:19, where the angel first appears, and Exodus 14:24, where God looks through the pillar to confuse the Egyptians. It is possible, too, that Philo's emphasis on the invisibility of the angel may suggest the influence of Moses and God's negotiation on Mt. Sinai, in which angel and *pānîm* appear together, if in competition, and God denies Moses the opportunity to view the *pānîm,* which presumably must remain invisible.[130] Whatever motivated Philo, his summary is a brilliant effort to homogenize the cloud, the pillars (both of them), the angel, possibly the *pānîm,* and perhaps even God's riding in the pillars[131] and looking through the pillar.[132] Absent, however, is the spirit and, with it, the likelihood that Isaiah 63:7-14 or Haggai 2:5 have exercised any influence over Philo's reflection.

Slightly later, Philo turns to Exodus 14:19. In his version of that last night, Philo recounts how "the guiding cloud, which at other times stood in front, turned round to the back of the multitude to form its rearguard, and thus posted between the pursuers and pursued regulated the course of the latter and drove them before it under safe protection, but checked and repelled the former when they strove to advance."[133] In this reprisal, the pillar features, though not by standing as a protective barrier; instead, the cloud, and the cloud alone, *drives* the Israelites from behind, like a herder, while simultaneously repelling the Egyptians. No angel drives or leads them in Philo's version. Philo also excises God, who, in a confusing narrative detail in the exodus story, confused the Egyptians by looking through the pillar of cloud and fire. In Philo's streamlined version, the spectacle of the cloud itself confused the Egyptians and terrorized them, causing them to tumble over one another, while the Hebrews fled.[134] God did not, in some awkward way, look through the pillars of cloud and fire in order to confuse the Egyptians during the morning watch.[135] In all of this interpretive work, which simplifies the biblical narrative, Philo does not introduce the spirit.

Another storyteller, at some point perhaps during the first century C.E., composed the Liber Antiquitatum Biblicarum, which abbreviates the three-month period between escape through the Sea and the sojourn at Mt. Sinai: "Now he led his people out into the wilderness; for forty years he rained down for them bread from heaven and brought quail to them from the sea and brought forth a well of water to follow them. Now with a pillar of cloud he led them by day, and with a pillar of fire he gave them light by night."[136] This is the bare-bones story. There is no evidence, as there may be in Jubilees, of the impress of Isaiah 63:7-14; there is certainly no holy spirit or divine *pānîm* at the helm. Nor is there evidence of other agents, as in Philo's effort to tell the story in less cluttered terms than his source. The pillars alone survive in this ancient Jewish retelling of the exodus story.

Only in the angel of the presence in Jubilees is there a glimpse of Isaiah 63:7-14, and there the glimpse is of the angel rather than the spirit.[137] By way of contrast, several other first-century Jewish authors, whose compositions are included in the New Testament, feature the spirit in the context of the exodus story. The primary story, of course, is the story of Jesus and the faith of his followers, but these are depicted with overtones of the exodus. A few touchpoints stand out as examples of how subtly these first-century authors may have incorporated the spirit in a story infused by the exodus; these examples make it possible to discern the impress that the association of the spirit with exodus had on at least some postbiblical authors.

In a letter to followers of Jesus in Galatia, the apostle Paul launches a volley of images to argue that something fundamental has changed in the lives of believers. He reasons:

> My point is this: heirs, as long as they are minors, are no better than slaves, though they are the owners of all the property; but they remain under guardians and trustees until the date set by the father. So with us; while we were minors, we were enslaved to the elemental spirits of the world. But when the fullness of time had come, God sent his Son, born of a woman, born under the law, in order to redeem those who were under the law, so that we might receive adoption as children. And because you are children, God has sent the Spirit of his Son into our hearts, crying, "Abba! Father!" So you are no longer a slave but a child, and if a child then also an heir, through God.[138]

This argument makes good enough sense in light of Roman laws of slavery, manumission, adoption, and inheritance, yet there may also be an exodus subplot, a subterranean conviction that God is about the business of stimulating a new exodus. Paul, according to N. T. Wright, "is doing his best . . . to place the present predicament and puzzlement of the Galatian Christians on to the well-known map of the exodus narrative, in order to draw the moral: don't go back to slavery, but go on to your inheritance, led by that indwelling divine presence."[139] This appeal is rife with allusions, both distant and close, to the exodus.[140] Like the Israelites, the Galatians are the heirs of Abraham.[141] Like the Israelites, the Galatians were once slaves.[142] Like the Israelites, whose liberation marked the fullness of time,[143] the Galatians have been liberated—male and female, slave and free, Jew and Gentile. Like the Israelites, the Galatians were redeemed.[144] And, like the Israelites, the Galatians are no longer slaves but children and, if children, then heirs.[145] It is high time they accept their inheritance rather than, like the Israelites in an agonizing desert sojourn, yearn to return to the fleshpots of Egypt.[146] The only movement can be forward.[147]

Yet there is more to this appeal than a general sense that the Galatians can experience a new exodus. The claim to God as father takes readers back to the first such claim in the Jewish Scriptures—in Isaiah 63:16, where a prophetic appeal to God as father arises from the pungent sense of divine presence in the past, which the lament in Isaiah 63:7-14 articulates. A few short lines after the prophet recalls the presence and guidance of God's spirit, he pleads, "For you are our father, though Abraham does not know us and Israel does not acknowledge us; you, O LORD, are our father; our Redeemer from of old is your name." These prophetic lines—a continuation of the lament, perhaps—may anchor Paul's claim to God as father in a context of redemption, in which he remembers the exodus and imagines the promise of a new exodus.[148]

Compelling, too, is the spirit sent into the heart of the people in a context bubbling up with exodus undertones. The spirit sent deep into the hearts of once-upon-a-time slaves does not mimic but does match the conviction, expressed in the prophetic lament, that God put the holy spirit within a people[149] who passed through the Sea. If God put the holy spirit into the hearts of slaves in Egypt—slaves who would rebel against God's holy spirit—then this same God can send the spirit of the son into the hearts of people enslaved to the elements of the cosmos, including failed obedience to Torah.[150]

This is the sort of coalescence of ingredients that prompts N. T. Wright to make the bald but credible claim that "anyone familiar with second-Temple Jewish writing, with its complex webs of allusion and echo, will recognize at once that this is indeed a compact exodus-story. Here is a group of slaves; here is the sovereign God, acting 'in the fullness of time'; he redeems the slaves, and addresses them as his 'sons.' Every element of this rings with exodus-echoes."[151] Add to this the recognition of God as father and redeemer, alongside the sending or setting of the spirit deep within, and the source may not be merely "a compact exodus-story" but the plaintive lament of an exilic or postexilic prophet who sought to detect the presence of God in an age of absence.[152]

What Paul expresses compactly in Galatians often appears less densely in his letter to the Romans. Small wonder, then, that this cluster of themes reemerges in Romans 8:14-17, in which Paul may appeal yet again to the story of the exodus to pry believers from anything less than a life of grace.[153] "For all who are led by the Spirit of God are children [sons] of God," Paul reminds his readers. "For you did not receive a spirit of slavery to fall back into fear, but you have received a spirit of adoption. When we cry, 'Abba! Father!' it is that very Spirit bearing witness with our spirit that we are children of God, and if children, then heirs, heirs of God and joint heirs with Christ—if, in fact, we suffer with him so that we may also be glorified with him." Slavery, the peril of falling back into slavery, sonship, fatherhood, inheritance—these are familiar themes reminiscent of the exodus, set now in the context of the grand scheme of salvation for a world beyond Israel.[154]

To this exodus story must be added the spirit. "All who are led by the Spirit . . . are children [sons] of God." In the exodus story, the pillars lead. The angel leads. God leads. But not the spirit. Yet in the Old Greek of Isaiah 63:14, the spirit unequivocally leads: "A spirit came down from the Lord and guided them. Thus you led your people, to make for yourself a glorious name." The verbs *lead* or *guide* are common enough, but the story of redemption from slavery, in which they are situated, both in Isaiah 63 and Romans 8, is not.[155] This is Israel's story and now, claims Paul, the nations' story.[156]

The spirit has another purpose in Paul's letter to the Romans: the spirit "helps us in our weakness," interceding with sighs too deep for words for those who "groan inwardly while we wait for adoption, the redemption of our bodies."[157] Redemption. Adoption. And groaning in weakness, like the Israelites, whose redemption began with the groans of slavery. "I have observed the misery of my people who are in Egypt; I have heard their cry on account of their taskmasters. Indeed, I know their sufferings."[158] "The cry of the *sons of Israel* has now come to me; I have also seen how the Egyptians oppress them."[159] The redemption of Israel begins with a cry, a groan. Believers, too, moan, as they await further redemption—a new exodus—of their bodies. Exodus, in other words, brings new exodus, which brings an even newer exodus to come. Throughout all of this, from Isaiah 63 to Galatians 4 to Romans 8, the spirit is pivotal, giving life within, leading, and interceding.

This is not the whole of the story, with its images of endless slavery without the slightest chance of manumission, hope for a renewed creation, and the promise of glory culled from a variety of visions in Israelite literature. But the exodus story likely underlies this text, giving resonance to such realities as slavery, fear, the threat of retreat into slavery, redemption, adoption, sonship, an inheritance to claim—and the spirit within, groaning and guiding to a promised land void of pain and suffering but rich with glory and solace.

The impact of Isaiah 63, though again probably not Haggai 2, extended beyond Paul's fertile imagination. It seeps as well into the telling and retelling of Jesus' baptism, not so much in Mark's gospel as in Luke's and Matthew's versions. In all three gospels, the spirit descends, as in the Greek version of Isaiah 63:14. In Matthew and Luke's gospels, the spirit then leads Jesus, either *up* to the wilderness at the start of the forty days (Matthew) or *in* the wilderness for the entire forty days of testing (Luke). The pattern is clear: descent of the spirit followed by leading. This is a general pattern that need not be tied to Isaiah 63:14, though the lament, in the Greek, at least, preserves this pattern quintessentially: "A spirit came down from the Lord and guided them."[160]

While the spirit casts Jesus out, like a demon or an unwelcome guest, in Mark's version, the image is altogether different in the Gospel of Matthew, in which "Jesus was led up by the Spirit into the wilderness to be tempted by the devil. He fasted forty days and forty nights, and afterwards he was famished."[161] In this portrait of testing, Jesus takes on the role of fledgling Israel, though without succumbing to hunger and idolatry. His forty days in the wilderness recall, of course, Israel's forty years in the wilderness. More emphatically, the quotations he selects to counter the devil are plucked from the story of Israel's deliverance, as it is told in Deuteronomy.[162]

With such rich resonance of the exodus, the verb *lead up* inevitably recalls the leading (ἤγαγεν) of Israel in Deuteronomy 8:2. Perhaps the addition of the preposition *up* in the verb that describes Jesus' journey of ascent from the Jordan (ἀνήχθη) is simply the product of topography. More likely, it recalls the exodus, in which God led Israel up from Egypt.[163] Perhaps it recalls in particular the intense negotiation between Moses and God that followed the debacle of the idolatrous calf, when Moses protested: "Look, you say to me, 'Lead up [ἀνάγαγε] this people!' but you did not disclose to me whom you would send along with me."[164] Then again, "If you yourself do not go, do not lead me up [ἀναγάγῃς] from here."[165] Like a dog with a bone, Moses would not let go. If they are to be led up from Sinai to the land of promise, God—and no less—must go.

At stake in this negotiation is whether God's angel or *pānîm* would accompany Israel. In the story of Jesus, the *spirit* leads Jesus up into the wilderness. For this shift, the Greek version of Isaiah 63:13-14 may supply an apt antecedent. God "led [ἤγαγεν] them through the deep like a horse through a wilderness [ἐρήμου], and they did not become weary, and like cattle through a plain. A spirit came down from the Lord and guided [ὡδήγησεν] them. Thus you led [ἤγαγες] your people, to make for yourself a glorious name."[166] In this lament, the spirit takes on the role of the angel and the presence or *pānîm* of God. Similarly, at the baptism of Jesus, the spirit takes on their role, as it leads Jesus up to be tested for forty days. Moses had begged for God's presence, for divine *pānîm*, but had been rebuffed. Jesus, unlike Moses, receives divine assurance when he is led up by the spirit into the desert to succeed where Israel had failed.

According to Luke's Gospel, Jesus, "full of the Holy Spirit, returned from the Jordan and was led by the Spirit in the wilderness, where for forty days he was tempted by the devil."[167] The spirit did not lead Jesus *up* into the wilderness, as in Matthew's Gospel; the spirit led him *in* the wilderness for forty days. Israel's baseline of leading in the wilderness is straightforward: God led Israel with pillars.[168] Yet the memory of leading was, as we saw, more complicated, even more convoluted, than that. Still, one dimension of this conviction is undeniable: *the spirit* did not lead Israel *except according to Isaiah 63:7-14*. In the Greek translation of the lament, without a doubt, the spirit guided (ὡδήγησεν) them and God led (ἤγαγες) them. Now, in the Gospel of Luke, the spirit leads Jesus in the wilderness.[169]

The extent of this interpretation may reach even one of the thorniest sayings in the Gospels. When, in the heat of controversy, Jesus forgives the sins of the paralyzed man whom he heals, the scribes inquire, "Why does this fellow speak this way? It is blasphemy! Who can forgive sins but God alone?"[170] Not long after, his family thinks he is out of his mind,[171] and the scribes from Jerusalem, somewhat less sympathetically, charge, "He has Beelzebul, and by the ruler of the demons he casts out demons."[172] Jesus turns the tables and charges them with blasphemy: "Truly I tell you, people will be forgiven for their sins and whatever blasphemies they utter; but whoever blasphemes against the holy spirit can never have forgiveness, but is guilty of an eternal sin."[173]

Matthew preserves this saying about blasphemy against the holy spirit in a slightly different form, with an added reference to this age and the age to come, perhaps as a nod to the words *eternal sin* in Mark's gospel. "Whoever speaks a word against the Son of Man will be forgiven, but whoever speaks against the Holy Spirit will not be forgiven, either in this age or in the age to come."[174]

Luke's version is similar to Matthew's: "And everyone who speaks a word against the Son of Man will be forgiven; but whoever blasphemes against the Holy Spirit will not be forgiven." Yet Luke connects it to another saying altogether, which has to do with the faithful witness of Jesus' followers, with the result that it becomes a warning against the failed witness of believers under duress rather than a threat to opponents.[175]

These are not the only versions of this saying that circulated in the early church. The gnostic Gospel of Thomas includes a third version:[176] "Jesus said, 'Whoever blasphemes against the Father will be forgiven, and whoever blasphemes against the Son will be forgiven, but whoever blasphemes against the Holy Spirit will not be forgiven, either on earth or in heaven.'"[177] The addition of the father is new, as is the reference to heaven and earth, but the gist of the saying remains intact: *blasphemy against the holy spirit will not be forgiven*. All three Synoptic Gospels—the Gospel of Thomas, too—contain this saying, and each does something different with it, presumably in an effort to make sense of such a grim, unfathomable saying.

The solution, if a solution is to be found, may lie in this lament and its antecedent—the angel of the exodus, on behalf of whom God had warned, "I am going to send an angel in front of you, to guard you on the way and to bring you to the place that I have prepared. Be attentive to him and listen to his voice; do not rebel against him, for he will not pardon your transgression; for my name is in him. But if you listen attentively to his voice and do all that I say, then I will be an enemy to your enemies and a foe to your foes."[178] In the lament, this promise is transposed to the holy spirit, about whom the prophet despairs: "But they disobeyed and provoked his holy spirit; therefore he turned to them in enmity, and he himself warred against them."[179] In Exodus, there is no pardon for those who rebel against the angel. In Isaiah, God becomes the enemy of those who rebel against God's holy spirit.

Because the promise of the angel and the lament about the holy spirit have to do with Israelites, the force of Jesus' saying, in light of Isaiah 63:10, applies equally to Jesus' opponents and the followers of Jesus, since both constitute the people of God, the heirs of the lament. On the one hand, the Pharisees demonstrate that they are enemies of Jesus because they attribute his exorcisms to Satan rather than the holy spirit. In this way, they rebel against God's holy spirit, with the result that, as in Isaiah 63, God becomes their enemy. They can be forgiven for their rejection of Jesus' Sabbath practices,[180] for their dismissal of his healings on the Sabbath,[181] for their refusal to acknowledge that Jesus is David's son,[182] even for speaking against the son of man.[183] They cannot be forgiven, however, for their failure to reckon with the holy spirit, for attributing Jesus' exorcisms to the prince of demons rather than the holy spirit. They cannot be forgiven for this precisely because of what their own tradition says, that God becomes the enemy of those who rebel against the holy spirit. On the other hand, Jesus' saying can serve as a warning as well to followers of Jesus. This is the tack Luke takes by tethering the warning against blasphemy to Jesus' promise, "When they bring you before the synagogues, the rulers, and the authorities, do not worry about how you are to defend yourselves or what you are to say; for the Holy Spirit will teach you at that very hour what you ought to say."[184] The warning is clear: when believers find themselves in times of trial, they must not do what Israel did and rebel—blaspheme, as Jesus put it—against the holy spirit. The gist of blasphemy is, in Luke's scenario, a failure to wait upon the spirit for faithful witness.[185]

Israel's mixed memories of guidance in its earliest days are difficult to untangle. Yet key figures emerged as agents of guidance: the pillars, the angel, the presence or *pānîm*, perhaps even the cloud. These were neither discrete nor discreet; they kept Israel alive, and it is this salient conviction, rather than an ability to create tidy boundaries between these agents, that holds this diverse collection of narratives, prophecies, and psalms together. Second Temple interpreters, from the author of the book of Nehemiah to Josephus, also held firmly to a belief in God's guidance during those troubled early days, though they, too, were not homogeneous in their belief. Some gave priority to the pillars, another to an angel, another to an amalgamation of these agents, still another simply to providence rather than agents of guidance.

The impress of the promise in the book of Haggai is negligible, while the impress of the lament in Isaiah 63:7-14 is marginally more visible in Second Temple texts. The book of Nehemiah has the ingredients of pillars and the spirit, but they coexist in a way to suggest minimal influence, if any, of the lament in Isaiah. There is nothing in the prayer to suggest that the spirit is the angel apart from the vague word *good*. The book of Jubilees embraces, as its preeminent mediator of revelation, the angel of the presence, which preserves the language of Isaiah 63:9. Otherwise, the impact of the lament in Isaiah, in general, is minimal.

Until, that is, the early church. The apostle Paul fitted his schema of salvation to the exodus with signal words such as *slavery* and *redemption*. The leading of the spirit, which responds to human groans, is a natural expression of the exodus, once it is refracted through the lens of Isaiah 63. The handlers of the gospel tradition, as well, bent the baptism and wilderness testing of Jesus to the arc of the exodus, not least in Jesus' trio of responses to the devil; in this context, it is not an angel or a pillar that guides Jesus but the spirit, even as the spirit led Israel. Once again, the exodus, pressed through the sieve of this lament, infiltrates the story of Jesus. Finally, Jesus' saying about blasphemy against the holy spirit, thorny and baffling though it be, gains traction against a background of Israel's capacity to rebel against or grieve or resist the holy spirit, which prompted God to become their enemy.

The impress of Isaiah 63:7-14, then, is evident principally in the writings preserved by the movement that would emerge full-blown in Christianity. This is hardly surprising, given their nearly ubiquitous claims to the spirit, their keen sense that they were part of a new exodus, and their relentless effort to ground the story of Jesus in the Jewish Scriptures. It was there, among the followers of Jesus, where Isaiah 63 would exercise its most palpable, if still muted, influence on postbiblical Judaism.

This realization does not shatter the foundations of contemporary pneumatology. There is no axe at the root of the tree. Yet it would perhaps be ill-advised to create a future for pneumatology void of the experience of exodus because not once but twice the origin of pneumatology lay there—first in the throes of exile and restoration, then again in the thrall of death and resurrection. At both moments, exodus and spirit fused.

The two texts to which we can trace the origin of pneumatology, we should remind ourselves, were not especially conspicuous. They evoke the drama of human experience, tied as they are to anguish and tethered to anticipation, but neither is the sort of text that drew attention to itself—which is, of course, as it should be, given the subtlety of the spirit, who, in the darkest of nights, stands watch, if unwatched, along the edge of despair and hope.

EXCURSES

Excursus 1

Hans Leisegang and the Freedom of Inquiry

Hans Leisegang's life is a testimony to human tenacity and integrity. The renowned and popular philosophy professor had been warned not to resist the rising tide of National Socialism. He paid no heed. He refused the offer from Nietzsche's sister to produce an edition of Nietzsche's works amenable to the propagandistic aims of the National Socialists.[1] He resisted a decision of the university senate in Jena to dissolve and to hand authority to a director from the National Socialist party. He received a phone call from the principal National Socialist minister, a Herr Stier, alerting him to the unacceptable statements he had made. He was even warned by the university rector, Herr Esau, to be more cautious—*vorsichtiger*—a warning the professor soundly rejected, with these words: "Herr Rektor Esau hat mir im Sommersemester 1934 durch den Senior der Fakultät sagen lassen, ich möchte bei meinen Äußerungen in meinem Kolleg '*vorsichtiger*' sein. Ich habe ihm bestellen lassen, dass ich als Professor der Philosophie . . . nicht 'vorsichtig' in dem gemeinten Sinne sein könne und nichts gesagt hätte, was ich nicht vor jedem wissenschaftlich gebildeten Menschen verantworten könne. Die Universität sei keine Volksversammlung, in der man auf jedes mögliche Mißverständnis primitiver und aufgeregter Seelen Rücksicht nehmen könne."[2]

On August 2, 1934, as he stood in the Jena marketplace, listening to National Socialist eulogies for General Field Marshal Hindenburg, he is reputed to have said, amid the clatter and chaos of the market, something derogatory. By

November, even as he anticipated exoneration for such shaky charges, he was sentenced to six months in prison—and the loss of his post at the University of Jena.[3] Hans Leisegang was forty-four years old. This was the first time he would lose a post.

Neither Leisegang nor his wife, Erna Leisegang, had expected to find him in this godawful pit, this *Kaff*. When she walked into the prison, Erna Leisegang saw her husband immediately run away from her to the farthest corner of the room, where, she recalled in her journal—in a letter she could never send—"I could take you in my arms, speak well with you, and stroke you. The torment in your eyes, the emotional shock, I will never forget."[4]

After the war, which he spent earning a doctorate in physics and working in industry, Leisegang resumed his university post in Jena, which now lay under Soviet control.[5] Yet again he butted up against totalitarian efforts to control academic freedom. Again, he resisted. Urged to be a delegate for the doubtful Volkskongreß, he refused and fell under suspicion for his failure to participate in party politics.[6] Then, in a referendum on Leisegang, the Soviet-controlled student council manipulated a meeting to rid themselves of him. It did not work. The lecturer, to whom students swarmed, received 1,097 student votes of support, 282 of rejection, and 113 abstentions—all of this in a toxic atmosphere that required students to display their identities; those who supported him essentially declared their opposition to the Soviet party. These numbers, therefore, are stunning.[7] The results were not. Though he had already been offered the position of rector at the Free University in Berlin, along with a chair in philosophy, Leisegang opted to stay in the east, in Jena, because, as he saw it, his students there needed him more than those in Berlin. The Soviet minister of culture, a Frau Torhorst, was unimpressed. She accused him of yelling at her in private conversation—*bawling* at her, as she put it—and he was summarily dismissed, *fristlos entlassen*. The charge? He was *antidemocratic*.[8] So off finally went Hans Leisegang and his family to Berlin, with nothing in tow but his library.

Hans Leisegang's scholarship is important and erudite—though wrong, I think, about the origin of pneumatology—but his integrity, his intensity, these are the qualities that endure. I am touched by them, by the settled commitment to academic freedom he never yielded even in the havoc of life.

Excursus 2

Locating Influence

It is important to point out that this study follows the same vein as S. Olyan by regarding exegesis as a principal impulse for the developments that take place in Haggai 2:5 and, especially, Isaiah 63:7-14, which refers in the Hebrew to *the angel of his presence*. Olyan's proposal is worth quoting in full because it provides an apt introduction to this study:

> Exegesis is at least a major aspect, if not the most significant component, of the elusive framework sought by scholars in order better to understand the development of ideas about angels in late biblical and post-biblical texts. Exegesis has great potential as an alternative to the problematic thesis of the distant and inaccessible God, with all its theological baggage. No doubt a number of different influences played a part in the articulation of the angelic host, as many have argued, but no general understanding of the growth of ideas about angels will be possible until sufficient attention has been paid to various inner-Jewish developments, especially the rise and triumph of exegesis in all its varied aspects.[9]

In particular, Olyan points to the penchant for dealing with what J. Kugel calls "surface irregularities in the text."[10] The first chapter of this book, on the traditions of presence in the exodus, explores myriad surface irregularities in stories of the agents—pillars, angel, and *pānîm*—of the sort that prompted unprecedented reflection, especially in Isaiah 63:7-14.[11]

This study's approach derives not so much from a theoretical conviction that inner-biblical developments rather than external influences explain the developments in Haggai 2:5 and Isaiah 63:7-14, but from observations that demonstrate, to my satisfaction at least, that the fusion of the exodus tradition and a robust belief in the spirit explain what happened in Israel during the Babylonian and Persian eras. Further, at the start of this research, I wrote to scholars with facility in Babylonian and Persian literature. Both cautioned me about trying to identify Persian influence on Israelite religion and culture. Bruce Lincoln, Caroline E. Haskell Distinguished Service Professor Emeritus of the History of Religions in the Divinity School of the University of Chicago, responded in detail to my initial query. In the context of a lengthy pair of thoughtful e-mails, he wrote,

> I don't think you'll find anything helpful in the Achaemenid evidence, but what we have there is very limited. The Zoroastrian tradition offers more, although there the category of spirit (Avestan mainiiāva, Pahlavi mēnōg) simply delineates the non-material dimensions of existence. One might also consider the way "wind" (Avestan vaya, vayu; Pahlavi wēh) is theorized, as this has some similarities to some uses of Hebrew ruah as life breath, vital spirit, inspirational and animating force. Even so, I'm not sure how relevant this is or how much help it might give you.

Jason Sion Mokhtarian, associate professor in the Department of Religious Studies and Borns Jewish Studies Program at Indiana University, cautioned as well, "Personally, I would not read too much into potential Achaemenid religious influences; it is not impossible, but the spheres of influence were more in the realm of politics than religion per se, at least according to the evidence that is available from the Achaemenid period."

Excursus 3

The Identity of the Angelic Messenger

The identity of the angelic messenger of the exodus is difficult to determine.[12] B. Childs refers to "the virtual identification of the angel with God."[13] J. Durham views the angel as "an extension of the Divine Presence"[14] and "an extension of Yahweh's own person and Presence," "virtually an assertion of equivalence: the 'messenger' = Yahweh."[15] G. von Rad sees the angel and God as "obviously one and the same."[16] The imprecision of words such as *virtual, extension, virtually,* and *obviously* suggest how difficult it is to determine the relationship that exists between the angel and God.

B. Stein[17] offers a clue to just how difficult this task is with his effort to explore what he calls *Identitätstheorie*—the belief that God and the angel were one and the same. W. G. Heidt analyzes angels of the heavenly court, angelic relations with humankind, and the peculiar challenges of interpreting references to the "angel of YHWH." He, like Stein, explores the "identity theory," that is, whether the angel is a visible manifestation of God or, rather, as he puts it, "a created spirit." In his conclusion to the analysis of Exodus 23:20-23, 32:32-33, and 33:2-3, Heidt inadvertently reveals how difficult it is to answer this question in any sort of satisfactory way. He must separate Exodus 23 from Exodus 32–33 to come to what he considers to be a suitable example of the identity theory: "Consequently an exceedingly strong argument in favor of the Identity explanation of the *mal'akh Yahweh* texts lies in the above passages. Read out of context the single verses may readily receive other interpretations. Read in context the most reasonable explanations sees [*sic*] two significations in the word *mal'akh,* i.e., the visible manifestation of Yahweh in Exodus 23:20, 23, a created spirit in Exod. 32:34; 33:2. And when the whole series of texts under consideration is kept in mind our conclusion becomes inescapable."

G. Juncker delivers detailed analyses of key texts, though always, like Stier and Heidt, with an eye toward the identity between God and the angel—for Juncker, to anticipate New Testament Christology.[18] Juncker points out parallels between Exodus 23:20-23 and other texts to identify the angel with God. He refers, first, to Genesis 28:15, in which the Lord—the angel of the Lord, according to Juncker—appears to Jacob and says: "Know that I am with you and will keep you wherever you go, and will bring you back to this land; for I will not leave you until I have done what I have promised you."[19] The elements of walking or traveling, of being "along the way," of keeping or guarding, and of bringing to the promised land, tie this text about Jacob's encounter with the LORD to the promise of the angel. He looks, second, at parallels between Exodus 23:20-23 and Exodus 15:26, in which the LORD refers to the self in the third person: "If you will listen carefully to the voice of the LORD your God, and do what is right in his sight, and give heed to his commandments and keep all his statutes, I will not bring upon you any of the diseases that I brought upon the Egyptians; for I am the LORD who heals you." Third, Juncker identifies parallels between this angelic promise and the role of the angel in the story of Balaam (Numbers 22), including the phrase *in the way* (Exodus 23:20; Numbers 22:22, 23, 31, 34). He concludes, "Balaam has had a personal encounter with the 'vanguard' angel of the exodus (Exod 23:20-23; Num 20:16); and Balaam has been the recipient of a theophany."[20] Juncker discerns evocative parallels but fails to come to grips with God's eventual distancing from the angel in Exodus 33:2-4. In fact, oddly enough, with respect to a text rife with tension over whether God's angel or presence will lead—they seem to be in competition with one another—Juncker sees *angel* and *face* as identical ways "of referring to the presence of YHWH."[21] Determined to iron out the wrinkles in the text—exactly what I propose ought *not* to be done—he identifies the angel, the pillar, and God with one another. "There is fluidity in all of these, to be sure," he admits. "But the fluidity is not between YHWH and the angel (as is commonly alleged) but between YHWH, the angel, and the pillar of cloud and fire. A satisfactory solution will account for all three, and the most satisfactory solution will equate all three (at least at the denotative level). An appearance of this angel like an appearance of the pillar of cloud and fire is properly understood as a theophany." I do not find this solution satisfactory at all. Juncker continues with what seems to me to be a constrictive approach: "The quasi-independent existence of this angel at the verbal level is carefully circumscribed or relativized at the contextual level by the ubiquitous stress on the presence of YHWH himself and by the association of the angel with an *Erscheinungsform* that is not only impersonal but that has no independent existence whatever. What the agency language would force apart the context forces together. The texts are still problematic," he admits, "in the sense that YHWH cannot literally send himself or dwell in himself. But in spite of this, perhaps even because of this, the texts succeed by periphrasis and circumlocution in communicating two theological profundities: YHWH is personally present with his people; and YHWH transcends his personal presence with his people." This is a complex approach to the text, single-mindedly aimed at demonstrating the identity of God and the angel.

H. Ausloos explores the possibility that the angel is the product of a "(post-) Deuteronomistic redaction or edition." He begins by analyzing various proposals of a (largely) post-Deuteronomistic provenance, including those of W. Johnstone, E. Blum, H.-D. Neef, and R. Kratz.[22] He boils the main reasons for these proposals down to two: (1) the relationship between Exodus 23:20-33 and a Deuteronomistic text, Judges 2:1-5, suggests that Exodus 23 is also Deuteronomistic in character; and (2) the resemblance of Exodus 23 to other Deuteronomistic texts, such as Genesis 24:7, Exodus 32:34, 33:2, and Numbers 10:16 also suggests that Exodus 23 is Deuteronomistic.[23] Ausloos then notes that there is no such messenger in the book of Deuteronomy; it is difficult to see the messenger or angel as a Deuteronomistic element. In fact, Deuteronomy 4:37-38 says the opposite: "And because he loved your ancestors, he chose their descendants after them. He brought you out of Egypt with his own presence, by his great power (וַיּוֹצִאֲךָ בְּפָנָיו בְּכֹחוֹ הַגָּדֹל), driving out before you nations greater and mightier than yourselves, to bring you in, giving you their land for a possession, as it is still today." He then suggests that Isaiah 63:9 is an indication of postexilic discussion and debate about the angel, though his discussion is marred by his translation, without rationale, of a hybrid between the Old Greek and the Hebrew: "It was no angel or messenger but his presence that saved them." On this basis, Ausloos deems it "rather plausible that Second Isaiah was favouring Deuteronomy's theology in Deut. iv 37 and thus reacted against the presentation of the מלאך as representing YHWH."[24] Ausloos continues by discussing efforts to view the messenger statement in Exodus 23 as Deuteronomistic, despite the absence of such a messenger or angel in Deuteronomy. Some scholars say the messenger is human, though this seems unlikely in light of the authority of the angel. Ausloos correctly points out, God's name is *in* the angel, but the angel does not speak *for* God.[25] Finally, Ausloos points out the differences between Exodus 23 and Judges 2. They are not part and parcel of the same redaction. They may, in fact, reflect different layers in a Deuteronomistic redaction, with Judges 2 being far more representative of Deuteronomistic theology than Exodus 23. I would suggest that it is possible to ask whether Exodus 23:20-33 is Deuteronomistic at all.[26]

The confusion created by Exodus 23:20-23 prompts W. Propp to pose a series of questions:

> At least in the composite text, it is a little surprising that Yahweh promises a Messenger at this late point. An angelic cloud has already led the Israelites to Sinai and will accompany them to Canaan. . . . Is this the same entity . . . ? It sounds like something new. Are we in a different literary source? Might the Messenger in question be Yahweh's "terror" (v 27) or the . . . "hornet" (?)? Moreover, in 33:2-3, Yahweh seems to send his Messenger as a punishment for the Gold Calf affair, in lieu of his "Face," i.e., his fuller presence. . . . How does that Messenger relate to this Messenger? Is the envoy of 23:20 Yahweh's hypostatic Name?

Propp then proffers a solution to this robust series of rhetorical questions: "The simplest answer—admittedly a dodge—is that Yahweh is deliberately Delphic.

While reassuring the people that, come what may, he will not abandon them, the Deity keeps his options open."[27] God, given the uncertain nature of the relationship with Israel, holds out an ambiguous promise of divine presence.

Is God deliberately Delphic? Perhaps not to the extent Propp suggests. Propp's instincts, nevertheless, are correct: the relationship between this angel and the pillars is difficult to determine. It remains unresolved throughout Torah. Still, it is possible to clear away some brush and discover the characteristics, responsibilities, and prerogatives of the angelic messenger, which will dissipate slightly later in the story, in Exodus 32–33, but reemerge in full force in Isaiah 63:7-14. It is possible, as well, to discern Israel's responsibility toward this angel. It is possible, finally, to suggest the nature of the relationship between God and the angel.

Excursus 4

God and Moses' Conversation in Exodus 32–33

Given how knotted this conversation is, unraveling, as it does, by fits and starts, it may be beneficial to chart the stages of the conversation:

1) Exodus 32:34; 33:2: God repeats the promise of an angel to go before the people into a land of milk and honey.
2) For the first time, God distinguishes God's personal presence-face (פָּנַי) from the angel who had once been the bearer of God's word, a traveler alongside God,[28] and a guard who would stand in the breach between Egypt and Israel.[29]
3) Exodus 33:7-11: A parenthetical episode in the story reveals how, when the pillar of cloud descended at the gate of the tent of meeting, Moses would enter the tent and speak to God face to face, as to a friend. But this apparently is not enough for Moses.
4) Exodus 33:12: Therefore, in one of the most inscrutable lines in the Jewish Bible, Moses—witness to the pillar(s) of cloud and fire going before Israel, witness to the pillar of cloud's descent at the tent of meeting, witness to the angel who went before Israel and, when needed, tucked itself between Israel and Egypt—risks it all by complaining, "You have not let me know whom you will send with me." God has sent pillar(s) and angel, but Moses tosses these guides aside. They are not enough. He wants more.
5) Exodus 33:15: Perhaps Moses should not be blamed. God, not Moses, had introduced the distinction between the angel and God's presence-face.[30] Moses simply exploits it, calling God's bluff: "If your presence will not go, do not carry us up from here."
6) Exodus 33:17: God concedes, though without any clear reference to the people whom Moses had wanted to be included in the equation.

Adopting only the second-person singular, not the plural—though this itself is not an unambiguous indication that the Israelites are excluded—God promises ambiguously, "I will do the very thing that you have asked; for you have found favor in my sight, and I know you by name."

7) Exodus 33:18: Moses, too, concedes. Presumably aware that the fate of Israel is no longer the topic of conversation, he asks now only for himself: "Cause me to see your glory, please."
8) No. God will not. Goodness, yes. Grace, for sure. Mercy, too. Name, as well. What lies behind God, even. But not God's presence-face. Not even Moses can see this and live.
9) Moses has forfeited the promise of the angel and the leading of the pillar(s) in pursuit of God's own presence-face in Israel's midst. He has gotten no further vis-à-vis Israel: God leaves them out of the equation. He is not even permitted himself to see God's presence-face.
10) Exodus 33:21-23: Still, it looks as if Moses has won. Even at the end, God covers Moses and lets Moses see. But what does Moses see?
11) Exodus 33:23: Not God's presence-face, which is all that Moses requested. Despite God's concession and promise to give Moses what he requests—the accompaniment of God's presence-face—in the end, God does not allow it. If the presence-face of God goes with Moses, or in the off chance the presence-face is found in Israel's midst, it cannot be seen. Not the face. Only the back. Is Moses, for all of his conjuring, badgering, and wrestling, any better off? Is Israel?
12) The negotiation ends, the conversation closes. God's ambivalence toward Israel yields a peculiar air of ambiguity to this unforgiving and inconclusive negotiation. Friends still perhaps—they meet at the tent and talk as friends—but uneasy allies, too.

Excursus 5

The Cloud in the Wilderness

If Exodus ends on a relatively tidy note, the first mention of the cloud of the Lord (it is called that in Numbers 10:34) in the book of Numbers is tidier still. In fact, four references to the cloud in close succession occur in a summary of what normally took place.

> On the day the tabernacle was set up, the cloud covered the tabernacle, the tent of the covenant; and from evening until morning it was over the tabernacle, having the appearance of fire. It was always so: the cloud covered it by day and the appearance of fire by night. Whenever the cloud lifted from over the tent, then the Israelites would set out; and in the place where the cloud settled down, there the Israelites would camp. At the command of

> the LORD the Israelites would set out, and at the command of the LORD they would camp. As long as the cloud rested over the tabernacle, they would remain in camp. Even when the cloud continued over the tabernacle many days, the Israelites would keep the charge of the LORD, and would not set out. Sometimes the cloud would remain a few days over the tabernacle, and according to the command of the LORD they would remain in camp; then according to the command of the LORD they would set out. Sometimes the cloud would remain from evening until morning; and when the cloud lifted in the morning, they would set out, or if it continued for a day and a night, when the cloud lifted they would set out. Whether it was two days, or a month, or a longer time, that the cloud continued over the tabernacle, resting upon it, the Israelites would remain in camp and would not set out; but when it lifted they would set out. At the command of the LORD they would camp, and at the command of the LORD they would set out. They kept the charge of the LORD, at the command of the LORD by Moses.[31]

T. Mann refers to this section as a compact paradigm of divine presence and guidance:

> It becomes immediately apparent from the rest of vss. 15-23 that the initial setting up of the tabernacle is not the subject, but rather the way in which the tabernacle is connected with the means of divine guidance for the extended period of Israel's march from Sinai. This is evident simply by the use of frequentative verbs throughout the passage. In this way vss. 15-23 provide a compact paradigm of the motif of divine presence and guidance, reminding us once again of Exod 13.21-22 and 33.7-11. The paradigmatic nature of this passage is almost painfully clear from the way in which the author answers hypothetical questions. What if the cloud remained for a very long time over the tabernacle? What if it was there only overnight? What if it did not descend at evening and the people had to march all night? The answer to all of these questions is the dogged repetition of the author's point: the people followed the command of Yahweh as it was demonstrated in the movement of the cloud, no matter how inconsistent that movement might be.[32]

The summary begins with a straightforward description of the day on which the tabernacle was first set up: "On the day the tabernacle was set up, the cloud covered the tabernacle, the tent of the covenant."[33] Immediately, however, the verbs turn from the perfect to the imperfect—iterative imperfects that describe what occurred over the course of time: "It was always so: the cloud covered it by day and the appearance of fire by night."[34] This summary has the benefit of retrospect. Untethered to a single event, it softens otherwise harsh edges and blunts awkward ones in important ways.

First, it may blunt the strangeness of a phenomenon that could be a cloud by day but a fire by night. (Some interpreters, we may recall, thought it was a cloud on one side and fire on the other—a strange phenomenon indeed.) This oddity is not resolved by returning to the two pillars of Exodus 13:21-22; the cloud is no longer a pillar at all. It is resolved by the introduction of the word *appearance*, in the phrase *having the appearance of fire* (מַרְאֵה־אֵשׁ). What is to be made of the word *appearance*, with respect to fire by night? Certainly not that all of this was an illusion. In Numbers 12:8, in fact, God contrasts speaking with Moses face to face, in "appearance—not in riddles." The word, in this context, appears to suggest ultrareality through an intense apprehension of the divine. Still, there is a measure of distancing here: the cloud was *not* fire at night, though it *appeared* to be. Propp's interpretation of the cloud in Exodus 40:34-38, though imprudent, is instructive:

> It seems that Exod 40:38 finally explains the nature of the cloud-fire pillar. The cloud is Yahweh's vehicle, while the fire is his Glory. . . . Once the Tabernacle is ready, God's fiery presence, as it were, parks its cloud vehicle on the roof (Num 9:15-23). After the Tent and clergy are purified and consecrated, the Glory leaves the cloud to fill the Tabernacle (Exod 40:34-35), igniting the wood upon the Altar to inaugurate worship (Lev 9:24). . . . When it is time to leave, the Glory reenters the cloud and together they take off (Exod 40:36; Num 9:15-23). Once again, the fire, i.e., the Glory, is visible only at night, shining through the cloud.[35]

Although Propp fills in too many gaps in the scene, his effort to connect the fiery appearance with the fire of the tabernacle altar is commendable. Were the cloud a dense presence that completely overshadowed the tabernacle, then the fire's reflection would be visible in the cloud at night. In this way, the cloud, though not on fire, would have the *appearance* of fire. By referring, then, to the appearance of fire at night rather than a cloud of actual fire, this summary points the way to a simple explanation of the otherwise baffling portraits of pillar(s) of cloud and actual fire in the book of Exodus: at night, the altar fire—or simply campfires—reflected on the dense cloud and gave it the appearance of fire.

Second, this summary resolves the difficulty prompted by the lack of travel directions in Exodus 40:34-38, where the cloud ascends and descends—but does not lead. While in Exodus 40, descent signals encampment and ascent embarkation, it is not clear where the Israelites are to go. In Numbers 9, the answer is clear in two respects. First, the Israelites encamped wherever, on the journey, the cloud descended on the tabernacle.[36] But where did they travel when they broke camp? This is resolved by the second detail. They encamped and set out by the command—literally, mouth—of the Lord.[37] There existed, then, an implicit symbiosis between the cloud's ascent or descent and the mouth or command of God. This relationship explains not only when Israel camped or journeyed but also, it would seem, *where* they journeyed.

Third, in this summary, the cloud is not entirely an active agent of God's presence. It *covers, is, settles,* and *is for a long time* upon the tabernacle,[38] but the cloud's ascent is depicted, as in Exodus 40:36, by the Hebrew niphal stem, which may suggest a certain passivity.[39] This point must not be pressed too far, but the niphal stem may explain the symbiosis between God's active command and the cloud's more passive ascent: the niphal points to an actor no less than God, whose command lay behind the ascent of the cloud.

Fourth, while it is perhaps irresistible in the interpretation of a journey narrative to focus upon where the cloud led, especially since the original purpose of the pillar(s) was to lead and protect Israel, central to this summary is the explanation of why Israel did *not* travel. Why did they not hurry to the promised land? Why did their journey take so long? Because they were attentive to the charge of God, marked both by God's command and the descent of the cloud, which compelled them to remain encamped for periods of time, both long and short.

This summary in the book of Numbers, then, resolves key elements of Israel's journey narrative. How could the (pillar[s] of) cloud be cloud by day and fire by night? What role did the cloud have in leading Israel along the way? In what ways was God present during the journey? And why did the journey take so long? Of course, as with Exodus 40:34-38, this resolution comes at a cost. Gone are the pillars that led Israel at the start. Gone is the pillar that moves about. Gone is the angel appointed to lead Israel. Gone even is the glory of Exodus 40:34-38. Still, the scenario of unremitting guidance and divine presence in a world centered on the tabernacle now lies at the forefront of Israel's journey.

Mann analyzes other aspects of this text as well. He summarizes:

> The Priestly material in Num 9.15-23 presents us with another paradigm of divine presence and guidance that utilizes the image of the cloud. The Priestly author has combined older traditions (Exod 13.21-22; 33:7-11) in order to demonstrate his view that the cultic institution of the Tabernacle itself is now the means through which not only Yahweh's presence, but also his guidance, is made manifest. The spatial as well as the theological centrality of the Tabernacle has resulted in the attenuation of the vanguard motif, but the use of standards by each of the subsidiary camps, and the fact that the march of Israel moves "at the command of Yahweh," indicate that the Priestly understanding of Israel's march through the wilderness resembles the march of the Assyrian army as we have seen it in the annals.[40]

When the cloud next appears, it does precisely, at a point in time, what the summary suggests: "In the second year, in the second month, on the twentieth day of the month, the cloud lifted [niphal stem, 'was lifted'] from over the tabernacle of the covenant. Then the Israelites set out by stages from the wilderness of Sinai, and the cloud settled down in the wilderness of Paran."[41]

The pattern continues with another instance:

> So they set out from the mount of the Lord three days' journey with the ark of the covenant of the Lord going before them three days' journey, to seek out a resting place for them, the cloud of the Lord being over them by day when they set out from the camp. Whenever the ark set out, Moses would say, "Arise, O Lord, let your enemies be scattered, and your foes flee before you." And whenever it came to rest, he would say, "Return, O Lord of the ten thousand thousands of Israel."[42]

This iteration contains a few variations. First, the cloud is now "the cloud of the Lord," though its presence is still without agency; this time, in fact, there is no verb at all. Second, this scene dispels any ambiguity about the location of the cloud. It was upon them. The cloud, unlike the pillar(s) and angel, did not proceed in front of them. Third, the movement of the cloud is now coordinated with the movement of the ark, which, like the Israelites, sets out and comes to rest.

The elasticity of the tradition is apparent again in Psalm 99, which praises the God of Israel by connecting worship at the tent or tabernacle with worship in the temple. The new wrinkle in this psalm is that God speaks out of a pillar of cloud: "He [God] spoke to them in the pillar of cloud; they kept his decrees and the statutes that he gave them."[43] Typically, the pillars are agents of guidance in the tradition, unlike the cloud, which ascends and descends. This distinction is especially clear in Numbers 14:14: "for you, O Lord, are seen face to face, and your cloud stands over them and you go in front of them, in a pillar of cloud by day and in a pillar of fire by night." Nonetheless, in Exodus 33:7-11, the pillar of cloud, and not just the cloud, descends, though it stands not within the tent but as a barrier at the entrance of the tent. Similarly, in Deuteronomy 31:15, "The Lord appeared at the tent in a pillar of cloud; the pillar of cloud stood at the entrance to the tent."

Psalm 99:7 reveals a tension in the tradition. The pillar(s) led Israel. That much is certain. Yet, when the pillar of cloud descended, did it provide a *barrier* on the other side of which, inside the tent, God spoke with Moses? Or did God speak *out of* the pillar of cloud? God appears often enough in a cloud,[44] but nowhere, other than Psalm 99:7, does God speak out of a *pillar* of cloud.

Excursus 6

The Dubious Preference for Greek Isaiah 63:7-14

Many interpreters do not explain, in any meaningful way, why they opt for the Greek reading rather than the Hebrew of Isaiah 63:9. C. Westermann offers no explanation for accepting the Greek reading.[45] Nor does P. Hanson.[46]

S. Paul offers as rationale for this decision references to Isaiah 18:2 and Proverbs 25:13, in which צִיר and מַלְאַךְ are synonyms. To defend having the plural noun פָּנָיו the subject of a singular verb, הוֹשִׁיעָם, Paul refers to Lamentations 4:16. Paul then builds upon this interpretation, which is based less on the Hebrew than the Greek, a lengthy statement about anti-angelic polemic.

> A scathing polemic against the belief in angels as emissaries between the Lord and His people is reflected in these verses. The roots of this polemic are already apparent in the earliest layers of tradition regarding the exodus. On the one hand, the Elohistic source (E) emphasizes in Exod 14:19: "The angel of God, who had been going ahead of the Israelite army, now moved and followed behind them"; 23:20: "I am sending an angel before you to guard you on the way"; 32:34: "See, My angel shall go before you"; Num 20:16: "We cried to the Lord and He heard our plea, and He sent a messenger who freed us from Egypt." On the other hand, other traditions negate any type of angelic intercession and emphasize God's sole responsibility for the redemption of His people. Thus according to this tradition God, following the sin of the golden calf, punished Israel by informing them that He shall no longer guide them, and instead appoints an angelic emissary (Exod 32:34, 33:2-3). Upon Moses' intervention (33:12-13), however, God relents; 33:14-15: "And He said, 'I will go (פָּנַי) in the lead.' . . . And he said to Him, 'Unless You (פניך) go in the lead, do not send us up from here;'" The same motif of the Lord's presence, i.e., the Lord Himself leading the nation, appears also in Deut 4:37: "And because He loved your fathers, He chose their children after them. He Himself (בפניך), in His great might, led you out of Egypt." This anti-angelic ideology reverberates in the Passover haggadah (based on *Mekilta de-Rabbi Ishmael, Bo, Pisḥa*, 7 [ed. Horovitz-Rabin, 23]). Compare also *y. Sanh.* 2:1, 20a; *Hor.* 3:1, 47a: "The Lord took us out of Egypt, not by means of an angel, nor through an emissary, nor through a messenger, but it was the Holy One blessed be He by Himself." Compare also *Sifre Deuteronomy* 42 (ed. Finkelstein, 88): "I will grant the rain for your land in season (Deut 11:14). I will grant it, not by an angel, nor by an emissary, nor through a messenger"; *Sifre Deuteronomy* 325 (ed. Finkelstein, 376): "'To be My vengeance and recompense' (Deut 32:35). I shall avenge Myself upon them on My own, not through an angel nor through a messenger."[47]

P.-E. Bonnard explains the textual options but does not offer a clear rationale for his translation, which, he says, follows the *kethiv* reading (see pp. 172–73n10 in this volume) and the Greek.[48] J. Morgenstern joins the chorus of "practically all modern scholars" and interprets verse 9 as the continuation of verse 8 "to regain the proper stichos." Why he prefers צִיר to צָר, he does not explain.[49] L. Brisman writes: "The Septuagint allows us to glimpse what is undoubtedly an earlier version of the text: 'In all their troubles, not a mediator or angel; His Presence saved them—in His love and mercy He saved them.'" He continues with an interpretation, based upon the Greek, "which yields an original text that takes us back to Exodus 33. God's mercy is shown by His willingness to accede to Moses' request, to forget about substituting a minister or angel and to allow *panav*, His face, His Presence, to accompany the people and save them."[50]

J. Goldenstein offers a thorough defense of the preference for the Greek text: "Insofern hat die LXX den glatteren, kunstvolleren Text," notes Goldenstein. The Septuagint also dispenses with "die merkwürdig anmutende und sonst im Alten Testament nirgends belegte Konstruktion des 'Angesichtsengels' Jahwes." Goldenstein concedes that the connection of angel (Engel) and presence (Angesicht) is natural—"Genetisch ist sie vermutlich erklärbar"—based upon passages in Exodus, Numbers, and Deuteronomy, but he demurs and concludes ultimately, "Dennoch bleibt die Formulierung . . . 'Engel seines Angesichts' gleichermaßen einmalig wie sachlich schwierig."[51] Most important for Goldenstein, the theology of the Septuagint, in which the accent lies upon the work of God alone, without the aid of messengers and angels, perfectly fits Isaiah 63:7–64:14. He continues: "In die enge und einzigartige Beziehung zwischen Vater und Sohn bzw. Söhnen will sich die explizite Entsendung eines 'Engels seines Angesichts . . . kaum einfügen."[52] Goldenstein argues that the personal pronoun, הוא, in the following phrase in Isaiah 63:9, can refer to God and God alone, so that "angel of his presence" does not fit. There is simply no room for a mediator; God alone redeems, lifts, and carries Israel.

It is possible to make a few more minor observations about Goldenstein's thoroughly argued but questionable preference for the Septuagint. First, Goldenstein's contention that the pronoun הוא in Isaiah 63:9 excludes the possibility of a mediator figure—God alone lifts and carries and saves Israel—ignores the relationship we observed between the angel and God in our analysis of Exodus 23 and other passages, in which the angel is described with the same verbs as God and in which God's name is said to be in the angel. To suggest that God's lifting Israel is incompatible with the angel of God's presence is to suggest something that violates the presence of divine agents throughout the exodus story. Goldenstein could argue that what is true for Exodus may not be true for Isaiah 40–66, in which God alone saves. This possible response, however, leads to a second smaller point: the spirit functions as just such a mediator in Isaiah 63:14: תֵּרֵד רוּחַ יְהוָה תְּנִיחֶנּוּ. We examine this clause closely elsewhere; for now, it is enough to observe that the spirit descends in order to lead or to give Israel rest. The spirit, in other words, is part and parcel of divine rescue. It looks, therefore, as if Goldenstein and others have driven too sharp a wedge between divine rescue and rescue by divine agents in their preference for the Septuagint over the Hebrew. Such a wedge is not necessary—not from the perspective of the Torah or from the perspective of Isaiah 63 in Hebrew. Third, Goldenstein has already pointed out one of the difficulties of the Septuagint. The juxtaposition of πρέσβυς and ἄγγελος is puzzling, since the angel in the exodus tradition is a divine agent, while an ambassador is invariably, according to Goldenstein, a human agent. Goldenstein, while noting this incongruity, suggests that earthly and heavenly spheres may be represented by this pair, so he offers this paraphrase: "Weder ein Mensch noch ein Engel noch irgendeine andere Macht hat Israel gerettet, sondern allein Jahwe."[53] Fourth and finally, the putatively felicitous pairings Goldenstein identifies in the Old Greek do not necessarily produce a felicitous rhythm, at least according to Blenkinsopp, who finds in Greek Isaiah 63:8b-9a "a very irregular meter and dubious syntax."[54]

If we scan the landscape of this issue, it is possible to see that, when scholars offer a rationale for preferring the Greek reading, it is typically due to the novelty of the Hebrew expression *the angel of his presence*. Blenkinsopp, following the proposal of B. Duhm, who preferred the Old Greek to the Masoretic Text (represented by the *qere* text), offers a clear explanation of this issue. "I note in passing," writes Blenkinsopp, "an interesting issue involved in the much-disputed verse, 63:9a. . . . According to the LXX, Israel was saved not by a messenger or an angel but by the Lord himself. Duhm reproduced this reading: *Nicht ein Bote und ein Engel, sein Angesicht rettete sie* ('It was neither a messenger nor an angel; his Face rescued them'), preferring the LXX to the Masoretic reading represented by the Qere, which corrects the consonantal text.[55] The reason given, that the expression *mal'ak pānîm*, 'the messenger of the Face/Presence,' is unattested, was enough to convince many commentators to follow Duhm's example."[56] Along the same vein, M. Kuntzmann notes that "seule la Vulgate, par une insistance sur la racine *sar* (9a-9b), introduit une phrase nouvelle avec *9a*: 'In omni tribulatione eorum non est tribulatus, et angelus faciei eius salvavit eos.'" He continues vaguely, "Cette solution, cependant, pose des problèmes pour la traduction de l'ensemble du verset."[57] The novel phrase—and novelty must mean unpalatability—must be *angelus faciei eius*. Whybray follows this path, too, though with a more explicit rationale, when he criticizes the Revised Standard Version for translating the *qere* text. He opts instead for the Old Greek, though this solution, he admits, is "not entirely free from difficulties." Still, the Old Greek, he thinks, solves difficulties with the Hebrew. "One of these is that the phrase *the angel of his presence* would be a unique and improbable concept in *OT* times."[58]

This rationale is thin. Many Hebrew phrases are unique, and the criterion of improbability, apart from not being a criterion at all, is so subjective as to be tendentious. As to improbability, this study demonstrates that the combination of angel, presence, and spirit was natural—and not improbable at all.

Excursus 7

Life in Babylon and Palestine during the Neo-Babylonian Era

J. Hayes and J. Miller,[59] I. Provan, V. Long, and T. Longman,[60] M. Moore and B. Kelle,[61] and O. Lipschits[62] deal with the use of extrabiblical data in reconstructing Israelite history. Moore and Kelle offer an excellent summary of how approaches to data lead to divergent opinions about life in Babylonian exile:

> New approaches are significantly reformulating the older consensus view concerning the nature of the Babylonian exile and the experience of the Judeans in that setting. Early in the twentieth century, scholarship reached the consensus view that the Babylonian exile was a reasonably tolerable experience in which the Judean deportees were not held as slaves, but maintained a decent level of freedom and prosperity. While one still finds this view among most historical studies, some recent works have drawn especially upon anthropological research and interdisciplinary reinterpretations of relevant biblical texts, in order to propose a new understanding of exile as a socio-psychological crisis that involved significant suffering and trauma and left an indelible imprint upon the faith and literature of ancient Israel.[63]

On the one hand, Jeremiah's famed letter to the exiles, urging them to build homes, marry, have children, plant gardens, and "seek the welfare of the city where I have sent you into exile, and pray to the LORD on its behalf, for in its welfare you will find your welfare,"[64] suggests that life in Babylon allowed deportees a range of freedom and upward mobility. Further, royal cuneiform tablets from Babylon refer to royal rations for Jehoiachin, once king in Judea: "10 (*sila* of oil) to . . . [*Ia*]-'-, *kin* of *Ia* . . . / 2½ *sila* (oil) to . . . [so]ns of the king of Judah . . . / 4 *sila* to 8 men from Judah."[65] This same Jehoiachin (if they are the same), according to 2 Kings 25:27-30, was released from prison in 561 B.C.E.; this act shows, it is suggested, leniency toward Babylon's captives. Further, among approximately 879 texts from the fifth-century B.C.E. Murashu family, a leading commercial family in Nippur, about eighty Jewish names occur—suggesting that exiles were active in the commercial life of Babylon at least a century later, when these texts were written. D. L. Smith-Christopher discusses the use of the Murashu texts for reconstructing exilic life.[66] Finally, the narrative of the return of exiles post-539 B.C.E., even if exaggerated, hints at the relative wealth of select returnees, who owned slaves[67] and "according to their resources they gave to the building fund sixty-one thousand darics of gold, five thousand minas of silver, and one hundred priestly robes."[68] These bits and pieces of evidence, it is argued, point to a measure of freedom for Babylonian exiles from Judea. Hayes and Miller[69] conjecture that Judean exiles settled in fortified towns that needed rebuilding. They supplied much-needed labor. "The appearance of the term 'tel' in various place names where Judean exiles lived (Tel-Melah, Tel-Harsha, Tel-Abib) could suggest that Judeans were sometimes settled on abandoned or destroyed sites, since 'tel' may mean 'mound' (often a city ruin). The prophet Ezekiel lived in Tel-Abib on the river Chebar (Ezek. 1:3; 3:15)."

On the other hand, these extrabiblical sources—biblical ones are nearly nonexistent—cannot easily be generalized to suggest that all exiles experienced freedom and flourishing. Jeremiah's letter is hardly a sign of success: gardens are to produce food to be eaten rather than sold; homes, while necessary, need not be large; even people in impoverished populations marry and have children; and seeking the welfare of the city in which one sojourns involuntarily is simply sage advice, perhaps even a sign of resignation. Jehoiachin's royal rations are an exception by any count; he was a king, after all. The Murashu texts characterize life a full century later, and the Judeans mentioned in them were small landowners or witnesses to contracts; they did not rise immediately to the upper echelons of Babylonian business.

Though they are scant, a few biblical texts do allow interpreters to tease out some insight into the rigors and restrictions of exilic life after 586 B.C.E. Ezekiel cites the threnody: "Our bones are dried up, and our hope is lost; we are cut off completely."[70] Lamentations charts the wrenching experience of devastation for those in Jerusalem. Add to that forced migration north through Riblah then southeasterly along the Euphrates River to the sacred Mesopotamian city of Nippur in Babylon—hundreds of miles to an unknown, foreign, and largely inhospitable destination. Moore and Kelle[71] suggest that prevalent references to slavery, imprisonment, and suffering in the late exilic poetry of Isaiah 40–55 may also be a lens to life in Babylonian exile.

It may not be possible to garner much about life in Babylon for the Judean exiles, but it is possible to garner several insights. First, the shift from Judea to Babylon was wrenching; the journey itself, even for affluent merchants, which the involuntarily transient Judeans were not, was treacherous and protracted. Second, members of different social classes were probably treated differently; Jehoiachin—if this is the Jehoiachin of 2 Kings—received royal rations, but there is no indication that others not of royal blood received the same treatment. Third, deportation yielded more than one response: Ezekiel would entertain grand visions of reunion, return, and rebuilding; Jeremiah, who was deported to Egypt rather than Babylon, advised caution and accommodation; Second Isaiah, decades later, envisioned a global movement centered upon Jerusalem and prompted by a Persian ruler. Fourth, some Israelites, at least, entered the stream of Babylonian commerce, even if only as small landholders. In short, exile was not a uniform experience; it had a variety of consequences for a diverse range of people.[72]

A brief description of life in the homeland, 586–539 B.C.E., appears in 2 Kings 25:9-26. Jeremiah 37–44 also contains valuable information on life in Palestine post-586 B.C.E., even if it is narrated through the experience of Jeremiah. Destruction was not uniform. According to a fascinating note in Jeremiah 41:4-5, "On the day after the murder of Gedaliah, before anyone knew of it, eighty men arrived from Shechem and Shiloh and Samaria, with their beards shaved and their clothes torn, and their bodies gashed, bringing grain offerings and incense to present at the temple of the LORD." Nebuchadnezzar did destroy many urban centers, but that devastation was not final. Hayes and Miller note:

> Evidence for destruction extends from Tell ed-Duweir (Lachish) in the west, to Arad and environs in the south, to En-gedi and Jericho in the east. This is not to suggest, however, that every Judean city was left in ruins. Primarily those cities that served as fortress towns and where anti-Babylonian sentiment was high would have been the most likely targets for the Babylonians. One area, however, is the exception to the rule. Cities north of Jerusalem, in the traditional territory of Benjamin, suffered little or no destruction.[73]

This means that a pattern of devastation in many Judean cities, including Lachish and Jerusalem, is not the whole story of life in Palestine after 586 B.C.E. P. M. McNutt notes that graves in the Hinnom Valley may mean that people lived outside of Jerusalem post-586 B.C.E.[74]

Another story, in fact, about the depth and breadth of destruction in Judea can be garnered, not by uncovering layers in devastated urban centers, such as Lachish and Jerusalem, and generalizing those findings to rural regions, but through survey-based archeology, which covers swaths of surface rather than discrete layers of remains. Based upon survey studies of pottery, and the like, some archeologists claim that the population growth in many cities remained stable after 586 B.C.E., while others, like Mizpah and other urban centers to the north of Jerusalem, actually progressed and grew. Mizpah, in fact, seems to have been an administrative center for Babylon—an urban locale that grew under Babylonian hegemony. Mizpah provides a subtle but important clue to life in Palestine—that military, commercial, and ritual life in Palestine persisted after the fall of Jerusalem. Hayes and Miller note that "Mizpah remained the political capital of Judah for over a century, from the days of Gedaliah until Nehemiah's refortification of Jerusalem. In support of his cause, Gedaliah seems to have been supported by a contingent of Babylonian (Chaldean) troops or at least advisers (see 2 Kgs. 25:24-25 and Jer. 40:10; 41:3)."[75] A certain Ishmael and his troops murdered the pro-Babylonian governor Gedaliah, his cadre, and the Babylonian military in Mizpah.[76]

Moore and Kelle identify still other sites, such as Ein-Gedi, that show signs of reoccupation during the decades after 586 B.C.E.[77] They go so far as to conclude their discussion of extrabiblical sources by saying that "an increasing number of interpreters assess the data gained through these methods [surface surveys] as indicating that a large percentage, perhaps the majority, of the population remained in Judah after 586, and that the basic societal and cultural life in Judah shows significant continuity with the situation before the Babylonian campaigns, despite the clear devastation that occurred at some major urban sites such as Jerusalem."[78]

Excursus 8

The Date and Provenance of Isaiah 56–66

For a variety of reasons, Isaiah 56–66, known among many scholars as Third or Trito-Isaiah, is notoriously difficult to interpret. First, it may be a composite work rather than the product of a single author; for instance, the unconditional promises of Isaiah 60–62 grate against various conditional promises, in which the people must relieve oppression if salvation is to arrive.[79] It would be simplistic, therefore, to interpret these chapters as the unified composition of a single Persian-era author. Second, there are insufficient historical markers to pinpoint the date of the work as a whole, let alone its parts. On the one hand, much in these chapters could easily be dated during the time of Haggai, circa 520 B.C.E., particularly the sense of poverty and discouragement that permeates these chapters. On the other hand, much could reflect the situation during the lifetime of Nehemiah, circa 445 B.C.E., such as the hope for rebuilding,[80] which is fundamental to Nehemiah's project. This lack of specificity makes it difficult to date these chapters; the championing of foreigners, for instance, could just as readily be understood as a reaction to the tendency of early returnees to be exclusive in worship[81] as to Nehemiah's stringent opposition to intermarriage.[82] Third, it does not look as if Isaiah 56–66 was simply appended to Isaiah 1–39 and 40–55; the scenario is more complicated. It looks as if an editorial hand or hands touched the entirety of the Isaiah corpus during the Persian era. The first and final two chapters of Isaiah as a whole, in fact, create what looks like an editorial "envelope," with themes from the beginning of the corpus reappearing at the end: idolatry in gardens,[83] self-centered choices of worshipers,[84] and the contrasting metaphors of a rotten tree and the tree that is like God's chosen.[85]

Excursus 9

Possible Dates of the Lament of Isaiah 63:7–64:11

Isaiah 63:7-14 provides the opening to a longer lament that spans Isaiah 63:7–64:11 (Hebrew; English 63:7-64:12). The provenance of this lament is notoriously difficult to pinpoint. When was it written, during the exile or after the return from exile? By whom was it written, by those in exile or by those who remained in the land (either before or after 539 B.C.E.)? At issue in particular are those statements that look to the destruction of Jerusalem:

> Your holy people took possession for a little while;
> but now our adversaries have trampled down your sanctuary.[86]
>
> Your holy cities have become a wilderness,
> Zion has become a wilderness,
> Jerusalem a desolation.
> Our holy and beautiful house,
> where our ancestors praised you,
> has been burned by fire,
> and all our pleasant places have become ruins.[87]

To which era in the desolation of Jerusalem do these statements refer? Goldenstein's excellent analysis identifies alternatives. (1) Goldenstein mentions the latest—and unlikeliest—dating: it is a reaction to Antiochus IV Epiphanes' impact on Jerusalem, during the years 175–164 B.C.E., which launched the Maccabean Rebellion.[88] If it was composed this late, how then was it incorporated into the book of Isaiah early enough to be included among the Isaiah scrolls of the Dead Sea Scrolls, some of which may have been copied as early as 125 B.C.E.? (2) Goldenstein cites O. Steck in suggesting a date more than a century earlier, that is, the incursion of Ptolemy I in Syria and Palestine in roughly 301 B.C.E. Goldenstein does not regard it as a separate composition that was later incorporated into Isaiah 56–66 but as an example of scribal prophecy, which gathered prior themes of the Isaiah corpus; in fact, according to Goldenstein, Isaiah 64 was the entire book's conclusion, before Isaiah 65 and 66 were eventually added.[89] (3) According to Goldenstein, T. Cheyne traces it to Artaxerxes III's response to rebellions in Palestine during the years 363 and 345 B.C.E., which led to the suppression of the temple.[90] (4) B. Duhm,[91] with J. Watts following him,[92] dates this lament prior to Nehemiah's mission, when Jerusalem lay in ruins, perhaps at the hands of the Samaritans. Duhm was the first to argue that Isaiah 56–66 is a postexilic composition. (5) J. Morgenstern dates these oracles slightly earlier, after an alleged destruction of Jerusalem under Xerxes in the year 485 B.C.E. He contends, "It can have been only the very same catastrophe to which unmistakable and vivid reference is made in Obadia; Joel 4.2-8; Ps. 44.10-15; 74.1-10; 79; 83.1-10 and in other psalms and likewise in other prophetic writings."[93] The date of this text, as this array of possibilities reveals, is difficult to confirm, rooted as its origins are in hazy memories and uncertain events. As Goldenstein, who opts for a date after 301 B.C.E., notes, "Die entscheidende Schwierigkeit aller Datierungsvorschläge, die sich auf eine Zerstörung oder Entweihung des *Zweiten* Tempels beziehen, ist die, daß die außerbiblischen Quellen so spärlich und oft so wenig zuverlässig sind, so daß es nicht gelingt, sich über die historischen Ereignisse dieser 'dunklen Jahrhundert[e]' ein präzises Bild zu verschaffen."[94]

Arguably the most influential interpretation of Isaiah 63:7–64:11 is the work of P. Hanson. In a thoroughly researched study, Hanson argues that this lament was composed later than Isaiah 40–55 *and* the earlier chapters of Isaiah 56–66—Isaiah 60–62 and 57:14-19. The lament, contends Hanson, reflects the experience of those who remained in Palestine, those who were *not* exiled. Those who remained in Palestine after the collapse of Jerusalem were particularly grieved by the state of the temple.[95] This lament, consequently, reveals "ominous signs that a fatal rift is threatening to divide the community" in the era post-539 B.C.E.[96] Those referred to as "Abraham" and "Israel" in Isaiah 63:5 are the Zadokite leaders, while the unusual reference to God as father[97] "arises from a desperate clinging to Yahweh by a group whose ancestral fathers (Abraham and Israel as eponyms of the nation) have rejected them."[98] Whose voice is heard here? It is "the group drawing upon the prophetic tradition of Second Isaiah in protesting the central community's failure to acknowledge their membership in Israel." "The party registering the protest in 63:7–64:11 against their exclusion from the cult included, perhaps among various other dissident elements, Levitical priests who found that the Zadokite program left no room for them in the restoration cult."[99] While Hanson dates this lament to the period 538–520 B.C.E., his interpretation is uniquely his own. The lament does not represent the voice of the community as a whole, certainly not the returnees, speaking in despair about the state of Jerusalem upon their return from exile. The lament reflects the voice of those whom the Zadokites rejected.

A fragile alliance of scholars contends that Isaiah 63:7–64:11 was composed at some earlier point, probably between 586 and 539 B.C.E. Goldingay writes: "The dissatisfaction that lies behind those chapters and is expressed in Lamentations 5, that Yhwh's inaction has gone on too long . . . implies a dissatisfaction with the fact that Yhwh is not acting in the manner described in 63.1-6."[100] Whybray sets this text after 586 B.C.E., though the absence of the harrowing closeness of Lamentations suggests for Whybray a date during the middle of exile rather than early exile.[101] H. Williamson offers the most substantial challenge to a postexilic date, particularly in the questions he raises about Hanson's reconstruction of the milieu of Isaiah 56–66. First, Williamson questions how reliable an analysis of meter can be to establish the origin of texts, despite Hanson's best efforts to use meter to locate Isaiah 63:7–64:11 in the earliest era of return from exile. Second, Williamson questions why ousted Levites would accord such revered names, Abraham and Israel, to the Zadokite returnees; he also notes how unlikely it is that those in the land would have conceded the name, Israel, to their Zadokite opponents. Third, and most important, Williamson questions why those who had remained in the land would be drawn to Isaiah 40–55, which is occupied with the promise of return from exile rather than prosperity in the land.[102] Why, asks Williamson, would ousted Levites "have been enthusiastic supporters of the return?" In fact, there is little literary evidence, notes Williamson, that they were. Following W. Zimmerli and H. Odeberg's detailed studies, Williamson discovers "very few reminiscences from earlier literature," not least Isaiah 40–55, in Isaiah 63:7–64:11, though on this count, the connections identified by R. Lessing[103] should be taken into consideration.[104]

More constructively, Williamson argues that Isaiah 63:7–64:11 "is a liturgical text from the Palestinian community during the time of the exile."[105] He contends that the historical survey, accompanied by a confession, in the lament's first lines, finds its best parallel in Psalm 106. "Ps 106 remains as the only Psalm in the Psalter to combine historical recital with confession in the manner of Isa 63,7–64,11." Psalm 106 then "draws our attention to the prayer of Neh 9," where further associations emerge, such as "a reference to God's Spirit in association with the wilderness traditions," along with various other elements that connect Isaiah 63:7–64:11 and Nehemiah 9.[106] Nehemiah 9, contends Williamson, is the product of a "Judaean community which was never exiled to Babylon but which continued to inhabit the decimated land during the period of the exile and after."[107] In essence, surmises Williamson, "if, as seems probable, those commentators are right who see Ps 106 as having a similar [late exilic] source, then all three historical recitals with confession [Psalm 106, Nehemiah 9, Isaiah 63:7-64:11] could be taken together as shedding light on the liturgical concerns of the late exilic period, very probably on the ruined site of the temple itself."[108] The difficulty with this sort of argument, of course, is its circularity; the dating of each text depends upon the dating of the others. Still, Williamson's vision of what took place in Palestine—not just among the exiles—is significant and falls in line with what many recent historians and interpreters have said. Israelite history and literature ought not to be based excessively upon clear divisions between preexilic and postexilic eras, since fewer people may have been transported to Babylon than the books of Ezra and Nehemiah may indicate and, equally important, people who remained in Palestine maintained worship, possibly centered in Mizpah, along with an agrarian lifestyle that, if not robust, was at least sustainable.

It may not be quite so important, then, to pinpoint a date of origin for Isaiah 63:7–64:11 in either the exilic or postexilic era; it may not even be possible. Some interpreters, in fact, conclude that the paucity of historical data in Isaiah 56–66 provides a heuristic key to these chapters, so that interpreters should *not* try to squeeze historical conclusions about date and provenance from these chapters. Lessing, for instance, argues that "excessive historical speculation on Isaiah 56–66 is not helpful. Efforts to ascertain historical specificity go beyond the design of the text. To conduct an overzealous search for chronological details is to read against the grain. The issues of dates and times must be subordinated to Isaiah's overarching theological concerns."[109] Even the desolation of the temple may not necessarily be considered an historical marker, notes J. Muilenburg, "since we are dealing with poetry in an eschatological context."[110]

Plausible chronological parameters for the composition of this lament consist probably of the fall of Jerusalem in 587 or 586 B.C.E. and the mission of Nehemiah in approximately 445 B.C.E. As to authorship, the lament's provenance could be among the exiles or the people who remained in the land. In this respect, the relationship to Isaiah 40–55 cuts both ways. A relative dearth of indisputable allusions to Isaiah 40–55 may point to a composition in Palestine rather than among the exiles, who produced Isaiah 40–55; the inclusion of this lament (if the lament was independent in the first place), on the other hand, in the Isaiah corpus may suggest that ancient interpreters had less difficulty with the inclusion of this lament after Isaiah 40–55 than do some modern interpreters.

In summary, some influential scholars regard Isaiah 63:7–64:11 (Hebrew; English 63:7–64:12) as an independent unit that was incorporated into the body of Isaiah 56–66. Given the fresh memory it preserves of the destruction of Jerusalem, some interpreters regard it as an exilic composition that predated 539 B.C.E. and became integral to Isaiah 56–66. Others tie this memory to the period just after the return from exile, while the temple still lay in ruins; these scholars see this as part and parcel of the postexilic composition identified as Isaiah 56–66. Still other scholars tie Isaiah 63:7–64:11 to later events that entailed the devastation of Jerusalem. In light of the looseness with which it is necessary to hold positions on the origin of this lament, including its exilic or postexilic date and its Palestinian or exilic provenance, it may be judicious simply to concede that it is a product of the late Babylonian or early Persian eras, composed and edited either in exile or Palestine. From the standpoint of this study, this may be enough: *Isaiah 63:7–64:11 contains an opening lament written before—possibly nearly a century or more before—the mission of Nehemiah in 445 B.C.E.*

Excursus 10

The Vision of the Temple in Isaiah 56–66 and Zechariah 1–8

Though they play no key role in the present study, the oracles in Zechariah 1–8, from a presumed Persian-era prophet, should be mentioned. Like Isaiah 56–66, Zechariah sees the need for a combination of justice and fasting. Zechariah asks whether the people should fast, as they had during exile. The answer is yes. The obligation to fast was given to prophets long before exile.[111] Then, immediately on the heels of this support for the continued practice of fasting, come these words:

> The word of the LORD came to Zechariah, saying: Thus says the LORD of hosts: Render true judgments, show kindness and mercy to one another; do not oppress the widow, the orphan, the alien, or the poor; and do not devise evil in your hearts against one another. But they refused to listen, and turned a stubborn shoulder, and stopped their ears in order not to hear. They made their hearts adamant in order not to hear the law and the words that the LORD of hosts had sent by his spirit through the former prophets. Therefore great wrath came from the LORD of hosts.[112]

The prophets who commended fasting were precisely the prophets whom Israel resisted through a rejection of justice toward the poor. By implication, the continued practice of fasting during the Persian era was to be accompanied by a keen commitment to justice.

The relationship between fasting and justice is bolder and less stereotypical in Isaiah 56–66 than in the prophecy of Zechariah. Still, both draw that connection, just as both support a commitment to sustained worship in the temple, though the commitment of Isaiah 56–66 is muted and occasional, as opposed to Zechariah 1–8, in which temple worship is a central element of the prophecy. Isaiah 56–66 also points away from the earthly temple in ways that Haggai and Zechariah do not. God inhabits "eternity" and dwells "in the high and holy place" and with the "contrite and humble in spirit."[113] The high and holy place is not Mt. Zion but a heavenly sanctuary. Later, in lament, God is asked to "look down from heaven and see, from your holy and glorious habitation."[114] In other contexts, such as Psalm 46, these words refer without doubt to the earthly temple; they do not here. Finally, Isaiah 66:1-2 implies that God no longer dwells in a temple made with hands:

> Thus says the LORD:
> Heaven is my throne
> and the earth is my footstool;
> what is the house that you would build for me,
> and what is my resting-place?
> All these things my hand has made,
> and so all these things are mine,
> says the LORD.
> But this is the one to whom I will look,
> to the humble and contrite in spirit,
> who trembles at my word.

This point of view is rooted in Solomon's claim at the dedication of the first temple that God is not confined to anywhere on earth;[115] Solomon, according to the story of the temple dedication, recognized this while championing the earthly temple. Isaiah 66 makes no room for an earthly temple at all. Isaiah 66:1-3 also has antecedents in Ezekiel's prophetic impulse. Ezekiel saw God enthroned on a chariot with wheels that traveled simultaneously in every direction[116] and was no longer limited to the earthly temple in Jerusalem; he saw, too, the glory depart in stages from the earthly temple because of its gross and growing sinfulness.[117] Yet Ezekiel still envisaged a rebuilt temple, ideal in lines with a priesthood holy in lineage, but a temple nonetheless.[118] The prophet of Isaiah 66 imagines no such temple, no equivalent resting place for God.

Excursus 11

Second Exodus in Isaiah 40–55

B. Anderson lists several texts as exemplars of the second exodus theme: Isaiah 40:3-5; 41:17-20; 42:14-16; 43:1-3; 43:14-21; 48:20-21; 49:8-12; 51:9-11; 52:11-12; 55:12-13. Not all of these, however, are undisputed references to a second exodus.[119] Recently, the presence of a second exodus theme in Isaiah 40–55 has come under severe scrutiny. H. Barstad, for instance, argues that

> as everyone familiar with the message of Second Isaiah will well know, the desert, or the wilderness, plays an important role in this prophet's message. Quite commonly, these occurrences of the "desert motif," as well as of other, "related" texts, are being referred to by biblical scholars as "exodus texts," and viewed as giving expression to the return of the exiled Judeans through the desert from Babylon back to Jerusalem, thus constituting a "new exodus." Those scholars who refer to these texts as "exodus texts," however, have failed to recognize the strongly metaphorical character of these texts.[120]

O. Lund comes to a similar conclusion:

> Previous exegesis has, in the main, sorted [verses] into two distinct groups, and these two groups of verses are treated in different ways and with clearly varying interest. In the first group one finds verses that, one assumes, help to create an implied story. This story imagines and describes a forthcoming second Exodus from Babylon to Jerusalem. It is assumed that the relevant way-passages in this interpretation refer to physical roads, preferably in an actual desert between Babylon and Jerusalem. It is assumed, further, that these verses predict that YHWH will transform this actual desert into fertile land to give the people water. In addition, YHWH will provide roads in the desert to ease the people's journey between Babylon and Jerusalem. One assumes, in this interpretation, that the main intention of the book is, primarily, to convince the people that YHWH both can and will lead them back to Jerusalem, and, further, that the people are to be ready now to go at the command of YHWH.[121]

Lund documents the scholarship that follows this interpretative trajectory. Another group of so-called way texts, according to Lund, scholars treat as metaphorical.[122]

A pivotal example of the important effort to undermine the view that a new exodus theme permeates Isaiah 40–55 occurs right away, in the opening oracle, Isaiah 40:3-5. Recent scholars have argued that this text, notwithstanding a reference to a way in the wilderness and the glory of God, does not contain an explicit reference to the return of Babylonian exiles. Barstad notes: "Of all the passages in Second Isaiah that have been taken as allusions to the return of the exiles from Babylon to Jerusalem through the desert, the most famous, and the one most frequently quoted, is undoubtedly Is 40:3-11." He cites a list of scholars who hold to this opinion.[123] He then argues:

> The message of this prophet is really very simple: Again and again he is trying to persuade his audience that Yahweh has forgiven them, and that they must put their trust in him as their god. If they do this, the nation will prosper again, and the inhabitants of Jerusalem and Judah shall raise [*sic*] from the wretched state in which they now find themselves. Within the context of national restoration there belongs also the return to Zion of Judeans from abroad. This event, however, comprises the return of exiles not only from Babylon, but from the whole of the diaspora. The return from the diaspora, again, constitutes only a part of the total restoration, which includes full political and religious restoration, victory over Yahweh's enemies, etc.[124]

As to whether this is a prediction of return from exile, J. Blenkinsopp writes:

> It is not stated, here at the beginning, that the message is an assurance of a proximate return to the homeland addressed to Judeo-Babylonians [exiles]. Juxtaposition with the prediction of exile in Babylon immediately preceding (39:5-8) might suggest this, as also the summons to leave Babylon with which this section ends (48:20-22). But for the moment all we are told is that Jerusalem, representing the people, has served its time of indentured service. . . . There is no mention here of preparing a route for return from exile in Babylon. It is, rather, that a processional way is to be prepared for the return of Yahveh to his people. Given what we imagine to be the state of roads at that time, this would have been normal procedure in preparation for the visit, the *parousia,* of a dignity.[125]

Several aspects of the argument against seeing a second exodus as a theme in Isaiah 40–55, though valid in undeniable ways, should, I propose, be nuanced. The first has to do with the presumed Babylonian origin of these chapters. It is argued that the idea of a second exodus would be important principally from a Babylonian, exilic perspective, but a Babylonian origin, while possible, is anything but certain. Nonetheless, a return from the diaspora to Jerusalem would naturally have been a part—perhaps an essential part—of restoration, just as a reuniting of the northern and southern kingdoms could be a part of restoration (e.g., Amos 9). In fact, Barstad, though opposed to the importance of a second exodus for Isaiah 40–55, admits, "Within the context of national restoration there belongs also the return to Zion of Judeans from abroad."[126]

The second argument in need of nuance is the distinction between metaphorical and historical. Scholars opposed to a second exodus theme tend to accuse their predecessors of failing to see the metaphorical dimension of the putative second exodus texts in Isaiah 40–55. In my opinion, the distinction between metaphorical and historical, between ways of living and actual physical ways or roads, seems to lack a certain resilience. In fact, it distorts our perception of Isaiah 40–55, where redemption, a way in the sea, a path in the waters, the death of chariot and horse, a way in the desert, and water in the wilderness are elements that evoke the exodus and, more important, are projected onto a future action of salvation, in which Babylon will be broken. This is indeed a second exodus and a second act of provision in the desert, though, of course, not exactly in the same way, since the sea and desert must by historical circumstance be different. The allusions are so strong, however, that it is imperative to see the future event imagined by the author of Isaiah 40–55 as similar in scope to the event of liberation from Egypt and provision in the wilderness. It was possible, in my opinion, for authors ca. 550 B.C.E., whether in Palestine or Babylon (or Egypt, for that matter), to regard anticipated liberation as analogous to the exodus and the occupation of Palestine. The category of allusion, in fact, bypasses the bifurcation of metaphor and history. It might have been possible to believe that God was about to do something akin to the exodus without actually imagining which road God would reconstruct through whichever desert in order to transport exiles to Jerusalem.

Third, scholars such as Barstad and Lund are right to issue a word of caution about seeing new exodus as a, perhaps *the*, dominant theme of Isaiah 40–55. This consensus, thanks in large measure to their work, may have seen better days. Yet there is no reason to throw out the baby with the bath; there may in fact still be, in certain texts, the conviction that God was about to do something along the lines of the exodus for a population—especially devastated *urban* segments of that nation, including Jerusalem—disrupted by exile. Other texts in Isaiah 40–55 must not be overlooked in an effort to debunk a long-held scholarly consensus that Isaiah 40–55 is rife with the language of a new exodus.

Fourth and finally, it is important to take into consideration that other authors before and after the author of Isaiah 40–55 saw the possibility of restoration in terms of a new exodus. Ezekiel and Jeremiah, like Hosea centuries earlier, had found hope in the possibility of a new exodus and a new Sinaitic covenant. Even the author of Ezra–Nehemiah would portray return from exile with the hues of exodus. The situation is not as if the author of Isaiah 40–55 were a lone voice; he or she was not.

Excursus 12

Haggai 2:4-5 as a Gloss

Satisfactorily resolving the matter of the Hebrew original—the textual issue—does not lead to a dismissal of literary questions, the most significant of which W. Beuken raises when he argues that nearly all of Haggai 2:4-5 is the product of the so-called Chronicler's final redaction of the book of Haggai.[127] This, we should note, does not damage the thesis of this study of the spirit; it simply sets these words a century or so later than the period 538–516 B.C.E. The origin of pneumatology still lies within the purview of the Persian era.

Beuken sees Haggai 2:4-5 as a later redaction for several reasons. First, more generally, the book is written in the third person, which suggests the hand of an editor. It is possible, of course, that the prophet wrote in the third person; it is more likely that an editor included chronological data and addressees. This observation opens the door to the likelihood of later editing.

Second, these particular verses, contends Beuken, interrupt the clear flow of Haggai 2:3 and 6-9. Without Haggai 2:4-5, these verses read:

> Who is left among you that saw this house in its former glory? How does it look to you now? Is it not in your sight as nothing? For thus says the Lord of hosts: Once again, in a little while, I will shake the heavens and the earth and the sea and the dry land; and I will shake all the nations, so that the treasure of all nations shall come, and I will fill this house with splendor, says the Lord of hosts. The silver is mine, and the gold is mine, says the Lord of hosts. The latter splendor of this house shall be greater than the former, says the Lord of hosts; and in this place I will give prosperity, says the Lord of hosts.

Several words recur in verses 3 and 6-9: *this house*, *glory*, and *former*.

Beuken's third observation concerns the language of Haggai 2:4-5, which, he contends, reflects the language of 1–2 Chronicles. The absolute use of the verb עשׂה occurs in 1 Chronicles 22:11-16, 28:10; 28:20; 2 Chronicles 19:11; and Ezra 10:4. Equally significant, the form of these sayings Beuken characterizes as an Amtseinsetzungsschema; this form authorizes those in leadership to *do* (עשׂה) something. "Es kann sein," proposes Beuken, "das wir hier es mit einer chronistischen Formvariante zu tun haben, erkennbar am absoluten Gebrauch von עשׂה, das in nichtchronistischen Anwendungen des Amtseinsetzungsschemas nie vorkommt."[128] He concludes more certainly about this intrusive but significant statement in Haggai 2:4-5: "Es liegt darum auf der Hand, im Rahmen von so vielen anderen Hinweisen auf eine chronistische Endredaktion von Haggai, anzunehmen, daß dieses Stück aus einem chronistischen Milieu stammt, umsomehr als es durch seinen Inhalt nicht gut ins Ganze dieses Komplexes paßt."[129]

The Chronicler has not, however, invented this saying entirely. Originally a statement directed to "all you people of the land," it was not yet an *Amtseinsetzungsschema*. That transformation took place only when the editor added references to the governor, Zerubbabel, and the high priest, Joshua. Only then did this invest the saying with a sense of official authorization, argues Beuken. "Auf diese Weise erweiterte er das Prophetenwort zu einem Amtseinsetzungsschema, wie es auch anderswo im chronistischen Werk gebraucht wird."[130] This transformation, which resulted in conformity between the Chronicler's perspective and this saying, also had the less felicitous effect of producing an awkward transition by interrupting the literary flow between Haggai 2:3 and 2:6-9.

This transformation of the original statement had serious theological consequences, says Beuken. The reference to the spirit's standing does *not* comprise an allusion to the pillars of the exodus, notwithstanding commentators' tendency to discern a relationship between the exodus and Haggai 2:4-5. This, Beuken contends, places too much emphasis upon the Chronicler's gloss, with its reference to the exodus. Much more important is the role of the spirit in the Chronicler's history, where the primary connection is between the spirit and the prophet's word. In Nehemiah 9, for instance, the reference to the spirit has to do with Moses the prophet. On a related note, exilic prophets connected the spirit to the expectation of salvation. Therefore, "der Chronist, im Bewußtsein lebend, daß die neue Heilzeit, wenngleich noch nicht vollkommen, durch den Geist schon begonnen war, betrachtete die Prophetie, heute und in der Vergangenheit, als Wirken Jahwes."[131] This statement has profound implications for understanding Haggai 2:4-5, which is not, according to Beuken, a statement about God's spirit in the context of liberation from Egypt; the promise of Haggai 2:4-5, contends Beuken, "schließt ein, daß er durch seinen Geist, d.h. durch das begeisternde Wort der Propheten, die Träger der Autorität, die jetzt ihre Amtseinsetzung empfangen, und die neu gebildete Kultgemeinschaft zu Jerusalem wieder führen werde."[132]

With this interpretation of Haggai 2:4-5 as a gloss that transforms a statement to the whole of the people into official authorization of the prophets, Beuken identifies the work of the spirit in Haggai 2:4-5 with the *prophetic* word. Gone is the allusion to the exodus. Absent is the connection to the pillars that provided protection and guidance. This is an authorizing word for prophets—one prophet, in particular, according to Beuken. "Durch seine Propheten wird Jahwe die ganze Gemeinschaft führen. Das ist schon greifbar geworden im Beschluß, den Tempel wieder aufzubauen: das Volk wurde durch das Wort Haggais dazu bekehrt, die Initiative dazu lag bei den Führern."[133]

A couple of potential weaknesses in Beuken's argument should be noted. First, redactional interpolations are notoriously difficult to identify, void of textual evidence. What appears to be an intrusion to an interpreter such as Beuken may seem like a natural movement to another interpreter.

Second, and more to the point, it may be errant to view the reference to the exodus as a gloss, which interrupts the flow from Haggai 2:3 to Haggai 2:6-9, as Beuken does. This argument against Beuken's point of view develops in three stages. (1) Beuken himself notes that Haggai 2:6-9 corresponds to Haggai 2:20-23; they comprise dual pillars of the book.[134] (2) Haggai 2:20-23, to which Haggai 2:6-9 corresponds, contains allusions to the exodus tradition.

> The word of the LORD came a second time to Haggai on the twenty-fourth day of the month: Speak to Zerubbabel, governor of Judah, saying, I am about to shake the heavens and the earth, and to overthrow the throne of kingdoms; I am about to destroy the strength of the kingdoms of the nations, and overthrow the chariots and their riders; and the horses and their riders shall fall, every one by the sword of a comrade. On that day, says the LORD of hosts, I will take you, O Zerubbabel my servant, son of Shealtiel, says the LORD, and make you like a signet ring; for I have chosen you, says the LORD of hosts.

There is no need to point out the parallels between Haggai 2:6-9 and Haggai 2:20-23, as they are obvious. It is no stretch to agree with Beuken that these are the pillars of the book of Haggai in its present form. What does need to be pointed out is the presence of exodus language, such as the overthrow of chariots and riders (Exodus 15:4), of horses and riders (Exodus 15:1), in Haggai 2:20-23. Simply put, future salvation is portrayed with language reminiscent of the exodus. Even the language of chosenness is reminiscent of the first reference to chosenness in the book of Deuteronomy, in which direct appeal is made to the exodus: "And because he loved your ancestors, he chose their descendants after them. He brought you out of Egypt with his own presence, by his great power."[135] (3) If Haggai 2:20-23 contains allusions to the exodus, then it is entirely possible that Haggai 2:4-5, which precedes Haggai 2:6-9, to which Haggai 2:20-23 corresponds, also contains allusions to the exodus. In other words, there is no need to posit that the allusion to the exodus in Haggai 2:4-5 is a gloss when Haggai 2:20-23 also contains allusions to the exodus.

D. Peterson offers a concise summary of Beuken's argument, though without the level of critique I have offered.[136] R. Mason offers a critical appraisal of Beuken in general.[137] The burden of proof, in my opinion, lies with Beuken, who discerns in Haggai 2:4-5 a gloss composed by the hand of the Chronicler. It is entirely possible—it is even likely, in my view—that his hypothesis stretches beyond the evidence—and that the allusion to the exodus in Haggai 2:4-5 belongs where it is.

Excursus 13

Ezekiel and the Torah

In an effort to establish the chronological relationship between the book of Ezekiel and the Deuteronomic and the Priestly sources of the Mosaic Torah, R. L. Kohn attempts to identify a combination of Priestly and prophetic traditions in the book of Ezekiel. She identifies: (1) legal citations in Ezekiel to Priestly laws;[138] (2) "terms or expressions used with a specific meaning in P which appear with a skewed or antithetical meaning in Ezekiel";[139] and (3) terms and expressions from the exodus and wilderness periods adopted by Ezekiel, such as tabernacle language, oddly enough, used in contexts other than the vision of the restored temple.[140] Often, notes Kohn, "numerous terms and expressions with positive connotations in P exhibit negative overtones in Ezekiel. It is as if Ezekiel parodies P language by using terms antithetically. This is especially true of language describing P's Exodus."[141] This suggests for Kohn that borrowing is from the Priestly source to Ezekiel rather than vice versa. "Ezekiel, writing in exile, reevaluated P's portrayal of Israel's uniqueness, cynically inverting these images such that what was once a 'pleasing odor to Yahweh' now symbolizes impiety and irreverence." In terms of dependence with respect to the theme of a new exodus, Kohn argues:

> Ezekiel, like Jeremiah and Second Isaiah, envisions the future restoration of Israel as a "Second Exodus" where Yahweh, through various miracles and wondrous feats, will once again rescue the Israelites from oppression in exile. Thus, terms and concepts found in reference to the first Exodus experience and Yahweh's original covenant with Israel are recycled in prophetic visions of the future. One of Ezekiel's sources for the Exodus/Wilderness event appears to be P. The prophet's recollections of these events and his subsequent hope for a "Second Exodus" must logically be based upon P's initial telling of the story.[142]

The reverse scenario, that P's account of the Israelite exodus from Egypt is modeled primarily upon Ezekiel's prophecies of restoration, is plausible, but the preponderance of evidence examined above, argues Kohn, suggests otherwise.

Further establishing this connection between the prophet and the Priestly Mosaic tradition, Ezekiel's language of restoration mirrors the original language of Israel's earliest experiences. In both exodus and restoration, "they will know that I am the LORD their God."[143] In both, they will dwell secure,[144] and God will dwell among them.[145] God even made a *covenant of peace* with Phinehas, Aaron's grandson; Ezekiel promises a *covenant of peace* to all Israel.[146]

Kohn makes these observations about the language of the Priestly material and Ezekiel.[147] She also examines what she considers the influence of

Deuteronomic material on Ezekiel. Kohn considers Ezekiel to be a liminal figure whose prophecy is a confluence of Deuteronomic and Priestly material intended to offer the exiles a hopeful future.[148]

> As a prophet of the Exile, Ezekiel was forced to confront, analyze and interpret Israel's past. In doing so, he looked back to Israel's written sources. Ezekiel's visions concerning the redemption and future restoration of Israel fuse Priestly and Deuteronomic concepts with many of the prophet's own ideas. The people will be redeemed by Yahweh who, "with an outstretched arm," will bring them to the land that was sworn to their forefathers (Ez 20,33-42). These visions of Judah restored amount to nothing less than a "Second Exodus," this time not from Egypt but from Babylonia. Like Jeremiah, Ezekiel foresaw a new covenant assuring the people's future well-being and security. While never mentioning Moses of old, Ezekiel in fact portrays *himself* as a new Moses.[149]

A range of studies of the relationship of Ezekiel to the Torah, such as J. Levenson's, exist. Among them, H. McKeating observes that Ezekiel's three key visions (Ezekiel 1–3, 8–11, and 40–48) correspond to Moses' visions first at the bush, then at Sinai, then on the final mountain (Nebo).[150] R. G. S. Idestrom limits her analysis to the book of Exodus but explores its relationship to the entirety of Ezekiel.[151] J. Evans looks more generally at the book of Ezekiel.[152] N. DeLapp offers a synthesis of secondary research.[153] In contrast to these wider-ranging studies of Ezekiel, Levenson principally compares Numbers with Ezekiel 40–48.[154]

NOTES

Chapter 1

1 E. Mesch, *Hans Leisegang: Leben und Werk* (Erlangen and Jena: Palm und Enke, 1999), 15. Leisegang was awarded the Bonitz Prize of 1200 Viennese krone from the Wiener Akademie der Wissenschaften on July 7, 1916.

2 H. Leisegang, in his preface to *Der heilige Geist: Das Wesen und Werden der mystisch-intuitiven Erkenntnis in der Philosophie und Religion der Griechen*, vol. 1, part 1, *Die vorchristlichen Anschauungen und Lehren vom ΠΝΕΥΜΑ und der mystisch-intuitiven Erkenntnis* (Leipzig: Teubner, 1919), iv. Translation mine, as are all translations of otherwise untranslated German works. Mesch (*Hans Leisegang*, 15–16) discusses Leisegang's military career.

3 Leisegang, *Die vorchristlichen Anschauungen und Lehren vom ΠΝΕΥΜΑ und der mystisch-intuitiven Erkenntnis*. See "Excursus: Hans Leisegang and the Freedom of Inquiry" for an overview of Leisegang's hard-won career. Throughout the book, excurses allow further scholarly consideration of discrete topics that are otherwise important but not essential to the narrative.

4 Anne Lamott talked about this dimension of writing as far as the headlights shine in a public lecture at Perkins School of Theology, Southern Methodist University, on November 14, 2017. This notion is consonant with her guidance on writing in *Bird by Bird: Some Instructions on Writing and Life* (New York: Pantheon, 1994).

5 While it would be simpler perhaps to refer to the holy spirit rather than to pneumatology, I use the latter term advisedly in order to reinforce that Israelite authors during the Babylonian and Persian eras understood the spirit in a way that later Christian authors would as well, that is, as other than an impersonal power or force. The study of the holy spirit in Israelite and Jewish texts is not merely prolegomenon to pneumatology. It *is* pneumatology proper. It is occupied with the holy spirit—*God's* spirit—acting on the plane of human history. Despite all of the provocations and problems it may raise, the term *pneumatology*, which is typically used to describe *Christian* pneumatology, allows

the opportunity to communicate that ancient Israelites and Jews were occupied with realities that would later occupy Christian authors.

6 Leisegang, *Der heilige Geist*, 4.

7 Leisegang, *Der heilige Geist*, 240. The principal ancient example of an author who used the Septuagint as a vehicle of Greco-Roman conceptions is first-century Alexandrian philosopher Philo Judaeus, who, according to Leisegang, proved to be the most important author in Antiquity for understanding the origin of Christian pneumatology because Greco-Roman conceptions of the spirit could be distilled from the Jewish veneer that overlay them in Philo's oeuvre. "Philos Anschauungen zwar tief im griechischen Volksglauben wurzelten, daß er aber die Volksvorstellungen bereits durchtränkt mit griechischer Philosophie übernahm und den Prozess der Veredelung und Vergeistigung des ursprünglich recht ungefügen und rohen Materials bis zu einer staunenswerten Verfeinerung fortführte, so daß sich der Volksglaube unter seinen Händen zu einer philosophischen Religion der Gelehrten umgestaltete."

8 This study is limited to texts from Israel and Second Temple Judaism, including ones included in the New Testament. The best starting points for postbiblical Jewish understandings of the spirit, in chronological order, include J. Abelson, *The Immanence of God in Rabbinical Literature* (London: Macmillan, 1912); H. Parzen, "The *Ruaḥ Haḳodesh* in Tannaitic Literature," *JQR* 20 (1929–1930): 51–76; P. Schäfer, *Die Vorstellung vom Heiligen Geist in der Rabbinischen Literatur* (Munich: Kösel, 1972); M. Isaacs, *The Concept of the Spirit: A Study of Pneuma in Hellenistic Judaism and Its Bearing on the New Testament* (London: Heythrop College, 1976); W. Davies, *Paul and Rabbinic Judaism: Some Rabbinic Elements in Pauline Theology*, 4th ed. (Philadelphia: Fortress, 1980), 177–226; G. Cage, *The Holy Spirit: A Source Book with Commentary* (Reno, Nev.: Charlotte House, 1995); M. Turner, *Power from on High: The Spirit in Israel's Restoration and Witness in Luke-Acts* (Sheffield: Sheffield Academic, 1996); J. Levison, *The Spirit in First Century Judaism* (Leiden: Brill, 1997); F. Philip, *The Origins of Pauline Pneumatology: The Eschatological Bestowal of the Spirit upon Gentiles in Judaism and in the Early Development of Paul's Theology* (Tübingen: Mohr Siebeck, 2005); V. Rabens, *The Holy Spirit and Ethics in Paul: Transformation and Empowering for Religious-Ethical Life* (Tübingen: Mohr Siebeck, 2010). The best starting points on the spirit in the Dead Sea Scrolls, which do not feature in this study, include O. Seitz, "Two Spirits in Man: An Essay in Biblical Exegesis," *NTS* 6 (1959–1960): 82–95; G. Johnston, "'Spirit' and 'Holy Spirit' in the Qumran Literature," in *New Testament Sidelights: Essays in Honor of Alexander Converse Purdy*, ed. H. McArthur (Hartford, Conn.: Hartford Seminary Foundation, 1960), 27–42; P. Wernberg-Møller, "A Reconsideration of the Two Spirits in the Rule of the Community in 1QSerek III,13–IV,26," *Revue de Qumran* 3 (1961): 413–41; H.-G. Kuhn, *Enderwartung und gegenwärtiges Heil: Untersuchungen zu den Gemeindeliedern von Qumran mit einem Anhang über Eschatologie und Gegenwart in der Verkündigung Jesu* (Göttingen: Vandenhoeck & Ruprecht, 1966); A. Sekki, *The Meaning of* Ruaḥ *at Qumran* (Atlanta: Scholars, 1989); R. Kvalvaag, "The Spirit in Human Beings in Some Qumran Non-biblical Texts," in *Qumran between the Old and New Testaments*, ed. F. Cryer and T. Thompson (Sheffield: Sheffield Academic, 1998), 159–80; J. Frey, "Flesh and Spirit in the Palestinian Jewish Sapiential Tradition and in the Qumran Texts: An Inquiry into the Background of Pauline Usage," in *The Wisdom Texts from Qumran and the Development of Sapiential Thought*, ed. C. Hempel, A. Lange, and H. Lichtenberger (Leuven: Leuven University Press, 2002), 367–404; J. Levison, "The Two Spirits in Qumran Theology," in *The Uniqueness of Qumran Theology*, vol. 2, *The Bible and the Dead Sea Scrolls*, ed. J. Charlesworth (Waco, Tex.: Baylor University Press,

2006), 169–94; E. Tigchelaar, "Historical Origins of the Early Christian Concept of the Holy Spirit: Perspectives from the Dead Sea Scrolls," in *The Holy Spirit, Inspiration, and the Cultures of Antiquity: Multidisciplinary Perspectives*, ed. J. Frey and J. Levison (Berlin: De Gruyter, 2014), 176–240.

9 Isaiah 63:11.

10 Haggai 2:5.

11 See "Excursus: Locating Influence."

12 I use traditional Christian language for the Jewish Scriptures here to underscore a typical Christian distinction.

13 Haggai 2:5.

14 Isaiah 63:11-14.

15 Throughout this study, I refer to various figures in the Hebrew Bible—the pillars of the exodus, the angel of the exodus, the presence-face or *pānîm* of God, and the spirit—as agents. I do not use this term in a technical sense. According to my colleague, philosophical theologian William Abraham, who has written *Divine Agency and Divine Action*, vol. 1, *Exploring and Evaluating the Debate* (Oxford: Oxford University, 2017); and *Divine Agency and Divine Action*, vol. 2, *Soundings in the Christian Tradition* (Oxford: Oxford University, 2017), with two further volumes on agency soon to appear, the notion of agency is a radically open concept, which defies definition. It leaves open possibilities ranging from impersonal (e.g., chemical) to personal agency. In the historical era that is the subject of our study, we discover an early intimation of the pillars, the angel, the *pānîm*, and the spirit as agents. What an agent is, however, is not entirely clear, not even to Abraham. Perhaps I can circumscribe how these ancient agents were understood by delineating how they were *not* understood. They are not metaphors of divine involvement; there are no literary clues to suggest they are metaphors. They are not speech acts, leading to personification. They are not hypostases or hypostatizations, unlike in later rabbinic and Christian thinking. (I address the inadequacy of the term *hypostasis* in the conclusion.) To quote my colleague, the stories and psalms and prophecies that refer to these ancient agents "articulate in a minimal fashion that we are dealing with a personal agent, distinct from YHWH, and intimately involved in the actions of YHWH in history." Much more could be said, but it is essential simply to lay down the parameters on agents and agency early in this study: the terms *agents* and *agency* are descriptive, deriving meaning principally from the ancient texts themselves. While I am aware that an interpreter brings a framework to his or her study, I have tried to create space in which the narratives, poems, and prophetic oracles of Antiquity can shape that framework in an ever-evolving conversation.

16 There is little precedent for a shared path, even in studies of divine presence that clear the way for collaboration between Jews and Christians. More than a century ago, a Welsh-born rabbi in England, Joshua Abelson, created a compendium on the topic, titled *The Immanence of God in Rabbinical Literature* (cited above). While he devoted more than one hundred pages to the holy spirit, Abelson discovered the immanence of God principally in the shekinah—God's abiding presence in Israel. Decades later, Jürgen Moltmann turned primarily to the shekinah as well in order to grasp the spirit of life in the Jewish Scriptures; Moltmann's pneumatology is discussed in the conclusion. Michael Lodahl, in *Shekinah/Spirit: Divine Presence in Jewish and Christian Religion* (New York: Paulist, 1992), discovers in the shekinah the presence of God that is accessible to Jew and Christian alike. While the word occurs 378 times in the Hebrew Bible, with 11 more occurrences in the Aramaic portions of the book of Daniel, *rûaḥ* still plays a subsidiary role to the

shekinah in Christian discussions of divine presence intended to embrace Judaism. The centrality of shekinah rather than *rûaḥ*, therefore, becomes a troubling cipher for the ambiguous place of the spirit in studies of the presence of God—and the challenge of generating a pneumatology that embraces both its Jewish point of origin and a long history of Christian reflection.

17 During the decades leading up to and throughout the research period of Marshall and Warren, the most common treatment of ulcer disease was the taking of antacids, which was followed by the first acid secretion–inhibition drug (cimetidine/Tagamet in 1976), followed by other drugs, such as Zantac and Pepcid, followed in the late 1980s by the first proton pump inhibitor—an even more potent acid secretion inhibitor—omeprazole/Prilosec, followed by still other drugs. It may be that pharmaceutical companies envisioned a long-term use of these acid-inhibiting drugs and were dismayed when it became apparent that there was an infectious cause of ulcers that could be cured with rather basic, nonexotic, oral antibiotics, removing the potential for lifelong use of acid inhibiting drugs.

18 A synopsis of this story can be found in P. Allen, "What's the Story *H. pylori?*" *Lancet* 357 (2001): 694. Marshall and Warren's first article on the topic appeared in the *Lancet* 323 (1984): 1311–15, titled "Unidentified Curved Bacilli in the Stomach of Patients with Gastritis and Peptic Ulceration."

19 This is the title of S. Terrien's significant study, *The Elusive Presence: Toward a New Biblical Theology* (San Francisco: Harper & Row, 1978).

Chapter 2

1 Isaiah 63:11-13, 15. Translations are normally from the NRSV, though I make many modifications. I will note when I offer my own translations and modifications.

2 In my prose, I avoid gendered language with respect to God, but it is extremely difficult to do so in the quotation of translations and, occasionally, in citations of the Hebrew text, such as this instance, where "God's" may say too much and "the" too little.

3 In beautifully crafted prose, professor of English Leslie Brisman identifies the multiple voices of the exodus tradition in "On the Divine Presence in Exodus," in *Exodus*, ed. Harold Bloom (New York: Chelsea House, 1987), 107.

4 Judges 2:1-4.

5 Psalm 78:14; 99:7; 105:39; Nehemiah 9:12, 19-20.

6 Numbers 14:13-14.

7 Brisman ("Divine Presence," 107), taking his cue from the consensus of scholarship, reflects on the eventual victory of the Priestly tradition: "The pillar of fire and cloud are spoils of the conquest. They are taken over from J by P and made to stand, at the very end of Exodus, for the triumph of Priestly vision." The alleged Priestly tradition, it should be noted, does not efface the others. It caps or concludes them, at least in this single book, but other traditions are left in place as testimony to God's implacable presence at the start of Israel's life as a nation.

8 Exodus 14:19-24.

9 Exodus 14:24.

10 Exodus 23:20-23.

11 Exodus 33:2-3, 14-15.

12 This unshakable question about God's elusive presence leads not to a seamless answer but to further questions concerning the manifestation of that presence. Was it an angel or a pillar—or both—that moved from the front of Israel to the rear to protect the fugitives

from their Egyptian pursuers (Exodus 14:19-20)? Could God's angel ever be an adequate agent of God's presence (Exodus 23:20-23; 33:1-15)? Was it not an agent at all that guarded Israel fore and aft but God, God's very self, as Isaiah 52:12 would have it? "For you shall not go out in haste, and you shall not go in flight; for the LORD will go before you, and the God of Israel will be your rear guard." Is this where theology should lead—to God and God alone sans a coterie of agents? Or is that the wrong way to put it? Was God's presence so identified with these agents, however uncertain their exact identities, that one would be remiss to distinguish God from God's agents?

13 Elements of other texts, such as Psalm 139:7, Psalm 143:10, and Nehemiah 9:12, 19-20, may represent the spirit in a similar way, though without the clarity of Isaiah 63:7-14 and Haggai 2:4-5.

14 T. Mann (*Divine Presence and Guidance in Israelite Traditions: The Typology of Exaltation* [Baltimore: Johns Hopkins University Press, 1977]) offers a thorough analysis of many of these elements, both exegetically and in the context of the Ancient Near East. He pays relatively little attention to the angel or messenger, interprets presence-face (*pānîm*) simply to mean "I," and devotes much more attention to the cloud than does this study. He ignores *rûaḥ* altogether. Laura Feldt discusses the relationship between the exodus tradition, autobiography, and collective memory in two articles. Without addressing the multiple agents of the exodus, she nonetheless deals with the nature of collective memory in interesting ways in "Exodus: Ritual, Cognition and Memory," *Collegium Biblicum Årsskrift* 15 (2011): 49–66. According to Feldt's analysis (50), Jan Assmann "distinguishes between two phases of collective memory: communicative memory, corresponding to the phase when multiple narratives by participants and eyewitnesses circulate and compete with each other, and cultural memory proper, corresponding to the much longer phase when all eyewitnesses and participants have died out and a society has only relics and stories left as a reminder of past experience." Traditions of divine agents defy this sort of development. All genres and phases of Israel's collective memory—prose, poems, and prophetic logia—preserve the characteristics of Assmann's earliest phase of memory, in which "multiple narratives by participants and eyewitnesses circulate and compete with each other." Israel's memory of divine agents never lost its sense of vitality and internal conflict. Feldt deals with this topic similarly in "Dis/orientations—Fantastic Memory in the Exodus Narrative," in *Literature and Memory: Theoretical Paradigms, Genres, Functions*, ed. A. Nünning and R. Sommer (Tübingen: Francke, 2006), 95–111.

15 Exodus 13:20, 14:2.

16 Exodus 13:21-22, modified.

17 Mann (*Divine Presence and Guidance*, 144) writes simply, "In Exod 13.21-22 the motif of divine presence and guidance was condensed in a passage that, in effect, constituted a paradigm. . . . [T]he same holds true for Num 9.15-23. In each of these passages, the frequentative aspect of the verbs shows that the authors were describing a customary mode of divine presence and guidance that, presumably, held true for Israel's entire journey through the wilderness. To this extent Yahweh was seen as being always present with his people."

While this study focuses neither upon the Ancient Near Eastern context nor upon putative sources (Exodus 13:21-22 is generally attributed to J, Exodus 13:17-18 to E), it is important to note correspondences with Ancient Near Eastern mythology. In this respect, Mann (*Divine Presence and Guidance*, 131) writes of Exodus 13:21-22: "Not only the highly poetic character of these lines, but also the particular image of 'going before' . . . in combination with 'cloud' and 'fire,' present remarkable similarities to the vanguard motif of the Near Eastern texts. Just as here, where it prepares us for the battle of the

Reed Sea, so in the Tukulti-Ninurta Epic the same type of imagery suddenly appears at the onset of the final battle with Kashtiliash. Assur leads in the vanguard . . . with a devouring flame. . . . Enlil is also there with a burning fire, and Adad uses the familiar flood . . . as his weapon. Behind this fearsome assembly the king marches to battle, just as the author of the biblical text pictures Israel marching behind the cloud and the fire in which Yahweh acts as their guide. As we have seen, very similar language is found in numerous other literary texts and in the Assyrian annals." Mann discusses Ancient Near Eastern texts in *Divine Presence and Guidance*, 27–105.

Mann discusses other dimensions of the pillar in "The Pillar of Cloud in the Reed Sea Narrative," *JBL* 90 (1971): 15–30: (1) the alleged provenance of the pillar in the Sinai theophany (15–19, where Mann discusses the proposals of M. Noth and W. Beyerlin); (2) the provenance of the pillar of cloud in Ugaritic texts, in which the cloud is a messenger of God (19–24, where Mann rejects the views of Beyerlin and Noth and suggests instead that the cloud's provenance "must be found in the Canaanite mythology surrounding the storm deity, his messengers, and weapons of divine warfare" [23]); (3) the relationship between the ark, the cloud, and the tent (24–30, where Mann traces the provenance of the cloud to the crossing of the Jordan River). Mann (25) notes the similarity between Exodus 33:14 and Numbers 10:33-34, the fact "that the cultic theophany connected with Yahweh's *pānîm* is directly related to the ark" (a view he attributes to W. Beyerlin), and the linking of the ark and the cloud via a background in the Canaanite storm motif. On this basis, he concludes "that the ark is to be understood as the cultic background of the J narrative of the Sea event, and that this narrative thus reflects the cultic background of Joshua 3-5 and Exodus 15" (27). In short, the background of the cloud and its "function in the J account of the Sea event also reflect the Jordan crossing from the *Sitz im Leben* of the ark cult at Gilgal." Mann's analysis is illuminating though not essential because the interest in this study lies in the *interpretation* of the exodus narrative rather than, as in Mann's study, its *origin*.

18 Still another question is whether the pillar is two sided, with light on one side and darkness on the other. W. Propp (*Exodus 1–18: A New Translation with Introduction and Commentary* [New York: Doubleday, 1999], 499) suggests that "rabbinic sources imagine the pillar as fire on the Israelite side and cloud on the Egyptian side." C. Houtman (*Exodus: Historical Commentary on the Old Testament*, 4 vols. [Kampen: Kok, 1993], 2:267) refers to the Targums, which suggest that the cloud was dark on one side and light on the other. The Targums to Exodus 14:20 read:

וְעָל בֵּין מַשְׁרִיתָא דמצראי וּבֵין מַשְׁרִיתָא דִּיִשְׂרָאֵל וַהֲוָה
עֲנָנָא וְקַבְלָא לְמִצְרָאֵי וּלְיִשְׂרָאֵל נָהַר כֹּל לֵילְיָא וְלָא
אִתְקָרַבוּ דֵּין לְוָת דֵּין כֹּל לֵילְיָא

Another possibility is that the pillar is two phased, giving light during the night and protection (e.g., from the desert sun) during the day. Propp (*Exodus 1–18*, 499) comments on Exodus 14:24: "But I find Bekhor Shor's solution the most attractive: at dawn, the pillar is in transition between its two aspects. The same notion might clarify 14:20." Regardless of how one resolves the nature of the pillars in Exodus 14, it is evident that only *one* pillar exists, in contrast to the dual pillars of fire and cloud in Exodus 13:21-22, and that this pillar is composed of fire *and* cloud. If Exodus 14:20 be understood in light of 14:24, it would seem that the narrator conceived of one pillar that could function as protector and illuminator—in short, as cloud and fire. This entire scene, however, resists easy resolution.

19 In Genesis 26:8, the king of the Philistines looked through the window and saw Isaac "playing with" Rebekah. In 2 Kings 9:30, 32, Jezebel saw Jehu through the window, and he saw her

through the window. The motif of looking through a window as a narrative device/metaphor for the confrontation of power, as in this text, can be illustrated by Michal's watching David through the window of the palace as he dances in the street in 2 Samuel 6:16.

20 Deuteronomy 1:33. I have retained the wording of NRSV, "who goes before you" (הַהֹלֵךְ לִפְנֵיכֶם), but changed the order because, in the Hebrew, only the pillar of fire seems to light the way.

21 The tradition of divine accompaniment continues in Deuteronomy. Divvied up into tribes under appointed administrators, the Israelites press on to Kadesh-barnea, south of the promised land, where they reject Joshua and Caleb's advice to take the land. For Moses, the God who carried them in the wilderness like a parent who carries a child (Deuteronomy 1:30), now goes before the Israelites and fights for them. The pillars, not incidentally, play no role in divine guidance at this point in Deuteronomy.

22 Psalm 78:14. This lengthy psalm twice narrates the guidance God provided from Egypt to the promised land (78:12-16 and 44-55), followed by Israel's unfortunate rebellion (78:17-20 and 56-58). Wedged between references to the splitting of the Sea (78:13) and the wilderness rock (78:15) occurs a reference to the cloud and fire. This is probably a northern psalm, composed prior to 722 B.C.E. but brought south after Assyrian destruction, where it was edited more extensively.

23 Psalm 105:39. My translation. On my preference for the translation *partition*, see below. It is not clear in this psalm whether the cloud and fire are separate entities, like the pillars of cloud and fire of Exodus 13:21-22, or one entity that is both cloud and fire, like the pillar of cloud in Exodus 14:19-24.

24 Nehemiah 9:19.

25 An intimate association between God and the pillars occurs both at the beginning and the conclusion of the first brief glimpse of the pillars. The description of God's guiding presence begins, "The LORD went *in front of* them." It ends by recalling that neither pillar departed "from *in front of* them." Is three a crowd in front of Israel? Two pillars and one God? No. The LORD was, as the text says clearly, *in* the pillars.

26 The root נחה, "to lead," was easily confused with the root נוח, "to rest." I will explore this in depth in the analysis of Isaiah 63:7-14.

27 A summary occurs in Numbers 14:14: "and your cloud stands over them and you go in front of them (הֹלֵךְ לִפְנֵיהֶם), in a pillar of cloud by day and in a pillar of fire by night."

28 According to Exodus 13:17, they could also avoid the Egyptians by taking a circuitous route, hence the need for guiding pillars. God avoids the direct route through Philistia, along the coast. God worries, apparently, that a war with the Philistines will discourage the Israelites and prompt a wholesale return to Egypt.

29 This emphasis upon *leading* is evident in the repetition of the verb הָלַךְ. The LORD traveled (הֹלֵךְ) in front of the people. And the pillars? The pillar of fire, in particular, brought light so that they, the people, could travel (לָלֶכֶת) by day and night. Apparently, the people did not set up camp in the evening and break it down in the morning; they traveled, escaped, fled by day and night, thanks to these pillars, which led them as they journeyed.

30 In Exodus 24, the experience is profound but short-lived, limited by a relatively brief trek up the mountain.

31 In Exodus 33:17-23, Moses' experience of God is fleeting and oblique.

32 In Numbers 11:16-30, seventy elders outside the camp, along with two who remain inside, are able to prophesy because God distributes the spirit that is upon Moses to them. Typically, prophecy is understood in this text to be ecstatic frenzy. I offer an alternative

interpretation, which ties this experience to that of Moses and the elders in Exodus 24, in "Prophecy in Ancient Israel: The Case of the Ecstatic Elders," *CBQ* 65 (2003): 503–21.

33 The occurrence of the participle rather than a verb in the perfect tense is an indication that God's journey was continual, God's presence constant.

34 This verb is not, as might be expected, a perfect tense; it is imperfect, יָמִישׁ, and should, consequently, probably be translated iteratively: "*would not leave* its place."

35 N. Sarna (*Exodus: The Traditional Hebrew Text with the New JPS Translation* [Philadelphia: Jewish Publication Society, 70]) observes how the participle suggests "continuous occurrence" and that Exodus 13:22 "emphasizes the uninterrupted nature of the manifested Divine Presence."

36 Exodus 15:22–18:27.

37 Exodus 33:3.

38 Numbers 11:1-3.

39 Numbers 11:34.

40 Numbers 14:12.

41 It is difficult to describe the nature of the pillars. Houtman (*Exodus*, 2:254) suggests that the pillar is a bank of clouds rather than a cloud. Sarna (*Exodus*, 70) views the pillars as "actually a diaphanous, luminescent mist visible both by day and by night."

42 Haggai 2:5.

43 Exodus 14:19-20, 24.

44 The verb נסע, translated "pulled out," typically occurs before Israel disembarks and moves ahead in their wilderness sojourn (Exodus 16:1; Numbers 10:5, 12, 17). In this passage, however, it communicates movement from one position to another—but not a sojourn.

45 The unbroken sequence of the story—from pillar of cloud to cloud—suggests that *cloud* is shorthand, in this scene, for *pillar* of cloud. They are one and the same. How does a pillar of cloud illuminate the night? This is an activity that might be expected of the pillar of fire, which is nowhere to be seen. The text of Exodus 14:20 reads literally, "And there was the cloud and the darkness, and it [the cloud or the darkness] illuminated the night, and this did not draw near to this all night" (Exodus 14:24, my translation). In light of Exodus 13:21-22, with its neat distinction between the pillars of cloud and fire, this description of the pillar of cloud as a night light is confusing. What has happened to the pillar of fire? According to Propp (*Exodus 1–18*, 499), "We receive the distinct impression from 13:21 that the pillar is *either* cloud or fire, not *both*." Naturally, tensions within the text lead to many interpretations. V. Hamilton (*Exodus: An Exegetical Commentary* [Grand Rapids: Baker Academic, 2011], 213) offers a lucid discussion. Houtman (*Exodus*, 2:268) and Propp (*Exodus 1–18*, 498) document further conjectures, including the interpretations of medieval commentators. Propp (*Exodus 1–18*, 549) also identifies the cloud as smoke, in which case, smoke (cloud) and fire are complementary images. For further discussion, see "Excursus: The Cloud in the Wilderness," below.

46 Nehemiah 9:19.

47 Numbers 14:14. All but effaced by the tradition of a dense cloud that covered the tabernacle by day and night, the pillars that appeared in Exodus 13:21-22, and just as quickly disappeared, once again see the light of day. Even the participial form of "travel" (הלך) and the prepositional phrase "in front of them," which were first used to describe God's traveling in the pillars, reemerges to describe how God is now traveling in the pillar. The parallel is striking.

48 Deuteronomy 1:33. This addition may be a matter of context. Deuteronomy 1:33 is set in a context of rebellion (Deuteronomy 1:26-33). The element of rebellion is traceable

to Numbers 14, where Joshua and Caleb speak to their recalcitrant and reluctant fellow Israelites, "Only, do not *rebel* [אַל־תִּמְרֹדוּ] against the Lord; and do not fear the people of the land, for they are no more than bread for us; their protection is removed from them, and the Lord is with us; do not fear them" (Numbers 14:9). In short, God can find suitable land for the people, just as God discovered encampments along the way.

49 Psalm 78:14, where the elasticity of the tradition once again comes to light. First, the psalmist leaves out that the cloud and fire were pillars, possibly to maintain the rhythm of the psalm. (On the dominant 3+3 meter, see H.-J. Kraus, *Psalms 60–150: A Commentary* [Minneapolis: Fortress, 1989], 122–23.) Second, he or she refers shorthand to a *light of fire*, a light that came from a fire, rather than a fire that gave them light. The ability to abbreviate Exodus 13:21 without explanation may indicate how embedded this element of the tradition was; readers of the psalm would have recognized in the "light of fire" the pillar of fire that gave their ancestors light.

50 Exodus 13:21-22; 14:20. This emphasis on duration throughout the night may be traceable to Exodus 14:20, in which the pillar of cloud left the front of the camp to maintain a position between Egypt and Israel. The cloud (it is one pillar of cloud, not two pillars, in Exodus 14:20) "lit up the night; one [camp] did not come near the other all night." The phrase "all night long" (וְכָל־הַלַּיְלָה), in Psalm 78:14 is identical to the phrase "all night" (כָּל־הַלָּיְלָה) in Exodus 14:20. Perhaps, then, the source of this emphasis is Exodus 14:20, though that verse is hardly necessary to explain why a poem might contain praise for a fiery light that illuminated the camp all night long during the journey from Egypt to the promised land.

51 Psalm 105:39. C. Broyles (*Psalms* [Grand Rapids: Baker, 2012], 330) and A. A. Anderson, (*The Book of Psalms*, 2 vols. [London: Oliphants, 1972], 2:734) think this is a reference to protection from the desert sun: God "spread a cloud for a covering" (NRSV).

52 Hebrew: מָסָךְ.

53 Exodus 27:16; 35:17; 38:18; 40:8; 40:33.

54 In the second line of Psalm 105:39, the purpose of the fire is "to give light by night." This brief statement does not offer immediate clarity on the purpose of the light—whether to illumine, protect, or lead. On the one hand, the Hebrew hiphil infinitive construct form of the verb in the psalm mirrors the hiphil infinitive construct in Exodus 13:21, "to give them light," which suggests that the purpose of the fire is to lead Israel along their journey to the promised land. On the other hand, the recurrence of the same verb in the hiphil stem in both this psalm and Exodus 14:20 is also noteworthy: "The cloud was there with the darkness, and it lit up the night." In light of the close association of the partition cloud with Exodus 14:20, it is probable that the purpose of the fire in Psalm 105:39 is principally to protect, rather than to lead, Israel, though these tasks are not mutually exclusive.

55 There is another option, as well. According to Exodus 33:9, "When Moses entered the tent [of meeting outside the camp], the pillar of cloud would descend and stand at the entrance of the tent, and the Lord would speak with Moses." Against this background, the simple statement that God "spread a cloud for a covering [*screen*]" recollects those times when Moses met with God face to face, with Joshua in attendance and the pillar of cloud marking the occasion at the tent's entrance. This allusion seems less likely, given that the emphasis in Psalm 105 lies upon God's protection and provision and, more significantly, that the events recounted recall Exodus 13–17.

56 Kraus (*Psalms 60–150*, 312) suggests that the cloud "is not (as in Exod. 13:21f.; Ps. 78:14) the cloud that led the way, but a covering, protective power (Exod. 14:19;

Wis. 10:17)." The fire, notes Kraus, serves a different purpose. "But the fire lights up the night (showing the way)." It may not be prudent to attribute different purposes to the cloud and fire, as Kraus does, given their reminiscence of Exodus 14:19. It is likely that Exodus 14 lies behind Psalm 105:39. The events cited in this section of the psalm follow the order of Exodus 13–14: silver and gold (Exodus 12:33-36), cloud and fire (Exodus 13:21-22, 14:19-24), quails (Exodus 16:13-21), water from the rock (Exodus 17:1-7). Given this explicit order, the reference to the cloud should probably be understood as a reflection of Exodus 13–14—especially 14:19-20, where the cloud forms a protective partition or screen between the Israelites and Egyptians.

57 Exodus 14:19-20.

58 A. Fischer ("Moses and the Exodus-Angel," in *Angels: the Concept of Celestial Beings—Origins, Development and Reception*, ed. F. Reiterer, T. Nicklas, and K. Schöpflin [Berlin: De Gruyter, 2006], 79–91) attributes the apparent redundancy to redaction. Fischer argues that all of the angel texts in Exodus belong to a supplementary redactional layer, the product of an "angel-redactor" (90).

59 The presence of the angel is attributable, on a source-critical level (if one accepts this analysis) to the presence of a second version of guidance. In the Jahwist's version, the pillars lead Israel; in the Elohist's (northern) version, the angel does. The angel, then, is included, though the primary story line belongs to the Jahwist.

60 William Shakespeare, *Macbeth*, 5.5.2382–83.

61 Isaiah 63:7-14.

62 See "Excursus: The Identity of the Angelic Messenger" for a consideration of various scholarly interpretations of the angel's function and relation to YHWH.

63 The Book of the Covenant (Exodus 20:22-23:33) is generally regarded as among the most ancient law codes in Israelite literature.

64 Exodus 23:20-24.

65 The position of this promise toward the conclusion of the Book of the Covenant is puzzling, since it is only loosely related to the laws in Exodus 20:19–23:33. This apparent dislocation prompts B. Childs (*The Book of Exodus: A Critical, Theological Commentary*, OTL [Louisville, Ky.: Westminster John Knox, 2004], 461) to this conclusion: "In my opinion, the passage was a sermon which once served a homiletical purpose in Deuteronomic circles in connection with the occupation of the promised land. It is much closer to Deut. 7 than Deut. 26. It was placed in its present position as a conclusion to the Book of the Covenant, but specifically because of the dominant emphasis on the land, which emerged in the last section (23:14ff.). The section is not really related to the whole Book of the Covenant—it is not a parenesis on obeying the law—but is a homily on the proper use of the land." Childs suggests that the older source includes Exodus 23:20-22, 25b-31a and that verses 23-25*aa* and 31b-33 comprise a Deuteronomic insertion. For further discussion, see "Excursus: Identity of the Angelic Messenger," below.

66 Exodus 23:20 reads: "it will guard you (לִשְׁמָרְךָ) on the way" to the promised land.

67 The angel will, literally, "cause [them] to come (וְלַהֲבִיאֲךָ)." Though this is a common expression, there is more than accompaniment here; there is cause as well, not least in the hiphil stem of the verb *to come*. The angel brings the people to the land.

68 Exodus 23:20, 23.

69 The phrase "my angel will *travel in front of* you" (יֵלֵךְ מַלְאָכִי לְפָנֶיךָ) is already familiar from Exodus 14:19, which describes, with a participle, "the angel of God who *was traveling in front of* the Israelite camp (מַלְאַךְ הָאֱלֹהִים הַהֹלֵךְ לִפְנֵי מַחֲנֵה יִשְׂרָאֵל)." That participle had occurred in Exodus 13:21-22 to describe the movement of God: "The Lord *was traveling in front of*

them (וַיהוָה הֹלֵךְ לִפְנֵיהֶם)." In Exodus 13:21-22 and 14:19, God and the angel took exactly the same action; here again, in Exodus 20:23, the angel similarly will travel in front of Israel.

70 The verb שָׁמַר, describes the actions of both the angel and Israel.

71 This inflection, תַּמֵּר, is difficult to parse. Its root, probably מָרַר, was easily confused with מָרָה, "to rebel." The Septuagint translators understood this verb as "rebel," ἀπείθει, as did the Greek translation of Aquila, the Syriac, and the Targums. This verse is missing from the Dead Sea Scrolls. Propp (*Exodus 1–18*, 136) discusses alternatives. The Targums understand the root as "to rebel," while adopting a different word: וְלָא תְסָרֵיב. W. Gesenius (*Genesius' Hebrew Grammar* [Oxford: Clarendon, 1988], paragraph 67g, y) regards this confusion as the effect of Aramaizing. He elsewhere discusses the close connection between מָרַר and מָרָה (77e).

72 Not only did God command this already (23:21); now the Hebrew form includes an infinitive absolute, שָׁמוֹעַ תִּשְׁמַע—a sign of emphasis that is difficult to translate (v. 22). Perhaps "You shall obey—absolutely obey him" conveys the strength of this syntax.

73 This nuance is unmistakable, for example, in Genesis 21:12; 27:8; and Exodus 18:19.

74 See "Excursus: The Identity of the Angelic Messenger."

75 Propp (*Exodus 1–18*, 288) elucidates Ibn Ezra's interpretation.

76 Houtman (*Exodus*, 3:275) ponders whether כִּי in Exodus 23:21 is causal or concessive. Must Israel obey *because* the angel will not forgive or *although* the angel will not forgive? Though the text can be interpreted to mean that Israel must obey *because* the angel will not pardon sins, Houtman wonders whether it should be read to mean that Israel must obey *although* the angel cannot pardon sins: such forgiveness is entirely God's prerogative. The following words, "since my name is in him," tip the balance toward the causal interpretation: Israel must obey because (כִּי) the angel will not forgive sins *because* (כִּי) God's name is in him.

77 Isaiah 63:10.

78 Exodus 32:7-14.

79 Exodus 32:15-24.

80 Exodus 32:25-29.

81 Exodus 32:30-31.

82 Exodus 32:33-34.

83 Exodus 32:35.

84 Hebrew: לֵךְ נְחֵה.

85 Hebrew: הֹלֵךְ.

86 Hebrew: לַנְחֹתָם.

87 Exodus 13:21. Moses would sing, after the escape from Egypt, "In your steadfast love you led [נָחִיתָ] the people whom you redeemed; you guided [נֵהַלְתָּ] them by your strength to your holy abode" (Exodus 15:13).

88 Exodus 32:35.

89 Exodus 33:1-2.

90 This may be a moot point because God's next statement is, if not a reversal, at least a drastic change of course. English translations of Exodus 33:3 smooth out the syntax; the Hebrew is edgier and more clipped:

> *English* (NRSV): Go up to a land flowing with milk and honey; but I will not go up among you, or I would consume you on the way, for you are a stiff-necked people.
>
> *Hebrew* (my translation): Go up to a land flowing with milk and honey, since I will not go up in your midst, since a stiff-necked people [are] you, lest I finish you on the way.

This statement, in Hebrew, if not in English translations, is disconcerting through and through. The beginning is disturbing: the Hebrew lacks an opening imperative. The start is jagged, rushed perhaps, maybe rude: "to a land flowing with milk and honey." The conclusion is just as jagged, rushed perhaps, maybe ominous: "lest I destroy you along the way." The opening and closing syntax anticipate the ragged, broken conversation that will transpire between God and Moses.

91 Exodus 13:21-22.

92 Exodus 14:24.

93 Hamilton, *Exodus*, 558.

94 W. Propp, *Exodus 19–40: A New Translation with Introduction and Commentary* (New York: Doubleday, 2006), 565. Propp summarizes Spinoza on this point: "by granting his people a Messenger (understood as a guardian angel) rather than his own presence, Yahweh demotes Israel to the status of other nations" (598). W. Beyerlin (*Origins and History of the Oldest Sinaitic Traditions* [Oxford: Basil Blackwell, 1965], 23) regards Exodus 33:3b-6 as characteristic of the perspective of the Elohist: God remains on Sinai, while the people, punished, are dismissed from where God dwells.

95 Exodus 33:4-6.

96 Numbers 20:14-16.

97 Theirs is a history in three simple stages: (1) adversity, with many days of ancestral oppression in Egypt; (2) liberation, when the Lord heard their cry, sent an angel, and brought them out of Egypt; (3) a journey, abbreviated so succinctly as to be assumed rather than described: "and here we are in Kadesh."

98 This angelic prerogative is apparent in Exodus 23:23, which reads: "When my angel goes in front of you, and brings you to the Amorites, the Hittites, the Perizzites, the Canaanites, the Hivites, and the Jebusites, and I blot them out." In the book of Numbers, Edom is the first nation Israel encounters in their orientation toward Canaan. Edom, however, is not one of those enemies in Canaan whom God will destroy, according to Exodus 23:20-23, so this answer to the question "Why the angel?" is somewhat unsatisfying.

99 In the episode that precedes Moses' recital to Edom, prior to arriving at Kadesh, Israel rebels against Moses and Aaron. As a result, Moses strikes the rock with his staff and produces water, though not before addressing the people as "those who rebel (הַמֹּרִים)" (Numbers 20:10). However, the onus lies too with Israel's leaders, whom God chides: "Because you did not trust in me, to show my holiness before the eyes of the Israelites, therefore you shall not bring this assembly into the land that I have given them" (Numbers 20:12). Then, in the episode that follows this recital, in which Israel sets out from Kadesh, Aaron dies. The explanation is put ambiguously. "Let Aaron be gathered to his people," God commands, "for he shall not enter the land that I have given to the Israelites, because you rebelled (מְרִיתֶם) against my command at the waters of Meribah" (Numbers 20:24). The verb, *you rebelled*, is a second-person plural addressed either to Moses and Aaron together or to Israel as a whole, whom Moses had characterized as "those who rebel." Regardless of whether the people as a whole or only Moses and Aaron are those who rebel, unambiguous references to rebellion precede and follow Moses' narration of Israel's past. These references to rebellion may explain Moses' inclusion of the angel, against whom the people should not rebel. "Be attentive to him and listen to his voice; do not rebel against him," warned God, "for he will not pardon your transgression; for my name is in him." Whatever the reason for the inclusion of the angel at this point in Israel's narrative, stories such as these provide concrete examples of what happens when Israelites, including Moses and Aaron, rebel against the angel whom God sent to liberate them.

100 It is difficult to know with what gender to refer to the angel. The neuter, *it*, seems too impersonal. Rather than alternating between *he* and *she* or using *he/she* (or some variation of it), I will resort simply to *he*, even if there is an off chance that the angel in these narratives is conceived of as feminine.

101 Judges 2:1.

102 Prior to this text, the final mention in Torah of an angel of God occurs in the story of Balaam (Numbers 22:35), though there is no direct connection here between that angel and the angel of the exodus. Neither Deuteronomy nor the book of Joshua makes mention of an angel that led Israel during the exodus and wilderness wanderings. In principle, Judges 2:1-5 could refer to any divine messenger that migrated from Israel's first place of worship in the land (Joshua 4:19; 5:9), where Joshua began to distribute the territories to the tribes (Joshua 14:6). The angel could be any divine messenger, since, according to T. Butler (*Judges*, WBC 8 [Nashville: Thomas Nelson, 2009], 39), the phrase *angel of Yahweh* appears fifty-eight times in the Jewish Scriptures, and the angel *of God* another nine times. The content associated with the angel's prerogatives, however, suggests otherwise. Further, Mann (*Divine Presence and Guidance*, 20) refers to Judges 2 in a discussion of Joshua 1:3-9: "It is significant that the form of divine presence in Exodus 23 (the *ml'k*) is not mentioned here [Joshua 1:3-9]. However, it is—almost certainly—a figure that appears in 5:13-15 (not D), 'the commander of the hosts of Yahweh. . . .' This passage is clearly a truncated example of the call narrative, and is very similar to Exod 3.1-6, and originally related the formal commissioning of Joshua. It is likewise related to Judg 2.1a, where the *ml'k yhwh* goes up from Gilgal to Bochim. Both texts are thus strategically placed at the moment when Israel is poised for the Conquest. But, whereas Josh 5.13-15 now is merged with the stunning victory in ch. 6, Judg 2.1a is joined to vss. 1b-5, which admonish Israel for covenant transgression in terms very similar to Exod 23.20-33." The similarities between Judges 2 and Exodus 23, of course, are not surprising, given the figure of the angel in both. See also "Excursus: The Identity of the Angelic Messenger" below.

103 Judges 2:1-3. G. Juncker ("Jesus and the Angel of the Lord: An Old Testament Paradigm for New Testament Christology" [Ph.D. diss., Trinity Evangelical Divinity School, 2001], 123–24) notes that what the angel says resumes prior statements, particularly Exodus 23:20-23, and that "in each instance, the words quoted were originally spoken by YHWH with no indication that an angel was speaking."

104 Exodus 14:19; 23:20-23; 32:34; and 33:2.

105 Exodus 14:19.

106 Exodus 23:20-23; 23:24.

107 Exodus 33:2.

108 An analogous move occurs in Deuteronomy 4:37, when the presence-face of God, which in Exodus led the people only from Sinai onward, became the agent of deliverance in Egypt. By collapsing exodus and land taking, it can be said that God "brought you out of Egypt with his presence, by his great power, driving out before you nations greater and mightier than yourselves, to bring you in, giving you their land for a possession, as it is still today" (Deuteronomy 4:37-38).

109 Exodus 23:22.

110 My preference for *presence-face* is due to the multivalence of the Hebrew פָּנִים. Despite some inelegance, this translation captures the *palpable* dimension of God's presence, which must be borne in mind by an interpreter, especially in light of Moses' demand in Exodus 33:14-15.

111 The words *holy spirit* occur elsewhere in the Hebrew Bible in Psalm 51.

112 See "Excursus: God and Moses' Conversation in Exodus 32–33."
113 Exodus 32:34; 33:2-3.
114 Exodus 33:4-6.
115 Exodus 33:7-8.
116 Exodus 33:12.
117 Exodus 33:14. Hebrew: פָּנַי יֵלֵכוּ וַהֲנִחֹתִי לָךְ.
118 Sarna (*Exodus*, 213) writes: "Moses, sensitive to God's omission of any mention of Israel, reacts immediately by stressing the people's interests, thereby affirming once again that he sees his own reputation inextricably bound up with the fate of his people."
119 Childs, *Exodus*, 566.
120 Exodus 33:15-16.
121 Exodus 33:17. God even agrees to Moses' unverified claim that God knows him by name: "I will do the very thing that you have asked; for you have found favor in my sight, and I know you by name." Earlier, Moses had claimed, "See, you have said to me, 'Bring up this people'; but you have not let me know whom you will send with me. Yet you have said, 'I know you by name, and you have also found favor in my sight.' Now if I have found favor in your sight, show me your ways" (Exodus 33:12-13).
122 J. Durham, *Exodus*, WBC 3 (Waco, Tex.: Word, 1987), 448. The sequence of this negotiation is clear even if its meaning is not: 1) Twice God reiterates the initial promise that the angel will lead Israel (Exodus 33:1-3). In the second iteration, however, God cajoles, "but I will not go up among you" (Exodus 33:3). This promise, notwithstanding the caveat of divine reclusion, would seem to be enough to cinch the negotiation. It is not. 2) Moses virtually ignores this firm promise—repeated by this point in the story three times—when he claims, "See, you have said to me, 'Bring up this people'; but you have not let me know whom you will send with me" (Exodus 33:12). Is this ingratitude? Insensitivity? Intentional obtuseness? 3) Whatever Moses' motivation, God promises God's presence-face: "My presence will go with you, and I will give you rest" (Exodus 33:14). With this concession, the real point of the negotiation comes to the fore: Will God accompany Israel—or just Moses? 4) Therefore, Moses presses God: "If your presence will not go, do not carry us up from here" (Exodus 33:15).
123 Even more puzzling, Moses claims that God did not communicate whom God would send, despite the promises of Exodus 23:20-23, 32:34, and 33:1-3: "See, you have said to me, 'Bring up this people'; but you have not let me know whom you will send with me" (Exodus 33:12). How can Moses say this in light of what God has promised three times? His statement is nothing short of inscrutable.
124 Exodus 23:20-23.
125 At stake in this negotiation is the question of whether God will accompany the whole of the people or just Moses. The second-person *singular* suffix throughout this negotiation, however, should not be regarded as a clear indication that Israel is excluded and Moses included. The promise of the angel in Exodus 23:20-23 had been expressed with the second-person singular: הִנֵּה אָנֹכִי שֹׁלֵחַ מַלְאָךְ לְפָנֶיךָ לִשְׁמָרְךָ בַּדָּרֶךְ. That promise recurs in Exodus 32:34 as מַלְאָכִי יֵלֵךְ לְפָנֶיךָ and in Exodus 33:2 as שָׁלַחְתִּי לְפָנֶיךָ מַלְאָךְ—both second-person singular. In Exodus 23:20-23, the second-person singular presumably refers to Israel as a whole; their sins are referred to with the second-person plural suffix, לְפִשְׁעֲכֶם (v. 21). The second-person singular in Exodus 33 can, therefore, refer to Moses or to Israel as a whole. Other indications in the context, identified above in this study, do suggest that Moses argues, against God, for the inclusion of Israel. It is possible that Moses rejects the promise of Exodus 32:34 and 33:1-3 because it excludes Israel, notwithstanding the use

of the second-person singular for all of Israel in Exodus 23:20-23, but this interpretation cannot be based exclusively on the second-person singular.

126 Exodus 33:18, my translation.

127 The Hebrew particle, נָא, often occurs in a request.

128 Exodus 33:19.

129 Hebrew: פָּנָי.

130 Exodus 33:20.

131 Mann (*Divine Presence and Guidance*, 157) contends that the expression *my pānîm* means "I": "The meaning is simply 'I myself will go (with you).' An interesting parallel is found in 2 Sam 17.11. In opposing Ahithophel's plan of taking a group of soldiers and quickly attaching the fleeing David, Hushai recommends that Absolom [*sic*] wait until the whole army can be gathered . . . 'then you yourself shall go in their midst.'" Several observations suggest that Mann is not correct at this point. First, there is a vast difference between the contexts of Exodus 33 and 2 Samuel 17; the former is preoccupied with whom God will send along the journey to Canaan. Will God go? The angel? The *pānîm*? The latter context is straightforwardly one of rebellion. Second, in Exodus 33, God does not need to import *pānîm* to mean "I"; earlier God readily used the first-person singular in self-reference: "But I will not go up among you" (לֹא אֶעֱלֶה בְּקִרְבְּךָ). The introduction of *pānîm* suggests that it probably means more than "I." Third, the tension in this negotiation between the angel and the *pānîm* suggests that the latter, like the former, is some sort of divine agent. On another note, whatever this means in Exodus 33—and I think Mann is incorrect—in the lament in Isaiah 63:7-14, *pānîm* is taken to mean other than God's self, as we will see. A. R. Johnson ("Aspects of the Use of the Term *pānîm* in the Old Testament," in *Festschrift Otto Eissfeldt zum 60 Geburtstag 1 September 1947*, ed. J. Fück [Halle: Max Niemeyer, 1947]) analyzes this term throughout the Hebrew Bible, though his treatment is rather cursory.

132 Propp (*Exodus 19–40*, 604) thinks it is "equivalent to 'Glory,' the aspect of Yahweh's presence visible to humans," though this is beside the point of its relationship to the angel, and too much is culled, anyway, from a reticent narrative.

133 Beyerlin (*Origins and History*, 106–11) suggests that Exodus 33:12-17 is a later stratum of the J material, which associates the *pānîm* exclusively with the covenant cult. Mann (*Divine Presence and Guidance*, 156–58) offers serious critiques of this limitation of the *pānîm* to the cult.

134 Exodus 32:18-19. Oddly enough, the rationale for this refusal is not rooted in glory but in goodness and God's presence-face: "I will make all my goodness pass before you, and will proclaim before you the name, 'The Lord'; and I will be gracious to whom I will be gracious, and will show mercy on whom I will show mercy. But,' he said, 'you cannot see my presence-face; for no one shall see me and live.'"

135 Exodus 33:21-23.

136 Exodus 33:23.

137 Two further questions arise from God's promise in Exodus 33:14: "My presence will go with you, and I will give you rest." First, does God promise to lead Moses or to give him rest? The verbs, give rest (הֵנִיחַ) and lead (נָחָה) are, in the hiphil stem (in Exodus 33:14, וַהֲנִחֹתִי) nearly identical. This form of the verb is understood as "giving rest" in Deuteronomy 3:20; 12:10; 25:19; Joshua 1:13, 15; 22:4; 2 Samuel 7:11; 1 Chronicles 22:9; Ezekiel 5:13; 16:42; 21:17 [Hebrew 22]. It is understood as "leading" in Exodus 13:17; 15:13; 32:34. The Septuagint translates this verb as "give rest" (καταπαύω); the Targums understand it similarly, though the Shekinah replaces the divine *I*: "My Shekinah will go, and I will give you rest" (וַאֲמַר שְׁכִינְתִּי תְהָך וַאְנִיחַ לָךְ). Second, who is the recipient of the promise?

Durham (*Exodus*, 447) supposes that this may be a personal promise to Moses, which excludes the Israelites: "I will dispel your anxiety." "In person I will go with you to give you a secure existence." Houtman (*Exodus*, 3:698) is in agreement. Or it may mean that God will give Israel—not just Moses—rest in the promised land, in which case the second-person singular suffix refers to Israel as a whole, as in the promise of the angel in Exodus 23:20-23. Either interpretation is possible. On the one hand, it may be that God offers Moses God's presence-face because Moses is caught in the gap, leading a recalcitrant people on behalf of an irascible God. On the other, it may be that God promises to take Israel into the land and settle them there, regardless of their insubordination. Along another vein, G. Coats ("An Exposition for the Wilderness Traditions," *Vetus Testamentum* 22 [1972]: 289–90) interprets נָחָה in terms of leadership in the wilderness.

138 Exodus 34:1-4.

139 Exodus 14:19.

140 Exodus 12:12; 12:23.

141 Exodus 34:6-7.

142 Hebrew: בְּפָנָיו.

143 Deuteronomy 4:37. This is the second of two flashbacks to the exodus. In a tight sequence of divine liberation—creation (Deuteronomy 4:32), Sinaitic theophany (4:33), exodus from Egypt (4:34), Decalogue (4:35), Sinai again (4:36), exodus again (4:37), land taking (4:38)—the whole sweep of God's activity flashes before Israel's eyes. The first flashback to the exodus gathers together the vocabulary of Exodus 1-15: "Or has any god ever attempted to go and take a nation for himself from the midst of another nation, by trials, by signs and wonders, by war, by a mighty hand and an outstretched arm, and by terrifying displays of power, as the Lord your God did for you in Egypt before your very eyes?" (Deuteronomy 4:34).

144 Exodus 33:14.

145 Exodus 33:19-20.

146 Isaiah 63:7-14.

147 J. Luzarraga (*Las tradiciones de la nube en la Biblia y en el Judaismo primitive*, AnBib 54 [Rome: Biblical Institute, 1973]) offers a thorough analysis of the cloud. L. Sabourin ("The Biblical Cloud: Terminology and Traditions," *Biblical Theology Journal* 4 [1974]: 290–311) identifies the contributions of Luzarraga's study. Mann (*Divine Presence and Guidance*, 132–33) provides a shorthand discussion of cloud in its Ancient Near Eastern milieu, especially Ugaritic storm imagery.

148 Exodus 16:10.

149 Durham (*Exodus*, 220) may be correct with this conjecture, though there is precious little in the narrative itself to support it.

150 Exodus 19:9, 19; 24:15-16. Of the Sinaitic theophany, Mann (*Divine Presence and Guidance*, 138) writes that "a primary purpose of the Sinai theophany in Exodus 19 (20.18-21) is the legitimation of Moses as the leader of the people and the recognition of Yahweh as their sovereign. The motifs of divine presence play a major role in this dual exaltation, and present a balanced emphasis on both visual and auditory aspects. . . . It is clear that with Exodus 19 we have left any explicit reference to the other aspect of our study—that of divine guidance. Here the cloud does not go in front of the people on the march, but comes down so that Yahweh may speak with Moses. This other function of the cloud—divine communication and the legitimation of Moses—is central to Exod 33.7-11 and Numbers 11-12."

151 Exodus 34:5.

152 Exodus 24:15.

153 To these may be added the pillar of cloud, which iteratively descends and stands at the gate of the tent of meeting (Exodus 33:9-10).

154 Exodus 40:34-38. For a majority of scholars informed by historical criticism, this epilogue is typically attributed to Persian-era (postexilic) Priestly authors, whose devotion to cult, worship, and priesthood—the tabernacle in this story—eclipses an interest in the journey of Israel from Egypt to the promised land.

155 Exodus 14:19-20.

156 Psalm 105:39.

157 The cloud also resembles the presence-face of God by dint of its association with glory. In a dense negotiation, which ended when God refused to allow Moses to see the presence-face, Moses had begged God to see glory, and God had allowed glory to pass by, however surreptitiously (Exodus 33:22). Now God makes good on the promise of glory, when the cloud descends and glory fills the tabernacle, though in this case neither the people nor Moses can enter into that glory. In this instance, divine presence is a matter of simultaneous offer and refusal—an important reminder of what S. Terrien (*The Elusive Presence: Toward a New Biblical Theology* [San Francisco: Harper & Row, 1978]) designates "the elusive presence."

158 Sarna, *Exodus*, 237. Childs (*Exodus*, 638) concurs: "The presence of God which once abode on Mount Sinai, now dwells in the sanctuary and accompanies Israel on her way." The parallel with Sinai is evident in the recurrence of key terms from Exodus 24:15-17 in 40:34-38: glory, dwell or settle, cloud, cover, and fire. Moses, however, entered the cloud on Mount Sinai (24:18), but he cannot enter the tabernacle in Exodus 40 because of the cloud. This contrast may underscore the intensity of God's glory in the tabernacle, or it may suggest that Moses has lost the access he had at Sinai, or both. In any case, his inability to enter the tabernacle recalls, by way of contrast, his ability to enter the cloud on Sinai. Hamilton (*Exodus*, 620) notes that Moses was unable to come closer to the burning bush in Exodus 3:5; he also discerns several verbal connections to Exodus 24:16.

159 See "Excursus: The Cloud in the Wilderness" for a sustained examination of the cloud's evolution in Israelite tradition.

160 Exodus 13:21-22.

161 Exodus 14:19-24.

162 Exodus 33:9-10.

163 Exodus 33:9-10.

164 Exodus 14:19-24.

165 Deuteronomy 1:33.

166 Psalm 78:14.

167 Exodus 14:19-20.

168 Exodus 23:20-23.

169 Exodus 32:24; 33:2-3; 33:14-15.

170 Numbers 20:16.

171 Exodus 13:21-22; 14:19-24.

172 Exodus 33:7-11.

173 Psalm 99:7.

174 Exodus 40:34-38; Numbers 10:11-12, 34.

175 Exodus 13:21-22.

176 Exodus 14:19-20.

177 Numbers 9:16.

178 Exodus 13:21-22.
179 Exodus 13:21-22.
180 Deuteronomy 1:33. A northern provenance for the book of Deuteronomy is not essential to this study; it is rather a matter of loose scholarly consensus. Regardless of the provenance reflected by the Deuteronomic tradition, that tradition is both related to but different from the traditions in the books of Exodus and Numbers.
181 Deuteronomy 4:36-37.
182 Deuteronomy 31:15

Chapter 3

1 M. Müller (*The First Bible of the Church: A Plea for the Septuagint*, JSOTSup 206 [Sheffield: Sheffield Academic, 1996], 47) discusses the (mistaken) identity of Demetrius of Phalerum.
2 Among a swath of studies should be included the classic study by S. Jellicoe, *The Septuagint and Modern Study* (Oxford: Clarendon, 1968); and the accessible introduction by K. H. Jobes and M. Silva, *Invitation to the Septuagint* (Grand Rapids: Baker Academic, 2000).
3 Letter of Aristeas 302.
4 Philo, *On the Life of Moses* 2.37–40.
5 Josephus, *Antiquities* 12.11–118, especially 12.57 and 12.86.
6 Hebrew: מִזְבֵּחַ; Greek: βωμόν and θυσιαστηρίου κυρίου.
7 See "Excursus: The Date and Provenance of Isaiah 56–66" and "Excursus: Possible Dates of the Lament of Isaiah 63:7–64:11" for a discussion of the various issues at stake in determining the point of origin and process of development for this indispensable witness to the exilic period.
8 S. Paul (*Isaiah 40–66: Translation and Commentary* [Grand Rapids: Eerdmans, 2012], 573) notes that the Masoretic pointing of this verb (וַיִּזְכֹּר) suggests that God is its subject: "Even as He was transformed into the nation's adversary, He remembered the days long past when he had had a loving relationship with the people (vv. 8b-9)." Paul also recognizes that, "on the basis of the rest of the verse, however, it seems more probable that the subject of the verb is the nation . . . and the Masoretic vocalization should be emended to the plural. . . . For the same expression with the nation as the addressee, see Deut 32:7: 'Remember the days of old'; see also Amos 9:11; Mic 5:1; 7:14; Mal 3:4." Watts (*Isaiah 34–66* [Waco, Tex.: Word, 1987], 893) translates, "Then he remembered days of (that) age: Moses, his people." Watts accepts the Masoretic pointing and views God as the subject: "The OT often depicts memory as a key motivation for God to act. When he remembers Abraham, he moves to get Israel out of Egypt (Exod 2:24). Here, he remembers the age of Moses and his people" (901).
9 Isaiah 63:7-14 (modified from NRSV).
10 The first five words of the Hebrew text of this line—בְּכָל־צָרָתָם לֹא (לוֹ) צָר—can be translated in different ways.

- Many interpreters see the beginning of verse 9 as a continuation of verse 8. P. Hanson (*Dawn of Apocalyptic: The Historical and Sociological Roots of Jewish Apocalyptic Eschatology* [Philadelphia: Fortress, 1975], 80), translates, "and he became their savior in all their distress. Not a messenger, nor an angel, but his own Presence saved them." C. Westermann (*Isaiah 40–66: A Commentary* [Philadelphia: Westminster, 1969], 385) translates similarly:

"And he became their savior in all their afflictions. Neither envoy nor messenger—he himself saved them." Both authors follow the Old Greek version in their translations of Isaiah 63:9.

- Other interpreters distinguish between verses 8 and 9, so that a new clause begins with the beginning of verse 9, at בְּכָל. Watts (*Isaiah 34–66*, 893), for instance, translates, "So he became their savior. In all their affliction he did not afflict." J. Goldenstein (*Das Gebet der Gottesknechte: Jesaja 63,9-64:11 im Jesajabuch* [Neukirchen-Vluyn: Neukirchener, 2001], 53) translates, "in all ihrer Not war keine Bedrängnis."
- Still other interpreters follow the read text (*qere*), which contains לוֹ, rather than the written (*kethiv*) text, which contains לֹא. In this case, the negative particle, *not*, is read as the inseparable preposition with the third-person masculine pronoun "to him." J. Blenkinsopp (*Isaiah 56–66: A New Translation with Introduction and Commentary* [New York: Doubleday, 2003], 252), for instance, translates, "So he became for them a savior. In all their afflictions he too was afflicted." Paul (*Isaiah 40–66*, 571) translates "So he became a deliverer for them; in all their trouble it became troublesome for him." R. Lessing (*Isaiah 56–66* [St. Louis: Concordia, 2014], 341) translates, "So he became their Savior. In all their anguish he had anguish." J. Goldingay (*A Critical and Exegetical Commentary on Isaiah 56–66* [London: Bloomsbury, 2014], 377) translates, "So he became a deliverer for them; in all their trouble it became troublesome for him." The *qere* version changes the point of reference. In the *kethiv* (according to the interpretation that begins a new clause in verse 9), the affliction is Israel's—or, better said, is not Israel's: in all their affliction, there was not [for Israel] affliction. The implied subject may be God: God did not afflict Israel. Or the subject may be impersonal: there was no affliction for Israel. In either case, the affliction is Israel's. In the *qere*, affliction reflects God's empathy: "In all their affliction, there was to him [to God] affliction." Whenever Israel experienced affliction, according to the *qere* reading, God experienced affliction along with them. Goldenstein (*Gebet*, 53) explains, "Diese Lesart setzt einen ganz anderen inhaltlichen Akzent; sie macht den Satz zu einer Aussage über das Mitleiden Jahwes. Gott und sein Volk werden dabei so weit miteinander identifiziert, daß die Not, die dem Volk widerfährt, de facto als Gott selbst treffend gedacht wird."

11 The Old Greek interprets לֹא צָר as לֹא צִיר, and translates the words as οὐ πρέσβυς, "not an ambassador." On the *qere* and *kethiv* readings of this verse, see note 10.
12 Exodus 23:20-23; 32:34; 33:1-3.
13 Exodus 33:14-15.
14 Some English translations, including the Protestant New Revised Standard Version and Catholic *New Jerusalem Bible*, suggest that the Greek represents the earlier text form with this translation: "It was no messenger or angel but his presence that saved them."
15 My translation based upon Goldenstein's translation (*Gebet*, 54).
16 See "Excursus: The Dubious Preference for Greek Isaiah 63:7-14" for the most common arguments in favor of a Greek original.
17 Qumran text: ויהי להמה למושיע בכול צרתמה לוא צר ומלאכ פניו הושיעמה

Masoretic text: וַיְהִי לָהֶם לְמוֹשִׁיעַ׃ בְּכָל־צָרָתָם׀ לֹא [לוֹ] צָר וּמַלְאַךְ פָּנָיו הוֹשִׁיעָם
18 The full context reads: "For he said, Surely they are my people, sons who will not deal falsely; and his Memra became their Saviour. In every time that they sinned before him

so as to bring affliction upon themselves, he did not afflict them, an angel sent from him saved them; in his love and in his pity upon them he delivered them; he lifted them up and carried them all the days of old." Translation by B. Chilton, *The Isaiah Targum: Introduction, Translation, Apparatus and Notes* (Wilmington, Del.: Michael Glazier, 1987), 121. B. Chilton (*The Glory of Israel: The Theology and Provenience of the Isaiah Targum* [Sheffield: JSOT, 1983]) offers an introduction to this Targum, including (48–52) an incisive discussion of the term *holy spirit* in relation to prophets, *shekinah*, and eschatology.

19 The Old Greek does not simply represent the Hebrew text repointed, as J. Kellas ("Note on Isaiah lxiii 9," *ExpTim* 18 [1907]: 384) argues.

20 In Isaiah 57:9, it occurs with the second feminine possessive pronoun as צִרַיִךְ.

21 Watts (*Isaiah 34–66*, 895) makes note of this addition.

22 Goldingay (*Isaiah 56–66*, 393) suggests, "While Exodus 33:14-15 can speak of Yhwh's face 'going' (cf. 2 Sam 17.11), it would be a unique usage for 'face' to be the subject of a verb such as 'deliver.['] More likely LXX, like K [*kethiv*], issues from discomfort with Q's [*qere*] reading and/or from a reading in the light of Exodus 33:14-15."

23 See "Excursus: The Dubious Preference for Greek Isaiah 63:7-14."

24 Watts (*Isaiah 34–66*, 898) sees these as unique formulations of Deuteronomic themes. Goldingay (*Isaiah 56–66*, 384) concurs: "At the same time, the imagery and ideas are innovative and distinctive, for instance in the description of the divine aide (63.9), the reference to Yhwh's holy spirit and to its capacity to be hurt (63.11), the description of the Reed Sea event and the time in the wilderness (63.12-14), the reference to Yhwh as father and to Abraham and Israel (63.16; 64.7 [8]), the declaration about Yhwh's making the people wander (63.17) and causing the people to sin through being angry with them (64.4 [5]), and the description of the people as like something taboo and like menstrual clothing (64.5 [6])." Verses 11–14 are particularly original. Westermann (*Isaiah 40–66*, 386) notes that "both the diction of the verses [11-14] and the stamp which they bear are odd. Nothing like them is found elsewhere."

25 Exodus 23:20-23.

26 Greek, ὑποστείληται. The *New English Translation of the Septuagint* reads: "For he shall not hold you in undue awe." Translations of the ancient Greek versions are usually from A. Pietersma and B. Wright, eds., *A New English Translation of the Septuagint and the Other Greek Translations Traditionally Included under that Title* (New York: Oxford University Press, 2007).

27 Other similar examples occur as well. In the Hebrew version of Gideon's story, God and the angel alternate as speakers. The Greek is more consistent, reading "the angel of the Lord" throughout, until Judges 6:23, by which point Gideon hears only God's voice.

28 Vulgate: *et angelus faciei salvavit eos.*

29 2 Kings 23:31-35.

30 2 Kings 24:1: "In his days King Nebuchadnezzar of Babylon came up; Jehoiakim became his servant for three years; then he turned and rebelled against him."

31 The account of Nebuchadnezzar's exploits in 597 B.C.E. is vivid: "He carried off all the treasures of the house of the Lord, and the treasures of the king's house; he cut in pieces all the vessels of gold in the temple of the Lord, which King Solomon of Israel had made, all this as the Lord had foretold. He carried away all Jerusalem, all the officials, all the warriors, ten thousand captives, all the artisans and the smiths; no one remained, except the poorest people of the land. He carried away Jehoiachin to Babylon; the king's mother, the king's wives, his officials, and the elite of the land, he took into captivity from Jerusalem to Babylon" (2 Kings 24:13-15). It is essential to note that Nebuchadnezzar did not ravage

Jerusalem; he carried off its leading political, military, and skilled leaders. Nebuchadnezzar then appointed Zedekiah in Jehoiachin's stead over an intact Jerusalem. I. Provan, V. Long, and T. Longman (*A Biblical History of Israel* [Louisville, Ky.: Westminster, 2015], 381–82), as well as M. Moore and B. Kelle (*Biblical History and Israel's Past: The Changing Study of the Bible and History* [Grand Rapids: Eerdmans, 2011], 352–59) offer further analysis.

32 2 Kings 24:20. Moore and Kelle (*Biblical History and Israel's Past,* 344) discuss how "an Egyptian priestly composition (the Rylands IX Papyrus) describes a victory tour through Syria-Palestine by Pharaoh Psammetichus II around 592, an event that may have contributed to King Zedekiah's willingness to enter into open rebellion against Babylonia shortly thereafter."

33 2 Kings 25:1-7.

34 2 Kings 25:9-12, 22-26.

35 2 Kings 25:13-21.

36 The brevity of the narrative in 2 Kings 24-25 belies a vitality catalyzed by the need to adjust to seismic shifts in reality. For the following half century, until 539 B.C.E., events and experiences must be teased out because both biblical and extrabiblical sources offer few stakes in the ground, many of them ambiguous, like signposts in the Cascade Mountains, which are puzzling to the casual hiker. Consequently, the era that precipitated extraordinary transformations of the exodus tradition and conceptions of the spirit is shrouded in uncertainty. If we cannot here dispel that uncertainty altogether, we can perhaps point to a few markers to frame the history that may have yielded such a stunning step in the origin of pneumatology.

37 Ezekiel 37:11.

38 The brief biblical detail that "high and low and the captains of the forces set out and went to Egypt; for they were afraid of the Chaldeans" (2 Kings 25:26) reveals the limits of a simplistic binary portrayal of exile in terms of the poor left in the land and the wealthy exiled to Babylon. Others—Jeremiah with them involuntarily—went to Egypt. This detail, in the main, is authentic. Hundreds of contractual and commercial Aramaic documents from a Jewish community have been found in Elephantine, a commercial hub in Egypt. There was even a temple there by the fifth century B.C.E., which points to migrations during the sixth century B.C.E., as this biblical text says. G. Granerød (*Dimensions of Yahwism in the Persian Period: Studies in the Religion and Society of the Judaean Community at Elephantine* [Berlin: de Gruyter, 2016]) offers insight into the Jewish community in Elephantine. J. Hayes and J. Miller (*A History of Ancient Israel and Judah,* 2nd ed. [Louisville, Ky.: Westminster John Knox, 2006], 496–97) provide a succinct summary of the Egyptian Diaspora.

39 See "Excursus: Life in Babylon and Palestine during the Neo-Babylonian Era" for a discussion of theories and findings for the Jewish experience in this pivotal period.

40 Hayes and Miller (*History of Ancient Israel,* 481) conjecture, "Such deportations frayed the total fabric of society, siphoning off many of the upper and artisan classes. At the same time, such deportations would have led to some redistribution of Judean property and wealth and thus benefited portions of the lower classes. Those left behind could occupy the land of those taken into exile (see Ezek. 11:15), and debtors may have been left suddenly without creditors to whom they were indebted." Hayes and Miller (*History of Ancient Israel,* 479–80, 482–87); Provan, Long, and Longman (*A Biblical History of Israel,* 382–83, 386–88); and Moore and Kelle (*Biblical History and Israel's Past,* 351–59, 367–79) offer informed portrayals of life in Palestine post-586 B.C.E.

41 In the mid-twentieth century, M. Noth (*The History of Israel*, 2nd ed. [New York: Harper & Row, 1958], 296) attributed to the so-called Chronicler (1–2 Chronicles, Ezra, and Nehemiah) the misguided tendency to see the center of gravity in the fifth century B.C.E. in Babylon rather than Palestine. "The Chronicler," wrote Noth,

> basing himself on a conception of legitimacy which is understandable in the context of his own age, and in very marked antithesis to the Samaritan schism, so portrayed the course of events as to suggest that the real history of Israel after the fall of Jerusalem may be traced by way of the "Babylonian exile" of the Judaeans and the later return of these "exiles" to the province of Judah. This view of things, which has become traditional under the influence of the Chronicler, is one-sided. Certain though it is that very important developments in life and thought took place among those deported to Babylon, which were to influence the whole later history of Israel, nevertheless even the Babylonian group represented a mere outpost, whereas Palestine was and remained the central arena of Israel's history, and the descendants of the old tribes who remained in the land, with the holy place of Jerusalem, constituted not only numerically the great mass but also the real nucleus of Israel.

42 E. Meyers and C. Meyers (*Haggai, Zechariah 1–8: A New Translation with Introduction and Commentary* [Garden City, N.Y.: Doubleday, 1987], xxix) describe this creative impulse.

> When the neo-Babylonian armies of Nebuchadnezzar wrought havoc upon Jerusalem in 587 or 586 B.C.E., and thousands of Judeans were taken captive and marched to Babylon, the story of Israel could well have ended. Instead, a uniquely creative epoch in Judean history began, ironically, in the diaspora and in exile, as the survivors of the Babylonian conquest sought to examine the causes of the calamity that had destroyed their holy city and the Jerusalem temple and had made so many homeless and impoverished. With Judeans dispersed into many new lands besides Babylon—into trans-Jordan, Egypt, and Syro-Phoenicia—the familiar sociohistoric framework of Israel, which had been limited to the southern tip of the Syro-Palestinian corridor from the thirteenth century B.C.E. until the Exile, was shattered once and for all.

D. Carr (*Holy Resilience: The Bible's Traumatic Origins* [New Haven, Conn.: Yale University Press, 2014], 75–76) puts the impact of Babylonian conquest succinctly and carefully, though in terms only of the exiles in Babylon, and particularly in terms of the formation of the Hebrew Bible:

> The Old Testament is, in large part, a collection of writings by these Judean exiles and their descendants. After all, the leaders that the Babylonians removed in wave after wave from Judah were exactly the sorts of people who would have been literate in the ancient world: priests, officers, bureaucrats, and royalty. . . . In a stroke, King Nebuchadnezzar of Babylon had created an unusually highly literate exiled Judean community.
>
> Little did Nebuchadnezzar know, but this tiny community of Judean exiles would be the incubator for a set of scriptures that would long outlast his empire. Over the coming decades Babylon successfully extended its imperial reach to Egypt in the west and Persia in the east. Babylon's Ishtar temple became a wonder talked about for centuries, and Babylon's texts were the jewels of the Mesopotamian

library. Yet less than fifty years after Jerusalem fell, Babylon was conquered by Cyrus the Persian (538 BCE). Within a few centuries, the tables of Babylon's libraries were buried in sand, their script and language forgotten. Meanwhile, like many people affected by trauma, the Judean exiles were coming to a fundamentally new understanding of themselves, one that would ultimately outlast empires like Babylon and its successors. The Hebrew Bible contains the deposit of their work. Virtually every book shows the impact of the Babylonian exile. This was the time, for example, when older prophecies of judgment, such as those by Amos, Micah, and Hosea, became the common focus of an exiled people trying to understand what had happened to them. Seized by the self-blame endemic to trauma, the exiles took to heart such previously marginalized judgment prophets and saw the exile as God's promised judgment for their sins. In addition, Judah's story of Israel's destruction and Judah's survival up through the reign of Josiah had to be modified in light of Jerusalem's subsequent destruction. It would no longer do to have the books of Kings end, as they probably originally did, with Josiah's covenant with God, purification of Jerusalem and land surrounding, and celebration of Passover. So Judean authors in exile added onto the end of the books of Kings to provide an answer. They argued that, in the end, even Josiah's great faithfulness was not enough to outweigh the disobedient acts of his father, Manasseh, before him.

43 Amos 3:1-2.
44 Hosea 2:14-15.
45 Hosea 11:1.
46 Deuteronomy 7:7-8.
47 Micah 6:3-4.
48 Isaiah 10:26-27. Cf. also the oracle against Egypt in Isaiah 19, especially Isaiah 19:19-20.
49 Jeremiah 7:21-26.
50 Ezekiel 16; 20; 23. C. Patton ("'I Myself Gave Them Laws That Were Not Good': Ezekiel 20 and the Exodus Traditions," *JSOT* 69 [1996]: 73–90) discusses Ezekiel's use of traditions in these historical surveys, as well as Ezekiel 40–48.
51 Ezekiel 16:3-5.
52 Ezekiel 20:25-26.
53 Ezekiel 23:8.
54 Ezekiel 1:12, 20, 21; 10:17.
55 Ezekiel 3:12, 14; 8:3; 11:1, 24; 37:1.
56 Ezekiel 11:5.
57 Ezekiel 36:25-26.
58 Ezekiel 36:25-26.
59 Ezekiel 37:1-14.
60 Ezekiel 39:28-29.
61 Ezekiel 18:2. Ezekiel's older contemporary, Jeremiah, also quotes this maxim. According to Jeremiah, in essence, God has broken down and destroyed; God will build and plant. In those days, no one will any longer quote this maxim, and people will die for their own sins. Death will be dispelled by a new covenant, which God will initiate; God will write Torah on Israel's hearts, and Israel will no longer even need teachers (Jeremiah 31:27-34).
62 Ezekiel 18:31; Hebrew: לֵב חָדָשׁ וְרוּחַ חֲדָשָׁה.
63 Ezekiel 18:31-32 (modified from NRSV).
64 Ezekiel 8:1-11:25.

65 Hebrew: לֵב אֶחָד וְרוּחַ חֲדָשָׁה.
66 Ezekiel 11:17-20.
67 Hebrew: וְנָתַתִּי לָכֶם לֵב חָדָשׁ וְרוּחַ חֲדָשָׁה אֶתֵּן בְּקִרְבְּכֶם.
68 Hebrew: וְאֶת־רוּחִי אֶתֵּן בְּקִרְבְּכֶם.
69 Ezekiel 36:24-28. This promise did not emerge from thin air but from Ezekiel's fidelity to the Deuteronomic tradition:

> When all these things have happened to you, the blessings and the curses that I have set before you, if you call them to mind among all the nations where the Lord your God has driven you, and return to the Lord your God, and you and your children obey him with all your heart and with all your soul, just as I am commanding you today, then the Lord your God will restore your fortunes and have compassion on you, gathering you again from all the peoples among whom the Lord your God has scattered you. Even if you are exiled to the ends of the world, from there the Lord your God will gather you, and from there he will bring you back. The Lord your God will bring you into the land that your ancestors possessed, and you will possess it; he will make you more prosperous and numerous than your ancestors. (Deuteronomy 30:1-5)

Although Ezekiel is faithful to this tradition, the dire situation brought about by the fall of Jerusalem propels him to transpose this tradition into a higher key. While Deuteronomy 30 promises restoration without cleansing, Israel's experience of protracted exile evokes from Ezekiel a more radical solution of purification: "I will sprinkle clean water upon you, and you shall be clean from all your uncleannesses, and from all your idols I will make you clean" (Ezekiel 36:25).

70 Ezekiel 11:14-21.
71 Ezekiel 18:30-32.
72 Ezekiel 36:25-26. Further analysis of the development in these three texts is available in J. Levison, "The Promise of the Spirit of Life in Ezekiel," in *Israel's God and Rebecca's Children: Christology and Community in Early Judaism and Christianity (Essays in Honor of Larry W. Hurtado and Alan F. Segal)*, ed. D. Capes, A. DeConick, H. Bond, and T. Miller (Waco, Tex.: Baylor, 2007), 247–59.
73 Ezekiel 11:24-31; 18:30-32.
74 Ezekiel 36:25-26.
75 The Deuteronomistic redaction (one layer of it, at least) may be an example of this effort to assess Israel's exilic present in light of their traditions.
76 The pillar and cloud are first mentioned in Exodus 13:21-22, the pillar alone in 14:19.
77 Exodus 14:19.
78 Exodus 23:20-23.
79 Exodus 32:34.
80 Exodus 33:2.
81 Numbers 20:14-16.
82 Judges 2:1.
83 Numbers 14:14.
84 Psalm 78:14; 99:6-7; 105:39.
85 Exodus 33:12.
86 Exodus 33:14-15 (modified from NRSV).
87 Exodus 33:20 (modified from NRSV).
88 Exodus 14:19; also 23:23.

89 Exodus 23:21-22.
90 Judges 2:1.
91 Goldingay (*Isaiah* 56–66, 393) sees in Isaiah 63:9 an identification of God with God's aide: "In other words [Exodus, etc.], 'God's very self' will be with them. It was Yhwh in person who delivered the people, in the person of the aide. It was he . . . who thus restored them. The Exodus passages express themselves in such a way as both to declare that Yhwh in person accompanied the people and also to deny that this is so. The need for the denial now issues from the people's waywardness as well as from their mere createdness, yet the reality of Yhwh's accompanying the people also needs safeguarding. Exodus attempts this by speaking in terms of Yhwh's aide and of Yhwh's face accompanying the people. This line in Isaiah combines the expressions."
92 Goldingay (*Isaiah* 56–66, 392) discerns a further possible allusion to Exodus 23:20-23 in the "trouble" referred to in Isaiah 63:9. "While strictly these words [in Exodus] likely need to be related to *sarar* III 'show hostility to' rather than *sarar* 'trouble,' the links with Exodus 23 in the context suggest that the prophet recognized the possibility of understanding Yhwh to be promising, 'I will trouble their troublers' and recalling how Yhwh became a trouble or enemy for them when they were in trouble or were experiencing enmity."
93 Blenkinsopp (*Isaiah* 56–66, 260) writes: "These statements may be taken to reflect learned theological discussions about the historical traditions going on among scribes, including Deuteronomic scribes (cf. Deut 4:37 . . .). The phrase *mal'ak pānîm* ('the angel of the Face') in Isa 63:9a may therefore represent a compromise solution to the exegetical problem posed by Exod 33, one which consisted in reconciling these alternative expressions of divine agency." He continues: "The association of the Spirit with the Presence or the Face of God (also in Ps 139:7) indicates that the Spirit . . . has now become the object of theological reflection" (261).
94 Isaiah 63:9.
95 Exodus 14:19.
96 Exodus 2:17; 4:30.
97 Exodus 14:27-29.
98 Exodus 14:30-31. These verses provide an inclusio to the crossing, along with Exodus 14:13, which reads: "But Moses said to the people, 'Do not be afraid, stand firm, and see the deliverance that the LORD will accomplish for you today; for the Egyptians whom you see today you shall never see again.'"
99 Small wonder, given this shift, that the Old Greek translators effaced the angel and opted for another alternative: God alone saved them. The translators of the Old Greek, however, preserved the centrality of God in the original story at the expense of the angel of God's presence in the lament. Embracing God entailed effacing the angel.
100 Isaiah 63:10.
101 Isaiah 63:10.
102 Isaiah 63:11.
103 Psalm 51:11 (Hebrew 51:13).
104 Interpretations of this line vary, based upon the *kethiv* and *qere*, as noted above.
105 Isaiah 63:9b-10 (modified from NRSV).
106 Though unlikely from a literary standpoint, it is possible to distinguish the angel of God's presence from God's holy spirit, as if they were two distinct agents. It may be that the prophet conceives of two separate agents: an angel that saved Israel and a holy spirit, against which Israel rebelled. There were, after all, various agents active in the liberation of Israel—the pillars, the cloud, the angel, the presence-face of God, and perhaps, in

some form, glory and another cloud. To suggest this, however, is to overlook the clear sequence in this lament. W. Wilder (*Echoes of the Exodus in the Context and Background of Galatians 5:18* [New York: Peter Lang, 2001], 130–48) analyzes this lament in detail but without noting this sequence. His analysis begins in earnest at Isaiah 63:11 rather than 63:9.

107 In Exodus 23:21, Israel is commanded either "do not rebel against him" or "do not embitter him." The consonants for both translations are the same: תמר. The Masoretes pointed these consonants to mean, "do not embitter," based upon the root מרר, but these consonants could just as easily be pointed to mean, "do not rebel against," based upon the root מרה. (Gesenius, *Hebrew Grammar*, paragraph 67y, writes: "אַל־תַּמֵּר Ex 23:21, but read אַל־תֶּ֫מֶר from מָרָה.") The author of the lament, using an unpointed text, would easily have read this command as "do not rebel" and accused Israel of having rebelled against God's holy spirit. In fact, the Greek translation of Exodus 23:21 agrees with Isaiah 63:10 by understanding the verb in Exodus 23:21 in terms of rebellion (מרה) rather than embitterment (מרר): καὶ μὴ ἀπείθει αὐτῷ. The Targum also interprets this verb in Exodus 23:21 as rebellion rather than embitterment by translating it with תְסָרֵיב, which connotes refusal. In Targum Deuteronomy 1:26, the same verb, "refuse" (סרב), translates the Hebrew verb "rebel" (מרה), which occurs in Isaiah 63:10. Targum Deuteronomy 1:26 reads, וְלָא אֲבֵיתוֹן לְמִיסַק וְסָרֵיבתוּן עַל מֵימְרָא דַיוי אֱלָהֲכוֹן. סרב is therefore an apt translation of מרה. Vulgate reads *contemnendum putes*.

108 Isaiah 63:10.

109 Exodus 23:22.

110 I am not willing to go so far as to argue for identification, given the ambiguity of the narratives and this prophetic lament. I prefer to refer to an *association*. On the so-called identification theory, see "Excursus: The Identity of the Angelic Messenger."

111 Exodus 14:19; 23:20-23.

112 The verb "they rebelled" (מָרוּ) occurs often in various exodus traditions, *always* with God as the one against whom Israel rebelled. In Numbers 20:10, 24, and 27:14, Israel rebelled over the bitter waters at Meribah. In Deuteronomy 1:26, Israel rebelled against God's command by not entering the land after spies Joshua and Caleb told them to enter. In Deuteronomy 1:43, Israel went, against God's command, into the hill country to fight the Amorites. Deuteronomy 9:7 contains a sweeping indictment of Israel's rebellion "in the wilderness; you have been rebellious against the Lord from the day you came out of the land of Egypt until you came to this place." Ezekiel, in his second gruesome transformation of Israel's history into an uninterrupted experience of disobedience, traces Israel's rebellion to Israel's unwillingness to forego the idols of Egypt (Ezekiel 20:8) and to the wilderness, where they rejected God's ordinances and profaned the Sabbath (Ezekiel 20:13, 21). Psalmists recount the rebellion of Israel's "ancestors" (Psalm 78:8), who "rebelled against" God "in the wilderness" (Psalm 78:17, 40 [modified from NRSV]), as well as in the land by building idols (Psalm 78:56-58). Psalm 106:7, like Ezekiel, traces that rebellion to Egypt and sees it continuing long afterward, even to the period of the judges: "Many times he delivered them, but they were rebellious in their purposes, and were brought low through their iniquity" (Psalm 106:43). Psalm 107:10-11 describes prisoners in misery and irons, "for they had rebelled against the words of God, and spurned the counsel of the Most High." The prayer of Ezra in Nehemiah identifies rebellion once people were in the land, when "they were disobedient and rebelled against you and cast your law behind their backs and killed your prophets, who had warned them in order to turn them back to you, and they committed great blasphemies" (Nehemiah 9:26).

113 Psalm 78:40.

114 Isaiah 63:7.

115 Isaiah 63:11-13.

116 The shape of the exodus tradition in this lament is influenced in part by Jeremiah 2:6-8. Paul (*Isaiah 40–66*, 572) documents this influence. "The prophecy in Jer 2:6-8," writes Paul, "left a decisive impression on the language and the content of these verses. Jeremiah complains that the nation had alienated itself from God: 'They never asked themselves, "Where is the Lord who brought us up (אַיֵּה הי המעלה) from the land of Egypt, and led us through (המוליך) the desert (במדבר)? Where is (אַיֵּה) the Lord?" The shepherds (הרעים) rebelled against Me.' Employing the same expressions, Deutero-Isaiah maintains that after their rebellion against God and His transformation into their enemy, they asked the very same questions: 'Where is He who brought them up (אַיֵּה המעלם) from the sea along with the shepherd (רֹעֶה) of His flock? Where is (אַיֵּה) He . . . who led them . . . in a desert (במדבר . . . מוליכָם)?' The two sections feature two identical איה queries and the image of a shepherd . . . (albeit in different contexts): Jer 2:8: 'The shepherds [= rulers] rebelled against Me' – v. 11: 'along with the shepherd of His flock.'"

117 Deuteronomy 34:9. The related text is Numbers 27:18, in which God commands Moses: "Take Joshua son of Nun, a man in whom is the spirit, and lay your hand upon him." I interpret these texts in *Filled with the Spirit* (Grand Rapids: Eerdmans, 2009), 70–74.

118 Exodus 31:1-5; 35:30-35; also 28:3. I interpret these texts in *Filled with the Spirit*, 51–65.

119 Numbers 11:16-30. I have analyzed this story in "The Case of the Ecstatic Elders," *Catholic Biblical Quarterly* 65 (2003): 503–21. J. Morgenstern ("Isaiah 63.7-14," *Hebrew Union College Annual* 23 [1950–1951]: 194n12) enthusiastically endorses the view that "the reference is unmistakable to the incident recorded in Num. 11.16-17, 24-30, and particularly, so it seems, to vv. 26-29." Morgenstern overstates the case because the spirit, according to Numbers 11, comes *upon* the elders rather than *in* them—and, to all but two of those elders, *outside* the camp, where the bulk of the Israelites remained. The mode of inspiration is a matter of distribution upon a select group of sequestered elders rather than placement within Israel as a whole.

120 The word רוּחַ does occur in Exodus 14:21 as a strong east wind. It is difficult to see how the prophet would have construed this as the setting of God's holy spirit in Israel's midst.

121 The question is more than wedged into this context. It is integral to, even determinative of, this context. The first of two questions beginning with the interrogative "Where?" exclusively addresses rescue through the Sea: "Where is the one who brought them up out of the sea?" The second, "Where is the one who put within them his holy spirit?" is so closely allied to the first that, without evidence to the contrary, it should be read as a question about the same event. Even more decisive for the locus of the question, "Where is the one who put within them his holy spirit?" is what follows. In a series of clauses, each of which begins with a participle, the focus lies upon the principal act of deliverance through the Sea. (1) "Who caused his glorious arm to march at the right [hand] of Moses." God promises Moses an outstretched arm and mighty acts of judgment that will lead to Israel's deliverance from Egypt (Exodus 6:6). Deuteronomy 4:34 makes an incontrovertible reference to the plagues against Egypt: "Or has any god ever attempted to go and take a nation for himself from the midst of another nation, by trials, by signs and wonders, by war, by a mighty hand and an outstretched arm, and by terrifying displays of power, as the Lord your God did for you in Egypt before your very eyes?" (2) "Who divided the waters before them" is an obvious reference to the parting of the sea. In fact, the root, בקע, refers to the dividing of the sea in Exodus 14:16, 21;

Psalm 78:13; Nehemiah 9:11. (3) "Who led them through the depths" is similar to the depiction of the sea as the depths (תְּהֹמוֹת) in Psalm 106:9, in which God "rebuked the Red Sea, and it became dry; he led them through the deep [תְּהֹמוֹת] as through a desert." This use of *depths* is ripe with irony; the Egyptians were the ones found, to their detriment and death, in the depths of the sea (Exodus 15:5). The Israelites, the lament recalls, walked through those same depths to salvation. In summary, the question about the holy spirit is so tautly tied to its context that the clear focus of the question must be rescue through the waters of the Sea.

122 Exodus 14:19.

123 Isaiah 63:14. There is nothing surprising in the reversion from the novel expression "holy spirit" to the more traditional epithet for the spirit, רוּחַ־יְהוָה. There is certainly no reason to distinguish the holy spirit from the spirit of the Lord, as if they were two different divine agents. The expression רוּחַ־יְהוָה occurs in a wide swath of contexts. It rushes or comes upon Israel's heroes, its judges and kings, in Judges 3:10, 6:34, 11:29, 14:6, 14:19, 15:14; 1 Samuel 10:6, 16:13. It falls upon Ezekiel (11:5) and brings him in visionary transport to a valley of very many, very dry bones: "the hand of the Lord came upon me, and he brought me out by the spirit of the Lord" (Ezekiel 37:1). In literature of the Persian era, רוּחַ־יְהוָה comes upon Jahaziel in 2 Chronicles 20:14. The language is traditional, but the content is not; Jahaziel delivers an inspired speech that combines traditional Priestly vocabulary with precise and, it turns out, effective, military instructions. I analyze this text in *Inspired: The Holy Spirit and the Mind of Faith* (Grand Rapids: Eerdmans, 2013), 132–34. A variety of other verbs are associated with רוּחַ־יְהוָה, which moves ambiguously in Samson, stirring him (Judges 13:15); departs from a disobedient Saul (1 Samuel 16:14); inspires a psalm of David—"the spirit of the Lord speaks through me, his word is upon my tongue" (2 Samuel 23:2); carries prophets like Elijah and Elisha away (1 Kings 18:12; 2 Kings 2:16); crosses over from one person to another, according to Zedekiah, ringleader of the king's company of prophets, who slaps Micaiah ben Imlah and asks, "Which way did the spirit of the Lord pass from me to speak to you?" (1 Kings 22:24; also 2 Chronicles 18:23); and rests on the anointed ruler whom Isaiah predicts (Isaiah 11:2). The phrase רוּחַ־יְהוָה is used variously: God's counselor (Isaiah 40:13); wind (Isaiah 40:7, 59:19; Hosea 13:15); God's patience (Micah 2:7); even an evil spirit of the Lord (1 Samuel 19:19).

124 There is justifiable debate about the meaning of the verb תְּנִיחֶנּוּ, because in the form תניחנו the hiphil stem of the root נוח, "to rest," is nearly identical to the hiphil stem of the root נחה, "to lead." In fact, if the hiphil of נחה were written defectively, without the *yodh*, they could be identical. This may be why the Old Greek (ὡδήγησεν), Vulgate (*doctor eius fuit*), and Targum (דַבַּרתָּהִי) understand the verb to mean "lead" rather than "cause to rest." The Old Greek differs from these versions by associating the verb *descended* not with Israel, which descended like cattle into the valley, but with the spirit: κατέβη πνεῦμα παρὰ κυρίου καὶ ὡδήγησεν αὐτούς. The spirit both descended and led Israel. The pointing of the Masoretic text and the Qumran text (תניחנו), on the contrary, read, "caused to rest."

125 Exodus 33:1-3.

126 As I noted in the second chapter, in Exodus 33:4-11, two scenes interrupt this conversation; one portrays apparently sincere repentance on Israel's part, while the other describes how amiably God and Moses met at the tent of meeting to talk as friends, face to face. This conversation is hardly amicable, though it is honest, the sort of negotiation that takes place in the context of candor—even trust.

127 Exodus 33:14-15.

128 The question of whether the presence-face of God would accompany Moses alone or Israel with him remains unresolved even in this lament. The singular suffix in תְּנִיחֶנּוּ can refer to Moses alone or to Israel. Though the suffix is singular, the context in Isaiah 63:13-14 refers to "your people" (עַמְּךָ), who "did not stumble" (יִכָּשֵׁלוּ).

129 The association of God's spirit and God's presence occurs also in two psalms. Psalm 51:11 (English) reads: "Do not cast me away from your presence, and do not take your holy spirit from me" (Hebrew 51:13: אַל־תַּשְׁלִיכֵנִי מִלְּפָנֶיךָ וְרוּחַ קָדְשְׁךָ אַל־תִּקַּח מִמֶּנִּי). Psalm 139:7 reads: "Where can I go from your spirit [מֵרוּחֶךָ]? Or where can I flee from your presence [מִפָּנֶיךָ]?"

130 Exodus 23:21; Isaiah 63:10.

131 Exodus 14:19; Isaiah 63:11.

132 Exodus 33:14; Isaiah 63:14.

133 Josephus (*Antiquities* 12.256) describes this gruesome punishment, brought about under the heinous reign of Antiochus IV Epiphanes.

134 Mann (*Divine Presence and Guidance*, 202) observes an analogous development with respect to the Torah in the Deuteronomistic editing of Joshua 1:5-9: "For the Deuteronomist, the Torah has, in effect, become the divine guide to supersede those colorful agents from Israel's remote past. This is brought out in a stunning way when we compare the above lines from Joshua [1:7-8] to the ancient paradigm of divine guidance found in Exod 13.21-22. There Yahweh goes in front of the people in the pillar of cloud and fire, and, like the Torah, it does not depart . . . but remains day and night. . . . Similarly, in Exod 23.20-21, it is Yahweh's *ml'k* who goes before the people and to whom they are answerable. In a very creative way, the Deuteronomist has appropriated this language and adapted it to fit his covenant theology. Now it is in following Torah that one will know the way to go. Now it is with the statutes that Israel's distinctiveness among the nations is so closely tied, and with which the nearness of Yahweh's presence is associated (Deut 4.5-8; cf. Exod 33.16; Num 14.14). The Deuteronomist could also accept the guidance of the ark under a similar rubric, for in his view, at least, the ark was the receptacle of the tablets of the Torah. Thus, as S. Dean McBride has suggested, although the ark was clearly redefined by the deuteronomistic school, it was, nonetheless, still connected with divine presence. Indeed, the tablets themselves are now 'the immediate manifestation of divine indwelling in Israel's midst.'" The McBride quotation is from private communication between him and Mann.

Chapter 4

1 Josephus, *Antiquities* 11.1.

2 Cyrus Cylinder, trans. from J. Pritchard, *Ancient Near Eastern Texts Relating to the Old Testament*, 3rd ed. (Princeton, N.J.: Princeton University Press, 1969), 316.

3 Josephus, *Antiquities* 11.6.

4 Isaiah 45:1.

5 Jeremiah 29:1-23.

6 Isaiah 44:28.

7 The book of Ezra preserves two decrees dated to the first year of Cyrus' rule, probably 539 or 538 B.C.E. In the first, in Hebrew, Cyrus states that the Lord has charged him with the task of rebuilding the temple, all Judeans are permitted to participate in rebuilding, and those who do not return can still contribute to the cost of rebuilding the temple and restoring the cult of offering and sacrifice (Ezra 1:2-4). The second,

recorded in Aramaic, details three elements of rebuilding: the temple should be rebuilt to certain specifications in terms of size and materials; royal funds should be tapped; vessels removed by the Babylonians should be restored (Ezra 6:1-5). The first decree focuses on the return of exiles without specifics about temple restoration; the second focuses on the specifics of restoration without a reference to exiles. These decrees seem to serve separate purposes, but together they reinforce the reality of Cyrus' policy of allowing captives to return to their homelands and restore their local shrines. J. Hayes and J. Miller (*A History of Ancient Israel and Judah*, 2nd ed. [Louisville, Ky.: Westminster John Knox, 2006], 505–8) discuss the character of the Cyrus Cylinder, which released captives to return to their homelands.

8 Hayes and Miller (*History of Ancient Israel*, 509–10) discuss how Cyrus' successor accomplished what Cyrus had not when he attacked and conquered Egypt. After the death of Cyrus in battle in the east, Cambyses conquered the east. Five years later, in 525 B.C.E., he conquered Psammetichus III in Egypt as well. Cambyses remained in Egypt for three years. While he tended to place severe restraints on local shrines and their personnel—they proved to be a substantial and reliable source of income—he did visit the temple of the goddess Neith, the mother of the sun god Re, in Sais, where he restored priests and outlawed foreigners.

9 According to Ezra 5:1, Yehud is the name the Persians assigned to the province formerly known as Judah.

10 Hayes and Miller (*History of Ancient Israel*, 498–500) explain how difficult it is to get a bead on the nature of this turmoil because the sources for the exilic, or Neo-Babylonian, and postexilic, or Persian, periods of Israelite history are scant, selective, biased, and hard to date with certainty. Sources include primarily the narrative books of Ezra and Nehemiah, the prophetic books of Haggai and Zechariah (1–8), the apocryphal book of 1 Esdras, and Josephus' *Antiquities*, book 11, which contains some material, reliable or not, not contained in his biblical sources. These sources tell the story of rebuilding from the perspective of exiles who returned from Babylon to Yehud. It is especially difficult to reconstruct Israelite history after 538 B.C.E., in part because two key sources, the books of Ezra and Nehemiah, are so difficult to correlate chronologically. The biblical books themselves suggest an overlap between their public vocations during the single reign of Artaxerxes (Ezra 7:7-8; Nehemiah 2:1), though they do not say which Artaxerxes ruled. First Esdras mentions Ezra but not Nehemiah. Josephus dates them consecutively during the reign of Xerxes I (486–465 B.C.E.).

11 M. Moore and B. Kelle (*Biblical History and Israel's Past: The Changing Study of the Bible and History* [Grand Rapids: Eerdmans, 2011], 425–31) discuss the disputed issue of population; in general, they note, recent scholars tend to think that Yehud was largely rural and smaller in population than during the years prior to exile in 597 and 586 B.C.E. K. G. Hoglund (*Achaemenid Imperial Administration in Syria-Palestine and the Missions of Ezra and Nehemiah* [Atlanta: Scholars, 1992]) offers further detail and analysis.

12 Ezra 4:3 reads: "But Zerubbabel, Jeshua, and the rest of the heads of families in Israel said to them, 'You shall have no part with us in building a house to our God; but we alone will build to the LORD, the God of Israel, as King Cyrus of Persia has commanded us.'" Hayes and Miller (*History of Ancient Israel*, 511–12) discuss the relatively small number of those who returned.

13 Various views of this opposition arise in the book of Ezra, though their relationship to one another is not clear. According to Ezra 4:4-5, their opposition began with a bribe to slow the restoration project. It continued with a letter, perhaps during the year of

the Egyptian rebellion, 486 B.C.E., warning of the infidelity of the returnees; this letter would paint the returnees, like Egyptians who rebelled, as threats to Persian peace. Finally, the officials of the province Abir-Nari wrote sternly to warn Persia that the returnees, once the temple was built, would withhold their tribute and taxes.

14 Ezra 6:21.

15 Nehemiah 13:25.

16 Ezra 5:16. Only decades later did a concerted effort to rebuild the temple take place. Nearly a century later, the temple would stand poorly restored. According to the book of Ezra and the apocryphal book of 2 Esdras, Ezra led the restoration. According to 2 Maccabees 1:18–2:15, Nehemiah led the project. First Esdras, Josephus, following 1 Esdras, and bits of Ezra, Haggai, and Zechariah, see Zerubbabel as the leader of temple restoration. Historians Hayes and Miller (*History of Ancient Israel*, 512–13) identify three stages of restoration, based upon Ezra 1–6: (1) Ezra 1 and 5:6-17: Sheshbazzar led the restoration during the reigns of Cyrus and Darius I (522–486 B.C.E.). Sheshbazzar was probably not a returnee but led restoration nonetheless with the imprimatur of the early Achaemenid rulers. (2) Ezra 3 and 6:19-22: Zerubbabel and Joshua led the restoration. (3) Ezra 5:1-5 and 6:1-18: Zerubbabel, Joshua, with prophets Haggai and Zechariah, led the restoration project.

17 P. Hanson, in *Dawn of Apocalyptic: The Historical and Sociological Roots of Jewish Apocalyptic Eschatology* (Philadelphia: Fortress, 1975), discerns two opposing factions in Yehud during the Persian era: (1) the *hierocratic* party, rooted in Ezekiel's vision of the temple purified and restored (Ezekiel 40–48), consisting of priests who had returned from Babylon and attempted to wrest control of Jerusalem in order to restore pure worship; (2) the *visionary* faction, rooted in Isaiah 40–55, consisting of disenfranchised Levites who had been excluded by the hierocratic party from worship. Wide in scope and masterful in execution, notwithstanding the justifiable critiques it has garnered, this is an indispensable study of the Persian era. G. Emmerson (*Isaiah 56–66* [Sheffield: JSOT, 1992], 85–90) offers a brief and beneficial summary.

18 Emmerson (*Isaiah 56–66*, 90–94) documents other scholars after Hanson who have argued that these divisions are too rigid, though few scholars deny that tensions were real, whether or not they could be imputed to distinct sects or factions.

19 Haggai 1:2.

20 Haggai 1:4-6.

21 Haggai 1:9-11.

22 Isaiah 62:9.

23 Isaiah 65:11.

24 Isaiah 56:3.

25 Isaiah 58:6-7.

26 Isaiah 58:8-9.

27 Isaiah 58:12.

28 Isaiah 58:11.

29 The word *breach* conjures images of Jerusalem's broken wall. Ezekiel had said, "You have not gone up into the breaches, or repaired a wall for the house of Israel, so that it might stand in battle on the day of the Lord" (Ezekiel 13:5). Nehemiah would come to the point in his project when "I had built the wall and that there was no gap [breach] left in it" (Nehemiah 6:1).

30 For Zechariah, the people run the risk of setting aside justice even as they hope in the promise that the temple will be rebuilt (e.g., 1:16).

31 E. Meyers and C. Meyers (*Haggai, Zechariah 1–8: A New Translation with Introduction and Commentary* [Garden City, N.Y.: Doubleday, 1987], xxxix) propose this chronology. D. V. Edelman (*The Origins of the "Second" Temple: Persian Imperial Policy and the Rebuilding of Jerusalem* [London: Equinox, 2005], 104–6) considers this date to be historically unreliable; in her opinion, the dedication of the temple is placed there in order to fit the seventy years of Jeremiah's prophecy.

32 If Hanson is correct, then this division can be accounted for because Haggai is a spokesperson for the returnees, the prophet of Isaiah 56–66 for the people of the land, whose ancestors were not exiled in the first place. Haggai asks the returnees to roll up their sleeves, to give, to labor. Isaiah 56–66 only briefly mentions the restoration of the temple; the primary concern here is to offer hope by urging the people to fast with justice and to give pride of place to those who were traditionally excluded from the life and worship of Israel. See "Excursus: The Vision of the Temple in Isaiah 56–66 and Zechariah 1–8" for a comparative analysis of this element of Isaiah 56–66.

33 Meyers and Meyers (*Haggai, Zechariah 1–8*, xl–xli) lend insight to the peculiarities of the situation during the Persian era:

> The preexilic prophets had little use for Assyria and Babylonia except as instruments of divine punishment, but Persia was a different matter altogether for the postexilic prophets. Both Haggai and Zechariah [1–8] placed their prophetic office in support of the reestablished province of Yehud. Zechariah in particular viewed Persia as an instrument of divine will. A kind of realistic, pragmatic viewpoint therefore is assumed by each prophet as he tried to assist his fellow Yehudites in the difficult transition back to "normalcy."
>
> But the normalcy of the Second Temple was not to be that of the First Temple, and the premonarchic pattern of dual leadership in civil and religious affairs gained new meaning and cogency. It was an enormous challenge for the two prophets to sensitize their audience to the traditional authority and the feasibility of the new pattern of leadership. At the same time, the temple still lay in ruins. The prophets provided that crucial measure of support for the enterprise of rebuilding that tipped the balance in favor of the temple's restoration being achieved. Haggai in particular is almost singlehandedly responsible for inspiring his countrymen to get about the task of actual labor on the temple. More than the accounts in Ezra (5:1 and 6:14) of those days, the Book of Haggai provides vivid testimony of the effect his words had on the people (Hag 1:12-13): the people heeded the words of Haggai and set about their task of rebuilding the temple. Since the two prophets Haggai and Zechariah overlap in their ministries, and since Zechariah presupposes that temple work had already recommenced, we can assume that the building efforts had been brought about by Haggai's exhortations.

34 Meyers and Meyers, *Haggai, Zechariah 1–8*, xxix.

35 Meyers and Meyers, *Haggai, Zechariah 1–8*, xliii–xliv.

36 D. Carr, *Holy Resilience: The Bible's Traumatic Origins* (New Haven, Conn.: Yale University Press, 2014), 129.

37 Ezekiel 20:33-35. The Exodus language is unmistakable here: causing them to come out (e.g., Exodus 7:4), a mighty hand and outstretched arm (Deuteronomy 4:34; 5:15; 7:19; 11:2; 26:8; 1 Kings 8:42; Jeremiah 21:5; 32:21; Psalm 136:12), the wilderness, and a face-to-face encounter (Exodus 33:11).

38 Ezekiel 20:36.

39 Ezekiel 40–48.

40 J. D. Levenson, *Theology of the Program of Restoration of Ezekiel 40–48* (Cambridge, Mass.: Scholars, 1976), 25–36.

41 Levenson, *Program of Restoration*, 7–24. Levenson makes a careful distinction between understanding Ezekiel 40–48 as an eschatological vision or a practical program (44–49). Levenson recognizes that this is an eschatological vision of divine grace, "one which can occur only through the type of divine action described in chs. 33–37" (45). This vision must not be confused with historical impulses (e.g., the early Calvinists' effort to establish the kingdom of God in Geneva). Still, surmises Levenson, "the highly specific nature of the description of the Temple, its liturgy and community bespeaks a practical program . . . not a vision of pure grace. For example, when the text says that eight steps led up to the vestibule of the inner court (Ezek. 30:31), can this be other than a demand that the new Temple be constructed just so?" (45). Levenson contends that "in sum, the order defined by the vision is still a goal to be effected through human striving and was understood as such by the tradition" (46). D. Block (*The Book of Ezekiel, Chapters 25–48* [Grand Rapids: Eerdmans, 1998], 504–6) also discusses whether the vision is purely eschatological or a blueprint for the future; he concludes that it should be understood "ideationally," that is, "not physical geography but spiritual realities" (505).

42 This discussion focuses exclusively upon the temple vision in Exodus 40–48. Others have looked more broadly at the question of whether Ezekiel is a prophet like Moses—or even a second Moses. See "Excursus: Ezekiel and the Torah."

43 Levenson (*Program of Restoration*, 38) draws this parallel between Ezekiel 43:18-27 and Leviticus 8 and 9. He writes: "Whoever the authors of chs. 40–48 be, the role of Moses falls upon the prophet Ezekiel. Ezek. 40–48 is the only corpus of legislation of the Hebrew Bible which is not placed in the mouth of Moses" (39). H. McKeating ("Ezekiel the 'Prophet like Moses'?" *JSOT* 61 [1994]: 101) calls attention to Ezekiel 44:15-31. He concludes that "the parallelism is close. Both Ezekiel 44 and Exodus 28–29 devote about half their space to the question of priestly garments. The other half, in Exodus, is devoted to the consecration of priests, that is, how they are made holy; in the Ezekiel passage the other half of the space is devoted to how their holiness is maintained."

44 McKeating ("Ezekiel the 'Prophet like Moses?'" 100) makes this rather obvious but significant observation: "Thus Moses, like Ezekiel, or Ezekiel, like Moses, goes up a high mountain, sees a vision of what the sanctuary is meant to be like, and beholds the glory of the Lord. The parallelism at this point is uncannily close."

45 Levenson (*Program of Restoration*, 39) notes how the detailed blueprint in Ezekiel 40–42 has its closest correspondence in the blueprint (תַּבְנִית) of the tabernacle.

46 Ezekiel 40:2; Numbers 27:12-13; Deuteronomy 32:52. Levenson (*Program of Restoration*, 42–44) explores the relationship between Ezekiel and Moses in relation to Priestly material. In general, Levenson writes: "Ezekiel is allowed to see the Land about which all his preaching has centered, but only in an inspired vision. He is not allowed to settle there, but must instead return to Babylonia to tell the exiles of his vision and to communicate to them the laws revealed to him. This motif has only a single close biblical parallel—Moses' one glimpse of the Promised Land before his death" (42) (Numbers 27:12-13; Deuteronomy 32:52). Moses' experience, contends Levenson, "had special relevance to the Exile. Through the experience of the prophet, Israel could receive a vicarious taste of the symbol of unmerited divine benefaction, the Promised Land" (43). McKeating ("Ezekiel the 'Prophet like Moses?'" 103) contends similarly, "What Moses does for the first tabernacle and the first settlement, Ezekiel is attempting to do for the second temple and for the restoration."

47 More tentative suggestions have been made. (1) McKeating ("Ezekiel the 'Prophet like Moses?'" 102–3) compares instructions about the so-called prince in Ezekiel 45:7-17 and 46:16-18 with limits on the king in Deuteronomy 17:14-20. (2) W. Zimmerli (*Ezekiel 2: A Commentary on the Book of the Prophet Ezekiel Chapters 25–28* [Philadelphia: Fortress, 1983], 430), following F. Baumgärtel, notes the use of prophetic language to introduce legal contents in both Exodus and Ezekiel, as well as possible dual introductions to Numbers 19 and Ezekiel 43:18-27, in which Zimmerli sees parallel developments in Ezekiel and Priestly materials. (3) C. Patton ("'I Myself Gave Them Laws that Were Not Good': Ezekiel 20 and the Exodus Traditions," *Journal for the Study of the Old Testament* 69 [1996]: 89) argues that Moses is a negative figure. "If Ezekiel knew of Moses, Moses was not just irrelevant; he mirrored the deceived prophet of 14.9 who gave laws that led to violation, separation, death." Therefore, argues Patton, Ezekiel's Torah must be "a complete reorganization of Israelite society" (88).

48 Zimmerli (*Ezekiel 2*, 330) discusses various ways to read the Hebrew text: either as the tenth month or the tenth day of the month (i.e., Passover).

49 Levenson (*Program of Restoration*, 43–44), notes, "Thus, the P material between the command to Moses to ascend the mountain and his death bears a not incidental similarity to the material of Ezek. 40–48." Details in the following notes are from Levenson's list of similarities.

50 Numbers 28–29; Ezekiel 45:18-25; 46:1-15.

51 Numbers 32; 33:50-56; Ezekiel 47:13–48:29. Numbers 34:1-15 delineates boundaries, as does Ezekiel 47:13-20.

52 Numbers 35; Ezekiel 45:1-6; 48:13-14.

53 Numbers 36; Ezekiel 46:16-18.

54 Levenson (*Program of Restoration*, 43–44) also notices differences. "In short, from the time Moses is commanded to climb Abiram until his death, the only P material unparalleled in Ezek. 40–48 is Nu. 30 (laws about vows), Nu. 31 (the raid on Midian, in which the theme of allocation of booty among the clans is paramount), and Nu. 33:1-50 (stations of the Exodus)." Block (*Ezekiel 25–48*, 501) includes a helpful comparison of "Mosaic Torah and Ezekielian Torah."

55 Jeremiah 16:14-15. This is repeated nearly verbatim in Jeremiah 23:7-8, where it better suits the context. Jeremiah 16:14-15 may be a later Deuteronomic insertion. W. McKane (*Jeremiah*, vol. 1, *1–25*, ICC [Edinburgh: T&T Clark, 1986], 373–76) offers a thorough discussion of these two texts, including their relationship to one another.

56 Jeremiah 31:32. The influence of Hosea 2:25 may be evident here. W. McKane (*Jeremiah*, vol. 2, *25–52*, ICC [Edinburgh: T&T Clark, 1996], 817–27) offers an illuminating discussion of the text in Jeremiah. Once again, questions arise over whether this is a preexilic statement (with no explicit reference to exile), a post-586 B.C.E. claim, or a later Deuteronomic redaction, either exilic or postexilic.

57 See "Excursus: Second Exodus in Isaiah 40–55" for a consideration of the arguments for and against reading Isaiah 40–55 in light of exodus traditions.

58 Isaiah 43:15-17.

59 H. Barstad admits that Isaiah 43:14-21 contains an allusion to the exodus. "The exodus tradition, being one of the most important and most influential of all the ancient biblical traditions, is, of course, also to be found in Is 40–55. If this had not been the case, it would indeed have been remarkable" (*A Way in the Wilderness: The "Second Exodus" in the Message of Second Isaiah* [Manchester: University of Manchester Press, 1989], 93). Nevertheless, he claims that "the motif of the passing through the Red Sea only serves the function

of a hymnic *Götterepithet*, aimed at convincing the prophet's audience that Yahweh, the mighty god that once saved his people from the Egyptians in a miraculous way, again will act on behalf of his chosen people. He shall now save them from the Babylonian yoke. . . . [T]here is no relating of the exodus event to the actual release of the Israelites from Babylon, nor any reference to any wandering through the desert back to Jerusalem, modelled on the wilderness wanderings of the Pentateuchal traditions" (97). In this rejection of the new exodus motif, Barstad's constrictive interpretation of the theme comes to the fore. No, the prophet does not imagine an actual (Barstad's word) release, an actual desert, an actual sea. No desert, in fact, was crossable between Babylon and Palestine. No sea, in fact, separated Babylon from Palestine. It is possible to imagine, however, that God would do a work akin to the exodus without positing that they had to look exactly alike. Allusion does not demand that. Certainly the words "redeemer," "makes a way in the sea, a path in the mighty waters," and "chariot and horse," which "lie down, they cannot rise," are evocative of the exodus. God will not repeat the same actions, but the actions the prophet imagines will be similar in scope and significance to the exodus. In this respect, they will be a new exodus.

Barstad continues along an equally narrow vein when he writes: "We notice further that we in Is 43:14-21 also find other motifs, well known to us from the Second Isaian corpus: the reference to the old and the new things, to the way in the desert, to the water in the wilderness, and to Yahweh's election of the Israelite people. But again, none of these different motifs has anything to do with any 'new exodus.' They are all poetical metaphors, giving expression to the future of salvation of the Judean people, i.e. their national restoration, their ingathering from the golah (not only from Babylon), and, last, but not least, victory over their enemies. In sum, all of these ideas constitute *the* theological and political program of the prophet Second Isaiah. Rather than to any 'new exodus' we find in these texts allusions to the 'new Israel'" (97). The special pleading in this case is hardly difficult to pinpoint. First, the distinction between a new exodus and a new Israel is forced; surely there is overlap between them. Second, while it is true that these motifs could be general in nature, in a context that contains clear elements of the exodus, it is sounder exegetically to interpret a way in the desert and water in the wilderness within the scope of that story. What may be a general metaphor elsewhere in Isaiah 40–55 (if one concedes this to Barstad) need not be a general metaphor in a context permeated by elements of the exodus. Third, the distinction between metaphor and an actual, historical event that matches the exodus—an event which Barstad quite correctly rejects—is unnecessary (see "Excursus: Second Exodus in Isaiah 40–55").

60 Isaiah 43:19-20.

61 J. Blenkinsopp (*Isaiah 40–55: A New Translation with Introduction and Commentary* [New York: Doubleday, 2002], 227–28) puts the matter well when he writes: "The argument here draws on analogy rather than prophecy. What God did in guiding his people en route to Canaan and providing them with life-giving water (Exod 15:22-27; 17:1-7; Num 20:2-13) is paradigmatic of what God does whenever he acts to save or redeem his people." Blenkinsopp goes on to say, "The point is made with a fine subtlety by the use of present participles in vv 16-17a" (228). Much more could be said about this text: the baptism of hope in tradition—liberation from Babylon rooted in liberation from Egypt—but with the surprising proviso to stop thinking about the past and to look instead to the future; the use of the particle "now" (Isaiah 43:19a); the inclusion of animals in restoration; and the background of a diaspora that extended beyond Babylon (e.g., Isaiah 41:9; 43:5; 49:12). K. Baltzer (*Deutero-Isaiah: A Commentary on Isaiah 40–55* [Minneapolis: Fortress, 2001]

175) wraps up his comment on this text with a sense of admiration for it: "This text is a model for the function of biblical tradition. The experience of the past helps toward an understanding of things in the present. The continuity of God's faithfulness makes hope for the future possible. This is in itself an exposition of tradition. But there are no superficial quotations. What we are offered is a further transmission of the testimony that this is 'the fulfillment of the Scriptures.'" P. Hanson (*Isaiah 40–66* [Louisville, Ky.: Westminster John Knox, 1995], 72) offers insight into why the prophet tells the people not to forget the past and to look ahead. The familiarity of the exodus tradition "would have had a lulling effect, evoking the feelings of the 'old-time religion' and giving comfort to a people battered on all sides by a threatening world filled with unfamiliar gods, rulers, languages, and customs." While there is nothing wrong with such retreat, it can become "a habit of mind and a permanent posture," "spiritual escapism." For the prophet, this posture was not an option. "Destiny hung in the balance with earthshaking events unfolding around them. The Jewish community was being engulfed by international developments that threatened to obliterate its identity and vocation as God's people. Accordingly, right at the point when his audience would have begun to yield to the soothing effects of the recitation of the traditional images of the exodus, Second Isaiah introduces a clashing dissonance with the words: 'Do not remember the former things, or consider the things of old.'"

62 Isaiah 48:20-21. Barstad (*A Way in the Wilderness*, 101) again imports questionable categories to discount the value of a text that relates the exodus to a future act of liberation from Babylon. He does admit, "Contrary to all the texts which we have dealt with above, the passage Is 48:20-21 *could* be read as a reference to a new exodus the way some scholars have understood this particular motif." Still, he refuses to concede defeat in the pursuit of his goal: "But this is not what the passage is all about. The basic context of these verses is not the return of the chosen people to Zion *an sich*, but rather a word of doom against Babylon. When the prophet addresses his fellow countrymen in Babylon with the request: 'Go forth from Babylon, flee from Chaldea', this should not be regarded as a request to run away from their captivity. We must here keep in mind that the context is that of a word of doom against Babylon. The meaning of the prophetic word is rather this: As Babylon is going to be destroyed by Yahweh, those of the people of Yahweh who soujourn [*sic*] there, either as a result of deportations, or as a result of voluntary migration, had better leave Babylon at once, or they will suffer with the Babylonians. . . . What we have here, is an indirect word of doom against the Babylonians rather than a reference to a 'new exodus.'" Again, this interpretation is too dichotomous to be valid. Barstad's rejection of this text in terms of a new exodus requires that an interpreter choose between a word of condemnation to Babylon and a word of second exodus to the exiles. They are, however, one and the same, just as escape from Egypt came simultaneously with the destruction of Egypt's army. True enough, this is not a prediction of which body of water and which desert will be crossed, but the prophet unmistakably links the command to flee Babylon with recollection of provision in the wilderness—in the most specific of terms. Barstad's dichotomy, which allows him to minimize the element of a second exodus, cannot stand close scrutiny.

63 This command may be based upon Jeremiah 50:8, which contains a similar command to flee Babylon.

64 The tradition of provision was remembered in two narrative versions (Exodus 17:1-7; Numbers 20:1-13), celebrated in the poetry of the psalms (Psalms 78:15-16; 105:41; 114:8), and recalled in Nehemiah 9:15. Baltzer (*Deutero-Isaiah*, 302–3) offers insightful comments on this text, including its reliance upon Exodus 17:1-7, as opposed to Numbers 20:1-13 and Psalm 78:15-16, 20.

65 Isaiah 51:9-11. Barstad is compelled to apply his constrictive lens to this text to exclude it from a possible emphasis in Isaiah 40–55 on a second exodus. Barstad (*A Way in the Wilderness*, 73) separates the exodus from a possible new exodus.

> The reference to the combat myth, and in that connection also the passing of the Israelites through the sea, serves the function of underlining, in a hymnic/rhetorical way, the mighty powers of Yahweh. In no way does the author of Is 51:9-11 intend any connection between the references to the combat/creation and the exodus with the exiles in Babylon, or with their home-coming alone. The home-coming, foreseen in v. 11, concerns the home-coming of exiles from all over the diaspora, forming a part of the restoration of the Judean nation. By referring to the mighty acts of salvation of Yahweh in the past, the prophet seeks to convince his audience of the reality of his saving words to Jerusalem and Judah, as well as of his words of doom regarding the foreign nations. So we do find an "exodus motif" in this text, but this is not an exodus motif relating to the concrete return of the exiles of Babylon through the desert back to Jerusalem. What is intended, is the restoring of the nation, brought about by, among other things, the destruction of the enemies of Israel, and the return of *all* exiles from the whole of the diaspora.

It is inconceivable, in my opinion, that Isaiah 51:10 and 51:11 should be unrelated, absent any sort of syntactical signal, and that the drying up of the sea so that the redeemed should cross would be distinct from the prediction that the ransomed of the Lord should return to Zion—except in the context of a strident scholarly agenda that seeks to eliminate any traces of a new exodus theme from Isaiah 40–55.

66 Blenkinsopp (*Isaiah 40–55*, 331-32) and C. Westermann (*Isaiah 40–66: A Commentary* [Philadelphia: Westminster, 1969], 240-42) illuminate the similarities between this type of liturgical composition in Isaiah 51:9-11 and Psalm 44 (especially verses 1-8 [Hebrew 1-9], 23 [Hebrew 24]), Psalm 74 (especially verses 12-17, 22), and Psalm 80 (especially verses 3, 8-13 [Hebrew 9-14]).

67 Hanson, *Isaiah 40–66*, 145. Isaiah 51:11 recollects Isaiah 35:10.

68 Isaiah 52:11-12. These strophes are similar to Isaiah 48:20-22.

69 U. Berges (*Jesaja 49–54* [Freiburg im Breisgau: Herder, 2015], 205) notes, "Die Exodusmetaphorik, die in V 11 bereits durchschien, bricht nun ganz durch und bestimmt diesen Schlussvers vollends."

70 Exodus 12:35.

71 Exodus 12:11; Deuteronomy 16:3.

72 Exodus 13:21-22; Numbers 14:14.

73 Exodus 14:19; 23:20-23; 32:34; 33:1-3.

74 The one possible glitch in the symmetry of God as front and rear guard is the word translated *rearguard*. As in Isaiah 43:9, this verb can mean simply "to gather": God will go before and gather from behind. Yet in other texts, in the piel stem, as in Isaiah 52:12, the word denotes a military rear guard. For instance, when the Israelites set out from Sinai, "the standard of the camp of Dan, acting as the rear guard of all the camps, set out, company by company" (Numbers 10:25). The army at Jericho had a rear guard: "And the armed men went before the priests who blew the trumpets; the rear guard came after the ark, while the trumpets blew continually" (Joshua 6:9). The symmetry of the promise in Isaiah 52:12—God's going before and behind—coupled with its reminiscence of the exodus, suggests that here, too, this word should communicate a rear guard.

75 Psalm 105:39.

76 The verb, עָלָה, occurs with reference to the exodus, in the hiphil stem, in Ezra 1:11; Exodus 3:8, 17; 33:1.

77 Ezra 1:6; Exodus 3:21-22; 11:2; 12:35-36; Psalm 105:37.

78 Isaiah 52:11-12.

79 Ezra 1:7-11.

80 H. Williamson, *Ezra and Nehemiah* (Sheffield: JSOT, 1987), 85.

81 Ezra 7:9. In Exodus 12:1-3, God speaks to Moses and Aaron: "This month shall mark for you the beginning of months; it shall be the first month of the year for you. Tell the whole congregation of Israel that on the tenth of this month they are to take a lamb for each family."

82 Williamson (*Ezra and Nehemiah*, 85–86) follows K. Koch ("Ezra and the Origins of Judaism," *Journal of Semitic Studies* 19 [1974]: 186) by arguing that "if, as v. 10 suggests, Ezra chose this date because of his study of the Torah, it was doubtless because of reflection in particular upon the date in Exod. 12.2." J. Blenkinsopp (*Ezra-Nehemiah: A Commentary* [Philadelphia: Westminster, 1988], 138–39) agrees: "That Ezra fixed the date of departure alerts us to the religious significance of these chronological indications. Like the exodus from Egypt, the departure is to be in the first month."

83 Koch ("Ezra and the Origins of Judaism," 184) sets out to demonstrate that "Ezra's march from Babylonia to Jerusalem was a cultic procession which Ezra understood as a second Exodus and a partial fulfilment of prophetic expectations." In addition to those already cited, he identifies other elements of a second exodus in Ezra. First, he argues that the detail of a delay at the River Ahawa because no Levite had arrived is "only conceivable against the order of the march through the desert after exodus, which required Levites (Num 10:13ff)" (187–88). Second, he argues that the description of occupation parallels the first occupation after the exodus (188–89). Third, he argues that the words, a "little renewal. For slaves we are . . ." in Ezra 9:8 comprise a recognition that the new exodus was only partial by comparison with the first. "But it must be remembered that there were surely not 60,000 exiles in Babylon, perhaps not even 20,000. So a second Exodus could not have the size of the first. This time it was not all the people who were in exile" (189). Koch summarizes, "All these details of the Ezra record are understandable only if the historical Ezra intended to fulfil the promises or, better, to be the instrument of fulfilment of the promises of the exilic prophets about a marvelous return of the exiles, which will be the foundation of a second Israel and the opening of a new *Heilsgeschichte*" (188). J. McConville ("Ezra-Nehemiah and the Fulfilment of Prophecy," *Vetus Testamentum* 36 [1986]: 205–24) develops this thesis in more detail.

84 If the passages that describe the architecture and building of the tabernacle are products of the Persian era, as they are often thought to be, then they provide clear testimony to a robust interest in the spirit after 539 B.C.E. I have analyzed these texts in detail in *Filled with the Spirit* (Grand Rapids: Eerdmans, 2009), 51–65.

85 Judges 3:9-12 (Othniel); 6:34 (Gideon); 11:29 (Jephthah); and 14:6; 14:19; 15:14 (Samson). The spirit *is upon* Othniel (וַתְּהִי עָלָיו רוּחַ־יְהוָה) and Jephthah (וַתְּהִי עַל־יִפְתָּח רוּחַ יְהוָה), *clothes* Gideon (6:34) (לָבְשָׁה), *rushes upon* (וַתִּצְלַח עָלָיו רוּחַ יְהוָה) Samson. In an ambiguous reference in Judges 13:25, the spirit begins to move (וַתָּחֶל רוּחַ יְהוָה לְפַעֲמוֹ) in Samson.

86 M. Welker (*God the Spirit* [Minneapolis: Fortress, 1994], 65 [emphasis in original]) offers an alternative reading of Judges by claiming that the judges restored solidarity rather than engaging in battle. "Even the early experiences of God's Spirit," claims Welker, "are *experiences of how a new beginning is made toward restoring the community of God's people.* They are *experiences of the forgiveness of sins, of the raising up of the 'crushed and oppressed,'*

and of the renewal of the *forces of life*." When the spirit clothes Gideon, he gathers the people together (Judges 6:34). When it comes upon Jephthah, he passes through Gilead and Manasseh (11:29). Yet, against Welker, the end to which the spirit comes or rushes upon the judges is not benign. When the spirit rushed upon Samson for a second time, for instance, "he went down to Ashkelon" and "killed thirty men" (14:19). A third time, the spirit gave him superhuman strength, causing what bound him to melt; immediately he found the fresh jawbone of an ass and killed a thousand people with it (15:14-15).

87 Hebrew: וַתִּצְלַח רוּחַ־אֱלֹהִים עַל־שָׁאוּל. The addition of the words, "in power," in NRSV, is unnecessary, so they are omitted in this translation.

88 This is only one dimension of Saul's story. Saul also prophesied and changed into another person when the spirit came upon him, presumably through contact with a company of prophets stirred by musical instruments (1 Samuel 10:6. Hebrew: וְצָלְחָה עָלֶיךָ רוּחַ יְהוָה. In 1 Samuel 10:10, וַתִּצְלַח עָלָיו רוּחַ אֱלֹהִים.). That spirit remained with Saul until his susceptibility to an evil spirit prompted the passing of the spirit from him to David (1 Samuel 16:13).

89 Though the language is slightly different, it may have surfaced in Ezekiel 11:4-5. Immediately after he was commanded to prophesy (לָכֵן הִנָּבֵא עֲלֵיהֶם הִנָּבֵא בֶּן־אָדָם), the spirit "fell upon" (וַתִּפֹּל עָלַי רוּחַ יְהוָה) Ezekiel. This claim is too short to determine whether the story of the judges or Saul influenced Ezekiel's claim. The Hebrew verb, furthermore, is different from the verbs in those stories. Whether it draws from the story of the judges or Saul, Ezekiel's claim, from the beginning of exile, anticipates a wrinkle in the Persian-era composition, 1–2 Chronicles, where individuals upon whom the spirit comes speak prophetic words.

90 In an interesting twist, this Persian-era revision of earlier materials omits the story of Saul, his transformation into another sort of human, and his dramatic surrender to spirits, both good and evil (1 Samuel 10–19). The story line begins with the anointing of David, though there is no hint even here of David's reception of the spirit (1 Samuel 16:13). These omissions render the addition of four references to the spirit more conspicuous.

91 The translation of the root, לבשׁ, in NRSV as "came upon" is puzzling. In Judges 6:34 and 2 Chronicles 24:20, the translators choose "took possession of." Here, in 1 Chronicles 12:18, they choose "came upon." Neither is adequate. "Took possession of" unnecessarily conjures images of spirit and demon possession; "came upon" is the translation of a different verb entirely, *to be*, as in 2 Chronicles 15:1: הָיְתָה עָלָיו רוּחַ אֱלֹהִים, rather than "clothed."

92 1 Chronicles 12:18; Hebrew: 12:19, וְרוּחַ לָבְשָׁה.

93 He claims, "We are yours, O David; and with you, O son of Jesse! Peace, peace to you, and peace to the one who helps you! For your God is the one who helps you." Without hesitation, "David received them, and made them officers of his troops" (1 Chronicles 12:16-18; Hebrew: 12:17-19).

94 2 Chronicles 15:1, my translation. Hebrew: הָיְתָה עָלָיו רוּחַ אֱלֹהִים.

95 2 Chronicles 15:8. His words, in fact, are referred to as a prophecy (הַדְּבָרִים הָאֵלֶּה וְהַנְּבוּאָה).

96 2 Chronicles 20:13-14 (modified from NRSV). Hebrew: הָיְתָה עָלָיו רוּחַ יְהוָה. Emphasis upon the public setting, "in the middle of the assembly," may comprise an allusion to Ezekiel 8:1, which refers to an experience in the presence of Israel's elders: "In the sixth year, in the sixth month, on the fifth day of the month, as I sat in my house, with the elders of Judah sitting before me, the hand of the Lord God fell upon me there."

97 2 Chronicles 20:20-28. Because of Jahaziel's advice, the people of Judah did not lift a finger; they looked on and sang praises while their enemies ambushed one another. His speech differs from the first two, which were delivered principally to kings. Jahaziel belongs to the sons of Asaph, whom David appointed, that they "should prophesy with lyres, harps,

and cymbals" (1 Chronicles 25:1). Jahaziel was, in short, one of Israel's trained musicians. For this reason, what follows Jahaziel's speech is hardly surprising. The king bowed down, face to the ground, as did all Judah and the inhabitants of Jerusalem, worshiping. The Levites and others stood "to praise the LORD, the God of Israel, with a very loud voice" (2 Chronicles 20:18-19).

98 2 Chronicles 24:20, my translation. Hebrew: וְרוּחַ אֱלֹהִים לָבְשָׁה.

99 2 Chronicles 24:21-22. This last inspired speaker in 1–2 Chronicles illustrates Israel's opposition to its prophets, to its priest-prophets, to men (and only men, apparently) of impeccable priestly, levitic, or military pedigree. The final word on inspiration in 2 Chronicles—in the entire Hebrew Bible—mirrors tragically other postexilic surveys of the history of Israelite prophecy:

> They abandoned the house of the LORD, the God of their ancestors, and served the sacred poles and the idols. And wrath came upon Judah and Jerusalem for this guilt of theirs. Yet God sent prophets among them to bring them back to the LORD; they testified against them, but they would not listen. (2 Chronicles 24:18-19)
>
> Many years you were patient with them, and warned them by your spirit through your prophets; yet they would not listen. Therefore you handed them over to the peoples of the lands. (Nehemiah 9:30)
>
> They made their hearts adamant in order not to hear the law and the words that the LORD of hosts had sent by his spirit through the former prophets. Therefore great wrath came from the LORD of hosts. (Zechariah 7:12)

100 It is not possible to provide an orderly chronology of literature from the Persian era. All that can be said with relative certainty is that both the book of Haggai and 1–2 Chronicles were composed and edited during the Persian era.

101 More detailed analyses are available in my *Inspired: The Holy Spirit and the Mind of Faith* (Grand Rapids: Eerdmans, 2013), 130–34.

102 Isaiah 32:15-30.

103 Isaiah 44:3-4.

104 Ezekiel 38:28-29.

105 Joel 2:28-29; Hebrew 3:1-2.

106 Zechariah 12:10. See also Isaiah 29:10, in which God pours out a spirit of deep sleep upon the prophets, Judah's seers.

107 Hebrew: עַד־יֵעָרֶה עָלֵינוּ רוּחַ מִמָּרוֹם.

108 Isaiah 32:15-18 (modified from NRSV).

109 Hebrew: אֶצֹּק רוּחִי עַל־זַרְעֶךָ.

110 Isaiah 44:3-5.

111 There may be something else new here: an appeal to foreigners. The claim "I am the LORD's" and the adoption of Israel's name transcends the replenishment of Abraham and Sarah's physical descendants by extending salvation to those who have not yet professed their faith in the God of Abraham and Sarah. The verb כנה, translated as "adopt," occurs in Isaiah 45:4 in a depiction of Persian ruler Cyrus: "I call you by your name, I surname [אֲכַנְּךָ] you, though you do not know me." The untamed torrents of the spirit, then, cannot be contained within Judah's family tree; they overflow to a world that has yet to follow Israel's God—including, just a few strophes later, Cyrus of Persia. The lavishness of this exilic promise contrasts with the earlier promise of Isaiah 32:15 in still another way. In the eighth-century promise, Isaiah chooses a verb (יֵעָרֶה) with the primary nuance of laying

bare (e.g., Leviticus 20:18; Isaiah 22:6) or emptying a vessel (e.g., Genesis 24:20) or even oneself (Isaiah 53:12); the spirit will be emptied onto the wilderness. The verb in the exilic prophecy communicates outpouring (אֶצֹּק), such as of oil (e.g., Leviticus 14:26; 21:10; 1 Samuel 10:1), water for cleansing or washing (e.g., 2 Kings 3:11), and sacrificial blood (e.g., Leviticus 9:9). This lavishness is especially accented by the presence of "torrents" in the desert: water on thirsty ground, torrents on dry ground. The shift from laying bare to outpouring matches the more drastic situation of the exile. No more is Judah in a state of mere political angst; now Judah has lost land, king, and temple. The outpouring must be full and final.

112 Ezekiel 39:28-29. Ezekiel's deep longing, expressed in nationalistic and land-based terms, is that God will never again desert Israel.

113 Joel 2:28-31; Hebrew 3:1-4. Joel imagines an indistinct day in the future, about which God promises, "Then afterward I will pour out my spirit on all flesh [אֶשְׁפּוֹךְ אֶת־רוּחִי עַל־כָּל־בָּשָׂר]; your sons and your daughters shall prophesy, your old men shall dream dreams, and your young men shall see visions. Even on the male and female slaves, in those days, I will pour out my spirit. I will show portents in the heavens and on the earth, blood and fire and columns of smoke. The sun shall be turned to darkness, and the moon to blood, before the great and terrible day of the Lord comes."

114 Zechariah 12:10. This final reference in the book of Zechariah occurs in the final six chapters of the book, which may have been originally separate from and later than the first eight chapters. C. Meyers and E. Meyers (*Zechariah 9–14: A New Translation with Introduction and Commentary* [New York: Doubleday, 1993], 15–45) discuss this issue. D. L. Peterson (*Haggai and Zechariah 1–8* [Philadelphia: Westminster, 1984], 110–25) offers a detailed analysis of Zechariah 1–8 and its formation.

115 Zechariah 12:10. It is a moot point to ask whether this has to do with the spirit of God or whether this merely means that God will pour out a disposition, a sense of compassion and supplication, upon certain people. The division between disposition or inspiration, human and divine spirit, attitude or possession, is one that certainly does not rise readily to the surface of the literature of ancient Israel. For example, if a wife is sexually unfaithful to her husband but undetected, "if a spirit of jealousy comes on him, and he is jealous of his wife who has defiled herself; or if a spirit of jealousy comes on him, and he is jealous of his wife, though she has not defiled herself; then the man shall bring his wife to the priest" (Numbers 5:14-15), who subjects her to an awful test in which she drinks the grain offering and reveals her guilt by causing her womb to drop or not. Is the spirit of jealousy an actual spirit that possesses the husband, or is this an expression for a jealous state? The story of Saul, in which an evil spirit from God torments him and causes him to rage against David, may weigh in on the side of actual possession. Still, if the spirit of jealousy comes from God, why is there any need to have the priest test the wife? Is the presence of a spirit of jealousy not enough? Another example of the ambiguity—or perhaps multivalence—of the notion of the spirit when it is attached to another noun—spirit of compassion and supplication, spirit of jealousy—is the description of an ideal ruler in Isaiah 28:5-6: "In that day the Lord of hosts will be a garland of glory, and a diadem of beauty, to the remnant of his people; and a spirit of justice to the one who sits in judgment, and strength to those who turn back the battle at the gate." Rich with metaphor, this text portrays God as a garland and a diadem, strength to warriors. Is the "spirit of justice" also a metaphor, or is this description to be understood in light of Isaiah 11:1-6, in which the spirit seems to be a presence that endows the ideal ruler with wisdom,

knowledge, etc.? It is extremely difficult, perhaps impossible, to decide. Nor is it necessarily advisable to decide, given the richness of the notion of *rûaḥ* in Antiquity.

116 A subsequent list of mourners (Zechariah 12:12-14) suggests who: the house of David (royalty), the house of Nathan (perhaps David's court prophet), and the house of Levi (priests and Levites).

117 Isaiah 32:15-20.

118 Isaiah 44:3-5.

119 Joel 2:28-32.

120 Hebrew: וְסָפְדוּ.

121 Isaiah 32:15.

122 Isaiah 44:3.

123 Ezekiel 39:28-29.

124 Joel 2:28-32.

125 Zechariah 12:10.

126 Isaiah 11:2. These are precisely the qualities that human beings can only pretend to exhibit. Assyria's arrogance impels it to make an ill-advised claim to wisdom and understanding (Isaiah 10:13). Judah's counsel (Isaiah 8:10) comes to nothing, and its mighty warriors fall in battle (Isaiah 3:25). As a consequence, Judah is void of knowledge (Isaiah 5:13) and pervaded by misguided fear (Isaiah 7:4; 8:12-13; 10:24). What nations, including Isaiah's own, lack, this inspired ruler embodies. This fourfold list of qualities—the spirit, justice, the spoken word, and might—is similar to Micah's conception of his prophetic role. The sole difference is that Micah already has the spirit within him as a permanent endowment, while the notion of the resting of the spirit upon the ideal ruler flows from the image of the king as one who is anointed with oil (e.g., 1 Samuel 16:13). In both instances, Micah's and this ruler's, the spirit is conceived of as a permanent endowment. Further analysis of Micah 3:8 is available in my *Filled with the Spirit*, 41–47.

127 This image of the spirit's resting also occurs in a succession narrative in 2 Kings. "When the company of prophets who were at Jericho saw Elisha at a distance, they declared, 'The spirit of Elijah rests [נָחָה] on Elisha.' They came to meet him and bowed to the ground before him" (2 Kings 2:15).

128 Isaiah 42:1. Hebrew: נָתַתִּי רוּחִי עָלָיו. It is difficult to identify this servant, who could variously represent: the nation Israel (Isaiah 41:8-10); a faithful remnant within Israel; a prophetic individual, presumably the prophet who delivers this oracle; Moses, who is explicitly identified as God's servant and who is associated with judgment and teaching; or even, though unlikely, Cyrus, the Persian ruler who is designated the Lord's anointed because he restores the exiles to the land (Isaiah 45:1). Any of these alternatives is possible, with telling implications, though there is a wide chasm between the identification of the servant, for example, as Moses or Cyrus. R. Collins ("Servant of the Lord, the," *NIDB* 5:192–95) analyzes the so-called Servant Songs in Isaiah 40–55.

129 The words "his teaching," in Hebrew are תּוֹרָתוֹ.

130 Isaiah 42:6-7.

131 Hebrew: רוּחִי אֲשֶׁר עָלֶיךָ וּדְבָרַי אֲשֶׁר־שַׂמְתִּי בְּפִיךָ.

132 Isaiah 59:21.

133 Ezekiel 36:26-28; Jeremiah 31:31-34. These sweeping promises envisage the restoration of Judah after Babylonian exile. At first blush, it looks as if the prophet of Isaiah 56–66 has followed the same hopeful vein and issued the promise of a renewed covenant to Israel.

134 2 Samuel 7:13-14.

135 Isaiah 11:1-9.

136 Each occurrence of *you* or *your* is in the second-person singular. Nonetheless, the second-person singular can refer to corporate entities. In Isaiah 44:3, God addresses the servant, Jacob, as if he were an individual, although Jacob clearly represents the entire nation, including proselytes who will join this nation. Still, other important reasons exist for understanding the recipient of the spirit in Isaiah 59:21 as an individual. First, in Isaiah 44:3, unlike Isaiah 59:21, Israel is understood eponymously, that is, as an individual who is identified variously as Jacob, Israel, and Jeshurun (Isaiah 44:1-2); naturally, then, the pronouns will be in the singular. This is not the case in Isaiah 59:21. Second, in Isaiah 59:21, the spirit will not so much be poured out as put upon someone; throughout the entire Isaiah corpus, the spirit rests exclusively upon individuals (Isaiah 11:2; 42:1; 61:1). Third, the placement of God's words in "your [singular] mouth" is the classic expression for the inspiration of an *individual* prophet. When a group is in mind, as in 1 Kings 22:23, God gives a lying spirit "in the mouth of all these your prophets."

137 Isaiah 61:1-3.

138 Isaiah 11:1-4.

139 Isaiah 42:1-7.

140 Isaiah 11.

141 Isaiah 42.

142 Isaiah 59.

143 Isaiah 61.

144 Isaiah 11.

145 Isaiah 42.

146 Isaiah 59; 61.

147 Isaiah 42.

148 Isaiah 61.

149 A burst of creativity occurs in the book of Ezekiel, written under the initial duress of exile. Even a cursory reading of Ezekiel reveals the presence of *rûaḥ* in Judah's present and future: *rûaḥ* in the wheels that moved in every direction at once (Ezekiel 1:12, 20, 21; 10:17); *rûaḥ* that lifted Ezekiel in visionary transport (3:12, 14; 8:3; 11:1, 24; 37:1); the falling of *rûaḥ* upon Ezekiel (11:5); the promise of a new *rûaḥ* and heart (36:25-26); the infilling of bleached bones through the *rûaḥ*-breath and the rush of the four *rûaḥ*-winds (37:1-14); and the outpouring of *rûaḥ* on the reconstituted people (39:28-29). The miseries of exile did not dampen Ezekiel's conviction that the spirit was—and would be—present among the exiles.

150 Isaiah 59:21; 61:1-3. This characterization applies even if these chapters are dated in the Neo-Babylonian era, since during that period, too, traditions were taken up and understood afresh.

151 Zechariah 4:6.

152 Zechariah 7:12.

153 Zechariah 12:10.

154 Exodus 19:3-6.

155 W. Wilder (*Echoes of the Exodus in the Context and Background of Galatians 5:18* [New York: Peter Lang, 2001], 124–30) analyzes this text; his interest lies principally in Pauline literature, so he concludes that the Hebrew, which has stronger allusions to the exodus, would have been the version to influence the apostle Paul. "If Hag 2:4-5 was at all influential in Paul's conception of the Spirit as typologically equivalent to the theophanic cloud of the exodus," writes Wilder, "it is likely to have been a result of Paul's knowledge of the Hebrew text, rather than the Greek" (130).

156 Naturally, the awkward start, with this particle, has spawned many proposed solutions. For example, P. Akroyd ("Some Interpretative Glosses in the Book of Haggai," *JJS* 7 [1956]: 163) believes that the word הַדָּבָר "has been attracted into the accusative by the following verb in the relative clause, which not unnaturally appears to govern it." Another solution is to suggest that the word אֶת should be read not as the sign of a direct object but as the preposition *with*, though "*with* the word that I made" is hardly more sensible than "the word that I made" in this context. Still another solution is to supply a verb, such as *remember*: "remember the word that I made." This addition, however, is arbitrary. Meyers and Meyers (*Haggai and Zechariah 1–8*, 51–52) suggest that the words, "the word I cut with you when you came out of Egypt," are related to the preceding verb, *do*, "do . . . the thing [אֶת־הַדָּבָר] I cut with you when you came out of Egypt." The intervening words, אִתְּכֶם נְאֻם יְהוָה צְבָאוֹת, make this less likely, though Meyers and Meyers appeal to Amos 6:14, in which a reference to God's authority divides a verb from its direct object: מֵקִים עֲלֵיכֶם בֵּית יִשְׂרָאֵל נְאֻם־יְהוָה אֱלֹהֵי הַצְּבָאוֹת גּוֹי. Here "raise up" and "nation" are divided by more words than divide subject and object in Haggai 2:4-5. They suggest, "While English syntax could not allow such displacement, its occasional use in Hebrew cannot be discounted" (51). If Meyers and Meyers are correct, the question must be raised, What particular *thing* from the exodus story does Haggai want the people to accomplish? Meyers and Meyers see this *thing* as the two tablets of stone (52). For evidence, they appeal to 1 Kings 8:9: "There was nothing in the ark except the two tablets of stone that Moses had placed there at Horeb, which the Lord cut [כָּרַת] with the Israelites, when they came out of the land of Egypt" (my translation). "Haggai is using somewhat elliptical language," they write, "referring, literally, to the doing of 'the Word [of the covenant] which I cut with you'" (52). This is possible but no more probable than referring the word to what follows: "My spirit stands in your midst. Do not fear." A. Petterson (*Haggai, Zechariah, & Malachi* [Downers Grove, Ill.: InterVarsity, 2015], 66), citing the grammar of B. Waltke and M. O'Connor (*An Introduction to Biblical Hebrew Syntax* [Winona Lake, Ind.: Eisenbrauns, 1990], 178), together with Zechariah 7:7, suggests that the sign of the direct object can be a demonstrative in Mishnaic Hebrew: *this* is the word.

157 This has proven to be difficult to explain. Akroyd ("Some Interpretative Glosses," 163) summarizes the complicated explanation of Köhler, in which *word* substitutes for *covenant*. Akroyd suggests, "It is perhaps desirable to clarify this by suggesting that this gloss—if we accept the M.T. and do not simply emend away the unusual expression—shows how the original sense of *karath* has been so lost that it is used with *davar* as object, and thus has the sense of 'to make a promise.'"

158 E. Tov, *Textual Criticism of the Hebrew Bible* (Minneapolis: Fortress; Assen: Van Gorcum, 1992), 123.

159 G. Howard, "The Twelve Prophets: To the Reader," in *A New English Translation of the Septuagint and the Other Greek Translations Traditionally Included under that Title*, ed. A. Pietersma and B. Wright (New York: Oxford University Press, 2007), 777.

160 J. Wagner's (*Reading the Sealed Book: Old Greek Isaiah and the Problem of Septuagint Hermeneutics* [Tübingen: Mohr Siebeck; Waco, Tex.: Baylor, 2013], 235) characterization of interpretation in the Old Greek of Isaiah as "elucidating its language, modulating its discourse and contextualizing its message" may be relevant to Haggai.

161 Howard ("The Twelve Prophets," 779) suggests that "the short reading of the Greek was caused by the translator's eyes jumping from the words, 'for I am with you, says the Lord of host,' to the parallel phrase, 'my spirit is present among you,' leaving out the intervening words." While certainly possible, this conjecture is not altogether compelling, in my

opinion, since these thoughts have little by way of vocabulary in common. They may be parallel thoughts, but they are not parallel phrases, such that a scribe's eye would jump from one to the other. Another text-critical possibility does commend itself, though it too is conjectural. The repetition of the word אִתְּכֶם, in verses 4 and 5, may have caused a scribe's eye to skip from the first to the second and inadvertently to omit the intervening words, נְאֻם יְהוָה צְבָאוֹת אֶת־הַדָּבָר אֲשֶׁר־כָּרַתִּי. This is most of what is missing from the translations.

162 Personal correspondence from Martin Abegg, November 1, 2017. He writes as well, "The only DSScroll that contains Hag 2:5 is Mur 88 which dates—according to Milik (DJD II, 183)—'assez semblable à celle du n° 1, mais pas identique,' which sends us back to p. 75: 'début du II siècle'."

163 My translation. The participle leaves open the question of whether the prophets *were* teaching or *are* teaching.

164 Hebrew אֶת־הַדָּבָר in Aramaic reads יָת פִּתְגָמָא.

165 Translational difficulties are apparent even in contemporary English translations. The New Revised Standard Version masks the difficulties in this line by adding "according to" at the start, translating *word* as "promise," and *cut* as "made": "according to the promise that I made you when you came out of Egypt." The New International Version begins with "this" and introduces the notion of a covenant, no doubt because of the verb *cut*, though in the Hebrew God cut a word rather than a covenant: "This is what I covenanted with you when you came out of Egypt." The Common English Bible takes a similar tack: "as with our agreement when you came out of Egypt." The Roman Catholic Jerusalem Bible and the Anglican New English Bible avoid such difficulties by excising this line altogether. It is not a long step from modern to ancient translations: for all of them, the difficulties of the Hebrew text demanded translational fidgeting or, better yet, surgical excision of the difficult text. Contemporary translations also reveal how easily allusions can be masked. The New Revised Standard Version, which reads: "My spirit abides among you," lacks even the slightest hint of the exodus. Nor is there an adumbration of the exodus in the New International Version, which reads: "and my Spirit remains among you." The Jerusalem Bible, too, contains no reminiscence of the exodus: "And my *spirit* is present among you." The Common English Bible, in contrast, does train a reader's eye on the exodus: "my spirit stands in your midst." The single word, *stand*, associated with the spirit, recalls the principal event of Israel's past. Coupled with the preceding line in Hebrew, "the word I cut with you when you came out of Egypt," the salutary word, *stand*, signals a rekindling of the exodus that is especially meaningful for the origin of pneumatology. See "Excursus: Haggai 2:4-5 as a Gloss."

166 Exodus 14:19-20a (modified from NRSV).

167 It is important to be reminded that the Hebrew word translated "pillar" is from the same root as the verb *to stand*.

168 Exodus 13:21-22 (modified from NRSV). This strategic role is central to the tradition (Deuteronomy 1:33; Psalm 78:14; 105:39).

169 I discussed the use of the imperfect tense in the first chapter.

170 Psalm 78:14.

171 Psalm 105:39.

172 In Deuteronomy 4:9-12, for example, the people of a later generation are positioned at Mt. Sinai.

173 Haggai 2:21-22.

174 Exodus 15:4. Horses and riders are overthrown in Exodus 15:1.

175 Exodus 33:9-10.

176 An analogous connection may exist between the glory that filled the tabernacle and the glory that, Haggai promises, will fill the temple once it is built. Just after issuing the promise of the spirit's standing in Israel's midst, Haggai speaks for God: "I will shake all the nations, so that the treasure of all nations shall come, and I will fill this house with splendor, says the LORD of hosts. The silver is mine, and the gold is mine, says the LORD of hosts. The latter splendor of this house shall be greater than the former, says the LORD of hosts; and in this place I will give prosperity, says the LORD of hosts" (Haggai 2:7-9). Though appealing in light of the new exodus overtones in the book of Haggai, this connection between the tabernacle and the temple Haggai imagines is tenuous. First, Haggai compares the "former glory" of the temple that was destroyed by Babylon with the glory of the rebuilt temple (Haggai 2:3, 7). This is the primary contrast in the words, "the latter *glory* of this house shall be greater than the former" (2:9). In view are two temples rather than an original tabernacle in the past and a rebuilt temple in the future. Second, 1 Kings 8:11 reads: "The priests could not stand to minister because of the cloud; for the glory of the LORD filled the house of the LORD." 2 Chronicles 7:2 reads similarly: "The priests could not enter the house of the LORD, because the glory of the LORD filled the LORD's house." The primary reference to glory in the book of Haggai, therefore, is to the temple, even if the glory of the temple is closely related to the glory of the tabernacle.

177 Exodus 14:13-14.

178 Cyrus Cylinder, trans. from Pritchard, *Ancient Near Eastern Texts*, 316.

179 Haggai 2:20-23.

180 Haggai 2:19.

181 Haggai 1:13.

182 Haggai 2:4.

Chapter 5

1 Amos 7:7-9.

2 P. Trible, *God and the Rhetoric of Sexuality* (Philadelphia: Fortress, 1978), 90, 140n13.

3 Göttingen: Vandenhoeck & Ruprecht, 1888. Ninety-one years after its appearance, R. Harrisville and P. Quanbeck II translated this slender volume into English, with the title, *The Influence of the Holy Spirit: The Popular View of the Apostolic Age and the Teaching of the Apostle Paul* (Philadelphia: Fortress, 1979).

4 Leading nineteenth-century New Testament scholar F. Baur, in *Paul the Apostle of Jesus Christ, His Life and Work, His Epistles and His Doctrine* (London: Williams and Norgate, 1875), had discussed the spirit under the rubric, "Principle of the Christian Consciousness." According to Baur, spirit denotes an "essentially spiritual principle, which forbids him [a Christian] to regard anything merely outward, sensuous, material as in any way a condition of his salvation" (126). Christian consciousness "is a truly spiritual consciousness, a relation of spirit to spirit, where the absolute spirit of God, in becoming the principle of the Christian consciousness, opens itself up to the consciousness of man" (128). Justification occurs when a person "has received the spirit into himself as the principle of his Christian consciousness and life" (140). From this perspective, Paul's "law of the spirit" "designates the principle of the Christian consciousness" (160).

5 H. Gunkel (*The Influence of the Holy Spirit*, 96) states his own point of view unreservedly: "The gifts of the Spirit in the apostolic age have vanished, though in isolated Christian circles something similar may perhaps be observed to this day. But we can also do without

these miraculous gifts. For even now we daily perceive other activities of the Spirit in our life. Even for us, the Christian is a miracle of God."

6 I have analyzed the contributions of Gunkel in "Assessing the Origins of Modern Pneumatology: The Life and Legacy of Hermann Gunkel," in *Christian Body, Christian Self: Essays on Early Christian Concepts of Personhood*, ed. J. Harrill and C. Rothschild (Tübingen: Mohr Siebeck, 2012), 313–31; and, with J. Frey, "The Origins of Early Christian Pneumatology: On the Rediscovery and Reshaping of the History of Religions Quest," in *The Holy Spirit, Inspiration, and the Cultures of Antiquity: Multidisciplinary Perspectives*, ed. J. Frey and J. Levison, with A. Bowden (Berlin: de Gruyter, 2014), 4–9.

7 Freiburg: J. C. B. Mohr (Paul Siebeck), 1899.

8 Oscar Holtzmann, *War Jesus Ekstatiker? Eine Untersuchung zum Leben Jesu* (Tübingen: J. C. B. Mohr [Paul Siebeck], 1903).

9 *Journal of Biblical Literature* 23 (1904): 13–67.

10 H. B. Swete, *The Holy Spirit in the New Testament: A Study of Primitive Christian Teaching* (London: Macmillan, 1909).

11 London: Macmillan, 1912. In 1876, Swete had already published *On the History of the Doctrine of the Procession of the Holy Spirit from the Apostolic Age to the Death of Charlemagne* (Cambridge: Deighton; London: G. Bell).

12 Tübingen: J. C. B. Mohr (Paul Siebeck), 1910.

13 J. Abelson, *The Immanence of God in Rabbinical Literature* (London: Macmillan, 1912), x.

14 Leipzig: Teubner, 1919.

15 Leipzig: J. C. Heinrichs, 1922. I have analyzed the contribution of Leisegang in "The Spirit in the Gospels: Breaking the Impasse of Early Twentieth-century German Scholarship," in *New Testament Greek and Exegesis*, ed. A. Donaldson and T. Sailors (Grand Rapids: Eerdmans, 2003), 55–76; and, with J. Frey, in "The Origins of Early Christian Pneumatology," 10–15.

16 At approximately the same time, E. de Witt Burton (*Spirit, Soul, and Flesh: The Usage of* Πνεῦμα, Ψυχή, *and* Σάρξ *in Greek Writings and Translated Works from the Earliest Period to 225 A.D.; and of their Equivalents* רוּחַ, נֶפֶשׁ, *and* בָּשָׂר *in the Hebrew Old Testament* [Chicago: University of Chicago Press, 1918]) offered an overview of the terms *spirit, soul,* and *flesh* in Greco-Roman and early Jewish literature, the Hebrew Bible, and the New Testament, as well as what he deemed to be "ethnic religious writings," including magical texts and hermetic literature.

17 F. Büchsel, *Der Geist Gottes im Neuen Testament* (Gütersloh: C. Bertelsmann, 1926).

18 H. von Baer, *Der heilige Geist in den Lukasschriften* (Stuttgart: Kohlhammer, 1926).

19 P. Volz, *Der Geist Gottes und die verwandten Erscheinungen im Alten Testament und im anschliessenden Judentum* (Tübingen: J. C. B. Mohr [Paul Siebeck], 1910), 144.

20 S. Heschel (*The Aryan Jesus: Christian Theologians and the Bible in Nazi Germany* [Princeton: Princeton University Press, 2008]) documents the activities of the Institute for the Study and Eradication of Jewish Influence on German Religious Life, in particular its influence upon German scholarship about the life of Jesus.

21 The portion of the study devoted to Geisthypostase concludes with a section (Volz, *Der Geist Gottes*, 169–95) that analyses related topics, such as the spirit in Babylonian and Persian literature, angels, Shekinah, and logos.

22 Several studies offer critical appraisals of the concept of hypostasis in Near Eastern Antiquity. G. Pfeiffer (*Ursprung und Wesen der Hypostasenvorstellungen im Judentum* [Stuttgart:

Calwer, 1967], 11–12) notes in particular how difficult scholars find it to distinguish between a poetic personification and an independent being. He also cautions against the distinction between "Personifikation" and "personifizieren" because of the potential anachronism inherent in the adoption of modern conceptions of personhood (15). He offers this provisional definition: "eine Größe, die teilhat am Wesen einer Gottheit, die durch sie handelnd in die Welt eingreift, ohne daß sich ihr Wesen im Wirken dieser Hypostase erschöpft" (15). P. Heinisch (*Personifikationen und Hypostasen im Alten Testament und im Alten Orient* [Münster: Aschendorff, 1921], 55) also notes how difficult it is to distinguish between poetic representations, which appear to be actual independent persons but are not: "Dichterisches Denken mußte leicht dazu führen, daß, wie man abstrakte Begriffe personifizierte, so besonders auch Eigenschaften der Gottheit als selbständig gefeiert wurden." H. Ringgren (*Word and Wisdom: Studies in the Hypostatization of Divine Qualities and Functions in the Ancient Near East* [Lund: H. Ohlsson, 1947]) offers an overview of the ancient Near East. His analysis of the spirit (165–71) is brief but useful as a summary. G. Juncker ("Jesus and the Angel of the Lord: An Old Testament Paradigm for New Testament Christology" [Ph.D. diss., Trinity Evangelical Divinity School, 2001], 25–26) avoids the use of the term *hypostasis*, because it is so difficult to define—and to distinguish from personification. For more theoretical studies, J. Barr's "Hypostatization of Linguistic Phenomena in Modern Theological Interpretation" (*Journal of Semitic Studies* 7 [1962]: 85–94) lays important groundwork. A. Gibson (*Biblical Semantic Logic: A Preliminary Analysis* [New York: St. Martin's Press, 1981], 60) distinguishes between a "hypostatized structure" (the product) and "collective hypostatization," in which "already hypostatized items are held up as markers of a typical set of functions in ancient language seemingly to characterize standard usage and often (alleged) ways of thinking in ancient times. If the components of such a linguistic calculation are hypostatized, then so must its conclusion be an hypostatization." Gibson's discussion offers caution in the use of words such as *hypostasis* or *hypostatization*, particularly, as with Pfeiffer, given the ease with which anachronism slips into the discussion. C. Gieschen (*Angelomorphic Christology: Antecedents and Early Evidence* [Leiden: Brill, 1998], 36–45) deems hypostasis a useful category, though his definition, "an aspect of the deity that is depicted with independent personhood of varying degrees" (45) reveals what a mare's nest the effort to define *hypostasis* is. Words such as *independent, personhood,* and *varying degrees* are not altogether accurate terms for describing phenomena in Antiquity.

23 T. Cheyne (*The Prophecies of Isaiah: A New Translation with Commentary and Appendices*, 2 vols. [London: Kegan Paul, Trench, 1884], 105) identified the spirit as "virtually equivalent to 'the Angel' or 'the Face' of Jehovah."

24 B. Duhm (*Das Buch Jesaia* [Göttingen: Vandenhoeck & Ruprecht, 1892], 437). He writes further, "Vor allen Dingen fast er den Geist als ein selbständiges Wesen auf, gleichsam als die Hypostase der Weissagung und Volksleitung."

25 Duhm (*Das Buch Jesaia*, 437) claims, "Weil er sonst kaum das Wort עצב, kränken, betrüben (vgl Eph. 4 30) hätte gebrauchen können." D. Marti (*Das Buch Jesaja* [Tübingen: J. C. B. Mohr (Paul Siebeck), 1900], 394) followed suit with similar logic: "Der heilige Geist . . . dem man widerstreben (vgl. Act 7 51) und den man selbst *betrüben* (Eph 4 30) kann, ist hier als ein selbständiges Wesen, als eine Art Hypostase gedacht, wohl fast zusammenfallend mit פְּנֵי י." Duhm (*Das Buch Jesaia*, 437) also discerned in Isaiah 63:10 an allusion to Numbers 11: "Mit dem heiligen Geist meint der Vf. nicht blos die persönliche Prophetengabe Moses, er denkt ohne Zweifel auch z. B. an die Erzählung Num. 11 25ff. (Dtn. 34 9)." Pfeiffer (*Ursprung und Wesen der Hypostasenvorstellungen*, 18)

concurs and discerns as well a hypostasis in Haggai 2:4-5: "Der Geist ist eng auf Jahwe bezogen, andererseits sehr selbständig aufgefaßt, so daß wir durchaus von einer Hypostase reden können. Der Geist ist als die Form der heilsmächtig wirkenden Gegenwart Jahwes inmitten seiner Gemeinde verstanden. Weitere Schlüsse verbietet freilich die Spärlichkeit der Aussagen."

26 As in Isaiah 63:10, the Hebrew verb is ambiguous: כִּי־הִמְרוּ אֶת־רוּחוֹ. The verb can be either מרר or מרה.

27 Psalm 106:33.

28 Volz (*Der Geist Gottes*, 145–46) writes: "Daß das Judentum den Geist (Gottes) als Hypostase betrachtet, ist zweifellos; aber es ist schwierig, genau zu sagen, wann diese Betrachtung einsetzt. Wir können nicht immer entscheiden, ob hypostatisch lautende Aussagen wirklich so zu fassen sind, ob mit 'Ruḥ Jahwes' an das in Jahwe ruhende Organ oder an die aus Jahwe hinaus projizierte Gestalt gedacht ist."

29 Volz (*Der Geist Gottes*, 145) writes: "Der charakterische Fortschritt der nachexilischen Periode innerhalb der Vorstellung von der Ruḥ ist aber die enge monotheistische Verknüpfung der Ruḥ mit Jahwe und die daraus hervorgehende neue Vorstellung von der Ruḥ-hypostase, der hypostasierten Natur und Kraft Jahwes."

30 Volz, *Der Geist Gottes*, 169. The full quotation in German reads: "Die Geisthypostase ist die nach außen projizierte Abstraktion des inneren Wesens Gottes, eine von Gott abgetrennte Potenz Gottes. In der Selbständigkeit gegenüber Jahwe, in der formalen Art der Benutzung des menschlichen Organs und in manchen Wirkungen berührt sie sich mit den altertümlichen Gestalten des personhaften Geistwesens und des Ruḥ-dämons, die daneben bis in die jüngste Zeit fortbestehen und nachwirken; im Wesen ist sie von diesen durch die monotheistische Verbindung mit Jahwe grundsätzlich verschieden. Sie ist nicht Person, sondern nur personifizierte Abstraktion, doch als eine selbständig neben Jahwe und außerhalb der Menschen für sich existierende Potenz gedacht."

31 The entry, "Hypostasis," in the *Concise Oxford Dictionary of World Religions*, ed. J. Bowker (Oxford: Oxford University Press, 2000), refers to "substantiation of a metaphysical reality"; "from this technical use [in theology], the term is applied to the substantiation of a metaphysical reality—e.g. the (possible) hypostasization of Wisdom in Jewish Wisdom literature" (332).

32 While Volz refers five times (*Der Geist Gottes*, 118, 121, 123, 124, 129) to W. Bousset's *Die Himmelsreise der Seele* (Darmstadt: Wissenschaftliche Buchgesellschaft, 1960 [originally published 1901]) and nowhere to his *Die Religion des Judentums im neutestamentlichen Zeitalter*, 2nd ed. (Berlin: Reuther und Reichard, 1906), the distinction between *person* and *personhaft* is not dissimilar to Bousset's description (*Die Religion des Judentums im neutestamentlichen Zeitalter*, 394) of a hypostasis: "Sie erscheinen als Mitteldinge zwischen Personen und abstrakten Wesen."

33 While the words themselves, cautions Volz, do not identify the spirit with certainty as a hypostasis, the connection of this lament to other texts does. A cluster of texts launches this perspective on the spirit. Psalm 139, in which the poet concedes that he or she cannot hide from God's spirit or flee from God's presence—the parallel is tantalizing—reveals a spirit that is a cosmic principle with a certain independence. Volz (*Der Geist Gottes*, 146) writes: "Die Ruḥ Jahwes ist hier in der Auffassung des Dichters wahrscheinlich eine kosmische Potenz mit einer gewissen Selbständigkeit neben Jahwe, ähnlich wie Panim Jahwes die Erscheinungsform Jahwes im Kosmos darstellend." In Psalm 139, the old pantheism mixes with newer monotheism. In a note, he asks whether this is an organ inside God or an independent power next to God, "eine Art hypostase im Universum."

Volz thinks the latter probable. As a parallel, he appeals to Wisdom of Solomon 1:7, though this, of course, is a much later Alexandrian composition.

34 Volz (*Der Geist Gottes*, 148) writes: "Der Wortlaut führt nicht mit zwingender Bestimmtheit dazu, in der Ruḥ Jahwes mehr als eben das innere Wesen Jahwes selbst zu sehen; doch spricht der Vergleich mit den verwandten Stellen dafür, sie auch hier als selbständigen Faktor zu fassen. Dann ist sie die unsichtbare, wunderbare Potenz, die in Israel waltet, Urheberin all der Kräfte, der besonderen Gaben und der Geistesmenschen Israels. Sie bekundet sich in den großen Religionsträgern des Volks, in Mose und seinen Nachfolgern, aber sie ist nicht an diese gebunden, auch nicht etwa bloß in der Körperschaft Israels wohnend gedacht, sondern eine selbständige Gestalt aus der höheren Welt, in der Gemeinde waltend." Ringgren (*Word and Wisdom*, 166) is not sure of this, and his comments reveal the difficulty of identifying a hypostasis. Of Isaiah 63:11, Nehemiah 9:20, Haggai 2:5, and Zechariah 4:6, he writes: "The hypostatization is not so apparent in these instances. In certain cases it can be doubted whether we have to do with a hypostasis or not. But we must say that there is a clear tendency to conceiving the Spirit as a concrete entity, emanating from Yahweh and connected with him, but which it is yet possible to separate from him." Clearly, a thin line separates a putative hypostasis from a concrete entity that emanates from God. He sees in these texts, as in Psalm 139:7, "characteristic ambiguity."

35 Why, wonders Volz, did Israel call this independent presence the spirit? Because of its relationship to prophecy. Prophets were the organs through which the spirit communicated, and prophets were closely identified with the spirit. Volz (*Der Geist Gottes*, 149) asks, "Warum nennt man diese Gemeindepotenz Ruḥ Jahwes? Einmal deswegen, weil ihre Wirkungen in erster Linie durch die Propheten vermittelt wurden und die Prophetie als die spezielle Erscheinung der Ruḥ gedacht war; so personifizierte man die prophetische Wirksamkeit in Israel zu der Gestalt der Ruḥ, die in all diesen durch die Jahrhunderte gehenden Erscheinungen und Personen sich manifestierte."

36 Volz (*Der Geist Gottes*, 149) writes: "Die Zaghaftigkeit, mit der unser Dichter den hypostatischen Charakter der Ruḥ ausspricht, beweist, daß wir uns noch im Anfang der Hypostasierung befinden." Still, Volz is able to garner from this lament several pivotal characteristics of the personified abstraction known as the spirit. (1) The spirit is a *hypostasis*, understood as the personification of the divine essence; this hypostasis, however, is not a person but a personification. (2) The principal aspect of God that the spirit expresses is *ethical*; therefore, the spirit functions in Israel predominantly in the ethical sphere. Volz writes: "Außerdem aber könnte diese Ruḥ auch eine Personifikation des sittlichen Wesens Jahwes sein; die Seite an Jahwe, von der die ethischen Wirkungen in Israel ausgehen und der das sittlich-religiöse Verhalten des Volkes korrespondiert, wird als selbständige Potenz aus Jahwe hinaus projiziert" (149). (3) The spirit functions primarily in the *community* rather than in individuals. (4) The spirit is more *passive* than God, who is more active in the national life of Israel. Volz writes: "Es werden nur passive Aussagen über sie gemacht und alle aktive Tätigkeit ist dem Jahwe beigelegt; doch denkt man wohl auch an Wirkungen der Ruḥ; sie umfassen das ganze Volksleben Israels, in erster Linie das sittliche Gebiet" (148). In this respect, the spirit is not identical to the angel of God's presence; the angel is more active in the sphere of national help and leading than the spirit. Nevertheless, suggests Volz, the warning not to rebel against the angel (Exodus 23:21) is, in the lament, expressed with reference to the spirit (150).

37 Volz (*Der Geist Gottes*, 150) connects Isaiah 63:10-11 with Haggai 2:5: "Wie in Jes 63 10f. ist sie die in der Gemeinde Israels waltende göttliche Potenz; sie hat auch hier etwas Personhaftes, sie 'steht mitten in' der Gemeinde. Sie wirkt physische und innerliche

Lebenskraft, verbürgt den Fortbestand und die Zukunft Israels, macht Israel gewissermaßen unsterblich und verleiht ihm göttliche Natur und göttlichen Anspruch in der Welt." This spirit, rather than Israel's fidelity, lends Israel its ethical and eternal character.

38 Volz, *Der Geist Gottes*, 150. The German reads: "Die Ruḥ erscheint durch dieses unmittelbar vorausgehende Wort als etwas neben Jahwe Selbständiges." I do not see the connection between the divine promise and the hypostatic character of the spirit.

39 Volz (*Der Geist Gottes*, 150) is not certain about the allusion to the exodus because of the absence of this phrase from the Septuagint.

40 Nehemiah 9:30.

41 Volz (*Der Geist Gottes*, 151–52) summarizes key points clearly:

> Die Ruḥ is personhafte Potenz und wirkt auf Jahwes Geheiß in Israel; sie ist nicht Ruḥ in den einzelnen Volksgliedern, sondern über Gesamtisrael übergeordnet; sie ist nicht auf einzelne Organe beschränkt, auch hier nicht bloß mit Mose verknüpft, sondern viel allgemeiner und umfassender die Urheberin alles geistigen und sittlichen Lebens in Israel. Sie benützt allerdings die Propheten als ihre Organe, wirkt aber ebenso auch im geschriebenen Gesetz und in den theokratischen Einrichtungen und äußert sich in jeder sittlich-religiösen Regung des Volkes. Ihr Zweck ist die Unterweisung in der heiligen Art Jahwes. Die Nehemia-stellen beleuchten den Gedanken von Jes 63 10 f. und bestätigen unsere dort gegebene Erklärung.

42 Volz, *Der Geist Gottes*, 152. The German reads: "Ein einheitliches Bild dieser in Israel stehenden und wirkenden Ruḥ-hypostase."

43 Volz (*Der Geist Gottes*, 152) writes: "Sie heißt immer Ruḥ Jahwes und ist personhaft geschildert. Sie ist gegenwärtig in Israel, wurde mit der Gründung des Volkes in Israel eingeführt und war in Israels Anfangszeit besonders kraftvoll."

44 Volz (*Der Geist Gottes*, 152) writes: "Sie steht mit den Propheten in besonderer Beziehung, ist aber nicht auf die Organe beschränkt, sondern ein Faktor für sich (vgl. besonders Hagg 2 5)."

45 Volz (*Der Geist Gottes*, 152) writes: "Sie ist eine Art Mittelwesen zwischen Jahwe und den theokratischen Organen bezw. dem Volk."

46 Volz (*Der Geist Gottes*, 152) writes: "Die Hypostase ist freilich noch nicht so weit fortgeschritten, daß der Ruḥ eine eigentlich aktive Tätigkeit neben oder statt Jahwe zugedacht werden könnte, sie ist nur Prinzip oder Ausdruck bestimmter Erscheinungen und Erfahrungen; Jahwe wirkt durch die Ruḥ, er unterweist und verwarnt durch sie das Volk, durch sie ist der Fortbestand des Volkes verbürgt."

47 Volz (*Der Geist Gottes*, 152) writes: "Hauptgebiet der Ruḥ ist das religiös-sittliche Leben, aber auch allgemeiner der Lebensbestand des Volkes."

48 Volz (*Der Geist Gottes*, 148) writes: "Es werden nur passive Aussagen über sie gemacht und alle aktive Tätigkeit ist dem Jahwe beigelegt; doch denkt man wohl auch an Wirkungen der Ruḥ; sie umfassen das ganze Volksleben Israels, in erster Linie das sittliche Gebiet."

49 Still, concedes Volz (*Der Geist Gottes*, 150), the warning not to rebel against the angel (Exodus 23:21) is, in the lament, expressed with reference to the spirit.

50 Volz (*Der Geist Gottes*, 152–53) concludes his discussion: "Man spürte, daß in der Gemeinde eine Kraft wehte, eine Gewissensstimme in ihr sich immer wieder regte, die von keinem Menschen herrührte . . . Diese Gedanken verknüpfte man mit der Idee der Ruḥ-hypostase und gab dieser die Funktion des personifizierten Gemeindeideals. Zwischen die Gemeinde und Jahwe bezw. zwischen die Propheten und Jahwe ist damit eine vermittelnde Potenz eingestellt und der Verkehr mit Jahwe verliert dadurch etwas

von der früheren Unmittelbarkeit; das entspricht der Erfahrung der nachexilischen Propheten, die nicht mehr in der Vertrautheit eines Jesaja oder Jeremia zu Jahwe standen."

51 W. Eichrodt, *Old Testament Theology*, 2 vols. (Philadelphia: Westminster, 1967), 2:60.

52 P.-E. Bonnard, *Le Second Isaïe, son disciple et leurs éditeurs* (Paris: Gabalda, 1972), 449. The full quotation reads: "Non certes deja une personne divine comme le precisera le dogme trinitaire, mais la personification d'un attribute divine: la Puissance de Dieu qui investit les hommes pour leur permettre de se depasser. Esprit, ce principe d'action est sourrle: comme le vent on ne sait pas d'ou il vient mais on constate ses effets. Saint, ce principe est divine."

53 R. Whybray, *Isaiah 40–66* (London: Oliphants, 1975; Grand Rapids: Eerdmans, 1981), 258.

54 J. Blenkinsopp, *Isaiah 56–66: A New Translation with Introduction and Commentary* (New York: Doubleday, 2003), 261.

55 B. Childs, *Isaiah* (Louisville, Ky.: Presbyterian, 2000), 524.

56 Goldingay's reference is to H.-J. Kraus, *Das Evangelium der unbekannten Propheten: Jesaja 40–66* (Neukirchen-Vluyn: Neukirchener Verlag, 1990), 227.

57 The reference is to A. Herbert, *Isaiah 40–66* (Cambridge: Cambridge University Press, 1975), 176.

58 J. Goldingay, *Isaiah 56–66: A Critical and Exegetical Commentary*, ICC (London: Bloomsbury T&T Clark, 2014), 396.

59 Note should be taken of M. Lodahl's important *Shekhinah/Spirit: Divine Presence in Jewish and Christian Religion* (New York: Paulist, 1992), in which he offers a blistering critique of the concept of hypostasis. Speaking largely of rabbinic Judaism, Lodahl asks, "What might this theological appropriation of the terms *ruach, pneuma* and *shekhinah* suggest for a reconstruction of Christian pneumatology? It is important to note, first, that these terms served as *ways of referring to God's presence and activity, rather than to a being or beings hypostatically distinct from God*. This, I would suggest, is an important consideration for a doctrine of the Holy Spirit written with attention to the context of Israel's history of interpretations of divine presence" (57). He summarizes this point similarly later when he claims "that the Jewish word-concepts *ruach, pneuma* and *shekhinah*, which provide the proper context for understanding what the phrase 'Holy Spirit' should mean for Christians, refer not to hypostases separate from God but provide ways for referring to God's dynamic presence and activity among the people and in creation generally" (65).

Lodahl clarifies these statements when he regards these terms not as "hypostases separate from God which mediate between God and the world." These terms, rather, "nearly always functioned as tropes for God's own active nearness to creation, to humanity, and particularly to Israel" (*Shekhinah/Spirit*, 67). This statement brings Lodahl into the same sphere as Goldingay: the spirit (the shekhinah, too, for Lodahl) is reduced to ways of portraying God's presence. While I agree with Lodahl that hypostasis is a troubling category, I would put greater emphasis upon the developments in Haggai 2 and Isaiah 63 and argue that the term *rûaḥ* is not merely a trope for God's nearness; the spirit's taking on the activities of the agents of the exodus suggests that the spirit is other than a trope. Nor, in light of these texts, should the spirit be replaced—or displaced—by Lodahl's concept of shekhinah.

60 Volz (*Der Geist Gottes*, 144) offers this programmatic statement:

> Die Gewohnheit, das ausgehende Judentum mit dem jungen Christentum zu vergleichen, hat stets dazu geführt, das erstere zu verkennen; das ist historisch ungerecht, und außerdem ist es viel wahrscheinlicher, daß die neue Religion aus

einer religiös beweglichen und tief empfindenden Zeit hervorging als aus einer erstarrten und erstorbenen. Vergleichen wir das Judentum etwa mit der heutigen Zeit oder sonst irgend einer Zeit der Menschheitsgeschichte, so bekommt man den Eindruck, daß ein verhältnismäßig reiches Leben des Geistes in der jüdischen Gemeinde der letzten vorchristlichen Jahrhunderte sich kundgab und daß sich die Juden auch hierin als das Volk der Religion erwiesen. Manches von dem was unter ihnen mit pneumatischem Bewußtsein auftrat, muß als edle Frucht des Geistes anerkannt werden, und der maßstab, mit dem das Judentum die pneumatischen Erscheinungen verwertete, bezeugt selbst am besten die Echtheit seiner Religion.

61 W. Brueggemann (*The Prophetic Imagination*, 2nd ed. [Minneapolis: Fortress, 2001], 39, 59, etc.) famously framed the prophetic task in this way.

62 It is important to repeat that the standing of the pillar on the eve of exodus is not the only standing in the exodus tradition; the cloud also stood at the entrance to the tent of presence, where Moses and God met. Either is possible, though my preference, given Haggai's precarious situation coupled with the command not to fear, is the former. Therefore, I return to that now, even if other possibilities remain.

63 The bibliography on hypostasis is extensive. A few significant studies may be found in G. Kittel and G. Friedrich, eds., "ὑπόστασις," *Theological Dictionary of the New Testament* (*TDNT*) 8:572–89; "Hypostasis (ὑπόστασις)," *Reallexikon für Antike und Christentum* (*RAC*) 16:986–1035; and G. L. Prestige, *God in Patristic Thought* (London: William Heinemann, 1938), 157–96. In an illuminating analysis, I. L. E. Ramelli ("Origen, Greek Philosophy, and the Birth of the Trinitarian Meaning of Hypostasis," *Harvard Theological Review* 105 [2012]: 309–11) reveals the lack of technical terminology among Christian thinkers prior to Origen. Ramelli outlines the philosophical background to Origen's conception of hypostasis (and thus, in her view, the Cappadocians); she accords particular possible influence to Philo Judaeus (e.g., *On the Eternity of the World* 88, 92), Soranus (e.g., *Gynecology* 2.27, 57), Sextus Empiricus (e.g., *Against the Mathematicians* 10.335–36), and Alexander of Aphrodisias (e.g., *Commentary on Metaphysics* [Aristotle] 180.4) (316–25). She identifies the second major source of Origen's understanding of hypostasis, in distinction from *ousia*, as Hebrews 1:3, in which the word occurs (337–45).

64 According to *RAC* 16:1004, Origen's earliest usage is found in his commentary on the gospel of John 2:75.

65 Ramelli, "Origen, Greek Philosophy, and the Birth of the Trinitarian Meaning of Hypostasis," 308.

66 Ramelli, "Origen, Greek Philosophy, and the Birth of the Trinitarian Meaning of Hypostasis," 306, citing *Commentarii in Romanos* 7.12.146-47. According to Ramelli, Origen opposed those who deemed the spirit simply "God's energy or activity, without a substantial existence of its own" (306).

67 *RAC* 16:1020–22 contains a helpful discussion of their distinctives. Gregory of Nyssa, for example, avoided the use of πρόσωπον because it smacked of Sabellianism.

68 Prestige, *God in Patristic Thought*, 189.

69 *RAC* 16:1026–27.

70 *RAC* 16:1027–28.

71 As I said in n15 of the introduction, agency is a radically open concept, which stretches from personal to impersonal agency. The meaning of agency in the lament of Isaiah 63 and promise of Haggai 2 derives from those figures that rescued Israel during the exodus and led them to the promised land. I have been careful to represent these agents as fungible, even interchangeable, and to propose that their particular exercise of agency shifts from

narrative to narrative, from oracle to poem. Despite the open-endedness of the words *agency* and *agents*, they have the advantage of not being principally Christian in orientation. Consequently, to use *agent* or *agency* of the holy spirit is not anachronistic, which is a fault toward which the use of hypostasis inevitably, in the light of history, bends.

72 Psalm 74:9; 1 Maccabees 4:46; 9:27; and 14:41; Josephus, *Against Apion* 1.37-41; Syriac Apocalypse of Baruch 85:3; Prayer of Azariah 15; and a rabbinic text, Tosefta Sotah 13:2-4.

73 "πνεῦμα," *TDNT* 6:385.

74 "Holy Spirit," *The Interpreter's Dictionary of the Bible*, ed. George A. Buttrick, 4 vols. (New York: Abingdon, 1962), 2:630.

75 G. Fee, *God's Empowering Presence: The Holy Spirit in the Letters of Paul* (Peabody, Mass.: Hendrickson, 1993), 914. Similar statements are myriad: C. K. Barrett (*The Holy Spirit and the Gospel Tradition* [London: SCM, 1947], 108–9) quotes G. Moore: "The Holy Spirit is so specifically prophetic inspiration that when Haggai, Zechariah, and Malachi, the last prophets, died, the Holy Spirit departed from Israel." J. Dunn (*Christology in the Making: A New Testament Inquiry into the Origins of the Doctrine of the Incarnation* [Philadelphia: Westminster, 1980], 135) cites these texts, adding Zechariah 13:2-6, to support the view that "with the rabbis the belief becomes very strong that Haggai, Zechariah and Malachi were the last of the prophets and that thereafter the Spirit had been withdrawn." In *Baptism in the Holy Spirit: A Re-examination of the New Testament Teaching on the Gift of the Spirit in Relation to Pentecostalism Today* (Philadelphia: Westminster, 1970), 27, he states that, at the baptism of Jesus, "the long drought of knowing the Spirit comes to an end." D. Hill (*New Testament Prophecy*, Marshall's Theological Library [London: Marshall, Morgan & Scott, 1985], 21) writes, "There can be no doubt that, long before the turn of the eras, the Jews believed that prophecy as such had ceased in Israel and that the prophetic Spirit had withdrawn." F. Horn (*Das Angeld des Geistes: Studien zur paulinischen Pneumatologie* [Göttingen: Vandenhoeck & Ruprecht, 1992], 31) finds evidence "des allgemeinen Bewußtseins der Prophetenlosigkeit oder Geistlosigkeit." J. Jeremias (*New Testament Theology* [New York: Charles Scribner's Sons, 1971], 81) subtitles section 9 "The Return of the Quenched Spirit," and writes: "With the death of the last writing prophets, Haggai, Zechariah and Malachi, *the spirit was quenched* because of the sin of Israel. After that time, it was believed, God still spoke only through the 'echo of his voice' . . . a poor substitute."

76 R. Leivestad, "Das Dogma von der prophetenlosen Zeit," *New Testament Studies* 19 (1972–1973): 288–99; D. Aune, *Prophecy in Early Christianity and the Ancient Mediterranean World* (Grand Rapids: Eerdmans, 1983), 103–6; F. Greenspahn, "Why Prophecy Ceased," *Journal of Biblical Literature* 108 (1989): 37–49; J. Levison, "Did the Spirit Withdraw from Israel? An Evaluation of the Earliest Jewish Data," *New Testament Studies* 43 (1997): 35–57.

77 Wright devotes two subsections of *Paul and the Faithfulness of God*, Christian Origins and the Question of God 4 (Minneapolis: Fortress, 2013) to Pauline pneumatology. The shorter section (*Paul and the Faithfulness of God*, 619–73) occurs in a section on monotheism, in which Wright demonstrates that "Paul clearly, solidly, skillfully and dramatically reworked exactly this 'monotheism' around Jesus the Messiah and also around the spirit. It is for the sake of Jesus, and in the power of the spirit, that Paul faces, and knows that his *ekklesiai* are facing, the equivalent challenges to those faced by the Maccabees before him" (634). Within this framework, he turns to "monotheism freshly revealed" and the spirit. The longer treatment (912–1038) occurs in an extensive section devoted to Paul's reworking of election, titled, "The People of God, Freshly Reworked" (774–1042). This section consists of Paul's "spirit-driven redefinition of election" (e.g., 1007). In the section "Election Reworked around the Spirit: The Messiah's Justified People," Wright discusses

Pauline pneumatology. I offer analysis and critique in "The Spirit in Its Second Temple Context: An Exegetical Analysis of the Pneumatology of N. T. Wright," in *God and the Faithfulness of Paul: A Critical Examination of the Pauline Theology of N. T. Wright*, ed. M. Bird, C. Heilig, and J. Hewitt (Tübingen: Mohr Siebeck, 2016), 439–62.

78 Wright, *Paul and the Faithfulness of God*, 759.

79 Wright, *Paul and the Faithfulness of God*, 711.

80 Wright, *Paul and the Faithfulness of God*, 712.

81 Wright, *Paul and the Faithfulness of God*, 712.

82 Wright, *Paul and the Faithfulness of God*, 712.

83 Wright, *Paul and the Faithfulness of God*, 716, on Ephesians 2:19-22. Elsewhere, Wright states simply, "The Shekinah dwelt in the tabernacle, separated from the people. Now, the divine spirit has come to dwell within the renewed people themselves" (983).

84 Wright, *Paul and the Faithfulness of God*, 716. S. Keesmaat (*Paul and His Story: (Re)interpreting the Exodus Tradition* [Sheffield: Sheffield Academic, 1999], 62–64), upon whom Wright claims (*Paul and the Faithfulness of God*, 71n306) to "owe a great deal," discusses the importance of Isaiah 63 for Pauline theology, though only briefly.

85 Wright, *Paul and the Faithfulness of God*, 711.

86 If, as Wright (*Paul and the Faithfulness of God*, 710) contends, "the Jewish context provided the framework for a thoroughly 'high' christology and pneumatology," that Jewish context antedated Paul by five centuries.

87 In this regard, Abelson's rather harsh but not entirely inaccurate comment, in the preface to *The Immanence of God in Rabbinical Literature* (v), though penned more than a century ago, may provide an apt starting point for the future of pneumatology. "The average Jew, unable to read the originals for himself, is, through a shortage of text-books, quite incompetent to pronounce an opinion of any worth upon the religion which has meant so much for his fathers and for the world. The average Christian DOES pronounce opinions, but as these opinions are drawn, neither from the originals nor from the few Jewish scholars who have written on these topics, they are invariably one-sided and incomplete. I believe that the silence of Jews about their own theology has been construed by many non-Jews into a proof that they really have no theology worth writing about."

88 Isaiah 63:7-14 is, in fact, a communal lament, like many communal laments in the Psalms.

89 As we saw, it is not entirely clear whether God put the holy spirit within Moses or the people, according to Isaiah 63:11. The Hebrew reads "in his midst" (בְּקִרְבּוֹ), which could easily refer to the people as a whole. The Greek adopts the plural, "in them" (ἐν αὐτοῖς).

90 Volz, *Der Geist Gottes*, 152.

91 Volz, *Der Geist Gottes*, 149.

92 J. Moltmann, *The Spirit of Life: A Universal Affirmation* (Minneapolis: Fortress, 1992), 7.

93 Moltmann, *Spirit of Life*, 8.

94 Throughout this discussion of Moltmann's theology, I will adopt the term Old Testament, which he uses, to refer to the Jewish Scriptures.

95 J. Moltmann, *God in Creation: A New Theology of Creation and the Spirit of God* (San Francisco: Harper & Row, 1985), 96. He continues: "It also means that this power is itself creative, not created, and that it has been 'breathed forth' by the Creator, that is to say, emanated. And this in its turn, means that in the Spirit the Creator himself is present in his creation. Through the presence of his own being, God preserves his creation against the annihilating Nothingness." Further,

> If we are to regard creatures in their plurality as the work of the Son both as deriving from God and among one another, and if the Son, as the Logos of

creation, is the principle of its order, by which all phenomena in their variety are related to one another, then, according to the biblical testimony, the Spirit of God is the life-giving principle, to which all creatures owe life, movement, and activity. This is particularly true of animals, plants, and humans, of which Ps. 104:30 says: "Thou sendest forth thy Spirit; they are created, and thou renewest the face of the ground." In keeping with this is the second creation account, which says that God "formed man of dust from the ground, and breathed into his nostrils the breath of life, and man became a living being" (Gen. 2:7; cf. Job 33:4). Conversely, all life perishes when God withdraws his Spirit (Ps. 104:29; Job 34:14f.). The souls of all living things and the breath of all people are in the hands of the Spirit (Job 12:10).

96 Moltmann, *Spirit of Life*, 39. He continues: "But we mean the reverse too: we can also mean an awareness of reality as history which emerges from experiences of God like this. Israel always linked its experiences of God with historical persons and historical happenings."

97 Moltmann, *Spirit of Life*, 39.

98 Moltmann, *Spirit of Life*, 40.

99 Moltmann, *Spirit of Life*, 42.

100 Moltmann, *Spirit of Life*, 43. He explains more fully: "To experience the *ruach* is to experience what is divine not only as a person, and not merely as a force, but also as space—as the space of freedom in which the living being can unfold." Since he has not spoken of the *rûaḥ* as a person in the Old Testament, this is probably a reference to Christian understandings of the spirit.

101 Moltmann's description of the spirit in postbiblical Judaism exhibits the same sort of imprecision—*a kind of counterpart*—that plagued commentators in their attempt to describe the spirit as a hypostasis. In the end, Moltmann (*Spirit of Life*, 47) is content to quote from E. Sjöberg's entry on πνεῦμα in Kittel's *TDNT*. "Where the later apocryphal and rabbinic literature of Palestinian Judaism is concerned, the following may be said: 'The way the spirit takes on independent form in Judaism is striking. In rabbinic literature, the spirit is very often talked about in personal categories . . . The essential point is that here the human being is face to face with a reality that comes to him from God, and in some sense represents God's presence, although the two are not identical.'" This statement is rife with imprecision: "*in some sense* represents God's presence, although the two *are not identical*." The relationship between God, spirit, and presence, Moltmann cannot pinpoint, nor can he say what that relationship is not.

102 Moltmann, *Spirit of Life*, 47. Moltmann explains this unambiguously: when Christian theologians offer "descriptions of Yahweh's *ruach* which we have cited as 'God's presence' or 'the confronting event of God's presence,'" these are "descriptions put forward by Christian theologians, and they cannot appeal to the special Israelite use of the term 'Holy Spirit'" (47). M. Lodahl (*Shekinah/Spirit*, 29–32) criticizes Moltmann for continuing with the language of the spirit in the context of trinitarian thought. Lodahl prefers to opt for a theology not just rooted in but circumscribed by the concept of shekinah. In light of Isaiah 63 and Haggai 2, this refocus of pneumatology is not necessary. What I have argued with respect to Moltmann applies a fortiori to Lodahl.

103 For example, in *Spirit of Life*, 49, Moltmann writes: "Ideas about the accompanying Shekinah and the indwelling Spirit of God certainly do not require a theological interpretation of this kind, but they do permit it. To say that the Shekinah is a divine attribute or a

divine emanation (interpretations also found), does not permit the full and real presence of God in his Shekinah and his Spirit to be thought. But the idea of 'God's self-distinction' makes this entirely possible."

104 Moltmann offers a lucid account of the historical emergence of shekinah theology during the exile in "Shekinah: The Home of the Homeless God," in *The Longing for Home*, ed. L. Rouner (Notre Dame, Ind.: University of Notre Dame Press, 1996), 170–84, especially 174–78. His *The Church in the Power of the Spirit* (New York: Harper & Row, 1977 [originally published in German in 1975]) is relevant to the topic, since he explores ecclesiology, in general terms, through the lens of Pentecost. Studies of Moltmann's theology are plethora; it may be helpful to identify just a few in chronological order. D. L. Dabney ("The Advent of The Spirit: The Turn to Pneumatology in the Theology of Jürgen Moltmann," *Asbury Theological Journal* 48 [1993]: 81–107) traces the evolution of Moltmann's pneumatology, from its relative absence in his early works to Moltmann's focus upon pneumatology in his later works. R. Bauckham (*The Theology of Jürgen Moltmann* [Edinburgh: T & T Clark, 1995], 161–66) offers a critical appraisal of Moltmann's perichoretic pneumatology. M. [Douglas] Meeks ("Jürgen Moltmann's *Systematic Contributions to Theology*," *Religious Studies Review* 22 [1996]: 95–102) offers a concise bird's-eye view of Moltmann's theology, including the realization that "the doctrine of the shekinah makes the personal character of the Spirit clear" (99). A. Johnson ("Shekinah: The Indwelling of God in the Theology of Jürgen Moltmann" [Ph.D. diss., Luther Seminary, Minneapolis, Minn., 2003]) discusses the relationship of shekinah and spirit, especially on pp. 107–24 and 142–58.

105 The shekinah, argues Moltmann, contributes three fresh dimensions to a holistic understanding of the spirit: (1) "The doctrine of the Shekinah makes the personal character of the Spirit clear. The Spirit is the efficacious presence of God himself. The Spirit is the presence of God in person. The Spirit is more than one of God's attributes, and more than a gift of God to what he has created. The Spirit is *God's empathy*, his feeling identification with what he loves" (*Spirit of Life*, 51). (2) "The concept of the Shekinah also draws attention to *the sensibility of God the Spirit*. The Spirit indwells. The Spirit suffers with the suffering. The Spirit is grieved and quenched. The Spirit rejoices when we rejoice. When it descends and takes up its habitation and indwelling in wandering and suffering created beings, the Spirit thrusts forward with intense longing for union with God, and sighs to be at rest in the new, perfected creation" (*Spirit of Life*, 51). (3) "The idea of the Shekinah points towards *the kenosis of the Spirit*. In his Shekinah, God renounces his impassibility and becomes able to suffer because he is willing to love. The theophany of the Spirit is not anthropomorphism, but is made possible through his indwelling in created being" (*Spirit of Life*, 51).

106 Moltmann, *Spirit of Life*, 62. Moltmann expands upon this: "How does the Spirit experience Jesus' living and his dying? This question is seldom asked. But if we remember Israel's concept of the Shekinah, we can say that if the Spirit 'leads' Jesus, then the Spirit accompanies him as well. And if the Spirit accompanies him, then it is drawn into his sufferings and becomes his *companion* in suffering."

107 Moltmann, *Spirit of Life*, 54–55.

108 Moltmann may be loath to concede that he was *forced* to introduce the shekinah into his pneumatology, a by-product of this study is the realization that his slightly inadequate understanding of *rûaḥ*, especially from the perspective of the exilic and postexilic eras, permits him, even if it does not force him, to attribute to the shekinah what the authors of Isaiah 56–66 and Haggai 2 attributed to *rûaḥ*. P. Althouse ("Implications of the Kenosis of the Spirit for a Creational Eschatology: A Pentecostal Engagement with

Jürgen Moltmann," in *The Spirit Renews the Face of the Earth: Pentecostal Forays in Science and Theology of Creation*, ed. A. Yong [Eugene, Ore.: Wipf and Stock, Pickwick, 2009], 155–62) offers a nuanced summary of spirit and shekinah, particularly in Moltmann's later works. Althouse notes, first, the relationship between Moltmann's concept of shekinah and Isaac Luria's concept of *zimsum* (158–59). He notes, second, the significance of shekinah for Moltmann's concept of kenosis, particularly the kenosis of Jesus (164). He offers, third, a summary of Moltmann's understanding of shekinah: (1) The shekinah is "the efficacious presence of the Spirit, not as an attribute of God, nor even as gift, but as God in person." (2) The shekinah is that which points to a "'sensibility,' in that the Spirit indwells, is grieved, is quenched. The Spirit rejoices with its creation and grieves in the suffering of the weak." (3) Returning to the theme of kenosis, Althouse identifies the shekinah as that which "coincides with kenosis in that divine love is a passable and suffering love. Theophanies of the Spirit are then not anthropomorphisms, but the presence of the indwelling Spirit. Images of the Spirit, such as 'outpouring,' 'flowing,' 'birth,' 'washing,' etc., are indicators of the Spirit's kenotic activity" (118).

109 Moltmann, *Spirit of Life*, 55.

110 Nehemiah 9:12.

111 Nehemiah 9:19.

112 Nehemiah 9:20.

113 Exodus 28:3.

114 In *Filled with the Spirit*, 51–67, I analyze Exodus 28–35 in some detail.

115 Hebrew: לְהַשְׂכִּילָם, in Nehemiah 9:20.

116 Hebrew: וְשׂוֹם שֶׂכֶל.

117 Nehemiah 8:8.

118 Nehemiah 8:13 (modified from NRSV). Hebrew: וּלְהַשְׂכִּיל אֶל־דִּבְרֵי הַתּוֹרָה.

119 I propose this interpretation in *The Spirit in First Century Judaism*, 194–97. W. Wilder (*Echoes of the Exodus in the Context and Background of Galatians 5:18* [New York: Peter Lang, 2001], 138–48) also draws this relationship between instruction and the spirit. His approach is different, however, in that he associates the spirit with the theophanic cloud on Sinai. He does caution that "the Spirit cannot simply be identified with the cloud in a kind of one-to-one correspondence as was possible in Hag 2:4-5 and Isa 63:11-14. However close the analogy may be between the two or to whatever extent the Spirit is implicitly cast in the role of the cloud, the two are still differentiated in this passage (9:19-20) and an account must be made of that distinction." I do not find Wilder's association of the spirit with the theophanic cloud compelling because the cloud does not instruct; God does. Further, his attempt to correlate the descent of God on Sinai with the implicit descent of the spirit in Nehemiah 9:20 is strained.

120 The shift from "the angel of his presence" to "the angel of the presence" seems to be incidental.

121 Jubilees 1:27 reads: "Write for Moses from the first creation until my sanctuary is built in their midst forever and ever." J. Kugel (*A Walk through Jubilees: Studies in the Book of Jubilees and the World of Its Creation* [Leiden: Brill, 2012], 129), following J. VanderKam (*The Book of Jubilees* [Louvain: Peeters, 1989]), interprets this as a command to dictate the book of Jubilees. Jubilees 1:29 continues: "And the angel of the presence, who went before the camp of Israel, took the tablets of the division of years from the time of the creation of the law and testimony . . . until the sanctuary of the Lord is created in Jerusalem upon Mount Zion." Then again, "And the angel of the presence spoke to Moses by the word of the Lord, saying, 'Write the whole account of creation, that in six days the

LORD God completed all his work and all that he created. And he observed a sabbath the seventh day, and he sanctified it for all ages. And he set it (as) a sign for all his works'" (2:1). Translations of the book of Jubilees are from O. S. Wintermute, "Jubilees," in *The Old Testament Pseudepigrapha*, ed. J. Charlesworth, 2 vols. (New York: Doubleday, 1983, 1985), 2:35–142.

122 Jubilees 48:12. Ethiopic manuscripts include "you," but Kugel (*Walk through Jubilees*, 196) does not: "'you,' although supported by all the Eth mss., seems unnecessary here (and is not found in Exod 14:19)."

123 According to Jubilees 48:10, these angels also fought the magicians of Egypt.

124 Exodus 13:21-22; 14:19.

125 The phrase occurs in the Dead Sea Scrolls in 1QSb 4.24-25: "May you be like an angel of the face in the holy residence for the glory of the God of the Hos[ts . . ." The phrase occurs in the plural in 1QH 14.13: "to all the men of your council and in the lot, together with the angels of the face, without there being a mediator between." S. Olyan (*A Thousand Thousands Served Him: Exegesis and the Naming of Angels in Ancient Judaism* [Tübingen: J. C. B. Mohr (Paul Siebeck), 1993], 104–9) discusses the angel(s) of the presence in some detail, including further references in Testaments of the Twelve Patriarchs (Testament of Judah 25:2; Testament of Levi 3:7). He tenders the suggestion that the name, Metatron Prince of the Divine Presence, in 3 Enoch can be traced (following P. Alexander's introduction to 3 Enoch in *Old Testament Pseudepigrapha* 1.252) to Isaiah 63:9. A. De Conick discusses this expression in "Heavenly Temple Traditions and Valentinian Worship," in *The Jewish Roots of Christological Monotheism: Papers from the St. Andrews Conference on the Historical Origins of the Worship of Jesus*, ed. C. Newman, J. Davila, and G. Lewis (Leiden: Brill, 1999), 328.

126 Philo, *On the Life of Moses* 1.166. Translations of the works of Philo Judaeus are from the Loeb Classical Library.

127 Exodus 13:21-22, 14:19, 14:24.

128 D. Runia (*On the Creation of the Cosmos According to Moses* [Leiden: Brill, 2001], 257–58) offers commentary on the Greek, ὕπαρχος.

129 Philo, *On the Life of Moses* 1.166.

130 Exodus 33:20.

131 Exodus 13:21-22.

132 Exodus 14:24.

133 Philo, *On the Life of Moses* 1.178.

134 Philo, *On the Life of Moses* 1.178.

135 Philo also interprets this story allegorically in *Who Is the Heir?* 203–4.

136 Liber Antiquitatum Biblicarum 10:7.

137 The pillars and angel disappear from Josephus' late first-century *Antiquities of the Jews* (2.315–46).

138 Galatians 4:1-7.

139 Wright, *Paul and the Faithfulness of God*, 657.

140 J. Scott (*Adoption as Sons of God: An Exegetical Investigation in the Background of* ΥΙΟΘΕΣΙΑ *in the Pauline Corpus* [Tübingen: J. C. B. Mohr (Paul Siebeck), 1992]) offers a thorough defense of this position, as well as an analysis of the Greco-Roman foreground, though he rejects it as the primary context of Galatians 4:1-7. R. Morales (*The Spirit and the Restoration of Israel: New Exodus and New Creation Motifs in Galatians* [Tübingen: Mohr Siebeck, 2010], 78–131) offers another thorough analysis. While differences divide Scott and Morales—for example, Morales thinks that Paul refers only to Jewish Christians in

Galatians 4:3—these differences do not undermine the essential point that a foreground, even if not the sole foreground, of Galatians 4:1-7 is the exodus story, refracted through the lens of Isaiah 63. Keesmaat (*Paul and His Story*, 155–215) also explores the exodus foreground of Paul's letter to the Galatians.

141 Galatians 3:27; 4:1. In Romans 9:4, adoption occurs in a list of Israel's prerogatives.

142 Galatians 4:1-2.

143 Galatians 4:4. Scott (*Adoption*, 140–45) refers specifically to the four hundred years of slavery in Genesis 15:13 and Exodus 12:40 (430).

144 Galatians 4:5 and, for example, Exodus 15:13.

145 Scott (*Adoption*, 129–30) refers to the use of νήπιος in the Greek translation of Hosea 11:1 in reference to the exodus.

146 Exodus 16:1-3.

147 A. Das (*Paul and the Stories of Israel: Grand Thematic Narratives in Galatians* [Minneapolis: Fortress, 2016], 125–33) offers a rigorous critique of Scott's *Adoption*. This critique seems misguided in that it is so granular as to fail to see the grand themes that permeate Paul's letters. Das argues *against* an exodus theme and for a Hellenistic legal foreground, although the exodus is evidently a key theme in Paul's letters. (See, in brief, W. D. Davies' classic *Paul and Rabbinic Judaism: Some Rabbinic Elements in Pauline Theology*, 4th ed. [Philadelphia: Fortress, 1980], 102–10). In my opinion, the alternatives are not mutually exclusive, as Das would have it. Das (*Stories of Israel*, 133–36) also critiques S. Hafemann ("Paul and the Exile of Israel in Galatians 3–4," in *Exile: Old Testament, Jewish, and Christian Conceptions*, ed. J. Scott [Leiden: Brill, 1997], 329–71) for seeing the reference to adoption as sons in Galatians 4:5 as evidence of an exodus typology in Paul's letter to the Galatians.

148 Morales (*Restoration of Israel*, 127) writes: "Less often noted, but no less significant for Paul's understanding of the outpouring of the Spirit, is Isaiah 63. Although Paul does not explicitly cite the text, a number of parallels with Gal 4:1-7 suggest that Paul interpreted the gift of the Spirit in terms of a new exodus." These parallels include: (1) the putting of the spirit within the Israelites; (2) the prayer of repentance, which "pleads for a new act of redemption based on the paradigmatic redemption of the exodus"; (3) God's role as father, a key feature of Galatians 4:4-6; (4) emphasis upon the hardness of Israel's heart, "perhaps drawing on the tradition of Deuteronomy that sees Israel's problem as one of the heart"; and (5) the goal of redemption as inheritance (Old Greek Isaiah 63:18) (128). A puzzling dimension of Morales' *Restoration of Israel* is his repeated references to the *sending* of the spirit as the *outpouring* of the spirit. Paul refers to sending, Morales to outpouring.

149 The Old Greek of Isaiah 63:11 reads: ποῦ ἐστιν ὁ θεὶς ἐν αὐτοῖς τὸ πνεῦμα τὸ ἅγιον.

150 It may be relevant to note, in relation to this discussion, that Wilder (*Echoes of the Exodus*, 182–88) views Psalm 143:10 as the primary background of Galatians 5:18. "It is our contention," he writes, "that the exodus background of Gal 5:18 is largely mediated through Paul's reflections on Psalm 143 and especially Ps 143:10 and therefore, that this psalm provides the key to understanding the relation of Gal 5:18 to its immediate context." His arguments, though ultimately, in my opinion, unsatisfactory, deserve summary. First, Psalm 143 belongs to those septuagintal texts that anticipate what Wilder sees as "Paul's typological equation of the Spirit and the exodus cloud (in 1 Cor 10:2 and 12:13)" (183). Second—and this is essential for Wilder—the psalm converts past physical leading into a "present and *ethically-oriented* experience of Spirit guidance" (183), just as Paul does. "Psalm 143:10 accomplishes this typological updating by, on the one hand, portraying the Spirit in terms and in a context strongly reminiscent of the exodus and its cloud, while, on the other

hand, explicitly identifying the guidance of the Spirit with the doing of God's will. The effect is to place the exodus-like Spirit-guidance of Ps 143:10 squarely within the ethical sphere also occupied by Gal 5:18 and its context. Thus, from a conceptual standpoint, Ps 143:10 contains immediate affinities to Gal 5:18 which commend it as a possible background text." The case for the background of Galatians 5:18 in Psalm 143 lies as well, for Wilder, in Paul's use of this psalm in Romans 3:20 and Galatians 2:16. Finally, reflection upon the psalm extended beyond Psalm 143:2; Wilder consequently conjectures, "the possibility cannot be overlooked that other elements from this psalm might well impinge upon Paul's thought and language in other places" (184). Das (*Stories of Israel*, 147–78) offers a withering critique of Wilder's interpretation of Galatians 5:18, though I find the substance of Das' critique to be attentive to detail at the expense of wider themes.

151 Wright, *Paul and the Faithfulness of God*, 656.

152 Paul's use of the verb *send* may provide an oblique pointer to the significance of Isaiah 63:7-14, in which God sets or places the spirit in Israel or Moses. It is important to note, therefore, that the verb *send* (ἀποστέλλω), is used of the *angel* in Exodus 23:20, whom the prophet in Isaiah 63:7-14 identifies first as "the angel of his presence" and then as "his holy spirit." In short, God promises to send an angel, who is the spirit of Isaiah 63; Paul says God "sent" (ἐξαπέστειλεν) the spirit. No taut argument can be made to identify spirit and angel in Paul's letters, but the use of a similar verb, even a common one, should not go unnoticed.

153 To say that the exodus story is the *only* story that illuminates this text would be misleading; images of slavery and adoption were evocative, even provocative, in other respects. I explore other dimensions of the relationship between the spirit, slavery, and sonship in *Filled with the Spirit*, 272–79.

154 Keesmaat (*Paul and His Story*, 54–154) analyzes in detail the possible exodus foreground of Romans 8:14-17 and 8:18-39.

155 Keesmaat (*Paul and His Story*, 62–63) suggests that Paul had both Deuteronomy 32 and Isaiah 63 in mind when he wrote his letters.

156 Keesmaat (*Paul and His Story*, 136) summarizes her interpretation:

> In my exploration of the themes of being led, of sons and sonship, of not having fear, of groaning, of being set free, of inheritance, even of the suffering of God, I have discovered that these themes find their roots in recollections of the exodus from Egypt and the wanderings in the wilderness towards the promised land. Moreover, all of these themes are linked with others also found in Romans 8, such as crying to God as father, the suffering of God and the people of God, having hope, the renewal of creation and the glorification of God and believers. These themes occur in portrayals of the new exodus event which was eagerly awaited by Jews within second temple Judaism.

She adds later, "In continuity with the prophetic books, Paul transforms the exodus tradition in such a way that it is not merely a recollection of past events but a type of the new event of salvation which is to come" (136).

157 Romans 8:26, 23. Keesmaat (*Paul and His Story*, 134) pays particular attention to the elements of suffering and crying out when she writes: "So we discover that underlying the various narratives of suffering, of groaning and bondage and liberation, lies the narrative of God, the God who felt the oppression of the Israelites in Egypt and liberated them, who grieved and mourned their disobedience and unfaithfulness throughout the prophetic literature, who continues to groan with her broken creation and people." This

groaning "not only evokes the groaning associated with the curse upon the woman in Genesis 3, but also the groaning of Israel in bondage to Egypt and other foreign overlords."

158 Exodus 3:7.

159 Exodus 3:9 (modified from NRSV).

160 J. Heil ("Jesus with the Wild Animals in Mark 1:13," *Catholic Biblical Quarterly* 68 [2006]: 63–78) argues for an exodus substratum in the baptism and temptation of Jesus. He discerns the influence of Isaiah 63:7-64:8, Greek Jeremiah 38:8-9, 19-20, and Isaiah 42:1 in the portrayal of Jesus as the son of the father. Heil notices in particular the elements of love (Isaiah 63:9), father (Isaiah 63:16; 64:7), and the people of Israel as children (Isaiah 63:7-8) in the baptismal scene (69–72).

161 Matthew 4:1-2.

162 D. Allison and W. D. Davies (*A Critical and Exegetical Commentary on the Gospel according to Saint Matthew* [Edinburgh: T & T Clark, 1988], 352) observe how

> in each temptation Jesus quotes from Deuteronomy, from Deut 8.3 in 4.4, from Deut 6.16 in 4.7, and from Deut 6.13 in 4.10. This is the key to the narrative: we have before us a haggadic tale which has issued forth from reflection on Deut 6-8. Jesus, the Son of God, is repeating the experience of Israel in the desert (cf. Tertullian, *De bapt.* 20). Having passed through the waters of a new exodus at his baptism (cf. 1 Cor 10.1-5), he enters the desert to suffer a time of testing, his forty days of fasting being analogous to Israel's forty years of wandering. Like Israel, Jesus is tempted by hunger. And, like Israel, Jesus is tempted to idolatry. All-important for a right understanding of our pericope is Deut 8.2-3: "And you shall remember all the way which the Lord your God has led you these forty years in the wilderness, that he might humble you, testing you to know what was in your heart, whether you would keep his commandments, or not. And he humbled you and let you hunger."

163 Greek Numbers 20:4-5 reads: "And why did you bring up the congregation of the Lord into this wilderness, to kill us and our animals? And why is it that you brought us up out [ἀνηγάγετε] of Egypt, to come into this evil place? A place it is where nothing is sown, neither figs nor vines nor pomegranates, nor is there water to drink." Greek 1 Samuel 12:6 reads: "And Samouel said to the people, saying, 'The Lord who made Moyses and Aaron is witness, who brought your fathers up out [ἀναγαγών] of Egypt.'" Greek Psalm 80:11 (Hebrew 81:10) reads: "For I am the Lord your God, who brought you up out [ἀναγαγών] of the land of Egypt. Open wide your mouth, and I will fill it."

164 Exodus 33:12.

165 Exodus 33:15 (modified from NRSV).

166 My translation.

167 Luke 4:1-2.

168 Greek Exodus 13:21 reads, ὁ δὲ θεὸς ἡγεῖτο αὐτῶν, ἡμέρας μὲν ἐν στύλῳ νεφέλης δεῖξαι αὐτοῖς τὴν ὁδόν, τὴν δὲ νύκτα ἐν στύλῶ πυρός.

169 Jesus' fullness with the spirit may possibly be explained, even in part, by Isaiah 63:11, according to which God placed within them (*him* in the Hebrew) the holy spirit. Now Jesus has within him the holy spirit. This may fit Luke's larger conception of Jesus as a new Moses—a topic developed at length by D. Moessner in *Lord of the Banquet: The Literary and Theological Significance of the Lukan Travel Narrative* (Minneapolis: Fortress, 1989). Moessner does not, to my knowledge, refer to Isaiah 63:7-14.

170 Mark 2:7.

171 Mark 3:21.

172 Mark 3:22.
173 Mark 3:28-29.
174 Matthew 12:32.
175 Luke 12:8-12.
176 Matthew and Luke's gospels preserve a similar version rather than two distinct ones.
177 Gospel of Thomas 44. Translation is from H. Koester and T. O. Lambdin, "The Gospel of Thomas," in *The Nag Hammadi Library in English*, ed. J. Robinson (New York: Harper & Row, 1981), 123.
178 Exodus 23:20-22.
179 Isaiah 63:10 (Greek). The decision of whether one accepts the Hebrew or Greek of Isaiah 63:9 does not have a direct impact upon the observation that the prerogatives of the angel (Exodus 23:20-23) are taken over by the holy spirit in Isaiah 63:10.
180 Matthew 12:1-8.
181 Matthew 12:9-14.
182 Matthew 12:23.
183 Matthew 12:32.
184 Luke 12:11-12.
185 Other texts may be related, too, to Isaiah 63. Isaiah 63:10 may have generated the command in Ephesians 4:30, "do not grieve the Holy Spirit of God, with which you were marked with a seal for the day of redemption." F. Thielman thinks this is the case (*Ephesians* [Grand Rapids: Baker Academic], 317–18). E. Best is skeptical because the verb *grieve* is akin to the Hebrew, while Best thinks the author of the letter to the Ephesians was dependent rather on the Greek Bible, which refers to rebellion rather than grieving. M. Barth considers this command to be a "stray element" in Ephesians, prompting him to suggest that this verse "was originally part of a liturgical confession." He suggests that "Eph 4:17-32 contains collected and re-edited pre-Pauline materials. However, the distinctive features of 4:30 are of greater than only formal or traditio-historical interest. By citing or alluding to a supposedly well-known line of prayer or confession, the author of Ephesians may wish to set forth the basis and motive for all ethics rather than to utter just one more special prohibition" (*Ephesians: Translation and Commentary on Chapters 4–6* [Garden City: Doubleday, 1974], 547–48). In short, this command may have been central to a well-known, pre-Pauline liturgy. It is unlikely that this saying is indebted to the blasphemy sayings of Jesus, since it refers, in its context, to damaging speech rather than blasphemy (*A Critical and Exegetical Commentary on Ephesians* [Edinburgh: T & T Clark, 1998], 457).

S. Currie argues that Greek Isaiah 63:7-10 belonged to a pre-Markan tradition, which "lies behind the Markan account of the Transfiguration" ("Isaiah 63:9 and the Transfiguration in Mark," *Austin Seminary Bulletin* 82 [1966]: 14). Presumably, Moses and Elijah were the ambassadors who did not save, but Jesus himself was the savior. Currie's proposal may work generally, but the *absence* of the spirit in a story that mirrors the baptism of Jesus is striking if indeed Isaiah 63:7-14 lies behind the transfiguration story in Mark's gospel.

An allusion to the words "shepherd of his flock" (τὸν ποιμένα τῶν προβάτων) in Isaiah 63:11 (Greek) may be detected in the words, "the great shepherd of the sheep" (τὸν ποιμένα τῶν προβάτων τὸν μέγαν) in Hebrews 13:20. As to Stephen's charge in Acts 7:51, this is probably an expression of the indictment that Israel resisted the prophets, which can be found in Nehemiah 9:30, 2 Chronicles 24:19, and Zechariah 7:12. Isaiah 63:10 does not belong to this trajectory of resistance to the prophets (despite what I wrote in *Filled with the Spirit*, 243n9).

Excurses

1 E. Mesch, *Hans Leisegang: Leben und Werk* (Erlangen and Jena: Palm und Enke, 1999) 95–100.
2 Mesch, *Hans Leisegang*, 102–5.
3 Mesch, *Hans Leisegang*, 107–8.
4 Mesch, *Hans Leisegang*, 112.
5 Mesch, *Hans Leisegang*, 133–43.
6 Mesch, *Hans Leisegang*, 149–65.
7 Mesch, *Hans Leisegang*, 165–70.
8 Mesch, *Hans Leisegang*, 199–204. In addition to the biography by Mesch, T. Litt offers a biographical sketch of Leisegang in "Zur ersten Wiederkehr seines Todestages am 5. April 1952," *Zeitschrift für philosophische Forschung* 6 (1952): 275–82.
9 S. Olyan, *A Thousand Thousands Served Him: Exegesis and the Naming of Angels in Ancient Judaism* (Tübingen: J. C. B. Mohr [Paul Siebeck], 1993), 11–12.
10 J. Kugel, "Two Introductions to Midrash," *Prooftexts* 3, no. 2 (1981): 144.
11 In his study of angels, P. Schäfer (*Rivalität zwischen Engeln und Menschen: Untersuchungen zur Rabbinischen Engelvorstellung*, Studia Judaica 8 [Berlin: de Gruyter, 1975], 1) appraises A. Kohut's *Die jüdische Angelologie und Dämonologie in ihrer Abhängigkeit vom Parsismus* (Leipzig: Brockhaus, 1866) by making much the same point as Olyan: "Diese These Kohuts wird, zumindest in ihrer radikalen Form, heute kaum noch von einem Forscher akzeptiert." The rationale for this consensus is that scholars tend to look more to inner-Israelite and Jewish developments than external influences:

> Neuere Untersuchungen auf verwandten Gebieten haben gezeigt, daß sehr viel mehr Vorstellungen, als lange angenommen wurde, aus innerjüdischen bzw. kanaanäischen Voraussetzungen zu erklären sind. Vermutlich wird eine (noch ausstehende) Zusammenfassung der nachexilisch-frühjüdischen Angelologie—statt allzu eilig nach "Fremdeinflüssen" zu fragen—sich verstärkt den kanaanäisch-altisraelitischen Wurzeln zuwenden müssen.

12 W. G. Heidt, *Angelology of the Old Testament: A Study in Biblical Theology* (Washington, D.C.: Catholic University of America Press, 1949), 82.
13 B. Childs, *The Book of Exodus: A Critical, Theological Commentary*, OTL (Louisville, Ky.: Westminster John Knox, 2004), 487.
14 J. Durham, *Exodus*, WBC 3 (Waco, Tex.: Word, 1987), 314n21a.
15 Durham, *Exodus*, 335.
16 *TDNT* 1:77–78.
17 B. Stein, "Der Engel des Auszugs," *Biblica* 19 (1938): 286–307.
18 G. Juncker, "Jesus and the Angel of the Lord: An Old Testament Paradigm for New Testament Christology" (Ph.D. diss., Trinity Evangelical Divinity School, 2001). Other studies include V. Hirth, *Gottes Boten im Alten Testament: Die alttestamentliche Mal'ak-Vorstellung unter besonderer Berücksichtigung des Mal'ak Jahwe-Problems* (Berlin: Evangelische Verlagsanstalt, 1975); and H. Röttger, *Mal'ak Jahwe, Bote von Gott: Die Vorstellung von Gottes Boten im hebr. Alten Testament* (Frankfurt am Main: Peter Lang, 1978).
19 Juncker, "Jesus and the Angel of the Lord," 85–88.
20 Juncker, "Jesus and the Angel of the Lord," 113.
21 Juncker, "Jesus and the Angel of the Lord," 89. In Exodus 33, Moses is told to go immediately without the tabernacle built, so that God cannot be in Israel's midst as they travel

to the promised land; thus, according to Juncker, the issue at stake has nothing to do with whether the angel will accompany Israel; the issue is whether they will build the tabernacle, in which God dwells, before embarking (99).

22 H. Ausloos, "The 'Angel of YHWH' in Exod. xxiii 20-33 and Judg. ii 1-5. A clue to the 'Deuteronom(ist)ic' Puzzle?" *Vetus Testamentum* 58 (2008): 1–6.

23 Ausloos, "'Angel of YHWH,'" 6–7.

24 Ausloos, "'Angel of YHWH,'" 8.

25 Ausloos, "'Angel of YHWH,'" 9.

26 Ausloos, "'Angel of YHWH,'" 10–11. Ausloos' analysis is a clear demonstration of how difficult it is to date Exodus 23:20-33. As we shall see, it is difficult to date Isaiah 63:7-14 as well; though included in a putatively Persian-era corpus, some scholars have argued that it is actually an exilic composition. Given the current state of affairs, there is little firm evidence, therefore, to prevent viewing the lament in Isaiah 63 as an interpretation of Exodus 23 (and other texts). See "Excursus: Possible Dates of the Lament of Isaiah 63:7–64:11."

27 W. Propp, *Exodus 1–18: A New Translation with Introduction and Commentary* (New York: Doubleday, 1999), 287.

28 See Exodus 13:21-22; 14:24.

29 See Exodus 14:19.

30 Exodus 33:3.

31 Numbers 9:15-23.

32 T. Mann, *Divine Presence and Guidance in Israelite Traditions: The Typology of Exaltation* (Baltimore: Johns Hopkins University Press, 1977), 164.

33 Numbers 9:15.

34 Numbers 9:16.

35 W. Propp, *Exodus 19–40: A New Translation with Introduction and Commentary* (New York: Doubleday, 2006), 674. Exodus 24:17, with glory and consuming fire, may be related to this text.

36 Numbers 9:17.

37 Numbers 9:18-20.

38 Numbers 9:15-17, 20, 22.

39 Numbers 9:17, 21-22.

40 Mann, *Divine Presence and Guidance*, 164–68.

41 Numbers 10:11-12.

42 Numbers 10:33-36.

43 Psalm 99:7.

44 E.g., Exodus 16:10; Deuteronomy 5:22.

45 C. Westermann, *Isaiah 40–66: A Commentary* (Philadelphia: Westminster, 1969), 385, 387–88.

46 P. Hanson, *Dawn of Apocalyptic: The Historical and Sociological Roots of Jewish Apocalyptic Eschatology* (Philadelphia: Fortress, 1975), 80.

47 S. Paul, *Isaiah 40–66: Translation and Commentary* (Grand Rapids: Eerdmans, 2012), 571.

48 P.-E. Bonnard, *Le second Isaïe, son disciple et leurs éditeurs: Isaïe 40–66* (Paris: Gabalda, 1972), 442–43.

49 J. Morgenstern, "Isaiah 63.7-14," *Hebrew Union College Annual* 23 (1950–1951): 188.

50 L. Brisman, "On the Divine Presence in Exodus," in *Exodus*, ed. H. Bloom (New York: Chelsea House, 1987), 120.

51 J. Goldenstein, *Das Gebet der Gottesknechte: Jesaja 63,9-64:11 im Jesajabuch* (Neukirchen-Vluyn: Neukirchener, 2001), 54.

52 Goldenstein, *Gebet*, 54–55. For this, he is dependent upon W. Lau, *Schriftgelehrte Prophetie in Jes 56-66: Eine Untersuchung zu den literarischen Bezügen in den letzten elf Kapiteln des Jesajabuches* (Berlin: de Gruyter, 1994), 290.

53 Goldenstein, *Gebet*, 55.

54 J. Blenkinsopp, *Isaiah 56–66: A New Translation with Introduction and Commentary* (New York: Doubleday, 2003), 254.

55 B. Duhm, *Das Buch Jesaja*, 4th ed. (Göttingen: Vandenhoeck and Ruprecht, 1922), 466.

56 Blenkinsopp, *Isaiah 56–66*, 260. In support of this position, Blenkinsopp lists J. Fischer, *Das Buch Isaias*, part 2 (Bonn: Peter Hanstein, 1939), 191; E. J. Kissane, *The Book of Isaiah*, 2nd ed., 2 vols. (Dublin: Browne and Nolan, 1960), 2:291, 296; J. L. McKenzie, *Second Isaiah: Introduction, Translation and Notes* (Garden City, N.Y.: Doubleday, 1968), 188; Westermann, *Isaiah 40–66*, 385–87; and R. N. Whybray, *Isaiah 40–66* (London: Oliphants, 1975), 257.

57 M. Kuntzmann, "Une relecture en *Is.*, 63, 7-14: Etude du vocabulaire," *Revue de Sciences Religieuses* 51 (1977): 24.

58 Whybray, *Isaiah 40–66*, 257. Many others follow this same track, including, for example, F. Nötscher, *"Das Angesicht Gottes schauen" nach biblischer und babylonischer Auffassung* (Würzburg: Becker, 1924), 51.

59 J. Hayes and J. Miller, *A History of Ancient Israel and Judah*, 2nd ed. (Louisville, Ky.: Westminster John Knox, 2006), 493–94.

60 I. Provan, V. Long, and T. Longman, *A Biblical History of Israel* (Louisville, Ky.: Westminster, 2015), 380–81, 385–86.

61 M. Moore and B. Kelle, *Biblical History and Israel's Past: The Changing Study of the Bible and History* (Grand Rapids: Eerdmans, 2011), 343–49.

62 O. Lipschits, "Shedding New Light on the Dark Years of the 'Exilic Period': New Studies, Further Elucidations, and Some Questions Regarding the Archaeology of Judah as an 'Empty Land,'" in *Interpreting Exile: Interdisciplinary Studies of Displacement and Deportation in Biblical and Modern Contexts*, ed. B. Kelle, F. Ames, and J. Wright (Atlanta: SBL, 2011), 57–90.

63 Moore and Kelle, *Biblical History and Israel's Past*, 330. For their full summary, see pp. 35–67.

64 Jeremiah 29:1-9.

65 Translation from J. Pritchard, *Ancient Near Eastern Texts Relating to the Old Testament*, 3rd ed. (Princeton, N.J.: Princeton University Press, 1969), 308

66 D. L. Smith-Christopher, *A Biblical Theology of Exile* (Minneapolis: Fortress, 2002), 69–71.

67 Ezra 2:65.

68 Ezra 2:69.

69 Hayes and Miller, *History of Ancient Israel*, 494.

70 Ezekiel 37:11.

71 Moore and Kelle, *Biblical History and Israel's Past*, 366.

72 Another important dimension of destruction and exile is the trauma it may have caused. D. Carr (*Holy Resilience: The Bible's Traumatic Origins* [New Haven, Conn.: Yale University Press, 2014], 67–127) offers a readable discussion of trauma and Israel's experience of exile.

73 Hayes and Miller, *History of Ancient Israel*, 479.

74 P. M. McNutt, *Reconstructing the Society of Ancient Israel* (Louisville, Ky.: Westminster John Knox, 1999), 184.

75 Hayes and Miller, *History of Ancient Israel*, 485.
76 Second Kings 25:25-26; Jeremiah 40:13–41:3.
77 Moore and Kelle, *Biblical History and Israel's Past*, 376.
78 Moore and Kelle, *Biblical History and Israel's Past*, 349. For an excellent compendium on archeology and surface surveys see pp. 374–79.
79 E.g., Isaiah 58:3-12. G. Emmerson (*Isaiah 56–66* [Sheffield: JSOT, 1992], 58, 63–67); and Westermann (*Isaiah 40–66*, 296–308) offer thumbnail sketches of the editorial history of Isaiah 56–66.
80 Isaiah 58:12; 60:10.
81 Ezra 4:1-3.
82 Nehemiah 13:23-27.
83 Isaiah 1:29-31; 65:3.
84 Isaiah 1:11, 29; 65:12.
85 Isaiah 1:30-31; 65:22. M. Sweeney (*Isaiah 1–4 and the Post-exilic Understanding of the Isaianic Tradition* [Berlin: de Gruyter, 1988]) analyzes this dimension of Isaiah 1–66.
86 Isaiah 63:18.
87 Isaiah 64:9-10 (Hebrew; English 64:10-11).
88 Goldenstein, *Gebet*, 233n8.
89 Goldenstein, *Gebet*, 233n7.
90 Goldenstein, *Gebet*, 233n6.
91 B. Duhm, *Das Buch Jesaia* (Göttingen: Vandenhoeck & Ruprecht, 1892), 390–91.
92 J. Watts, *Isaiah 34–66*, WBC 25 (Waco, Tex.: Word, 1987), 331.
93 Morgenstern, "Isaiah 63.7-14," 198–203 (198).
94 Goldenstein, *Gebet*, 234.
95 Hanson, *Dawn of Apocalyptic*, 86–87.
96 Hanson, *Dawn of Apocalyptic*, 92.
97 Isaiah 63:15-16.
98 Hanson, *Dawn of Apocalyptic*, 94.
99 Hanson, *Dawn of Apocalyptic*, 94–95.
100 J. Goldingay, *A Critical and Exegetical Commentary on Isaiah 56–66* (London: Bloomsbury, 2014), 387.
101 Whybray, *Isaiah 40–66*, 255–56.
102 H. Williamson, "Isaiah 63,7-64,11: Exilic Lament or Post-exilic Protest?" *Zeitschrift für die Alttestamentliche Wissenschaft* 102 (1990): 51–55.
103 R. Lessing, *Isaiah 56–66* (St. Louis: Concordia, 2014), 12–20.
104 Williamson, "Exilic Lament or Post-exilic Protest?" 54.
105 Williamson, "Exilic Lament or Post-exilic Protest?" 55.
106 Williamson, "Exilic Lament or Post-exilic Protest?" 56–57.
107 H. Williamson, "Structure and Historiography in Nehemiah 9," in *Proceedings of the Ninth World Congress of Jewish Studies: Panel Sessions; Bible Studies and Ancient Near East* (Jerusalem: World Union of Jewish Studies, the Magnes Press, the Hebrew University, 1988), 129.
108 Williamson, "Exilic Lament or Post-exilic Protest?" 58.
109 Lessing, *Isaiah 56–66*, 23.
110 J. Muilenburg, "The Book of Isaiah, Chapters 40–66," *Interpreter's Bible* 5:653, cited by Lessing, *Isaiah 56–66*, 23.
111 Zechariah 7:3-7.
112 Zechariah 7:8-12.

113 Isaiah 57:15.
114 Isaiah 63:15.
115 First Kings 8:27-30.
116 Ezekiel 1–3.
117 Ezekiel 8–11.
118 Ezekiel 40–48.
119 B. Anderson, "Exodus and Covenant in Second Isaiah and Prophetic Tradition," in *Magnalia Dei: The Mighty Acts of God; Essays on the Bible and Archaeology in Memory of G. Ernest Wright*, ed. F. Cross, W. Lemke, and P. Miller (New York: Doubleday, 1976), 339–60.
120 H. Barstad, *A Way in the Wilderness: The "Second Exodus" in the Message of Second Isaiah* (Manchester: University of Manchester Press, 1989), 5–6.
121 O. Lund, *Way Metaphors and Way Topics in Isaiah 40–55* (Tübingen: Mohr Siebeck, 2008), 1.
122 Lund, *Way Metaphors and Way Topics in Isaiah 40–55*, 2n3.
123 Barstad, *A Way in the Wilderness*, 15–16.
124 Barstad, *A Way in the Wilderness*, 19–20.
125 Blenkinsopp, *Isaiah 40–55*, 180–81. U. Berges (*Jesaja 40–48* [Freiburg im Breisgau: Herder, 2008], 103–4) argues similarly that

> eine zentrale Frage, nicht nur für die Auslegung dieser Angangsverse, sondern für Jes 40-55 insgesamt, ist die nach dem "Weg JHWHs" in Jes 40,3. Handelt es sich dabei um die Einspielung der "Exodus-Thematik," also um die Ankündigung eines zweiten Exodus, analog zur Herausführung der Söhne Jakobs aus Ägypten? Zielt diese Wegbereitung auf die Rückkehr der Exilsgemeinde aus dem feindlichen Babylon ab? Diese Auslegung, die in der Forschung lange Zeit unwidersprochen blieb, wird zusehends differenzierter betrachtet (dazu besonders *Lund*, Way). Denn zum einen geht es ausdrücklich um den Weg JHWHs, und an keiner Stelle ist expliziert, die exilierten Judäer würden auf dieser Straße den Rückweg aus Babel antreten. Zum anderen bietet auch die Metaphorik, von JHWH als königlichem Hirten (Jes 40,10-11) keinen Hinweis darauf, dass es um den Rückzug der babylonischen Gola ginge, zumal sich die Trostbotschaft ja gar nicht an sie, sondern an Zion/Jerusalem richtet! Von einem Rückzug der Gola durch die syrische Wüste nach Juda und Jerusalem ist *expressis verbis* nirgends die Rede.

Berges continues: "Entgegen der *opinio communis* bezeichnen Wüste und Steppe hier nicht die *arabica deserta* . . . also die *terra intermedia* zwischen Zweistromland und Palästina, sondern sind eine Metapher für den trostlosen Zustand Jerusalems und des Gottesvolkes in exilisch-frühnachexilischer Zeit" (104). The "way of the LORD" in the Hebrew Bible, contends Berges, is never concrete and spatial ("konkret-räumlichen") but always ethical and religious ("ethisch-religiösen").
126 Barstad, *A Way in the Wilderness*, 19.
127 W. Beuken, *Haggai-Sacharja 1–8: Studien zur Überlieferungsgeschichte der frühnachexilischen Prophetie* (Assen: Van Gorcum, 1967).
128 Beuken, *Haggai-Sacharja 1–8*, 53.
129 Beuken, *Haggai-Sacharja 1–8*, 54.
130 Beuken, *Haggai-Sacharja 1–8*, 56.
131 Beuken, *Haggai-Sacharja 1–8*, 58.
132 Beuken, *Haggai-Sacharja 1–8*, 58–59.

133 Beuken, *Haggai-Sacharja 1–8*, 60.
134 Beuken, *Haggai-Sacharja 1–8*, 79–83.
135 Deuteronomy 4:37.
136 D. Peterson, *Haggai and Zechariah 1–8: A Commentary* (Philadelphia: Westminster, 1984), 65–66.
137 R. Mason, "The Purpose of the 'Editorial Framework' of the Book of Haggai," *Vetus Testamentum* 27 (1977): 413–21.
138 R. Kohn, "A Prophet like Moses? Rethinking Ezekiel's Relationship to the Torah," *Zeitschrift für die Altestamentliche Wissenschaft* 114 (2002): 239–40.
139 Kohn, "A Prophet like Moses?" 240–42.
140 Kohn, "A Prophet like Moses?" 242–43.
141 Kohn, "A Prophet like Moses?" 244.
142 Kohn, "A Prophet like Moses?" 245.
143 Exodus 29:46; Ezekiel 39:28.
144 Leviticus 26:5; Ezekiel 28:26; 34:28; 39:6.
145 Exodus 25:8; 29:45-46; Leviticus 15:31; Numbers 5:3; 35:34; Ezekiel 37:26, 28; 43:7, 9.
146 Numbers 25:12; Ezekiel 34:25. "Covenant of peace" in Hebrew: בְּרִית שָׁלוֹם.
147 Kohn, "A Prophet like Moses?" 242.
148 Kohn, "A Prophet like Moses?" 246–48.
149 Kohn, "A Prophet like Moses?" 248–49.
150 H. McKeating, "Ezekiel the 'Prophet like Moses'?" *Journal for the Study of the Old Testament* 61 [1994]: 99.
151 R. Idestrom, "Echoes of the Book of Exodus in Ezekiel," *Journal for the Study of the Old Testament* 33 (2009): 489–510.
152 J. Evans, "An Inner-Biblical Interpretation and Intertextual Reading of Ezekiel's Recognition Formulae with the Book of Exodus" (Th.D. diss., University of Stellenbosch, 2006).
153 N. DeLapp, "Ezekiel as Moses—Israel as Pharaoh: Reverberations of the Exodus Narrative in Ezekiel," in *Reverberations of the Exodus in Scripture*, ed. R. Fox (Eugene, Ore.: Pickwick, 2014), 51–73. His synthesis of secondary research occurs especially on pp. 56–60.
154 J. Levenson, *Theology of the Program of Restoration of Ezekiel 40–48* (Cambridge, Mass.: Scholars, 1976).

SELECTED BIBLIOGRAPHY

This selected bibliography includes works that are relevant to this study. The disciplines of pneumatology in general and New Testament pneumatology in particular require their own discrete bibliographies. A good starting point for the spirit in the Hebrew Bible, early Judaism, and New Testament can be found in *Oxford Bibliographies Online*, for which Volker Rabens and I have compiled a preliminary annotated bibliography. In the following bibliography, I tend to exclude commentaries, except when they contribute pivotal arguments to which I respond at length (e.g., U. Berges and W. Beuken).

Abelson, J. *The Immanence of God in Rabbinical Literature*. London: Macmillan, 1912.

Akroyd, P. "Some Interpretative Glosses in the Book of Haggai." *Journal of Jewish Studies* 7 (1956): 163–67.

Allen, D. M. "'The Forgotten Spirit': A Pentecostal Reading of the Letter to the Hebrews?" *Journal of Pentecostal Theology* 18, no. 1 (2009): 51–66.

Althouse, P. "Implications of Kenosis of the Spirit for a Creational Eschatology: A Pentecostal Engagement with Jürgen Moltmann." In *The Spirit Renews the Face of the Earth: Pentecostal Forays in Science and Theology of Creation*, edited by A. Yong, 155–72. Eugene, Ore.: Pickwick, 2009.

Anderson, A. A. "The Use of 'Ruah' in 1QS, 1QH and 1QM." *Journal of Semitic Studies* 7 (1962): 293–303.

Anderson, B. "Exodus and Covenant in Second Isaiah and Prophetic Tradition." In *Magnalia Dei: The Mighty Acts of God; Essays on the Bible and Archaeology in Memory of G. Ernest Wright*, edited by F. Cross, W. Lemke, and P. Miller, 339–60. New York: Doubleday, 1976.

Aune, D. E. *Prophecy in Early Christianity and the Ancient Mediterranean World*. Grand Rapids: Eerdmans, 1983.

Ausloos, H. "The 'Angel of YHWH' in Exod. xxiii 20-33 and Judg. ii 1-5. A Clue to the 'Deuteronom(ist)ic' Puzzle?" *Vetus Testamentum* 58 (2008): 1–12.

Baer, H. von. *Der heilige Geist in den Lukasschriften*. Stuttgart: Kohlhammer, 1926.

Barr, J. "Hypostatization of Linguistic Phenomena in Modern Theological Interpretation." *Journal of Semitic Studies* 7 (1962): 85–94.

Barrett, C. K. *The Holy Spirit and the Gospel Tradition*. New York: Macmillan, 1947.

Barstad, H. *A Way in the Wilderness: The "Second Exodus" in the Message of Second Isaiah*. Manchester: University of Manchester Press, 1989.

Bauckham, R. "The Role of the Spirit." In *The Climax of Prophecy: Studies on the Book of Revelation*, edited by R. Bauckham, 150–73. London: T&T Clark, 1993.

Baumert, N. *Charisma-Taufe-Geisttaufe*. 2 vols. Würzburg: Echter, 2001.

Baur, F. C. *Paul the Apostle of Jesus Christ, His Life and Work, His Epistles and His Doctrine*. London: Williams and Norgate, 1875.

Berges, U. *Jesaja 40–48*. Freiburg im Breisgau: Herder, 2008.

Bertone, J. A. *"The Law of the Spirit": Experience of the Spirit and Displacement of the Law in Romans 8:1–16*. Studies in Biblical Literature 86. New York: Lang, 2005.

Betz, O. *Der Paraklet: Fürsprecher im häretischen Spätjudentum, im Johannes-Evangelium und in neu gefundenen gnostischen Schriften*. Arbeiten zur Geschichte des Spätjudentums und Urchristentums 2. Leiden: Brill, 1963.

———. *Offenbarung und Schriftforschung in der Qumransekte*. Wissenschaftliche Untersuchungen zum Neuen Testament 1/6. Tübingen: J. C. B. Mohr (Paul Siebeck), 1960.

Beuken, W. *Haggai-Sacharja 1-8: Studien zur Überlieferungsgeschichte der frühnachexilischen Prophetie*. Assen: Van Gorcum, 1967.

———. "The Spirit of God in Us Loathes Envy: James 4:5." In *The Holy Spirit and Christian Origins: Essays in Honor of James D. G. Dunn*, edited by G. Stanton, B. W. Longenecker, and S. C. Barton, 270–81. Grand Rapids: Eerdmans, 2004.

———. *The Theology of Jürgen Moltmann*. Edinburgh: T&T Clark, 1995.

Bonnard, P.-E. *Le Second Isaïe, son disciple et leurs éditeurs*. Paris: Gabalda, 1972.

Boring, M. E. *Sayings of the Risen Jesus: Christian Prophecy in the Synoptic Tradition*. Society for New Testament Studies Monograph 46. Cambridge: Cambridge University Press, 1982.

Bousset, W. *Die Himmelsreise der Seele*. Darmstadt: Wissenschaftliche Buchgesellschaft, 1960. Originally published 1901.

———. *Die Religion des Judentums im neutestamentlichen Zeitalter*. 2nd ed. Berlin: Reuther und Reichard, 1906.

Brisman, L. "On the Divine Presence in Exodus." In *Exodus*, edited by H. Bloom, 105–22. New York: Chelsea House, 1987.

Brodeur, S. *The Holy Spirit's Agency in the Resurrection of the Dead: An Exegetico-Theological Study of 1 Corinthians 15,44b–49 and Romans 8,9–13*. Tesi Gregoriana, Serie Teologica 14. Rome: Editrice Pontificia Università Gregoriana, 1996.

Brueggemann, W. *The Prophetic Imagination*. 2nd ed. Minneapolis: Fortress, 2001.

Büchsel, F. *Der Geist Gottes im Neuen Testament*. Gütersloh: C. Bertelsmann, 1926.

Bucur, B. G. *Angelomorphic Pneumatology: Clement of Alexandria and Other Early Christian Witnesses*. Supplements to Vigiliae Christianae 95. Leiden: Brill, 2009.

Bulgakov, S. *The Comforter*. Grand Rapids: Eerdmans, 2004.

Burton, E. *Spirit, Soul, and Flesh*. Historical and Linguistic Studies in Literature Related to the New Testament 2/3. Chicago: University of Chicago Press, 1918.

Buttrick, G. A. *The Interpreter's Dictionary of the Bible*. 4 vols. New York: Abingdon, 1962.

Cage, G. T. *The Holy Spirit: A Source Book with Commentary*. Reno, Nev.: Charlotte House, 1995.

Carr, D. *Holy Resilience: The Bible's Traumatic Origins*. New Haven, Conn.: Yale University Press, 2014.

Carson, D. A. *Showing the Spirit: A Theological Exposition of 1 Corinthians 12–14*. Moore College Lectures. Grand Rapids: Baker, 1987.

Castelo, D. *Pneumatology: A Guide for the Perplexed*. London: Bloomsbury, 2015.

Chevallier, M.-A. *Souffle de Dieu: Le Saint-Esprit dans le Nouveau Testament*. Paris: Beauchesne, 1990.

Christoph, M. *Pneuma und das neue Sein der Glaubenden: Studien zur Semantik und Pragmatik der Rede von Pneuma in Röm 8*. Europäische Hochschulschriften, Theologie 23/813. Frankfurt: Peter Lang, 2005.

Collins, R. "Servant of the Lord, the." In *New Interpreter's Dictionary of the Bible*, vol. 5, edited by K. Doob Sakenfeld, 192–95. Nashville: Abingdon, 2009.

Congar, Y. *I Believe in the Holy Spirit*. New York: Crossroad, 1999.

Cosgrove, C. H. *The Cross and the Spirit: A Study in the Argument and Theology of Galatians*. Macon, Ga.: Mercer University Press, 1988.

Crone, T. M. *Early Christian Prophecy: A Study of Its Origin and Function*. Baltimore: St. Mary's University Press, 1973.

Currie, S. "Isaiah 63:9 and the Transfiguration in Mark." *Austin Seminary Bulletin* 82, no. 3 (1966): 7–34.

Dabney, D. L. "The Advent of the Spirit: The Turn to Pneumatology in the Theology of Jürgen Moltmann." *Asbury Theological Journal* 48 (1993): 81–107.

Das, A. *Paul and the Stories of Israel: Grand Thematic Narratives in Galatians*. Minneapolis: Fortress, 2016.

Davies, W. D. *Paul and Rabbinic Judaism: Some Rabbinic Elements in Pauline Theology*. 4th ed. Philadelphia: Fortress, 1980.

DeLapp, N. "Ezekiel as Moses—Israel as Pharaoh: Reverberations of the Exodus Narrative in Ezekiel." In *Reverberations of the Exodus in Scripture*, edited by R. Fox, 51–73. Eugene, Ore.: Pickwick, 2014.

Dreytza, M. *Der theologische Gebrauch von* Ruaḥ *im Alten Testament: Eine wort- und satzsemantische Studie*. Giessen: Brunnen, 1990.

Dunn, J. D. G. *Baptism in the Holy Spirit: A Re-examination of the New Testament Teaching on the Gift of the Spirit in Relation to Pentecostalism Today*. Studies in Biblical Theology 2/15. London: SCM Press, 1970.

———. *The Christ & the Spirit: Collected Essays of James D. G. Dunn*. Vol. 2, *Pneumatology*. Edinburgh: T&T Clark, 1998.

———. *Jesus and the Spirit: A Study of the Religious and Charismatic Experience of Jesus and the First Christians as Reflected in the New Testament*. London: SCM Press, 1975.

Eichrodt, W. *Old Testament Theology*. 2 vols. Philadelphia: Westminster, 1967.

Engberg-Pedersen, T. *Cosmology and Self in the Apostle Paul: The Material Spirit.* Oxford: Oxford University Press, 2010.

Evans, J. "An Inner-Biblical Interpretation and Intertextual Reading of Ezekiel's Recognition Formulae with the Book of Exodus." Th.D. diss., University of Stellenbosch, 2006.

Fatehi, M. *The Spirit's Relation to the Risen Lord in Paul: An Examination of Its Christological Implications.* Wissenschaftliche Untersuchungen zum Neuen Testament 2/128. Tübingen: Mohr Siebeck, 2000.

Fee, G. D. *God's Empowering Presence: The Holy Spirit in the Letters of Paul.* Peabody, Mass.: Hendrickson, 1994.

Feldt, L. "Dis/orientations—Fantastic Memory in the Exodus Narrative." In *Literature and Memory: Theoretical Paradigms, Genres, Functions,* edited by A. Nünning & R. Sommer, 95–111. Tübingen: Francke, 2006.

———. "Exodus: Ritual, Cognition and Memory." *Collegium Biblicum Årsskrift* 15 (2011): 49-66.

Firth, D. G., and P. D. Wegner. *Presence, Power, and Promise: The Role of the Spirit of God in the Old Testament.* Downers Grove, Ill.: InterVarsity Press, 2011.

Fischer, A. "Moses and the Exodus-Angel." In *Angels: The Concept of Celestial Beings—Origins, Development and Reception,* edited by F. Reiterer, T. Nicklas, K. Schöpflin, 79–91. Berlin: de Gruyter, 2006.

Foerster, W. "Der Heilige Geist im Spätjudentum." *New Testament Studies* 8 (1961–62): 117–34.

Forbes, C. *Prophecy and Inspired Speech in Early Christianity and Its Hellenistic Environment.* Wissenschaftliche Untersuchungen zum Neuen Testament 2/75. Tübingen: J. C. B. Mohr (Paul Siebeck), 1995.

Fox, Michael, ed. *Reverberations of the Exodus in Scripture.* Eugene, Ore.: Pickwick, 2014.

Frey, J. "Flesh and Spirit in the Palestinian Jewish Sapiential Tradition and in the Qumran Texts: An Inquiry into the Background of Pauline Usage." In *The Wisdom Texts from Qumran and the Development of Sapiential Thought,* edited by C. Hempel, A. Lange, and H. Lichtenberger, 367–404. Bibliotheca Ephemeridum Theologicarum Lovaniensium 159. Leuven: Leuven University Press, 2002.

Frey, J., and J. R. Levison, eds., with A. Bowden. *The Holy Spirit, Inspiration, and the Cultures of Antiquity: Multidisciplinary Perspectives.* Ekstasis: Religious Experience from Antiquity to the Middle Ages 5. Berlin: de Gruyter, 2014.

Gibson, A. *Biblical Semantic Logic: A Preliminary Analysis.* New York: St. Martin's Press, 1981.

Gieschen, C. *Angelomorphic Christology: Antecedents and Early Evidence.* Leiden: Brill, 1998.

Gillespie, T. W. *The First Theologians: A Study in Early Christian Prophecy.* Grand Rapids: Eerdmans, 1994.

Goldenstein, J. *Das Gebet der Gottesknechte: Jesaja 63,9–64:11 im Jesajabuch.* Neukirchen-Vluyn: Neukirchener, 2001.

Greenspahn, F. "Why Prophecy Ceased." *Journal of Biblical Literature* 108 (1989): 37–49.

Gunkel, H. *Die Wirkungen des heiligen Geistes nach der populären Anschauung der apostolischen Zeit und nach der Lehre des Apostels Paulus*. Göttingen: Vandenhoeck & Ruprecht, 1888. English translation: *The Influence of the Holy Spirit: The Popular View of the Apostolic Age and the Teaching of the Apostle Paul; A Biblical-Theological Study*. Translated by R. A. Harrisville and P. A. Quanbeck II. Philadelphia: Fortress, 1979.

Hafemann, S. J. *Paul, Moses, and the History of Israel: The Letter/Spirit Contrast and the Argument from Scripture in 2 Corinthians 3*. Wissenschaftliche Untersuchungen zum Neuen Testament 1/81. Tübingen: J. C. B. Mohr (Paul Siebeck), 1995.

Halperin, D. *The Faces of the Chariot: Early Jewish Responses to Ezekiel's Vision*. Texte und Studien zum antiken Judentum 16. Tübingen: J. C. B. Mohr (Paul Siebeck), 1988.

Hanson, P. *Dawn of Apocalyptic: The Historical and Sociological Roots of Jewish Apocalyptic Eschatology*. Philadelphia: Fortress, 1975.

Hawthorne, G. F. *The Presence and the Power*. Waco, Tex.: Word Books, 1991.

Hayes, J., and J. Miller. *A History of Ancient Israel and Judah*. 2nd ed. Louisville, Ky.: Westminster John Knox, 2006.

Heidt, W. G. *Angelology of the Old Testament: A Study in Biblical Theology*. Washington, D.C.: Catholic University of America Press, 1949.

Heschel, S. *The Aryan Jesus: Christian Theologians and the Bible in Nazi Germany*. Princeton, N.J.: Princeton University Press, 2008.

Hildebrandt, W. *An Old Testament Theology of the Spirit of God*. Peabody, Mass.: Hendrickson, 1995.

Hill, D. *New Testament Prophecy*. Marshall's Theological Library. London: Marshall, Morgan & Scott, 1985.

Hirth, V. *Gottes Boten im Alten Testament: Die alttestamentliche Mal'ak-Vorstellung unter besonderer Berücksichtigung des Mal'ak Jahwe-Problems*. Berlin: Evangelische Verlagsanstalt, 1975.

Horn, F. W. *Das Angeld des Geistes: Studien zur paulinischen Pneumatologie*. Forschungen zur Religion und Literatur des Alten und Neuen Testaments 154. Göttingen: Vandenhoeck & Ruprecht, 1992.

Hurtado, L. W. *One God, One Lord: Early Christian Devotion and Ancient Jewish Monotheism*. Philadelphia: Fortress, 1988.

Idestrom, R. G. S. "Echoes of the Book of Exodus in Ezekiel." *Journal for the Study of the Old Testament* 33 (2009): 489–510.

Isaacs, M. E. *The Concept of Spirit: A Study of* Pneuma *in Hellenistic Judaism and Its Bearing on the New Testament*. London: Heythrop College, 1976.

Jeremias, J. *New Testament Theology*. New York: Charles Scribner's Sons, 1971.

Johnson, A. "Shekinah: The Indwelling of God in the Theology of Jürgen Moltmann." Ph.D. diss., Luther Seminary, 2003.

Johnson, E. A. *She Who Is: The Mystery of God in Feminist Theological Discourse*. New York: Crossroad Herder, 2001.

Johnston, G. "'Spirit' and 'Holy Spirit' in the Qumran Literature." In *New Testament Sidelights: Essays in Honor of Alexander Converse Purdy*, edited by H. K. McArthur, 27–42. Hartford, Conn.: Hartford Seminary Foundation, 1960.

Juncker, G. "Jesus and the Angel of the Lord: An Old Testament Paradigm for New Testament Christology." Ph.D. diss., Trinity Evangelical Divinity School, 2001.

Kärkkäinen, V.-M. *Pneumatology: The Holy Spirit in Ecumenical, International, and Contextual Perspective.* Grand Rapids: Baker, 2002.

Keesmaat, S. *Paul and His Story: (Re)interpreting the Exodus Tradition.* Journal for the Study of the New Testament Supplement 181. Sheffield: Sheffield Academic Press, 1999.

Koch, K. "Ezra and the Origins of Judaism." *Journal of Semitic Studies* 19 (1974): 173–97.

Koch, R. *Der Geist Gottes im Alten Testament.* Frankfurt: Lang, 1991.

Kohn, R. L. "A Prophet like Moses? Rethinking Ezekiel's Relationship to the Torah." *Zeitschrift für die Alttestamentliche Wissenschaft* 114 (2002): 236–54.

Kugel, J. "Two Introductions to Midrash." *Prooftexts* 3, no. 2 (1981): 131–55.

Kuhn, H.-W. *Enderwartung und gegenwärtiges Heil: Untersuchungen zu den Gemeindeliedern von Qumran mit einem Anhang über Eschatologie und Gegenwart in der Verkündigung Jesu.* Studien zur Umwelt des Neuen Testaments 4. Göttingen: Vandenhoeck and Ruprecht, 1966.

Kvalvaag, R. W. "The Spirit in Human Beings in Some Qumran Non-Biblical Texts." In *Qumran between the Old and New Testaments,* edited by F. H. Cryer and T. L. Thompson, 159–80. Journal for the Study of the Old Testament Supplement 290. Sheffield: Sheffield Academic Press, 1998.

Leisegang, H. *Der Heilige Geist: Das Wesen und Werden der mystisch-intuitiven Erkenntnis in der Philosophie und Religion der Griechen.* Vol. 1, part 1, *Die vorchristlichen Anschauungen und Lehren vom ΠΝΕΥΜΑ und der mystisch-intuitiven Erkenntnis.* Leipzig: Teubner, 1919.

———. *Pneuma Hagion: Der Ursprung des Geistbegriffs der synoptischen Evangelien aus der grieschischen Mystick.* Leipzig: J. C. Heinrichs, 1922.

Leivestad, R. "Das Dogma von der prophetenlosen Zeit." *New Testament Studies* 19 (1972–73): 288–99.

Levenson, J. D. *Theology of the Program of Restoration of Ezekiel 40–48.* Cambridge: Scholars, 1976.

Levison, J. R. "Assessing the Origins of Modern Pneumatology: The Life and Legacy of Hermann Gunkel." In *Christian Body, Christian Self: Essays on Early Christian Concepts of Personhood,* edited by J. Harrill, and C. Rothschild. 313–31. Wissenschaftliche Untersuchungen zum Neuen Testament 1/284. Tübingen: Mohr Siebeck, 2012.

———. "Did the Spirit Withdraw from Israel? An Evaluation of the Earliest Jewish Data." *New Testament Studies* 43 (1997): 35–57.

———. *Filled with the Spirit.* Grand Rapids: Eerdmans, 2009.

———. *Inspired: the Holy Spirit and the Mind of Faith.* Grand Rapids: Eerdmans, 2013.

———. "The Case of the Ecstatic Elders." *Catholic Biblical Quarterly* 65 (2003): 503–21.

———. "The Promise of the Spirit of Life in Ezekiel." In *Israel's God and Rebecca's Children: Christology and Community in Early Judaism and Christianity (Essays in Honor of Larry W. Hurtado and Alan F. Segal),* edited by D. Capes, A. DeConick, H. Bond, and T. Miller, 247–59. Waco, Tex.: Baylor University Press, 2007.

———. *The Spirit in First Century Judaism.* Leiden: Brill, 1997.

———. "The Spirit in Its Second Temple Context: An Exegetical Analysis of the Pneumatology of N. T. Wright." In *God and the Faithfulness of Paul: A Critical Examination of the Pauline Theology of N. T. Wright*, edited by M. Bird, C. Heilig, and J. Hewitt, 439–62. Wissenschaftliche Untersuchungen zum Neuen Testament 2/413. Tübingen: Mohr Siebeck, 2016.

———. "The Spirit in the Gospels: Breaking the Impasse of Early Twentieth-Century German Scholarship." In *New Testament Greek and Exegesis*, edited by A. Donaldson and T. Sailors, 55–76. Grand Rapids: Eerdmans, 2003.

———. "The Two Spirits in Qumran Theology." In *The Uniqueness of Qumran Theology*, vol. 2, *The Bible and the Dead Sea Scrolls*, edited by J. Charlesworth, 169–94. Waco, Tex.: Baylor University Press, 2006.

Levison, J., and J. Frey. "The Origins of Early Christian Pneumatology: On the Rediscovery and Reshaping of the History of Religions Quest." In *The Holy Spirit, Inspiration, and the Cultures of Antiquity: Multidisciplinary Perspectives*, edited by J. Frey and J. Levison, with A. Bowden, 1–37. Ekstasis: Religious Experience from Antiquity to the Middle Ages 5. Berlin: de Gruyter, 2014.

Lipschits, O. "Shedding New Light on the Dark Years of the 'Exilic Period': New Studies, Further Elucidations, and Some Questions Regarding the Archaeology of Judah as an 'Empty Land.'" In *Interpreting Exile: Interdisciplinary Studies of Displacement and Deportation in Biblical and Modern Contexts*, edited by B. Kelle, F. Ames, and J. Wright, 57–90. Atlanta: Society of Biblical Literature, 2011.

Lodahl, M. *Shekinah/Spirit: Divine Presence in Jewish and Christian Religion*. New York: Paulist, 1992.

Lund, O. *Way Metaphors and Way Topics in Isaiah 40–55*. Forschungen zum Alten Testament 2/28. Tübingen: Mohr Siebeck, 2008.

Luzarraga, J. *Las tradiciones de la nube en la Biblia y en el Judaismo primitivo*. Analecta Biblica 54. Rome: Biblical Institute, 1973.

Mann, T. *Divine Presence and Guidance in Israelite Traditions: The Typology of Exaltation*. Baltimore: Johns Hopkins University Press, 1977.

———. "The Pillar of Cloud in the Reed Sea Narrative." *Journal of Biblical Literature* 90 (1971): 15–30.

Manns, F. *Le symbole eau-esprit dans le judaïsme ancient*. Jerusalem: Franciscan Press, 1983.

Mason, R. "The Purpose of the 'Editorial Framework' of the Book of Haggai." *Vetus Testamentum* 27 (1977): 413–21.

McConville, J. "Ezra-Nehemiah and the Fulfilment of Prophecy." *Vetus Testamentum* 36 (1986): 205–24.

McKeating, H. "Ezekiel the 'Prophet like Moses?'" *Journal for the Study of the Old Testament* 61 (1994): 97–109.

Menzies, R. P. *The Development of Early Christian Pneumatology—with Special Reference to Luke-Acts*. Journal for the Study of the New Testament Supplement 54. Sheffield: JSOT Press, 1991.

Mesch, E. *Hans Leisegang: Leben und Werk*. Erlangen and Jena: Palm und Enke, 1999.

Mills, W. *The Holy Spirit—a Bibliography*. Peabody, Mass.: Hendrickson, 1988.

Moltmann, J. *God in Creation: A New Theology of Creation and the Spirit of God*. San Francisco: Harper & Row, 1985.

———. "Shekinah: The Home of the Homeless God." In *The Longing for Home*, edited by L. Rouner, 170–84. Notre Dame, Ind.: University of Notre Dame Press, 1996.

———. *The Church in the Power of the Spirit*. New York: Harper & Row, 1977.

———. *The Spirit of Life: A Universal Affirmation*. Minneapolis: Fortress, 1992.

Montague, G. T. *The Holy Spirit: Growth of a Biblical Tradition*. Peabody, Mass.: Hendrickson, 1994.

Moore, M., and B. Kelle. *Biblical History and Israel's Past: The Changing Study of the Bible and History*. Grand Rapids: Eerdmans, 2011.

Morales, R. J. *The Spirit and the Restoration of Israel: New Exodus and New Creation Motifs in Galatians*. Wissenschaftliche Untersuchungen zum Neuen Testament 2/282. Tübingen: Mohr Siebeck, 2010.

Morgenstern, J. "Isaiah 63.7-14." *Hebrew Union College Annual* 23 (1950–1951): 185–203.

Moule, C. F. D. *The Holy Spirit*. London: Mowbray, 1978.

Muñoz Leon, D. *Gloria de la Shekina en los Targumim del Pentateuco*. Madrid: Consejo Superior de Investigaciones Cientificas Instituto, 1977.

Neve, L. R. *The Spirit of God in the Old Testament*. Cleveland, Tenn.: Center for Pentecostal Theology Press, 2011.

Olyan, S. *A Thousand Thousands Served Him: Exegesis and the Naming of Angels in Ancient Judaism*. Texte und Studien zum antiken Judentum 36. Tübingen: J. C. B. Mohr (Paul Siebeck), 1993.

Parzen, H. "The *Ruaḥ Hakodesh* in Tannaitic Literature." *Jewish Quarterly Review* 20 (1929–1930): 51–76.

Patton, C. "'I Myself Gave Them Laws That Were Not Good': Ezekiel 20 and the Exodus Traditions." *Journal for the Study of the Old Testament* 69 (1996): 73–90.

Pfeiffer, G. *Ursprung und Wesen der Hypostasenvorstellungen im Judentum*. Stuttgart: Calwer, 1967.

Philip, F. *The Origins of Pauline Pneumatology: The Eschatological Bestowal of the Spirit upon Gentiles in Judaism and in the Early Development of Paul's Theology*. Wissenschaftliche Untersuchungen zum Neuen Testament 2/194. Tübingen: Mohr Siebeck, 2005.

Prestige, G. L. *God in Patristic Thought*. London: William Heinemann, 1938.

Provan, I., V. Long, and T. Longman. *A Biblical History of Israel*. Louisville, Ky.: Westminster John Knox, 2015.

Rabens, V. "Geistes-Geschichte: Die Rede vom Geist im Horizont der griechisch-römischen und jüdisch-hellenistischen Literatur." *Zeitschrift für Neues Testament* 25 (2010): 46–55.

———. *The Holy Spirit and Ethics in Paul: Transformation and Empowering for Religious-Ethical Life*. Wissenschaftliche Untersuchungen zum Neuen Testament 2/283. Tübingen: Mohr Siebeck, 2010.

Ramelli, I. L. E. "Origen, Greek Philosophy, and the Birth of the Trinitarian Meaning of Hypostasis." *Harvard Theological Review* 105 (2012): 302–50.

Ringgren, H. *Word and Wisdom: Studies in the Hypostatization of Divine Qualities and Functions in the Ancient Near East*. Lund: H. Ohlsson, 1947.

Robson, J. E. *Word and Spirit in Ezekiel*. Library of Hebrew Bible / Old Testament Studies 447. London: T&T Clark, 2006.

Röttger, H. *Mal'ak Jahwe, Bote von Gott: Die Vorstellung von Gottes Boten im hebr. Alten Testament*. Frankfurt am Main: Peter Lang, 1978.

Runia, D. *On the Creation of the Cosmos According to Moses*. Philo of Alexandria Commentary Series 1. Leiden: Brill, 2001.

Schäfer, P. *Die Vorstellung vom Heiligen Geist in der rabbinischen Literatur*. Studien zum Alten und Neuen Testament 28. Munich: Kösel, 1972.

———. *Rivalität zwischen Engeln und Menschen: Untersuchungen zur Rabbinischen Engelvorstellung*. Studia Judaica 8. Berlin: de Gruyter, 1975.

Schandorff, E. D. *The Doctrine of the Holy Spirit: A Bibliography Showing Its Chronological Development*. 2 vols. ATLA Bibliography Series. Lanham: Scarecrow, 1995.

Schweizer, E. *The Holy Spirit*. Philadelphia: Fortress, 1980.

———. "*Pneuma, Pneumatikos*." In *Theological Dictionary of the New Testament*, vol. 6, edited by G. Kittel and G. Friedrich, 332–455. Grand Rapids: Eerdmans, 1964.

Scott, J. *Adoption as Sons of God: An Exegetical Investigation in the Background of ΥΙΟΘΕΣΙΑ in the Pauline Corpus*. Wissenschaftliche Untersuchungen zum Neuen Testament 2/48. Tübingen: J. C. B. Mohr (Paul Siebeck), 1992.

Seitz, O. J. F. "Two Spirits in Man: An Essay in Biblical Exegesis." *New Testament Studies* 6 (1959–1960): 82–95.

Sekki, A. E. *The Meaning of* Ruaḥ *at Qumran*. Society of Biblical Literature Series 110. Atlanta: Scholars, 1989.

Shoemaker, W. R. "The Use of *Ruach* in the Old Testament, and of *Pneuma* in the New Testament: A Lexicographical Study." *Journal of Biblical Literature* 23 (1904): 13–67.

Smith-Christopher, D. L. *A Biblical Theology of Exile*. Minneapolis: Fortress, 2002.

Spawn, K. L., and A. T. Wright, eds. *Spirit and Scripture: Examining a Pneumatic Hermeneutic*. New York: T&T Clark, 2012.

Stanton, G., B. W. Longenecker, and S. C. Barton, eds. *The Holy Spirit and Christian Origins: Essays in Honor of James D. G. Dunn*. Grand Rapids: Eerdmans, 2004.

Stein, B. "Der Engel des Auszugs." *Biblica* 19 (1938): 286–307.

Stuckenbruck, L. T. *Angel Veneration and Christology: A Study in Early Judaism and in the Christology of the Apocalypse of John*. Wissenschaftliche Untersuchungen zum Neuen Testament 2.70. Tübingen: J. C. B. Mohr (Paul Siebeck), 1995.

Swete, H. B. *On the History of the Doctrine of the Procession of the Holy Spirit from the Apostolic Age to the Death of Charlemagne*. Cambridge: Deighton, Bell, 1876.

———. *The Holy Spirit in the Ancient Church: A Study of Christian Teaching in the Age of the Fathers*. London: Macmillan, 1912.

———. *The Holy Spirit in the New Testament: A Study of Primitive Christian Teaching*. London: Macmillan, 1910.

Terrien, S. *The Elusive Presence: Toward a New Biblical Theology*. San Francisco: Harper & Row, 1978.

Thiselton, A. C. *The Holy Spirit—in Biblical Teaching, through the Centuries, and Today*. Grand Rapids: Eerdmans, 2013.

Tibbs, C. *Religious Experience of the Pneuma: Communication with the Spirit World in 1 Corinthians 12 and 14.* Wissenschaftliche Untersuchungen zum Neuen Testament 2/230. Tübingen: Mohr Siebeck, 2007.

Tigchelaar, E. "Historical Origins of the Early Christian Concept of the Holy Spirit: Perspectives from the Dead Sea Scrolls." In *The Holy Spirit, Inspiration, and the Cultures of Antiquity: Multidisciplinary Perspectives*, edited by J. Frey and J. Levison, 176–240. Ekstasis: Religious Experience from Antiquity to the Middle Ages 5. Berlin: de Gruyter, 2014.

Timoner, R. *Breath of Life: God as Spirit in Judaism.* Brewster: Paraclete Press, 2011.

Turner, M. *Power from on High: The Spirit in Israel's Restoration and Witness in Luke–Acts.* Journal of Pentecostal Theology Supplement 9. Sheffield: Sheffield Academic Press, 1996.

———. *The Holy Spirit and Spiritual Gifts in the New Testament Church and Today.* Rev. ed. Peabody, Mass.: Hendrickson, 1998.

Verbeke, G. *L'évolution de la doctrine du* Pneuma: *Du Stoïcisme à S. Augustine.* Bibliothèque de l'Institut Supérieur de Philosophie, Université de Louvain. Paris: Desclée de Brouwer, 1945.

Volz, Paul. *Der Geist Gottes und die verwandten Erscheinungen im Alten Testament und im anschliessenden Judentem.* Tübingen: J. C. B. Mohr (Paul Siebeck), 1910.

Vos, J. S. *Traditionsgeschichtliche Untersuchungen zur Paulinischen Pneumatologie.* Assen: van Gorcum, 1973.

Waddell, R. *The Spirit of the Book of Revelation.* Journal of Pentecostal Theology Supplement 30. Blandford Forum Dorset: Deo, 2006.

Wagner, J. R. *Reading the Sealed Book: Old Greek Isaiah and the Problem of Septuagint Hermeneutics.* Supplements to Novum Testamentum 101. Tübingen: Mohr Siebeck, 2013.

Weinel, H. *Die Wirkungen des Geistes und der Geister im nachapostolischen Zeitalter bis auf Irenäus.* Freiburg: J. C. B. Mohr (Paul Siebeck), 1899.

Welker, M. *God the Spirit.* Minneapolis: Fortress, 1994.

Welker, M., et al., eds. *Heiliger Geist.* Jahrbuch für Biblische Theologie 24. Neukirchen-Vluyn: Neukirchener Verlag, 2010.

Wernberg-Møller, P. "A Reconsideration of the Two Spirits in the Rule of the Community in 1QSerek III,13–IV,26." *Revue de Qumran* 3 (1961): 413–41.

Wilder, W. *Echoes of the Exodus in the Context and Background of Galatians 5:18.* New York: Peter Lang, 2001.

Williamson, H. "Isaiah 63,7-64,11: Exilic Lament or Post-exilic Protest?" *Zeitschrift für die Alttestamentliche Wissenschaft* 102 (1990): 48–58.

Witt Burton, E. de. *Spirit, Soul, and Flesh: The Usage of* Πνευμα, Ψυχή, *and* Σάρξ *in Greek Writings and Translated Works from the Earliest Period to 225 A.D.; and of their Equivalents* רוח, נֶפֶשׁ, *and* בָּשָׂר *in the Hebrew Old Testament.* Chicago: University of Chicago Press, 1918.

Wright, C. J. H. *Knowing the Holy Spirit through the Old Testament.* Downers Grove, Ill.: InterVarsity Press, 2006.

Wright, N. T. *Paul and the Faithfulness of God.* Minneapolis: Fortress, 2013.

Yates, J. W. *The Spirit and Creation in Paul.* Wissenschaftliche Untersuchungen zum Neuen Testament 2/251. Tübingen: Mohr Siebeck, 2008.

INDEX OF SUBJECTS AND ANCIENT NAMES

INDEX OF MODERN AUTHORS

INDEX OF ANCIENT SOURCES

A. Hebrew Scriptures (MT)
B. Greek Versions of Hebrew Scriptures
C. Apocrypha
D. Pseudepigrapha
E. Josephus
F. Dead Sea Scrolls
G. Philo
H. Rabbinic Literature
I. Greek and Roman Authors
J. New Testament
K. Early Christian Authors

A. Hebrew Scriptures (MT)

B. Greek Versions of Hebrew Scriptures

C. Apocrypha

D. Pseudepigrapha

E. Josephus

F. Dead Sea Scrolls

G. Philo

H. Rabbinic Literature

I. Greek and Roman Authors

J. New Testament

K. Early Christian Literature